Fundamentals of

FARM BUSINESS MANAGEMENT

S.S. JOHL
Professor of Economics and
Head, Department of Economics
and Sociology (Retd.)
Punjab Agricultural University,
LUDHIANA

T.R. KAPUR
Development Officer (Retd.)
(*Agril. Finance*)
Punjab, Haryana, Himachal and
J & K Branches, Bank of India,
CHANDIGARH

KALYANI PUBLISHERS

LUDHIANA – NEW DELHI – NOIDA (U.P.) – HYDERABAD
CHENNAI – KOLKATA – CUTTACK – GUWAHATI – KOCHI

KALYANI PUBLISHERS

Head office :
B-I/1292, Rajinder Nagar, **Ludhiana**-141 008

Administrative Office :
4863/2B, Bharat Ram Road,
24, Daryaganj, **New Delhi**-110 002

Works :
B-16, Sector-8, **NOIDA (U.P.)**

Branches :
No.1, Mahalakshmi Street,
T.Nagar, **Chennai**-600 017
110/111, Bharatia Towers, Badambadi,
Cuttack-9 (Orissa)
3-5-1108,Narayanaguda, Hyderabad-500 029
10/2B, Ramanath Mazumdar Street,
Kolkata-700 009
Arunalaya, First floor, Saraswati Road,
Pan Bazar, **Guwahati**-781 001
Convent road, **Kochi**-682 035

S-36076 1

Reprinted, 2001
Reprinted, 2005
Revised Edition 2009
Reprinted, 2022

TYPESETTING AT
(09–FOFBM)
Gautam Graphic Printers
O/s Mai Hiran Gate, Jalandhar.

978-81-272-5223-6

Printed in India
At Process World (India), C-90 Sec 63, Noida

Preface

Until recently, the subject of farm management had been taught in the agronomy departments of the agricultural colleges in India. Economic analysis and its application in the teaching of farm management was limited. Now the teaching and research in this subject is progressively being located with the agricultural economists and departments of agricultural economics.

Although in India farm management teachers and researchers have produced a good deal of literature on different aspects, we do not find many books dealing with the subject comprehensively and systematically to meet the requirements of students. The available books on farm management contain material which has little relevance to Indian conditions. While teaching undergraduate and graduate courses over a number of years, we found ourselves handicapped due to this lack of teaching material on Indian conditions. This motivated us to collect data and information relevant to the management problems of Indian farms in order to illustrate the concepts of farm management in a simplified manner for the undergraduate and graduate students.

The main objective of this book is to discuss the subject of farm management under the Indian conditions with an emphasis on demonstrating the application of economic principles for the benefit of the students. It is our hope that the book will be useful to the teachers and students alike. Presentation of the material in this book has been deliberately kept simple so that it can also be understood and used even by literate progressive farmers who may not have any previous training in the subject. Extension specialists in farm management and other extension workers engaged in the development programmes can also benefit from this book. The value of this book for teachers, students, extension workers, bankers and farmers is especially enhanced because the analyses and illustrations have been based on the actual experience and data from the farms.

This book first deals with the fundamentals of farm management science. Discussion is pointedly focussed on the meaning of farm management, characteristics of farming as a business, basics of farm production decisions, application of farm management principles and the basic tools of farm business analysis. Here the book attempts to explain important farm management concepts which the students need to master before taking up advance courses. Next we discuss the principles of resource-use planning. Important farm inputs such as land, labour, machinery, buildings, etc., are dealt with in order to explain how best each of these resources can be managed. The management problems concerning different farm resources are identified and application of the management principles to solve these individual resource-use problems demonstrated. The last chapter deals with the subject of risk and uncertainty in agriculture as it affects the decisions of the farmer in a developing country.

We are thankful to the various research organisations and journals from where data have been used to write this book. Our thanks are also due to a number of colleagues, particularly Mr. H.S. Sandhu of Punjab Agricultural University and Dr. Edgar T. Shaudys of Ohio State University who read the manuscript and made many helpful suggestions on an earlier draft. We are grateful to Professor David H. Boyne, Chairman and his Department of Agricultural Economics and Rural Sociology of the Ohio State University (USA) for their inviting Professor Johl as Visiting Professor with them for one and a half year, which provided him with a congenial academic environment to work on this book.

We thank Mr. B.D. Tandon at Ludhiana and Mrs. Majel Haas at the Ohio State University who showed an extraordinary patience and accuracy in typing the manuscript of this book.

Punjab Agricultural University, Ludhiana — **S.S. JOHL**

Bank of India, Chandigarh — **T.R. KAPUR**

Contents

Chapter 1	**THE FIELD OF FARM MANAGEMENT** What is farm management ? What makes a successful farm manager ? Scope of Farm Management; Importance of the subject of Farm Management in India; Nature and characteristics of Farm Management science; Relationship of Farm Management with other sciences; Typical farm management decisions; Some farm management problems under Indian conditions; Development of Farm Management science in India.	**1—35**
Chapter 2	**CHARACTERISTICS OF FARMING AS A BUSINESS** Characteristics—Primay forces of production; Size of production unit; Climatic factors; Frequency and speed of decisions; Changes in prices; Standardization of practices and products; Turnover; Financing; Home and business; Fixed and variable costs; Inelastic demand; Time regidities in consumption of Agril. products; Changing economic environment and farming; Farmer's lack of knowledge; Management, learning and adjustment. Requirements in farming Profession.	**36—44**
Chapter 3	**BASICS OF FARM PRODUCTION DECISIONS** Production economics; objectives of production economics; Language of production economics.	**45—61**
Chapter 4	**PRODUCTION RELATIONSHIPS** Factor-product relationships; Production function; Types of production function, Relationship between total, average and marginal products, Elasticity of production; Three regions of production function; Impact of technological changes on production function.	**62—79**

Chapter 5	**PRODCTION AND COSTS** Concept of cost; Categories of cost; Opportunity costs; Cost function; Relationship among total fixed, total variable and total costs; Relationships among average, fixed variable and total costs; Relationships between average and marginal costs; Determination of net revenue as a function of output; Three zones of cost function and profit maximization; Minimum loss principle; Factor and product price change and production decisions.	**80—101**
Chapter 6	**FACTOR-FACTOR RELATIONSHIPS** Isoquants; Types of factor-factor relationship; Iso-cost lines; Least-cost combination; Isoclines; Expansion path; Ridge lines; Choosing the optimum level of output; Rational and irrational zones of production; Substitution curves; Input Price changes and least cost combination; Application of factor-factor analysis in cost-minimization problems.	**102—123**
Chapter 7	**PRODUCT-PRODUCT RELATIONSHIPS** Basic relationships; Production possibility curves; Shifts in production possibility curves; Ridge lines; Iso-clines for production possibility curves; Iso-revenue line; Determination of optimum production combination; Product Price changes and optimum combination of output; Expansion path in product-product analysis; Specialisation and Diversification.	**124—148**
Chapter 8	**PRINCIPLES INVOLVED IN FARM MANAGEMENT DECISIONS** Principle of variable proportion; Cost principle; Principle of factor substitution; Law of equimarginal returns; Opportunity cost principle; Principle of combining enterprises; Principle of comparative advantage; Time comparison principle; Limitations of the principles of farm management.	**149—175**
Chapter 9	**TOOLS OF FARM MANAGEMENT ANALYSIS** Farm Planning; How farm planning helps; Objectives of farm planning; why a written plan is needed; Principal characteristics of a good farm plan; Techniques of farm planning; Information needed for planning and budgeting;	**176—219**

	Production function analysis; Farm budgeting; Partial budgeting; Enterprise budget; Complete budgeting; Steps in farm planning and budgeting; An illustration on complete budgeting; Linear programming analysis.	
Chapter 10	**FARM BUSINESS ANALYSIS** Farm business analysis; Advantages of farm records and accounts; Problems and Difficulties in farm accounting; Levels of farm accountancy; Systems of book keeping; Types of farm records and accounts; Parts of a farm record system; Physical farm records; Production records, Labour records, Feed records; Financial records. Farm inventory; Methods of valuation; Methods of computing depreciation; Net worth statement; Farm Financial accounts: Income statement; Treatment and classification of special transactions for financial accounts; Farm efficiency measures; Measures for farm income and efficiency; Efficiency Measures and Business Decision; Evaluation of Records and Surveys for research.	**220—285**
Chapter 11	**FARM FINANCIAL MANAGEMENT** Importance of studying farm financial management; Role of credit in production and marketing; Economic feasibility tests of a farm credit proposal; Repayment plan; Use of farm financial budget and cash-flow chart in farm financial management; Methods and Mechanics of processing farm credit proposals; Farm credit analysis kit.	**286—321**
Chapter 12	**MANAGEMENT OF IMPORTANT FARM RESOURCES** Land management: Efficient farm layout, Remodelling of farm layout; Impact of mechanisation; Source of irrigation, Soil management : Management of soil resources; Fertilization management programmes; Weather and price risks in fertilizer use.	**322—342**
Chapter 13	**FARM LABOUR MANAGEMENT** The management problem; Labour problem under Indian conditions; Classification of farm labour; Composition of farm labour; Special features of Indian farm labour; Improving the efficiency of farm labour; Farm work simplification.	**343—355**

Chapter 14	**FARM MACHINERY MANAGEMENT** What cost to take into account ? Rate at which costs are to be charged; Selection of size of machine; Substituting machinery for labour; Tractor V/s Bullocks power; Changing the size of machine; Timeliness of operation; Hiring V/s owning a machine; Estimation of Break-even point for a farm machinery; Purchase of old V/s new machine; Basic information for farm machinery management decisions.	**356—386**
Chapter 15	**FARM BUILDINGS MANAGEMENT** Building as an input; Cost benefit Analysis; Designs; Flexibility; Durability.	**387—395**
Chapter 16	**RISK AND UNCERTAINTY** Product-Price uncertainty; Yield uncertainty; Profitability—a catch-all factor; Uncertain availability of inputs; Level of enterprise; Adjustments in planting time; Inputs application on growing crops.	**396—406**
	INDEX	**407—415**

1 The Field of Farm Management

WHAT IS FARM MANAGEMENT ?

Farm management comprises of two words : 'farm' and 'management'. Literally 'farm' means a piece of land where crops and livestock enterprises are taken up under a common management and has specific boundaries. 'Management' means the act or art of managing. Gray[1] states, the art of managing a farm successfully, as measured by the test of profitableness, is called farm management.

Although the farm is an economic and social institution developed over many centuries, the scientific management of farm as a business is relatively new. Because of its recent origin, the term 'farm management' conveys different meanings to different people. Some take it to be another name of production economics or agricultural economics, while others consider farm management is nothing more than the farmer's art of carrying out the daily routine. The daily work of supervision of farm labour and carrying out the directives of seniors by the public or private employed farm manager, is generally referred to as farm management. There is, in fact, no single definition that is acceptable to all. It is not very important too. More important is to understand as to what this term actually means.

Like any other economic problem, farm management is a rational resource allocation proposition, more particularly from the point of view of an individual farmer. On one hand, a farmer has a certain set of farm resources such as land, labour, farm buildings, working capital and farm equipment, etc; which are relatively scarce. On the other side, the same farmer has a set of goals or objectives to achieve, may be maximum family satisfaction through increasing net farm income. In between these two poles is the farmer himself with specific degree of ability and awareness. This gap is bridged by the mental exercise and concentration of desire and will power of the individual farmer, to use his scarce resources in a way that

1. Gray, L.C., "Introduction to Agricultural Economics" : New York: MacMillan, 1924, p.3.

desired objectives are achieved. This bridging up process necessitates taking a series of rational decisions in respect of farm resources having alternative uses and opportunities. This management process is illustrated in Fig. 1.1.

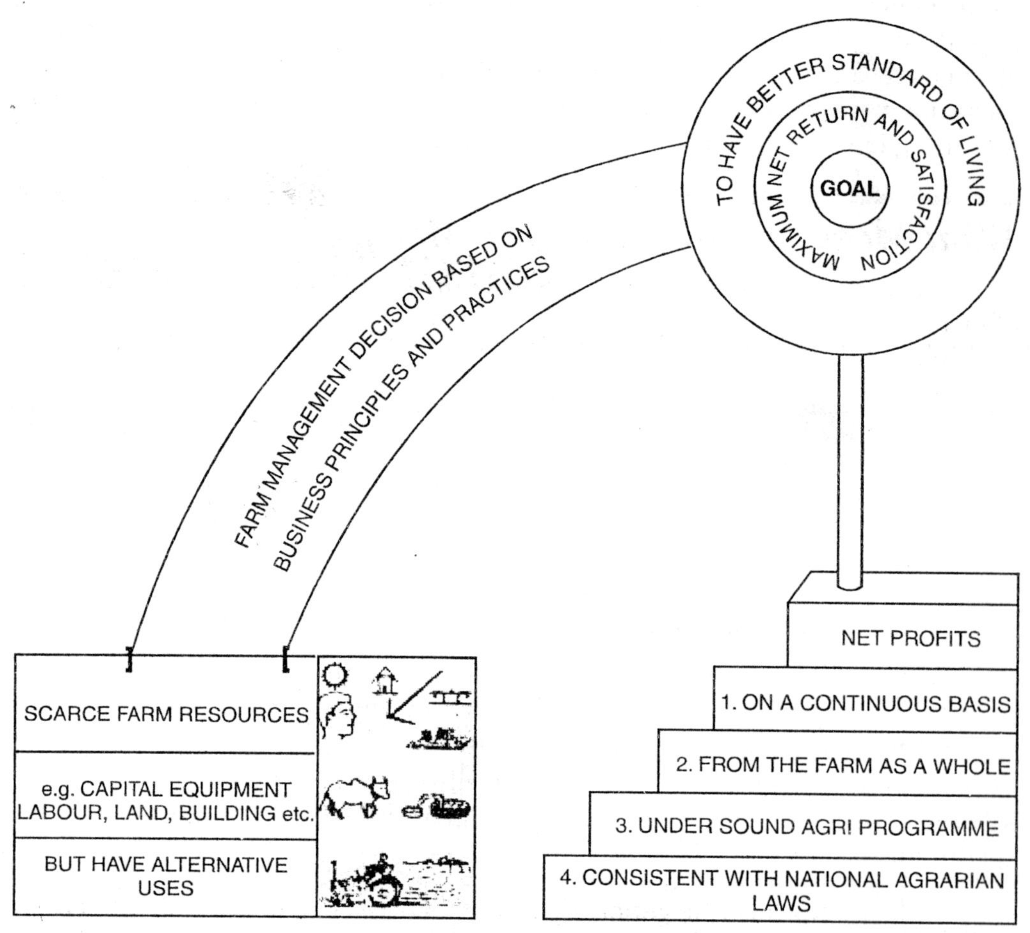

Fig 1.1. An Illustration of Farm management process.

Thus, in simple words, farm management can be defined as a science which deals with judicious decisions on the use of scarce farm resources, having alternative uses to obtain the maximum profit and family satisfaction on a continuous basis from the farm as a whole and under sound farming programmes. In other words, farm management seeks to help the farmer in deciding problems like what to produce, how much to produce, how to produce and when to buy and sell and in organization and managerial problems relating to these decisions. It is important to note here that farmer and his family may have many objectives. They may be concerned, for example, both with providing a certain amount of leisure and generation of maximum income. The goal of increasing income and leisure also depends upon the 'planning horizon' and personal values of the farmer.

Farm Management may, in short, be called a science of decision-making or a science of choice. It is to be emphasised that managing a farm is a continuous process of decision-making. The need for it arises out of changes in the farm conditions as well as changes occurring outside the farm; hence need of continuous adjustment of farm operations to these changes becomes inevitable. The principal changes frequently encountered by the farmer are : fluctuations in prices; weather variations; inventions in farming methods ; changes in socio-economic environment including changes in Government policies and social responses and values.

What Makes a Successful Farm Manager ?

Successful farm management requires the ability and capacity on the part of farmer not only to make decisions, but to make the correct decisions. This decision-making process is discussed below. To improve management ability, one needs a process-model to know what one is trying to improve.

Eight processes or functions have been proposed by Nielson[1] :

1. Formulation of the goals or objectives of the firm ;
2. Recognition and definition of a problem or opportunity;
3. Obtaining information-observation of relevant facts;
4. Specification and analysis of alternatives ;
5. Decision-making—choosing an alternative;
6. Taking action;
7. Bearing responsibility for the decision or action taken;
8. Evaluating the outcome.

Understandably, a manager may or may not consciously proceed systematically from first process to the last. However, the study of this model is useful for proper understanding of the process.

Since management functions are primarily a mental process, each choice and action that results is conditioned by the attitudes, values and goals of the manager. His goals and value systems unconsciously determine what he will observe, what variables he will consider, what information he will gather and which alternatives he will choose. Thus the formulation of these goals is essential in effective management because they give direction to the whole managerial process.

Problems need to be recognised and defined in order to produce the most acceptable results. Research has indicated that identification of problems in the farm business is surprisingly difficult for farmers[2]. Problems are recognized as a result of (1) a forced action situation, (2) a systematic study of farm operation, or (3) ordinary opportunities for action. Good managers will pinpoint more problems as a result of systematic farm-business analysis.

---

1. James Nielson, "Improvement of the Management Resource in Agriculture: Improved Managerial Process for Farmers". J. Farm Econ. 43: 1251, Dec. 1961.
2. Nielson, p. 1254

Closely allied with problem recognition is a systematic approach in selecting related information for alternative comparisons. The farm manager therefore needs to build up patterns of expected norms which are basic to the making of decisions.

Decision-making is one of the crucial process or function of management. A decision can be made to take no action and live with the status quo, to postpone a solution while obtaining further information, or to undertake a different course of action. Successful farm managers prefer to try alternative course of action, of course, within reasonable risk limits.

Good managers have not only the will and capacity to get the job done but also the fortitude to bear the responsibility for the actions they take. Evaluation is similar to search for alternative courses of action, and here management performs the role of scientific enquiry and analysis.

The managerial process can be improved and streamlined through research and educational programmes. Management of course, remains to be still an art in making choices, taking action and bearing responsibility for the action taken. In practice, management is a continuous process through observing and conceiving ideas, analysing the observations, making decisions on the basis of the analysis, taking action and accepting the responsibility. Management can be distinguished from entrepreneurship. The entrepreneurship is a pioneer, founding and developing activity. The manager is hired to manage an established business. Most farmers function in both capacities. A third category, the executive, carries out the orders of management.

SCOPE OF FARM MANAGEMENT

Farm Management is generally considered to fall in the field of micro-economics. It deals with the allocation of resources at the level of an individual farm. While in a way it is concerned with the problems of resource allocation in the agricultural sector, and even in the economy as a whole, the primary concern of farm management is the farm as a unit.

It covers aspects of farm business which have a bearing on the economic efficiency of the farm. Thus, the types of enterprises to be combined, the kind of crops and varieties to be grown, the dosage of fertilizer to be applied, the implements to be used, the way the farm functions are to be performed, all these fall within the purview of the subject of farm management. The subject of farm management includes; Farm management research, training and extension.

Farm Management Research

Solution of economic problems faced by a farmer is greatly facilitated through recording of data relating to the farm. These data have to be analysed with a view to identify causes of inefficient functioning of the farm. Remedial measures have to be then formulated. All this falls within the scope of subject of farm management.

Although the problems and their solutions will vary from time to time, in the developing countries, the following aspects need to be continuously researched :

(*a*) delineation of homogeneous type-of-farming-areas in various regions of the country.

(*b*) generation of input-output co-efficients and working out comparative economics of various farm enterprises.

(*c*) formulation of standard farm plans and optimum cropping patterns for different areas and types of farming.

(*d*) developing suitable models of mechanisation and modernisation; and

(*e*) evaluation of agricultural policies having a bearing on development and growth of the farm-firms.

Farm Management Teaching

Farm management is relatively a younger discipline and has come to its own only recently. Now, almost all the Agricultural Universities in India have one or more compulsory courses in farm management for the under-graduate students. In quite a few places, however, economic content of the subject is not appreciated and teaching of this course is placed with the Departments of Agronomy. The situation is, however, remedying fast because it is being realised that the training in farm management science is essential for agricultural graduates for understanding farmer's response to varying economic pressures and stimuli. With the new technological break-through in agriculture, the decision-making processes have become more complex on farm organisations. To help the farmer take right decisions as to what to grow, how much to grow, how to grow, when and where to buy and sell, higher training in this subject has become necessary. Recently, the Indian Agricultural Research Institute, New Delhi and the Punjab Agricultural University, in India, have started teaching advanced farm management as a major subject at M.Sc. and Ph. D. levels. Other agricultural universities are picking up in this direction.

Farm Management Extension

Once the results of a study are known, they are to be made available to the farmers. They have to be educated and trained also in the application or adoption of these results. Since many farmers in the developing countries do not have the requisite education to follow the results, findings of farm management research have to be demonstrated to convince the farmers of their utility and effectiveness. Experience shows that the managerial ability of farmers can be improved appreciably through extension education programmes in farm management.

Short course in farm management for progressive farmers engaged in various types of farm enterprises and for young farmers can be organised. The field extension service (as of Extension Specialists in Farm Management) can go a long way in improving the managerial ability of the farmers through district, block and village level training camps, other such extension training programmes and demonstration centres (farms).

Research, teaching and extension together thus seek improving the ability of the farmers to introduce desirable changes in the utilisation of scarce resources at the farm with a view to increase incomes and improve standards of living of the farmers.

IMPORTANCE OF THE SUBJECT OF FARM MANAGEMENT IN INDIA

Through the process of mechanisation, automation, commercialisation and modernisation, farming has gone beyond its framework of merely providing the necessities of life to the farm family. Now the farmer produces not only to meet his family subsistence needs, but at the same time he endeavours to produce maximm surpluses to be sold in the market to buy some non-farm products for fuller satisfaction of life. This has made agricultural production market oriented and has introduced a business content in the farming profession.

Scope of Increase in Farm Income Through Suitable Farm Adjustments

It has been tested in Ludhiana and other parts of the Punjab State, through farm management studies that the existing resource allocations and product combinations remain below optimum and need adjustments. These studies gave encouraging results in different regions and type of farming areas. For example, in Ludhiana district[1], the rational resource utilisation of farm resources with existing technology and existing resources promised an increase in the returns to fixed farm factors, on small, medium and large farms to the extent of 19.66%, 20.25% and 14.57% respectively. When the same situations were reorganised at improved level of technology with recommended farm practices, the returns to fixed resources increased by 99.46, 98.69 and 76.73 per cent respectively.

The major changes which promised higher incomes were reported as under :

1. Acreage under maize local (desi) was mostly replaced by maize hybrid except for a small area to meet the family consumption needs.
2. Area under *desi* cotton decreased.

---

1. Kapur, T.R. and Kahlon, A.S. "Optimum Cropping Patterns for Upper-dhia region of IADP Distt. Ludhiana", Ind. Jr. Agri. Econ. XXII (2) April-June 1967.

3. Irrigated groundnut acreage increased to the maximum permitted by land suitability whereas unirrigated groundnut areas remained constant.
4. Among rabi crops, area under barley, gram and mixtures was replaced with wheat.
5. Practice of keeping the land fallow was reduced to the minimum and cropping intensity increased.
6. Use of improved varieties of seeds, fertilizers and plant protection measures increased.

Another study[1] brought out that returns to fixed farm resources could be increased through rationalisation of resource use, with existing resources and technology by 84.77%, 79.88% and 52.25% under irrigated conditions and 34.66%, 37.51% and 31.53% under unirrigated conditions on small, medium and large farms respectively. A similar study conducted in Jalandhar district[2] on general crop farms and the farms in the vicinity of a sugar factory indicated that returns to fixed factors on around 10 acres modal farms when re-organised with existing resources at existing level of technology, would promise an increase of 45.7% and 25.7% respectively.

A more comprehensive view of the differences in farm incomes generated by the existing production programmes of the farmers and those promised by the optimum production programmes is provided in Table 1.1.

Technological Progress and Role of Farm Management

Evidences of a break-through in agricultural production technology are now available. This is especially true in the high production potential areas of the country like Punjab, Haryana, Western parts of U.P. and Andhra Pradesh.

This technological break-through has come about in two directions :

(*i*) a break-through in the use of divisible inputs and farm practices such as high yielding varieties seeds, fertilizers, insecticides, crop-rotations, etc; and

(*ii*) a break-through in the technology and use of lumpy resources such as tractors, pumping sets and tubewells, harvestors, thrashers and transportation facilities.

The impact of the divisible inputs has been felt irrespective of the size of holdings, particularly in those areas where assured irrigation facilities and production potentials exist. The input-use per acre has shot up and with that total farm production, as well as returns, have increased. Crop rotations are experiencing

1. Sidhu, Tehal Singh—M.Sc. Thesis 1966 P.A.U. Ludhiana (Unpublished).
2. Aulakh, Santokh Singh—M.Sc. Thesis 1966 P.A.U. Ludhiana (Unpublished).

TABLE 1.1*

Farm Income Potentials in Various Types of Farming Areas of Punjab, (Based on normative farm plans) at the Existing and Improved Levels of Technology

Study No.	*Region/ District.*	*Types of Framing Area*	*Particular Situation*	*Resource Description of each farm situation*	*Net Farm earnings (Rs.)*				
					Existing cropping pattern	*Optimum cropping patterns based on existing technology*		*Optimum cropping patterns based on improved technology*	
					1965-66	*Total*	*Percentage increase over the existing*	*Total*	*Percentage increase over the existing*
1	*2*	*3*	*4*	*5*	*6*	*7*	*8*	*9*	*10*
1	Ludhiana district	Upper Dhaia region	A	**Small Size Synthetic farm :** 10 acres; Bullock operated ; Persian wheel irrigation, soil-loamy to heavy loam.	4447.54	5593.01	25.75	10110.16	127.32
			B	**Medium Size Synthetic farm :** 16 acres ; Bullock operated; Tubewell irrigation; Soil-loamy to clayey.	6535.76	8437.30	29.09	15611.26	138.86
			C	**Large Size Synthetic farm :** 22 acres ; Bullock operated; Tubewell irrigated; Soil-loamy to clayey.	11072.89	13198.66	19.19	22039.97	99.03
2	Ludhiana district	Lower Dhaia Region	A	**Small farm :** 10 acres ; Bullock operated; Persian wheel irrigation; Soil loamy.	3103.66	—	—	5734.83	84.77

Source : 1. Kapur, T.R.—Optimum cropping pattern for I.A.D.P. District Ludhiana, M.Sc. Agri. Econ. (Farm Management) Thesis 1966 (Unpublished) P.A.U., Ludhiana.

2. Sidhu, T.S.—Standard Plans for Bullock operated general crop farm in Ludhiana M.Sc. Agri. Econ.(Farm Management) Thesis 1966 (Unpublished) P.A.U., Ludhiana.

* Reproduced from Johl, S.S. & Moore, C.V. "Essentials of Farm Financial Mangement." Today and Tomorrow Publishers, New Delhi, 1970.

			B	**Medium farm :** 18 acres ; Bullock operated; Tubewell irrigation ; Soil loamy sand.	8179.72	—	—	14713.96	79.88
			C	**Large farm** : 25 acres ; Bullock operated ; Tubewell irrigation; Soil sandy loam.	9123.17	—	—	13898.29	52.25
		Bet Region	A	**Small farm :** 8 acres ; Bullock operated; Persian wheel irrigation; Soil-loamy sand.	2382.73	—	—	3208.54	34.66
			B	**Medium farm :** 12 acres ; Bullock operated ; Persian wheel irrigation; Soil-sandy loam.	3129.78	—	—	4303.70	37.51
			C	**Large farm :** 20 acres ; Bullock operated; Persian wheel irrigation; Soil-loamy sand.	4583.13	—	—	6028.08	31.53
3	Ludhiana district	Upper Dhaia Region (Ludhiana Block)	A	**Small Sized holding :** 28.33 acres; Tubewell irrigation; 32 H.P. Massey Fergusen Tractor; Loamy soil.	11902.57	14526.42	22.04	19322.12	62.33
		Mechanized farm situation	B	**Medium Sized holding** : 40.19 acres; Tubewell irrigation; Soil loamy; 25 H.P. Zetor Tractor.	16766.73	22880.82	36.45	30875.91	84.12
			C	**Large Sized holding :** 65.10 acres; Tubewell irrigation; Soil sandy loam ; 32; H.P. Massey Fergusen Tractor.	28604.84	34502.56	20.62	48737.49	70.39

3. Bal H.S.—Optimum Resource Use Pattern for some mechanised farm situations in Ludhiana District M.Sc. (Agri. Econ. Farm Mgt.) Thesis (Unpublished) 1966.

4	Ludhiana district	Vegetable growing around Ludhiana city	A	Operational area 10 acres; 5 H.P. electric tubewell irrigation; Bullocks operated	12779.25	17730.50	58.74	19956.66	56.16
			B	Operational area 15 acres ; Tubewell irrigation by 5 H.P. electric motor ; Motive power-2 pairs of bullocks	24660.88	37854.78	53.50	40099.52	62.62
			C	Operational area 18 acres ; Tubewell irrigation by 5 H.P. electric motor; Motive power-one D.T. 14 Tractor.	29988.77	41131.95	37.16	49615.55	65.45
			D	Operational area 22 acres; Three tubewells irrigation by 5 H.P. electric motors each Motive power, one Massey Fergusen 35 H.P. tractor	44350.27	51554.25	16.24	64214.42	44.78
			E	Operational area 25 acres; loamy soil; One tubewell with 7 1/2 H.P. electric motor; Motive power-one Massey Fergusen Tractor.	35714.77	48061.02	34.57	63184.11	76.91
			F	Operational area 44 acres; Loamy soil; 3 tubewells irrigation with 5 H.P. electric motor; Motive power one Massey Fergusen 35 H.P. Tractor.	94078.44	107061.14	13.80	116854.58	24.21
5	Jalandhar district	General Crop-raising Area	A	Operational holding 11.50 acres; All irrigated; Bullock operated; Tubewell	6673.20	8589.30*	—	12081.93	81.05

4. Dhillon, Balkar Singh—"Alternative Farm Plans for vegetable Farms around Ludhiana City" M.Sc. (Agri. Econ. Farm Mgt.) Thesis 1966 (Unpublished).

5. Aulakh, Santokh Singh—Economic potentialities of farm adjustments in medium rainfall, medium temperature and non bet areas of Jalandhar District Farm Adjustments—M.Sc. (Farm Management) Thesis (Unpublished) 1966.

* This represents income with no change in cropping pattern but shift from existing technology to recommended technology.

		Sugercane Factory Area	B	Operational holding 8.07 acres of which 5.82 acre irrigated and 2.25 acres unirrigated; Bullock operated, Persian wheel.	3993.41	4963.57*	—	6902.82	73.02
		Vegetable Growing Area	C	Operational holding 7.43 acres all irrigated, bullocks operated, tubewells	6271.04	7476.07	—	13715.82	118.72
6	Ferozepur	Cotton Belt of Punjab with special reference to	A	**Small Size farm** (below 30 acres) 15 acres. Soil sandy loam ; Land very fertile; Irrigation-canal supply.	3927.15	5524.60	40.6	9380.99	138.8
		Ferozepur District	B	**Medium Size** :31.70 acres model class 40 acres. Soil sandy loam texture; Irrigation-canal but water availability was short by 42.5%.	11948.02	15247.85	27.6	25561.25	113.8
			C	**Large size** : 70 acres and above model class-120 acres soil sandy to sandy loam ; Irrigation-canal but water was short.	30909.16	35958.29	16.3	72051.70	133.1
7	Amritsar district	Water-logged area	A	**Small size farm :** 8.00 acres; canal supplemented by well irrigation; Bullock operated; water—logged area.	3816.16	4969.54	30.32	8118.86	112.72
			B	**Large size farm :** 30.14 acres-canal supplemented by well irrigation; Bullock operated-water-logged area.	13539.41	17841.05	31.77	29701.38	119.37

6. Gill, H.S.—Optimum Cropping Pattern for Cotton Belt of Punjab with Special Reference to Ferozepur District M.Sc. (Agri. Econ.) Farm Management Thesis—1966 (Unpublished) P.A.U. Ludhiana.
7. Chahal, T.S.—"Optimum Cropping Pattern for water-logged area of Amritsar"—M.Sc. (Agri. Econ.) Thesis, 1966 (Unpublished) P.A.U., Ludhiana.

* This representa income with no change in cropping pattern but shift from existing technology to recommended technology.

8.	Amritsar district	Specialised potato farms around Amritsar city.	A	**Small farm :** 8.5 acres; Electric tubewell; Irrigation tractor of bullock power to hired.	9665.20	14266.97	—	15781.34	63.28
			B	**Medium farm :** 14.30 acres, Tractor/Bullock power hired Tubewell irrigation.	18793.00	24497.72	30.35	25438.30	35.47
			C	**Large farm :** 24.63 acres. Perennial canal and tubewell irrigation; Tractor power hired; Soil loamy.	35525.70	41964.90	18.12	44780.95	26.05
			D	**Large farm :** 34.00 acres;Electric tubewell irrigated,, Tractor Fergusen 22 H.P.	45295.95	57668.18	27.31	61243.48	33.21
			E	**Large farm :** 46.50 acres; Perennial canal and tubewell irrigation; 32 H.P. Massey Fergusen Tractor.	61506.15	81882.65	33.13	84767.80	37.82
9	Hissar district	Bhakra Nangal canal irrigated area in Hissar-I and Barawala Blocks	A	**Small farm :** 13 acres : Canal water supply was considerably short; Bullock operated, land lift for all crops.	4970.60	N.A.	—	5670.51	14.08
			B	**Medium farm :** 21 acres; Canal irrigation with 65% irrigation intensity, Bullock operated	6426.97	N.A.	—	8771.63	36.48
			C	**Large farm :** 36 acres ; Canal irrigation very much restricted in summer season; Bullock operated.	9733.69	N.A.	—	15239.82	56.56

8. Khera, Gurnam Singh—"Some alternative plans for specialised potato farms around Amritsar city", M.Sc. Thesis 1965.

9. Kaushik, C.R.—"Farm Adjustment on introduction of new irrigational facilities in canal irrigated areas of Hissar District"—M.Sc. (Agri. Econ.) Farm Mgt. Thesis 1966 (Unpublished).

10	Gurgaon district	**Region—I** Gurgaon, Rewari and some parts of	A	**Small Synthetic farm :** 10.00 acres; 5.50 acres irrigated and 4.50 acres unirrigated; Bullock operated	1390.35	2737.20	52.95	4631.31	181.25
		Ballabhgarh tehsils of this district :	B	**Medium Synthetic farm :** 15.00 acres irrigated and 8.00 acres un-irri; Soil sandy to sandy loam; Bullock operated.	2642.67	3837.85	31.33	6398.97	142.54
		Persian Wheel and pumping set irrigated	C	**Large Synthetic farm :** 26.00 acres of which 11.50 acres irrigated and 14.50 acres unirrigated – soil sandy to sandy loam ; Bullock operated	3586.20	5275.22	51.52	9431.00	161.11
		Region—II Consists of Palwal and some parts of BallabhGarh, Nuh and	A	**Small Synthetic farm :** 8.00 acres of which 5 acres irrigated areas and 3 acres unirrigated, sandy loam to loam. Bullock operated.	1497.83	1769.44	20.00	2408.86	71.43
		Ferozepur Zhirka Tehsils Agra Canal irrigated.	B	**Medium Synthetic farm :** 13.00 acres of which 6.00 acres irrigated and 7.00 acres unirrigated, Bullock operated.	1783.47	2438.70	33.33	4744.48	108.00
			C	**Large Synthetic farm** : 25.00 acres of which 11.50 acres irrigated and 13.50 acres unirrigated, Soil loam to sandy loam, Bullock operated.	4468.74,	5539.93	20.20	9177.27	106.80

10. Himmat Singh—"Optimum Cropping Pattern for different areas of Gurgaon District"—M.Sc. (Agri.Econ.) Farm Mgt. Thesis 1966 (Unpublished).

a significant change with a high cropping intensity. The overall impact of this is an increase in the volume of business, which in turn has made adoption of lumpy technological improvements comparatively more economical. Most of these technological innovations available at this stage demand relatively more intensive use of labour. It looks to be paradoxical but is true that the farmers who are not able to mechanise their operations use less labour per acre. Where mechanisation of farm operations has taken place, labour use per acre has increased. No doubt, per crop-acre labour-use has marginally decreased but per cultivated acre labour requirements have increased due to intensive use of inputs and operations as well as increase in cropping intensity. All this requires farm organisation adjustments and better decision-making ability to make use of new technological improvements. Unfortunately, adjustment process is not automatic. With the initial adoption of a bunch of innovations, a different set of problems show up. The farmers' expectations rise. They eagerly look for new research results. In fact, an insatiable desire for new-finds gets created. Continuous adjustment in resource use, therefore, becomes very essential to take advantage of changing technology and farm management science has to play a pivotal role in bringing about these adjustments smoothly and efficiently.

Sometimes it is said that in India and other developing countries there is hardly any scope of the subject of farm management, because majority of small size holdings have to grow a given set of crops needed to meet their family needs. With the innovation of high yielding varieties, farmers in these countries can now produce the same quantities for their family consumption from a lesser area and released area can be used to produce for the market. There is also a scope of bringing about structural changes, and an ample scope is there to bring about changes in operational aspect of the farm business. Even where crop and other farm-enterprise specialisations are coming up, there is a good scope of making adjustment on operational aspects of farming. In specialised potato cultivation, for example, there are many ways and methods of sowing, hoeing, spraying and digging potatoes. One has to decide which method is more economical on a particular farm situation depending upon availability of labour, capital and other resources.

Industrial Development and Farm Management

Development of industry in a country enhances the scope of the application of the subject of farm management. Progressive industry puts forward many alternatives in relation to type and use of fertilisers, insecticides, implements and agricultural machinery, etc. This requires managerial skill to suitably adopt these new inputs and make other farm adjustments in order to rationalise the resource use under new set of alternatives.

Farm Management as an Educational Tool

Level of awareness of farmers increases with increased education facilities and extension programmes. To make full use of rapidly increasing new technology, the adoption process of agricultural practices need to be accelerated. Farmers learn more quickly if they are convinced on cost returns analysis of each suggested management action. Economic analysis makes the farmers learn more of alternative courses of action. The scientific management process acts as a useful educational tool through gathering more information on new alternatives and testing each recommendation on economic standards.

NATURE AND CHARACTERISTICS OF FARM MANAGEMENT SCIENCE

The farm management science has many distinguishing characteristics from other fields of agricultural science. A few of important characteristics are discussed below :

Practical Science

It is a practical science, because while dealing with the facts of other physical and biological sciences, it aims at testing the applicability of those facts and findings and showing how to put these results to use on a given farm situation. Threshing of wheat, for example, can be done by different methods, such as *Phalla* system, disc thresher, power thresher, tractor, fodder cutter, etc. All these methods have their own weak and strong points. A farmer has to select a method which is more practicable and economical to his particular farm situation, taking into consideration the volume of work and financial implications. Through a partial budgeting technique, the economic desirability of adopting a particular operation can be decided. Again, whether to purchase a new thresher or to get the threshing done on custom hire, is a decision falling under the subject of farm management.

Profitability Oriented

Farm management science alone is interested in profitability along with practicability of an idea. For example, physical scientists such as agronomists and plant breeders concern themselves with obtaining the maximum yield per acre irrespective of the profitability of inputs used but the farm management specialists always consider the costs involved in producing each unit of output in relation to returns and decides the optimum level of production. He has to consider all relevant factors such as financial implications, marketing, transportation and storage facilities and costs. In the decision-making process, profitability is thus the major criterion of selection/adoption of an enterprise or practice. Agricultural engineering science as another example may give the merits and demerits of a number of machines and power units. Which one or combination of those methods or materials is more profitable to adopt on a particular farm situation is the field of farm management. Farm management is thus interested in optimum results/yields which may not necessarily coincide with the maximum production point. In short, when other sciences deal with physical efficiency, the farm management concerns with economic efficiency.

Integrating Science

It is an integrating science in a sense that the facts and findings of other sciences are co-ordinated for the solution of various problems of individual farmers with a view to achieving certain desired goals. It considers the findings of other sciences in reaching its own conclusions. Most of the physical sciences throw out results having usefulness under specific set of conditions. The principles of farm management help integration of these results to reach at optimum combination of practices under the framework of restraints of individual farm situations.

Broader Field

Farm management decisions are made by getting information from more than one discipline. Most of the physical sciences concern themselves within narrower compartments of information. A farm management specialist has to know the broad principles of all other concerned sciences in addition to specialisation in the business principles of farm managment. It is thus a much broader field, because it has to gather knowledge from many other sciences for making its own decisions. A farm management specialist has to be thus a "Jack of many trades and master of one."

Micro-approach

Farm management has a micro-approach and it treats every farm unit unique in available resources, problems and potentialities. It recognises that no two farms are exactly identical with respect to soil, other production resources, farmers, managerial ability, etc. Each farm unit has to be, therefore, studied, guided or planned individually.

The major emphasis of this approach lies on treating the farm as an operational unit and tailoring the recommendations to fit into its resource position. Recommendations tailored to suit particular farm situations instead of blanket recommendation, is an important approach of the farm management extension education.

Farm Unit as a Whole

In farm management analysis, a farm as a whole is considered to be the unit for making decisions because the objective is to maximise the returns from the whole farm instead of only improving the returns from a particular enterprise or a practice. No agronomist will tell a farmer,how to utilise his surplus labour and scarce capital by taking up supplimentary enterprises. The sciences like Horticulture, Dairy, etc.; are similarly concerned with only one aspect of the whole farm business. Farm management considers all possible aspects and enterprises for the farm as a unit. It does not concern with merely one profitable enterprise, but with most profitable enterprise combinations to obtain maximum income from the farm as a whole on a continuous basis, exploiting the advantages of complementarity and supplementarity in the farm enterprises. It is much more concerned with total crop productivity instead of one crop productivity. A farmer may be declared *'Krishi Pandit'* because of highest per acre yield obtained of a particular crop but may be at the same time earning less than an average farmer of his group, because he may be allocating most of his resources to one crop and one plot instead of using each rupee or unit of labour and other resources where it adds to returns the most. This is more true where many of the farm resources are limited. The principles of Farm Management thus help reach the optimum enterprise-mix that would yield the highest income to the farmer from his total farm organisation.

RELATIONSHIP OF FARM MANAGEMENT WITH OTHER

Economic Theory

Farm Management as a subject matter is an application of business principles in farming from the point of view of an individual farmer. It is only a specialised branch of the wider field of Economics. The tools and techniques for farm management are supplied by the general economic theory. The law of variable proportions, the principles of substitution and the marginal analysis are all instances of tools of economic theory used in farm management analysis. It is an integral part of agricultural production economics. It is often difficult to make a distinction between the two.

Relationship of Farm Management with Other Sciences

Relationship between farm management and other sciences is interdependent as illustrated in the following chart.

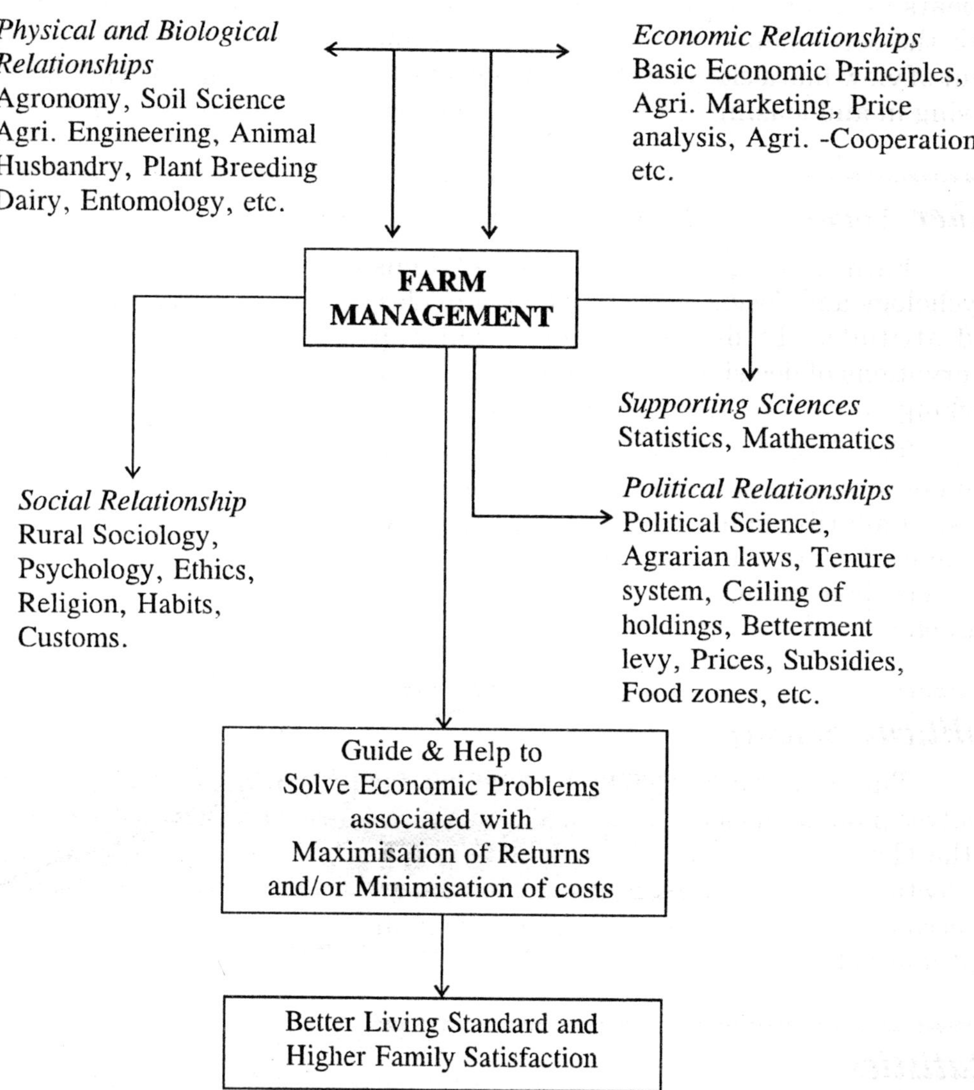

It is generally accepted that while farm management is concerned with the economic efficiency at the farm level, agricultural production economics deals with allocative efficiency in resources in agriculture as a whole. Thus farm management is an intra-farm science and agricultural production economics an inter-farm or inter-region science. This distinction cannot, however, be stretched too far. The emphasis is only relative. Various subject matter fields in the applied science of agricultural economics include agricultural finance, credit and co-operative marketing and land economics. In so far as these problems are dealt at the farm level, they become an important phase of farm management analysis. The acquisition and use of credit by the farmer for the production purposes logically appears to be within the realm of farm management. The land economics dealing with the settlement and tenure problems and trends in land use from national point of view has a close relationship with farm management decisions as it affects leasing in and leasing out activities of the farmers.

Other Social Sciences

Farm Management has close relationship with other social sciences like Psychology and Sociology. Psychology provides information on human motivations and attitudes. In decision-making, many psychological aspects and mental reservations of decision maker come in, such as attitude towards taking risks and working under conditions of uncertainty.

The farmer lives and works in a given social-matrix. His decisions are influenced by the customs, habits and cultural values of the society in which he lives. Similarily, many decisions are made by the family jointly. Rural Sociology which deals with the social problems, responses and reactions of the rural people vis-a-vis their main occupation *i.e.,* agriculture has a great bearing on the farm management decision the farmers make.

Political Science

The acceptance of new production techniques and methods in farming involves political aspects as well. Various pieces of legislation and political actions of the Government affect the production decision of the farmer such as scale of production, restrictions or encouragement on growing of certain crops such as poppy, tobacco in India, land utilisation, ceiling on land, minimum and maximum prices, food zones etc.

Statistics

Statistics is another science that has been used effectively and extensively by the agricultural economists and farm management specialists. This science is helpful in providing methods and procedures by which data regarding specific farm problems can be collected, analysed and evaluated.

Physical and Biological Sciences

Farm management has to heavily depend on other physical and biological sciences for its source material. More than any other field in agricultural economics, farm management relies closely on other branches of agricultural science such as soil science, agronomy, animal husbandry, agricultural engineering, forestry, etc.

These physical and biological sciences are not directly concerned with economic efficiency. They provide input-output relationships in their respective areas in physical terms *i.e.*, they define production possibilities within which various choices can be made. Such information is helpful, indeed is indispensable to the farm management specialist, in dealing with the problems of production efficiency. For example, physical input-output relationships in crop production are developed in agronomy. Animal Science tells about the rates of gain in live-weight associated with feed rations, age and breed of animal. Dairy science indicates the response of milk production to the feed intake by cows and other conditions associated with milk production. Agricultural engineering provides information on efficiency of various implements and machines in performance of various tasks. An agronomist cannot, however, tell the farmer as to what crops he should grow and in what combination for maximising returns. The soil scientist cannot indicate the optimum doses of fertilizer consistent with the input-output prices. The animal scientist cannot indicate the point of optimum feeding for beef cattle or milch animals. Of all branches of agriculture, it is agricultural economics and farm management which concern with the total profitability. Farm management specialist has to, however, depend heavily upon other disciplines for getting information on the technological relationships in agriculture. This only emphasises the fact that if farm management studies are to be meaningful and useful to the farmer, there should be co-operative team-effort between the farm management specialist and other physical and biological scientists.

Physical and biological sciences, thus specify the production possibilities, farm management economics defines optimum resource use within the framework of farm resource-restraints and the production possibilities, social sciences and political sciences figure out and place limitations on choice making through customs, habits, laws and other individual or group values.

Various sciences other than economics thus contribute to the solution of the economic problems of agriculture. It is the task of the farm management specialist and agricultural economist to determine how and to what extent the findings of these sciences should be used. This is by no means an easy responsibility.

TYPICAL FARM MANAGEMENT DECISIONS

As farm management is the science which concerns with making decisions and choices about combining different enterprises and optimal utilisation of resources available, it is necessary to understand the typical farming decisions. Decisions can be classified on the basis of characteristics like (1) importance, (2) frequency, (3) imminency, (4) revocability, and (5) available alternatives. For the purpose of obtaining proper sequence in production process the various typical farming decisions are discussed under three major heads (see chart on next page):

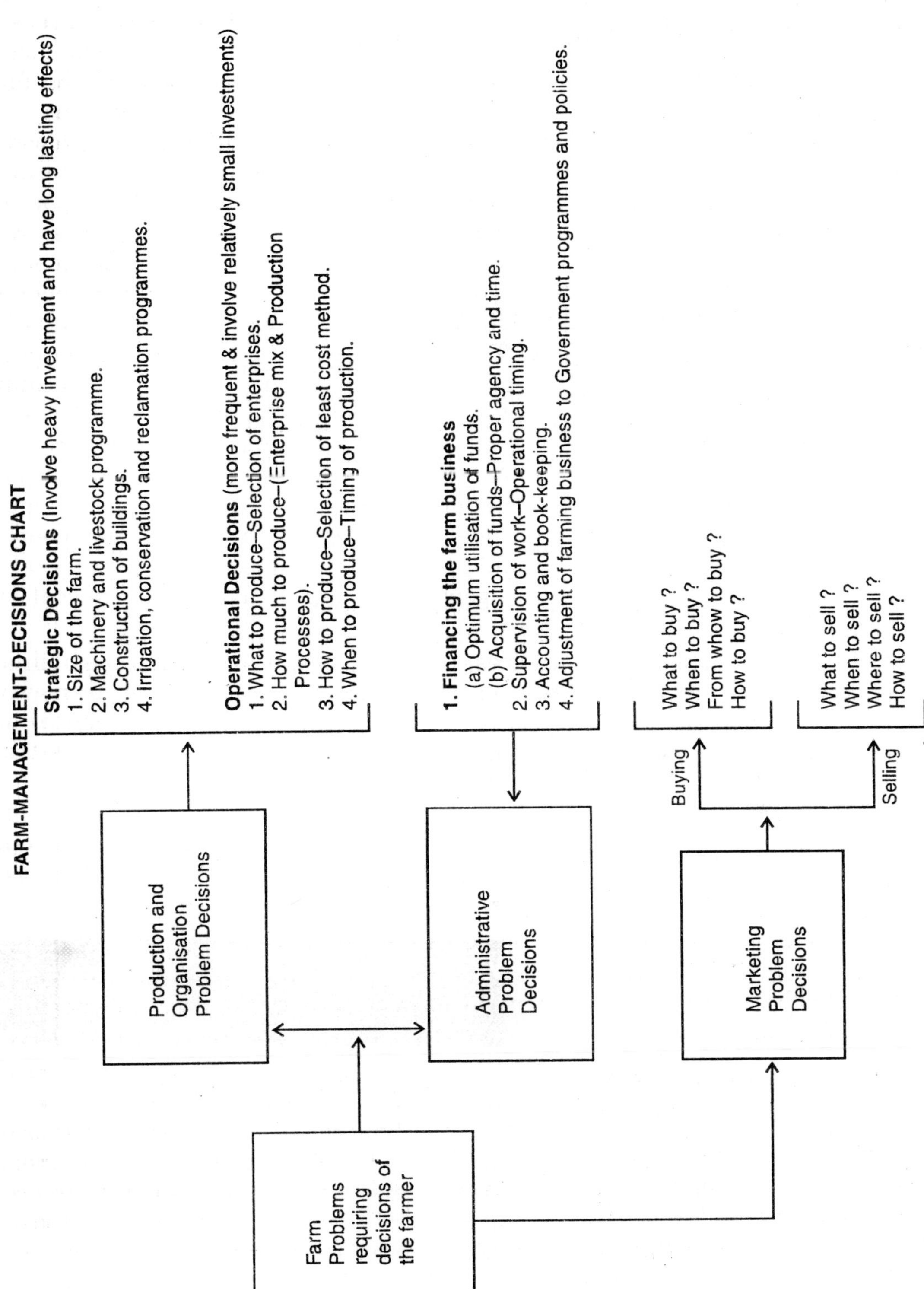
FARM-MANAGEMENT-DECISIONS CHART
Farm Problems requiring decisions of the farmer
Production and Organisation Problem Decisions
Administrative Problem Decisions
Marketing Problem Decisions
Strategic Decisions (Involve heavy investment and have long lasting effects)
1. Size of the farm.
2. Machinery and livestock programme.
3. Construction of buildings.
4. Irrigation, conservation and reclamation programmes.
Operational Decisions (more frequent & involve relatively small investments)
1. What to produce–Selection of enterprises.
2. How much to produce–(Enterprise mix & Production Processes).
3. How to produce–Selection of least cost method.
4. When to produce–Timing of production.
1. Financing the farm business
(a) Optimum utilisation of funds.
(b) Acquisition of funds–Proper agency and time.
2. Supervision of work–Operational timing.
3. Accounting and book-keeping.
4. Adjustment of farming business to Government programmes and policies.
Buying
What to buy ?
When to buy ?
From whow to buy ?
How to buy ?
Selling
What to sell ?
When to sell ?
Where to sell ?
How to sell ?

Production and Organisation Decisions

Farm manager must take decisions on certain fundamental questions regarding production of enterprises and organisation of his farming business. These questions involve his land resources, what to produce, and how to produce. He must decide what the scale of his farming operations will be and how to equip his farm business. Such decisions can be further categorised into two groups *i.e.*, strategic and operational decisions :

Strategic Management Decisions

These are the management decisions which involve heavy investment and have long lasting effect. These decisions give shape to overall organisation of the business. In turn, operational decisions get greatly influenced by the organisation. A few of the examples of strategic management decisions are detailed below :

1. *Deciding the best size of the farm*

Decisions on size of the farm depend on a number of factors such as type of farming area, type of business, land irrigated or unirrigated, level of mechanisation, intensity of land use, managerial ability of the farmer, etc. Farms of different sizes have thus both advantages and disadvantages in terms of costs and operational efficiency. The economic efficiency of each crop and/or livestock enterprise and their combination, when they are operated on different scales, are considered to decide the optimum size of the holding. The decisions here will partly determine how specialised or diversified the farm will be.

Appropriate size of farm is more important to a farmer than to most other businessmen because of slow turnover in agriculture and the durability of the farm investments. The most serious weakness of agriculture in India is that many of the farms are not large enough to utilise fully the available family labour. The major advantage of the large farms is greater labour and machinery efficiency. Trends indicate that operational size of farm is increasing. As new machinery and labour saving devices develop, the operational size of the holdings will continue increasing. A large holding in one period may turn out to be economically small in the future. Leasing in and leasing out activities can regulate the operational size of holdings.

2. *Decisions on farm labour and machinery programmes*

Deciding the most profitable combination of the factors to be used in producing a commodity is one of the important farm management decisions. Is there too much equipment in relation to the land and labour available on the farm ? Would it be profitable to vary labour or land to better utilise a given set of machinery ? What combination of farm labour and machinery should be adopted to get maximum returns ? These are a few of the questions on substituting machinery for labour and labour and vice versa so as to reduce the cost of production. Best machinery and labour programme should consider many other factors such as seasonal labour requirements against availability, financial position of the farmer, etc. As labour and machinery are substitutable, such decisions are taken in relation to size of the farm *i.e.*, volume of farm business.

Suppose, for example, there is a question of purchasing power- wheat-thresher on a farm situation where only 5 acres of wheat are grown. Threshing of wheat from 5 acres means work for only 1-2 days for the thresher, which is too less to justify the purchase. It may be, however, possible to get custom work, In this situation, purchase of thresher may be justified. In the absence of sufficient custom work, the purchase of power thresher may not be economical and consistent with the opportunity cost of capital.

3. *Decisions on construction of buildings*

Decisions on size and type of farm buildings involve heavy-investment which become fixed resource for the business. Kind of buildings, for the present pattern and level of production, depends upon the kind and level of crops or livestock produced. For example, different types of buildings are required for dairy enterprises, crop enterprises and vegetable enterprises. Once a particular building programme has been designed and executed it will be very difficult to bring about any change without heavy additional costs.

4. *Decisions regarding irrigation, conservation and reclamation programmes*

As improvements of alkalinity, salinity and other soil defects require heavy investments, soil conservation and reclamation programmes often have to be spread over years and choice of most economical method or a combination of methods has to be made from among mulching, contouring, strip cropping, bunding and terracing, In case of reclamation, decisions have to be made on chemical treatment, soil scraping, cultural practices, depending upon the feasibility and efficiency of a particular treatment.

Decisions on irrigation programme are very crucial because it involves heavy investment and it gives a flow service over long period of time and also improves the productivity of other associated inputs. Availability of underground water, field contour and availability of capital, influence the choice on type of irrigation.

Operational Management Decisions

Such decisions are continuously made in the day-to-day operations of the farm business. The frequency of these decisions is more as compared to strategic management decisions but the investment involved is relatively small and impact shortlived. These decisions are generally :

What to produce ?

How much to produce ?

How to produce ? and

When to produce ?

In this section, a discussion is made on these decisions ; risks and uncertainties are held constant. These will be discussed in later chapters.

1. *What to produce ?* (Selection of enterprises)

There can be many alternative enterprises available to a particular farm, consistent with the technical feasibility of such enterprises. Certain enterprises will yield higher production returns as compared to others, because of favourable climate, soil and topographical conditions. The law of comparative advantage will help decide here the crops to be grown or the livestock to be raised. For this, information on crop rotations, new varieties and physical requirements of different enterprises is essential. The relative profitability of these enterprises (based on cost-returns analysis) will determine as to what to produce and what not to produce ?

Crop rotation can be compared like single crop enterprises taking into consideration their technical feasibility and economic desirability. Certain crops may not, however, sometimes fit into a rotation because of different soil requirements. For example, Groundnut-wheat rotation cannot normally be compared with sugarcane, due to different soil requirements. Alongside technical feasibility and economic optimality, the personal preferences and prejudices of the farmer also influence selection of farm enterprises. However economical, a *Sikh*-farmer will not grow tobacco crop, a *Brahmin* cultivator will not prefer hog and poultry enterprise. Again a farmer seeking some leisure time will not prefer sugarcane crop. One may still grow some amber-coloured bold-grain local wheat for home consumption, though Mexican wheat may give twice high returns.

2. *How much to produce ?* (Enterprise-mix)

This decision has two aspects : Enterprise-mix and resource-use.

Product-mix

It involves degree of specialisation or diversification. Combination of crop and livestock enterprises will depend upon the level of resources available and land use capabilities in addition to existence of complementary and supplementary relationships.

Level of each enterprise will be decided on the basis of principle of substitution *i.e.*, the scarce farm resources are first considered for those enterprises which are most profitable and then the next best profitable enterprises are considered for inclusion. One cannot put all the acreage under one crop based on its individual profitability because one or the other resource will become a limiting factor, if production of that crop is expanded beyond a certain limit.

The factors influencing the farm enterprises-mix are generally labour availability, use of land, use of bye-product, maintenance of soil fertility, relative risks, distribution of income overtime and efficiency in the use of power, machinery and buildings.

Level of resource use

What amount of resources should one use with each acre of crop land or each animal is the second dimension of the problem. For every crop and livestock unit, one can use different amounts of labour, capital and other inputs to produce different levels of output per acre or per animal. For example, one may use small or large amounts of fertilizers, irrigation, labour or seeds according to their availability. Different levels of these inputs will yield different levels of output. It is, therefore, a management problem to decide on the combination and level of inputs-use which may be consistent with the overall goals of the farmer to maximise the returns and profits or minimise the costs and losses.

3. *How to produce ?* (Selection of least cost/ efficient method or practice)

There are many substitute practices and resources that can be used for the production of a unit of crop or livestock product. Decisions here are made on the best practice or combination of practices and methods. There is always a question of choice among different ways of doing the same operation. Technological advances are continuously putting new machines, new inputs and new methods at the disposal of the farmer. The choice making from among the various alternatives has, thus become a real management problem. For example, many methods of sowing of wheat such as *kera, pora, rabi* drill, automatic *rabi* drill, seed-cum-fertilizer drill etc. exist today. Although objective generally is to select the least cost or most efficient method keeping in view the amount of work to be done on a particular farm situation, the least-cost method or practice is not always the best choice. Because least-cost practice or combination of practices might have to be very often abandoned in favour of comparatively more costly, but a time saving practice or combination of practices.

4. *When to produce ?* (Timing of production)

Although this aspect is taken care of while deciding what to produce, how much to produce and how to produce, yet for emphasis on time, it is discussed separately. Different enterprises have different growth periods. For example, apples take 10 years to fruit, wheat takes six months, different vegetables crops need different growth periods to reach maturity. Different crops and fruit plants have varieties ; early season, normal season or late season. Prices differ during these periods. Farmers are frequently faced with questions, whether to produce normal, early or late variety of a crop or what combination thereof, because differences in yield in different period may not be balanced by the differences in prices during these periods.

Administrative Decisions

Along with production and organisation decisions, a farm manager has to take certain administrative decisions too. He must ensure, for example, that farm-work is done in time and in the way it should be done. He must foresee the need for and implement adjustments, sometimes quickly, in production and organisation strategies. Brief description of a few administrative decisions is as follows :

1. *Financing the farm business*

While some farmers have their own sufficient funds, others may have to borrow. The problem is two fold, (*i*) utilisation of funds within the farm business and (*ii*) acquisition of funds : proper agency, time and type of credit. Farm manager has to decide which agency will be more economical and efficient for getting loan when needed and of the type needed. What time will be appropriate for getting credit and how to plan repayments ? How much credit he should get within safe limits to secure the maximum benefit from the productive credit.

2. *Supervision of work*

The farm manager has to make sure that every job is done in time in the desired way and operationally most efficiently.

3. *Accounting and book-keeping*

Administrative responsibilities on the farm involve collecting, synthesising and analysing data to evaluate performance for making future decisions. Here decisions are to be made on the kind of farm records, time allocation and money to be spent on this activity; balancing these inputs with the utility of farm records maintained and analysed.

4. *Adjustments to Government programmes and policies*

Government programmes and policies place restrictions on farm production and marketing programmes. Food zones, restriction on product movements, price support policy, etc. are some of the examples of Govt. instruments used to regulate production, marketing and prices of farm products. The farmer has to decide on the level of production and resource use consistent with price and procurement policies. Again size of the holding has to remain within the ceilings imposed by the state, as is the case in India.

5. *Production for home consumption and the market*

The objective normally should be to earn highest profits and not to operate a self-sufficient unit. If the home-consumption enterprises interfere with this objective, these should be generally discarded in favour of buying the product from the market with the higher earnings from commercialisation of major farm enterprises.

Often, however, farm families prefer to produce some products for home consumption, even if they are not economically justified. Under such situations the farmer has to decide the proper combination of products for home consumption as well as for the market to achieve maximum family satisfaction.

Marketing Decisions

Decisions on buying and selling, *i.e.* to buy seeds, fertilizers, livestock equipment, etc. from the least cost source and in the least costly way and to sell the farm produce in a manner to get maximum profit are some of the very important decisions a farmer has to make. A brief discussion on buying and selling decisions of the farmer are as follows.

1. *Buying* (When to buy, where to buy and how to buy)

Farmers generally purchase a number of inputs for production of agricultural commodities. Attempt is always to purchase at the least cost. He, therefore, faces such questions as from where to buy ? When to buy ? and How to buy ? Suppose he has to purchase poultry feed to meet his requirements for one year. Choices before him are to : (*i*) buy maize grain immediately after harvest to get advantage of post harvest low prices and meet storage costs over time, (*ii*) spread his buying over different periods, pay higher prices and avoid storage costs and risks, (*iii*) purchase in bulk or in small lots at a given time—small and large transactions normally carry different prices and costs, (*iv*) purchase processed poultry feed or different components separately and mix them himself. These are a few of the lots of small decisions the farmers have to take which make the whole difference to the success or failure of their business.

2. *Selling* (When, where and how to sell farm products.*)

Although individual farmer has a little control over market prices, yet he can adjust the timings of his sales. He can sell in the lean period when the prices are higher, keeping in view the storage costs. Other alternatives are to sell immediately after harvest at lower prices. In principle if the market prices are expected to be higher than the storage costs, it would be profitable to store and sell in the lean period. Whether to sell in the village or city market, whether to sell as raw material or a processed product are some other such decisions the producer-seller has to make.

---

* Seldom in Agriculture these three functions get separated although it is sometimes done so in big businesses.

SOME FARM MANAGEMENT PROBLEMS UNDER INDIAN CONDITIONS

Farm management problems in India vary from place to place depending largely upon the degree of agricultural development and the availability of resources. The following are some of the most common problems in the field of farm management and planning in India :

Small Size of Farm Business

The average size of operational holding in India is 6.57 acres*. The holdings are fragmented too. Excessive pressure of population creates unfavourable man-land-ratio in most parts of the country. This combined with excessive family labour depending upon agriculture has weakened the financial position of the farmers and limited the scope for business expansion.

Farm As A Household

In most parts of the country family farms prepetuate the traditional combinations of crops and methods of cultivations. Work habits are closely associated with food intake, living conditions, sanitation, etc. Thus, the equation between agricultural labour and household labour becomes an identity. This makes it difficult for the farmer to introduce business content and incorporate new management ideas in his farm operations. Home management thus heavily influences and gets influenced by farm management decisions.

Inadequate Capital

Inadequacy of capital is a serious deficiency of Indian farms. Small size of farms and until recently unremunerative prices had kept the farmers under perpetual debt. In the recent years, due to increased productivity of crops through introduction of new varieties of crops and production oriented incentive prices, the situation has improved a great deal. Still, small farmers and tenant cultivators are not out of the woods. The new technology demands heavier inputs, such as more of fertilizers, plant protection measures, irrigation and better seeds, as well as investment on power and machinery. The small farmers have very low marketable surpluses. They cannot meet their farm financial requirements from their own funds. Low cost, adequate and timely credit is their most pressing need if they have to put their farm-firms on a growth path.

---

* India, 1971-72.

Under-Employment

Under employment results from : (1) small size of the farms, (2) large family labour supply, (3) seasonal nature of production, and (4) lack of subsidiary or supporting rural industries. Under-employment, in turn, breeds laziness, economic frustration and social tension. It also reduces efficiency and productivity of rural manpower.

Slow Adoption of Innovations

Small farmers are usually conservative and sometimes skeptical of new techniques and methods. However, once they try a new idea and find it effective, they get eager to adopt that. New researches offer many improved techniques of production and farm practices to farmers. The rate of adoption, however, depends largely on the farmer's willingness and ability to use the new information. Since established attitudes and values do not change overnight, the extension programmes take time to get the research results commercially exploited and adopted on the farms. It requires trained men and substantial financial investments. Yet, there is no better short cut to a more rapid adoption of agricultural innovations for increasing farm incomes.

Inadequacy of Input Supplies

Farmers may be willing to introduce change, yet they may face the difficulty in obtaining the required inputs of proper quality, in sufficient quantity, and on time to sustain the introduced changes. Shortages of foreign exchange in developing countries seriously limit importation of needed supplies and materials. Besides, domestic industries generally lack raw material, skills, capital or combination of these, to manufacture the needed farm supplies or inputs. India is, however, developing agricultural inputs fast and is also importing the materials not available in the country. Fertilizers, insecticides, pesticides and plant protection equipment manufactures are being expanded and are being imported. Tractor manufacturing is being expanded indigenously and also a large number of tractors are being imported from U.K., Germany, Italy and Russia mainly. Pumping sets and electricity, as well as oil engines to pump water and to do stationary farm jobs are being almost entirely produced indigenously.

Mangerial Skills

The most important and difficult problem for many years to come will be to improve the managerial skills of the large number of small farmers in the country.

This is necessary to make millions of ultimate users of research results develop progressive attitudes responsive to the technological changes. Education of the farmers on a mass scale is thus the most important need. Even illiterate people can be educated through demonstration of the application of new techniques and better ways of using the inputs available.

Communication and Markets

These are two important elements of infrastructure necessary for introducing economic content in the farm organisations. Lack of adequate communication systems and regulated market organisation stand as a major bottleneck in the way of improving the management of farms on business lines. Substantial investments, therefore, need to be made on roads, marketing systems and other communication facilities in almost all parts of the country.

DEVELOPMENT OF FARM MANAGEMENT SCIENCE IN INDIA

Various quotations are found in the Indian literature on the art and management of agriculture. Countries with old civilizations, such as India, China, Italy and Greece, acquired considerable skill in the art of farm management in the period when most of the countries now considered advanced were in a hunting stage. Development of farm management as specialised science, however, received attention only very recently. Although numerous efforts have been made from time to time, various organisations, institutions and individuals, the details of which are difficult to describe within the scope of this book, a brief survey of the development of the subject of farm management is discussed here under three headings, *viz* Research, Extension, and Teaching.

Farm Management Research

Research in farm management in India is of recent origin. Although studies pertaining to cost of production of various crops and cost surveys have been made by various organisations such as Punjab Board of Economic Enquiry, Indian Council of Agricultural Research, Gokhale Institute of Politics and Economics, Indian Central Jute Committee, Indian Central Cotton Committee and Indian Central Oil Seed Committee since 1923, these studies were more of the nature of cost of production surveys. Farm management studies in real sense for providing a basis for efficient farming decisions were taken up only very recently with the inception of a broad base programme of studies in "Economics of Farm Management" in five regions of the states *i.e* Punjab, U.P., W.Bengal, Maharashtra and Madras in 1954-55 through 1956-57, with another region added to it (in Maharashtra) in 1955-56. These studies were taken up jointly by the Directorate of Economics & Statistics, Ministry of Food & Agriculture and Research Programme Committee (R.P.C.) of the Planning Commission with two-fold objective :

(*i*) to provides a basis for formulation of agricultural policies and a farm management extension work, and

(*ii*) to compare cost accounting and survey methods in order to determine their place in future programmes of farm management research.

These studies were later extended to three more states *i.e.* Andhra Pradesh, Bihar and Orissa for the year 1957-58 with the additional objectives of appraising the availability of farm resources and their allocation under different farm situations as well as to study the input-output relationship on these farms. Farm management studies with only cost accounting technique were later extended to some other regions of Bihar for the period 1960-63, and in Punjab for 1961-64. They generated a wealth of information which could be used for various policy decisions as well as in appraisal of farm economy of the regions. These studies were not adequate, however, to suggest a basis for re-organisation of farms to improve efficiency standards in the business of agriculture. Although some research workers tried to demonstrate the use of these studies to develop alternative farm plans for the selected farmers, yet these data could not be realistically used to develop optimum farm plans which could be taken up by the individual cultivator. These studies lacked in identification of resource restrictions. Also, input-output relationships could not be detailed for individual farm situations.

The series of studies conducted by the Punjab Board of Economic Enquiry on farm accounts provided a very useful data based on farm records. These inquiries were started in the year 1923 with the major objectives of studying the costs and returns as well as farm resource use patterns in different regions of the state so that they serve as a basis for policy decision to the government. The objective of these studies has been to improve farm efficiencies which, however, could not be fulfilled because they lacked data on specific resource restrictions on the individual holdings. Also, the inputs used could not be classified into fixed resource inputs and variable resource inputs.

Another set of studies has been made by Agro-Economic Research Centres located in eight different regions of the country. These centres, since the year 1954-55 have been bringing out studies on almost all economic aspects of agriculture including food, policy, fair price shops, prices, marketing, irrigation, agricultural labour, co-operatives and other miscellaneous aspects. These centres conducted only a few pin-pointed studies in the subject of farm management and planning itself.

Recently, the interest has been shown in the subject by the various Agricultural Universities, Indian Agricultural Research Institute, and other economic Organisations, such as Institute of Economic Growth, Directorate of Economics and Statistics, Indian Council of Agricultural Research, Programme Evaluation Organisation & Research Programme Committee of the Planning Commission. In the universities, these studies have been mostly conducted on individual basis or as post-graduate student projects. There are quite a number of these studies which have centered attention on farm management and planning aspects. First attempts made in this direction were on exploring the potentialities of increasing farm incomes through re-organisation of the farm business at the existing level of technology and farm resources. Quite a few studies incorporated new and improved technology and resource variable programming. Pioneering work in this direction has been done by the department of Economics and Sociology of Punjab Agriucltural University, Indian Agricultural Research Institute, Directorate of Economics and Statistics, Ministry of Food and Agriculture and Institute of Economic Growth.

The farm management research thus made a beginning through farm surveys leading to farm accounting and farm business analysis. Actual farm management research goes back to hardly a decade or so. Through this short span of time, thinking has much cleared up. Now farm management research in India is using sophisticated mathematical tools of analysis such as linear programming, non-linear programming, as well as recursive programming. It may be a little early at this stage for an extended application of these refined tools of analysis for making any practical use of results on actual farm-firms, yet it augurs well that farm management researchers are improving and building up new techniques.

Farm Management Extension

In the subject of farm management, emphasis is now increasingly being placed on applied side of the techniques of farm planning and budgeting. Farm planning and management studies in different universities and agricultural economics research institutions are thus getting more importance. Under the Intensive Agriculture Districts Programme (IADP) use of farm planning and management techniques was made in seven districts in India in the year 1960-61 and later extended to other eight districts of the country. This was the first attempt at the application of the farm management and planning techniques on actual farm situations. Comprehensive farm planning techniques were first tried, but soon it was realised that the technical persons responsible for the job were not adequately trained and were not sufficient in number. Farm planning programmes were then classified into three stages.

In the first stage, simple crop plans (crop budgets) for some important crops were prepared with complete package of practices and tried on small plots. As many as 8,600,000 so called simple crop plans were prepared under I.A.D.P. in the country in the year 1963-64. In the second stage, such crop plans were developed for all the crop enterprises carried by the farmers. In the third stage, complete farm planning procedure was adopted on a few selected farms by the Agricultural Extension Officers, who are graduates in agriculture. Unfortunately, this attempt turned out to be a wide shot. The technical persons were too meagre in number to handle this project at such a wide scale and, above all, they were not trained in the subject of farm management.

In the year 1966-67, Agricultural University in Punjab initiated a programme of farm management extension education with Assistant Extension Specialists (Farm Management) located in all the districts and at important block headquarters of the state. This Assistant Extension Specialist (Farm Management) at each district headquarter is one of the line members of a team of specialists (University Farm Advisory Service) ; other four disciplines being soil science, agronomy, horticulture, and plant protection. This is a pioneering step in farm management extension education in India. It is expected that the example will be followed by other states especially where the Agricultural Universities are located with strong departments of agricultural economics. Broad job responsibilities of the farm management extension specialists are :

(*i*) Delineate-homogeneous type of farming areas with identical problems and potentials of growth,

(*ii*) develop standard production plans for guidance of the farmers with different size of farms and resource mix.

(*iii*) hold training camps and field days for the farmers of their areas.

(*iv*) introduce simple farm record books and assist the record keeping farmers in farm business analysis planning their farms.

(*v*) operate a few demonstartion centres (whole farm unit) with the assistance and collaboration of other subject matter specialists to demonstrate the practicability and profitability of the various recommendations of the university.

(*vi*) keep detailed records on the farming conditions of their area, including records on production, acreage under different crops, prices, marketing arrivals etc. and

(*vii*) serve as a live link between the university department of economics on one hand and farmers, government extension agencies and other institutions concerned with agricultural development on the other, for transmission of research results and feedback of the field problems.

Teaching of Farm Management

Farm management till recently was one of the many subjects taught to the under-graduate students in the Agricultural Universities and colleges in departments of agronomy. Subject matter never went beyond simple cost and returns calculations. At post-graduate level, farm management was taught only as minor part of the curriculum in the subject of agriculture economics. It was only in 1963, this subject as a specialised field of study was introduced at post-graduate level in some of the teaching institutions such as Indian Agricultural Research Institute and the Agricultural Universities. Under-graduate teaching also got transferred to the agricultural economics departments. However, in many universities, this subject is still being taught in the departments of agronomy. Punjab Agricultural University, introduced a special ad-hoc course in the subject of farm management and trained some 60 students in Master's programme by the year 1965-66. In this university and in some other too, subject of farm management is now a regular field of specialisation, Indian Society of Agricultural Economics supplements education programmes of the colleges and universities through short training courses designed to improve the competence of the teachers engaged in farm management research, teaching and extension.

Farm management research and teaching facilities and programmes are thus developing fast in India. The efforts and the resources allocated, however seem to be as yet inadequate to match the needs on farm management and planning work in the country.

1. *Define farm management ?*
2. *What is difference between management of a farm and farm management ?*
3. *Describe the relationship between farm management and other agricultural sciences, such as soil science, agronomy, agricultural engineering and dairy technology.*
4. *How would you differentiate between the subject of farm management and agricultural economics ?*
5. *What are the peculiar characteristics of farm management as a science ?*

6. ***What is the difference between farm management and production economics ?***
7. ***What are the bottlenecks in developing farm management on scientific lines in under-developed countries ?***
8. ***Review the historical development of farm management science in India.***

(Recommended Readings)

1. ***Bradford, Lawrence A. and Glenn L. Johnson, "Farm Management Analysis," New York, John Wiley and Sons, Inc. : 1953, Chapters 1, 2 & 3.***
2. ***Heady, Earl O and Harald R. Jenson, "Farm Management Economics," Englewood Cliffs, New Jersey, Prentice-Hall, Inc. ; 1954, Chapter 1.***
3. ***Forster, G.W., "Farm Organization & Management," New York, Prentice Hall, Inc.; Chapter 1.***
4. ***Gray, L.C., "Introduction to Agricultural Economics," New York, MacMillan; 1924, Chapter 1.***

2 Characteristics of Farming as a Business

For successful organization of a business and for optimum use of resources, it is important to first understand the characteristics of that industry or business. This chapter deals with the characteristics of farming as a business and farmer as a businessman. Discussion here will be directed to the special characteristics of farming that influence the actions of farmers.

CHARACTERISTICS

Farming as a business has many distinguishing features from most of other industries in their management methods and practices. Farm management principles cannot be, therefore, taken as a simple application of principles involved in managing other industries. The major differences between farming and most other industries are in :

(*i*) primary forces of production.

(*ii*) size of the production unit,

(*iii*) dependence on climate factors,

(*iv*) frequency and speed of decisions,

(*v*) changes in prices,

(*vi*) standardisation of practices,

(*vii*) turn-over,

(*viii*) financing,

(*ix*) inseparable home and farm business,

(*x*) nature of variable and fixed costs,

(*xi*) demand for farm products, and

(*xii*) time rigidity in consumption of agricultrual products.

(*i*) *Primary forces of production*

Agricultural production is primarily biological in nature. Farming deals with living enterprises (plants and animals). A slight change in the environment may, therefore, cause serious difficulties. One day of cold wave may, for example, destroy the whole of a standing crop. Unforeseen changes in environment such as plant or animal disease and storms can cause a considerable damage. Most of other industries are less affected by such circumstances ; they do have risks, but the degree is relatively low. The farmers, thus, have little control over production due to agriculture being seasonal and biological in character. Management practices in farming must, therefore, be adjusted to meet these conditions.

Agriculture, on the whole, requires a far larger proportion of land in relation to other factors of production than does industry. This is the underlying cause of many of the chief differences between agriculture and industry such as : (*i*) diminishing returns at an earlier stage, (*ii*) wide scatter of production, and (*iii*) greater importance of systems of land tenure.

(*ii*) *Size of the production unit*

Farming is, comparatively a small-sized business and thus provides little scope for division of labour. The farmer is generally both a labourer and a capitalist since he works on the farm, on which all his accumulated wealth and annual savings get invested. Most other industries, however, are organised on a large scale. Because of this difference in the size of the unit, management problems of agriculture vary greatly from those of many other industries.

Farming is not basically suited to large scale operations on a scale obtained in industries, because it is concerned with living things, plants and animals scattered over space, which need prompt attention and personal care of the farmer.

(*iii*) *Heavy dependence on climate factors*

Weather is a very important, but unpredictable variable in all farming operations. It is of less importance in most other business. Any sudden change in the weather-temperature, rainfall, or himidity, would involve readjustment of the entire day's work, perhaps the entire week's work on a farm, while it may mean only a minor inconvenience in many other industries.

Farming is, thus subject to a great risk and uncertainty on account of excess or failure of rainfall, drought, hail storm, floods, insect-pests and disease. As a result of dependence on climatic factors, management practices in farming must be much more flexible than in other industries.

(*iv*) *Frequency and speed of decisions*

Farming requires many and speedy decisions on the part of the farmer and farm workers. When a sudden rain floods all the crop land on a Saturday afternoon, there is no time to discuss the merits of paying one and a half time or double wages on Sunday. The fields must be drained immediately to save the growing crops, even if it takes all the night to do the job and costs tremendously.

(*v*) *Changes in prices*

Agricultural prices and production usually move in opposite directions. Because of the effects of climate and biological factors, a relatively large volume of production of a given farm commodity is usually followed by a decline in process; and a smaller volume results in increase in prices. This difference is due to the fact that in the short-run agriculture has little control over the volume of production resulting in inelasticity of supplies. Demand for agricultural products is also relatively more inelastic. Most other industries can apply checks over-production by adjusting their manufacturing schedules. Even in the long-run, it is comparatively more difficult in agriculture to adjust production to price variations.

(*vi*) *Standardization of practices and products*

Most of the non-agricultural industries are characterized by the production of a large volume of highly standardised single-line products. By the use of machines and trained personnel, it is possible to produce large volume of products exactly the same in size, form and quality. Such standardisation of practices is impossible in agriculture. In spite of years of intensive scientific breeding and selection of desirable potato varieties for example, there are no identical potatoes available. Although many different systems of classification and grading have been developed, absolutely uniform products have not been placed in the market. The management problems of the farmers thus differ from those of many other industries because of the marketing difficulties involved in small volumes of different-quality products.

(*vii*) *Turn-over*

Rate of capital turn-over is the gross returns on a farm as a percentage of total capital investment.

$$\frac{\text{Gross income}}{\text{Total farm Assets}} \times 100 = \text{Rate of capital turn-over.}$$

Rate of capital turn over is the basic measure of efficiency in the use of capital employed by the business. This means the speed with which the original capital investment is recaptured by receipts from the business. A higher turnover rate usually means efficient use of capital.

In retail business such as general merchandising, the turn over is normally quick *i.e.*, in one to three months total capital investment gets recaptured. In other words, the total receipts from the business equal short term capital investment.

In agriculture, this period varies from seven to ten years in general. For the usual diversified farm business including both crop and livestock enterprises, the capital is recaptured in approximately 5 years. Turn-over rate in most other types of business are 10 to 20 times as rapid as in agriculture.

This does not mean that agriculture is inefficient. The turn-over rate in agriculture is relatively slow because the production process ordinarily requires a period of several years. This does mean that the management problems of farmers in regard to capital use differ greatly from those of many other industries. It also implies that credit and financing problems of agriculture must be approached in a different manner.

(viii) Financing

Agricultural financing faces different problems than those faced in financing other types of business. Because farming is subject to many risks from storms, dry periods, insects-pests, diseases and such other exigencies, investment in agriculture goes comparatively more risky and therefore expensive. Also because of slower rate of turn-over, repayment provisions have to be different from those on other types of investments. Credit plan has to, therefore, provide for repayment time and rates according to the recovery rate on the capital used in agriculture which is generally periodic and spreads over a longer period.

(ix) Home and business

Farming is a unique industry in that it combines a mode of life with the business enterprise. This close interdependence no longer exists in present-day industries. In agriculture even some farm inputs may be partly used in the home such as : foodgrains feed grain transport-vehicles etc. Agriculture is, therefore often regarded as a way of life as well as a means of livelihood such that socio-psychological and financial considerations influence its organisation more than they do so in other forms of industries and business.

(x) Fixed and variable costs

Of the total costs, portion of fixed costs is more in agriculture than in industry. This high proportion of fixed costs tends to make adjustments in production more difficult. There thus enter rigidities in the production process and products. Their level and combinations cannot be changed quickly in response to changes in prices and economic environment.

(xi) In-elastic demand for farm products

Agriculture is mainly concerned with the production of food and raw-material. It is to be expected that as standard of living improves and income increases, the demand for agricultural products will increase less rapidly than those for industrial products. At the lower level, demand for agricultural products (especially food) is inelastic, but in the upper portion the curve becomes more elastic. This kink comes at a point where reasonable level of consumption (C_R) is reached as shown in Fig. 2.1.

This characteristic puts agriculture at a disadvantage. Higher production may reduce prices so low that total returns might not increase or may even decrease. On the other hand, if increased production comes from the decreasing marginal returns phase of the response curve, costs will go high.

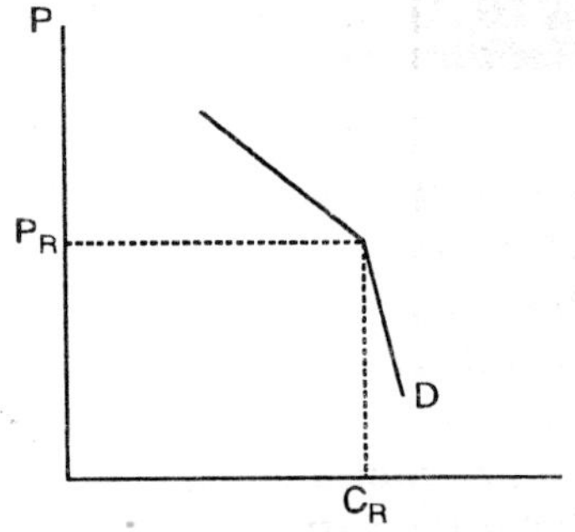

Fig. 2.1

(xii) Time rigidities in consumption of agricultural products

Agricultural products are generally perishable. It is not easy to postpone their utilisation. Partly as a result of this, and partly because of the small scale individual productions, the market intermediaries between the producers and the final consumers assume a place of particular importance. They come in to provide place, time and form utility to the farm produce to make it available to the consumer in the form, at the time and place required by them. The share of the producer in consumer's rupee, therefore, goes low in case of agricultural products.

CHANGING ECONOMIC ENVIRONMENT AND FARMING

The most important characteristics of farming business is continuous changes in the economic environment that influence production decisions. Changes occur in many areas, such as prices, production methods and responses and Government policies. There occur changes in relative prices of farm products *i.e*, product-product and factor-product price relations. Farmer has little immediate control over the market. He has to, therefore, keep making adjustments in his production programmes in response to changes in the market prices.

Technology also keeps changing. New varieties of crops such as wheat crosses and selection, hybrid maize and hybrid bajra may increase the yields manifold. With such new varieties, use of inputs such as fertilizers, irrigation and pesticides also increases. Production techniques keep changing in many other ways too ; such as methods of planting, application of insecticide, harvesting techniques, etc. Continuous farm adjustments to take full advantages of continuously changing technology thus becomes very important for a successful farm business. Government programmes and policies also keep changing and thus affect farmer's production programmes and business. Intensification of Government development efforts in certain areas (I.A.D.P. and J.A.A. programmes in India for example), betterment levies, ceilings on land holdings, food zones, floor and ceiling prices, etc. do influence farm organisation and production decisions.

FARMER'S LACK OF KNOWLEDGE

Farmer's lack of knowledge on the conditions affecting his farm business is as pronounced as the changes that continually occur. Imperfect knowledge lies in three areas, *i.e.* prices, production techniques, and production response. What he has to pay for inputs, especially in the long-run (level of factor and products prices) is difficult for him to foresee. Knowledge of expected production is never perfect in agriculture. Good or bad weather and biological factors such as diseases often result in production responses that differ widely from those anticipated by the farmers. New inventions and discoveries often render fixed investments obsolete. There is no way for the farmer to know immediately and exactly the response, performance, willingness and capacity of the people the farmer engages. It is more difficult for him to judge how other farmers will react and respond to a particular change. Knowledge about one's ownself even is not complete. The business of agriculture, thus, operates under a high degree of risk and uncertainty.

MANAGEMENT, LEARNING AND ADJUSTMENT

With continuously occuring changes and imperfect knowledge, farmers must continually keep learning from experience and keep adjusting their programmes to changing conditions. Successful farm management or decision-making process thus requires :

Learning. from other farmers, literature, extension workers and other such sources.

Risk-bearing. entrepreneurship and capacity to take calculated risk and

Mental alertness and imagination. Conceiving optimum plans out of many alternatives and narrowing their outcome to reasonably expected norms.

REQUIREMENTS IN FARMING PROFESSION

It is difficult to give a prepared set of requirements for a successful farming business, yet the following essentials, if properly checked and heeded to, can go a long way in avoiding failures.

Careful selection of the profession

Life of a successful farmer is a continuous process of decision- making. Selection of farming as a career is, therefore a crucial choice. Should one become a farmer or take up some other occupation ? The answer to this question will affect the entire life of the man. It will determine the income one realises and the enjoyment one gets out of life's work. One should, therefore think hard before deciding for or against farming as an occupation. Will comparatively low income from farming satisfy him ? Is he and his family qualified for farming ? Once one begins farming he is not very likely to retrace steps even if the work is harder and the income is lesser than expected. Income is not the only important consideration in determining whether one should become a farmer. We shall discuss below the personal, managerial and capital requirements for farming.

Personal Requirements

1. *Liking*

If one is going to farm, he must like farm work and farm life. In no other occupation "living and working" is so nearly identical. Good head, vigour, habit of working hard and ability to lead a rugged life and aptitude for farm work are some of the pre-requisites.

2. *Knowledge of farming and farm practices*

Knowledge of the theory and practices of agriculture business is essential and one must be and keep himself fully updated with all aspects of agricultural production and marketing.

3. *Managerial ability*

Even the beginning operator needs to have the basic qualities of management. He should have a keen eye to observe things, gather information, analyse the situation, make decision, take action and bear the responsibility.

4. *Business judgement*

There are many new ideas made available to the farmer. His success depends to a great extent on his ability to sort out the ideas that will work in his situation. Most farmers want to see an idea tested before they use it. Quick, premature adoption and undue delay in innovation, both are not conducive to good profits. There may be many experiments conducted on many different aspects of farming. The farmer has to decide : the results of which experiment will be best applicable to his farm situation. The decisions such as the number of cattle to be put on feed, on the number of acres to plant under cotton, for example, call for a good bit of judgement and ability to make right decisions.

Initiative and Ambition

The initiative and ambition to succeed are a driving force for exploring the possibilities of different enterprises, their combinations and searching the least cost production methods. For this, one needs study habits to read current farm magazines and literature in order to keep one updated and progressive.

Farm and Home

Most of the people like to work and interact with other people and take part in community activities. There is an ample such opportunity on the farms. There is no clear cut line to separate business from livings; dinner conversation may revolve as much around crop prospects, the rush season coming up or price outlook as around the neighbour's wedding ceremonies. Farming is a family partnership ; it succeeds best when wife, husband and children work in team. It requires perseverance, ambition and co-operation from each member of the family. Where the biological nature of farming calls for physical stamina, patience, family co-operation and ability to take some hard knocks, these same characteristics bring about advantages which appeal to many people. One is one's own master and has independence in making decisions ; many people go into farming because decision-making and some degree of risktaking is stimulating to them. The close interdependence between home and the business in agriculture has some other advantages too. Important among these are the fresh and wholesome product used directly in the household, and opportunities for the family to work, play and grow together.

1. ***Why is it that farmers find it difficult to change the volume and type of production with the change in demand ?***
2. ***What are the distinguishing features of farming as a business ?***
3. ***Why is financing of farming more risky as compared to other industries ?***
4. ***How price elasticities of demand and supply are important for farm products ?***
5. ***In what way, the integration of home and farm business is a problem in managing the farm ?***
6. ***What points should one consider in making a decision to take up farming as a profession ?***

1. *Bishop, C.E. and Toussaint, W.D. "Introduction to Agricultural Economic Analysis," New York, John Wiley & Sons, Inc., 1958, Chapter 2.*
2. *Heady, Earl O. and Harald R. Jensen, "Farm Management Economics" Englewood Cliffs, N.J., Prentice-Hall, Inc., 1954, Chapter 2.*
3. *Forster, G.E., "Farm Organization and Management," New York, Prentice-Hall, Inc., 1953 Chapter 2.*

3 Basics of Farm Production Decisions

Farm production decisions involve application of the principles of production economics. It is, therefore, essential for a farm operator or a planner to understand basic concepts, and relationships pertaining to the economics of agricultural production. This chapter deals with the meanings, objectives and languages of production economics.

PRODUCTION ECONOMICS

Meaning, Nature and Scope

Farm production economics is a broad division or field of specialisation within the subject of agricultural economics. It is concerned with the choice of production patterns and resources use in order to maximise the objective function of the farm operator, their families, the society or the nation, within a framework of limited resources. It is concerned with choosing of available alternatives or their combinations with a view to maximising the returns and/or minimising the costs.

Production economics is concerned with two broad categories of decisions in the production process. *i.e.* ;

(*i*) How to organise resources in order to maximise the production of a single commodity ? *i.e.* to make choices from among various alternative ways of using resources.

(*ii*) What combination of different commodities to produce ?

The goals of agricultural production economics are two fold :

(*i*) to provide guidelines in using the farm resources most efficiently, and (*ii*) to facilitate the most efficient use of resources from the stand point of the economy.

The Field of Agricultural Production Economics

With a view of optimising the use of farm resources on an individual farm-level and to rationalise the use of agricultural resources from a national angle, production economics involves analysis of relationships and principles of rational decisions.

It is concerned with productivity, *i.e.*, use of and incomes from production resources. Specifically stated, the subject matter of production economics includes such topics as : combination of farm enterprises, methods of production, size of the farms, returns to scale, leasing, production possibilities, farming efficiency, use of credit and capital, risk and uncertainty which affect decision-making.

Any agricultural problem that falls under the scope of resource allocation and marginal productivity analysis, is the subject matter of agricultural production economics. The production economist is, therefore, concerned with any phenomena which have a bearing on economic efficiency in the use of agricultural resources.

The Objectives of Production Economics

The laws of production economics explain the conditions under which the quantities can be maximised (profit, output, national income), or minimised (cost, use of physical input). The main objectives of production economics, therefore are ;

(*i*) to determine and define the conditions which provide for optimum use of resources.

(*ii*) to determine the extent to which the existing use of resources deviates from the optimum use,

(*iii*) to analyse the factors or forces which are responsible for the existing production patterns and resources use, and

(*iv*) to delineate means and methods for changing the existing use of resources to the optimum level.

The principles or laws that help attain these objectives are the same on a micro as well as on a regional or national level. On micro level where intra-farm resource allocation and production pattern are involved, it is the subject matter of farm management. When choice principles involve a broader field on a macro-level, the subject is known as production economics. The difference, however, does not exist in a very distinct manner. The economist who focusses his attention on individual farm cannot make rational recommendations unless he considers the aggregate or overall aspect of production. For example, if poultry is recommended to the farmers being a paying enterprise, this may increase the poultry production so high that through lower prices, farm incomes might subsequently decline. Similarly, Government programmes and policies affect the decisions on the individual farms. Production economist, therefore, must understand and be able to integrate both individual and aggregate aspects of agricultural resource use and production patterns. Still, it is essential to understand the basic difference in the approaches of the two fields of specialisation. Following examples will clarify the distinction further.

From the view point of agricultural production economics, it seems that not much can be done to improve the size of the farm in a country because neither land nor population change easily and quickly in a short period of time. From the view point of farm management on the other hand, farm income will vary with the size of the farm : old farmers retire or may be forced out of farming ; some farmers increase the size of their farms by renting more land and others decrease the size of their farms by selling land or renting out land. Hence, the size of an individual farm is not so fixed and it may be desirable to examine the possibility of adjusting the size for an efficient production. As another example, from a national view point, under the situation of relative inelasticity of demand for many important agricultural products, an increase in agricultural production may mean a decrease in farm income. Governments may, therefore, take measures to restrict crop acreage and livestock production. On the other hand, it may become all the more necessary for an individual farmer to raise crop yields and animal production for maintaining at lower prices.

Thus, while farm management is an intra-farm application of business principles, production economics involves inter-farm study and the economy of the region or the country as a whole. However, the distinction cannot be stretched too far.

LANGUAGE OF THE PRODUCTION ECONOMICS

Beginning with the study of a new subject, resembles visiting a foreign country without understanding its language. In the study of production economics and farm management, the first task should be, therefore to learn the language of the subject. Unless a sound understanding of the meaning of terms is acquired, one is likely to be misled. Before one attempts to understand the production relationships, basic terms, frame-work and economic concepts need to be understood. In fact, knowledge of these concepts is a pre-requisite for a purposeful analysis. Some of the frequently used terms in production economics analysis are :

Units of accounting. Application of inputs or measurement of output relate to a technical unit, plant or an economic unit.

Technical unit. Technical unit refers to a single, convenient unit in production for which technical co-efficient are calculated *e.g.*, an acre or a hectare of land, a cow, a trio or a unit of poultry birds etc.

Farm-firm. It is a production unit under one management and is also known as an economic unit referring to an aggregation of resources for which costs and returns are worked out as a whole *e.g.* A farm holding is an economic unit

Plant. Plant generally refers to a group of technical units such as a dairy, enterprise or say 15-acre farm. Each enterprise or plant is a part of the farm-firm. A farmer may have a dairy unit and a 20-acre-crop farm, for example. These are two plants of one farm-firm.

Production and resource relationships can be studied as they relate either to a technical unit, plant or economic unit or a farm-firm. We may note that distinction between a farm and a field is the same as between a firm and a plant in industry. Firm refers to a decision-making unit within an industry while the plants within a firm refer to units which are relevant in the production plan of the firm.

Resources and Resource Services

There are some inputs or resources such as fertilizers (N.P.K.) water, insecticides, which get consumed or transformed into products in the process of production. There are certain resources of which only services are available which are transformed into a product. Such resources are labour, implements, buildings, etc. For our analysis both resources or resource-services that enter into the production of a product are considered alike *e.g.,* even though labour and tractor fuel never enter physically into the transformation process, we still consider services of these resources to be transformed to a product.

Fixed and Variable Resources

Level of some resources such as buildings, machinery, implements is fixed over a planning period irrespective of the level of enterprise (s) taken up. These are known as fixed farm resources.

The resources such as fertilizers, seeds, feeds, etc. whose use varies with the level of enterprise(s) are known as variable resources. Some fixed resources, however, have a variable use, such as tractor services, bullock power. This distinction between fixed and variable resources or inputs is essential for computing technical co-efficients for farm management decisions and production programming.

Flow and Stock Resources

There are some resources, if their services are not used, these cannot be stocked. Services are forthcoming like a flow. These services are labour, buildings etc. If the services of a labourer are not used today, they cannot be stored until next day, month or the year. Such services are known as flow-resources. Some resources such as seeds, fertilizer, feeds, are however entirely used up in the production process. If these resources are not used in one period of production, they can be stored for a later period. These are known as stock-resources.

Some factors of production embody both flow and stock services such as machinery. In this case, depreciation is a function of both use and time. Whether a service should be defined as a flow or a stock depends partly on the length of time under consideration. A building which lasts for 50 years provides a flow of services in each of the individual years. It gives flow service each year but a stock service over say 10 years (life of a tractor). Sunshine on the other hand is purely a flow service as are such other services derived from the atmosphere.

The resources that give a flow service usually introduce elements of uncertainty in production planning. Stock services that are consumed up in one production period are, on the other hand, simple to reckon with.

Product or Production

Productions are the result of the use of resources or services of resources ; examples are wheat, maize, milk, eggs, etc. Production is a process of transformation of certain resources or inputs like land, labour (human and bullock, seeds, fertilizer, irrigation water into products like wheat, paddy, milk.

Production Function

Level of output of a particular commodity depends upon the quantities of inputs used for its production. This relation between inputs and outputs can be characterised as a production function. Production function is thus a technical and mathematical relationship describing the manner and extent to which a particular product depends upon the quantities of inputs (s) or services(s) of inputs used. In the production function, output is "dependent upon" or "determined by" or "related to" or is the "function of" input(s) or the use of resource(s). Production function is of two types : (1) Continuous function, and (2) discontinuous or discrete function. Continuous function can be explained by response of yield to fertilizer or seeds where the doses or levels of inputs and output can be split up into small units, *e.g.*, fertilizers can be applied to a hectare of land in quantities ranging from a fraction of a kilogram upto hundreds of kilograms. Labour is also quite divisible because it can be used in minutes or in terms of man hours. Indivisible inputs can also be used in divisible units. Example is of a tractor not so divisible as an input. If tractors are to be used in production, no less than one be employed. However, tractor input can be varied by using a tractor more or less number of hours per day, employing tractors of various sizes, substituting second-hand for a new tractor and hiring tractor services, etc.

Discontinuous or Discrete Function

Such a function is obtained for input factors or work units which are used or done in whole numbers such as one ploughing or a number of ploughings. One can only shift from one point to another. In discrete functions, the alternative decision points get limited, otherwise same method of analysis is followed in both continuous and discrete production functions.

Transformation of Production Period

Time required for a resource to be completely transformed into a product is referred to as transformation period or the production period. The production period varies with resources. The production of the transformation period gives rise to complexities in decision-making. Economic analysis would be simple if production is carried on with resources which are completely transformed in a single year. However, a farmer must own long lived resources such as machinery and buildings. These resources need heavy investments and decisions which extend over several years. The stock services used in any year or a production period become variable costs relating to the particular output, while the flow resources rise to fixed costs. Cost calculations thus become complex. Again, time excludes the possibility of perfect knowledge. Expectations and estimations enter into the decision-making process leading to risks and uncertainties.

SHORT AND LONG-RUN-PRODUCTION FUNCTION

Production function which relates to factors and products where some resources are fixed (regardless of the number of fixed resources and level at which each is held fixed) can be termed as short-run production function. Those input-output relations which permit variation in the input of all factors (none is fixed) can be termed as long-run-production functions.

A Choice Indicator

A product can be produced in many ways through different combinations of resources and techniques. The most desirable combination of products or factors can not be determined without a choice indicator, which moves production problem from the field of physical sciences to the field of economics. A choice indicator is a yardstick or an index or a criterion indicating which of two or more alternatives is optimum or will maximise a given end. Examples are price ratios, substitution ratios, etc.

Cost concepts

Corresponding to the fixed resources there are costs which are there irrespective of the level of the enterprise(s) or combination of enterprises. These are known as fixed costs. Examples are farm building, machinery investment, etc.

On the other hand, there are variable costs corresponding to variable resources which vary with the level of enterprise(s) or production. Examples are seed, feed, fertilizer costs. Fixed and variable costs put together amount to total cost of production.

Returns Concepts

Gross returns are equal to total production times the price. Returns to fixed farm resources are equal to gross returns minus variable costs. These are also known as returns over variable costs. Net returns are equal to gross returns minus all costs (fixed and variable ; cash and kind).

Farm Entrepreneur

Farm entrepreneur is the person (can be a group of persons also) who thinks of, organises and operates the business and is responsible for the results *i.e.*, losses and gains from the business. He is a pioneer in organising and developing the farm firm.

Farm Manager

He is a person (can be more than one) who manages or supervises the business according to the instruction of the entrepreneur. He is hired to manage the business. He is not generally responsible for any gain or loss to the business. To the extent he does so, he performs the entrepreneurial function.

Farm Executive

He (can be more than one person) carries out the orders of the management. A farmer may be performing all the three functions himself.

FRAMEWORK OF ANALYSIS IN PRODUCTION ECONOMICS

The analysis of production relationships can be made under.

(1) perfect knowledge situation, and (2) imperfect knowledge situation. In this section we will discuss only perfect knowledge situation, leaving the second situation (involving risk and uncertainty) to be dealt with in a later chapter.

In the first case, we make two simplifications as under :

(*i*) we consider a single production period which does not involve uncertainty or imperfect knowledge. This is realistic assumption because farmers reckon their income on specific period (annual/half yearly) basis. The analysis may be related either to ;

(*a*) a production period corresponding to the time required to completely transform the relevant resources into products. The particular production function will refer to a specific time period.

(*b*) a period of production long enough that the longest-lived resource is completely transformed into the product.

(*ii*) will also assume that the prices and input-output relationships are known with certainty before production process starts, (*iii*) we concern ourselves only with return forthcoming from the physical production process and the sale of commodities so produced on the farm. We ignore in our analysis here the gains or losses growing out of changes in the market value of the durable resources. The other assumptions are : Homogeniety of factors and products ; constant technology or single technique of production over a relevant production period.

In case of imperfect knowledge situations or under uncertain conditions, the above mentioned assumptions do not hold true. Under such a situation more complex type of analysis is required. In analysis under uncertain conditions, the above mentioned assumptions do not hold true. Under such a situation more complex type of analysis is required. Analysis under uncertain condition is given in later chapters.

GRAPHS IN PRODUCTION FUNCTION ANALYSIS

Graphs, illustrative tables and algebraic equations are the main expository devices used in the analysis of production relationships. While the illustrative tables are used to introduce a situation; graphs are to present a generalised version of the essential features of the situation. Illustrative tables hardly need any comments or explanation. It would be useful to get acquainted with some types of graphs and their relevant features which will be frequently used in the subsequent chapters where they will be discussed in relation to specific subject matter. Here only their forms are presented and their characteristic feature are pointed out.

In empirical economic investigations, graphs are a visual aid to understand the data. They help in bringing out certain relationships of particular interest.

For example input-output relationships between fertiliser (N) used on wheat and its yield can be represented as under.

Presentation of data on graphs is not possible if the quantities involved are more than three. Even in the case of three quantities, this representation gets quite complicated. As an example, a three dimensional diagram illustration of wheat yield response to various levels of nitrogen and phosphorous is provided in Fig, 3.1.

Yield Response of Wheat (Lerma rohjo) to Fertilizer (N) in Punjab 1965-66.

Input(X) *Fertilizer(N)* (Kgs./hectare)	*Output(Y)* *Yield of Wheat* *in*
0	12.41
40	22.96
80	35.96
120	45.20
160	50.85
200	59.76

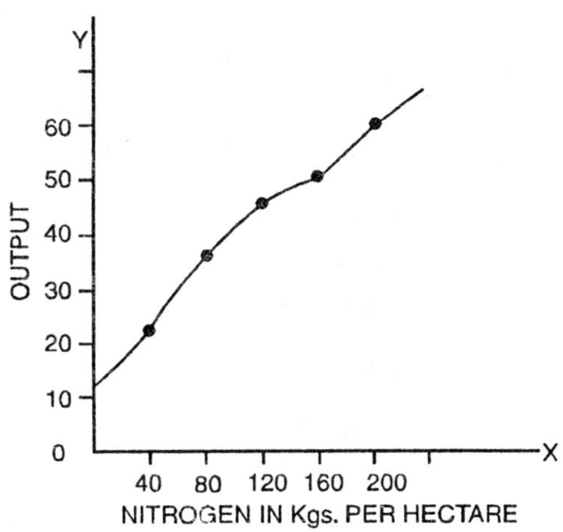

Fig 3.1. Response of wheat yield to fertilizer application

Yield Response of Wheat (Lerma rohjo) to Nitrogen and Phosphorous, Punjab, 1965-66*

Input(lbs/Acre)		*Output(lbs/Acres)*
N	*P*	*Yield*
X_1	X_2	Y
40	20	781
80	20	934
40	40	820
80	40	930

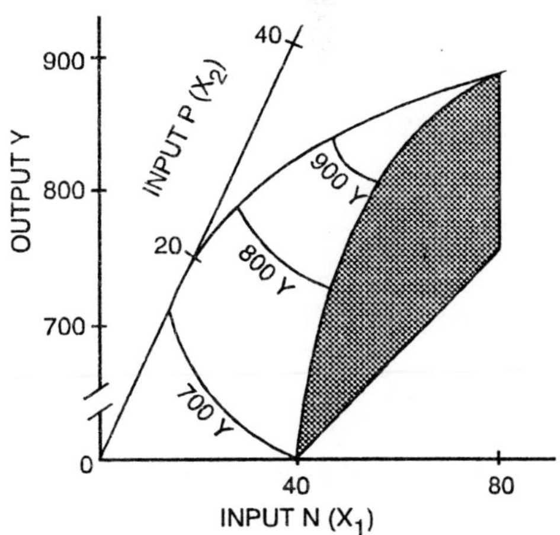

Fig. 3.2. Response of wheat yield to Nitrogen and Phosphorous

***Source.** Annual Report of Department of Soils, P.A.U., Ludhiana, 1965-66 p.87.

Some Graphic Presentations

Important relationships that can be depicted through graphs are :

(*i*) Linear relationships — *i.e.*, Straight line graphs.

(*ii*) Non-Linear relationships.

(*a*) Monotonic relationships—monotonic curves.

(*b*) Non-monotonic relationships—non-monotonic curves

Linear relationship graphs

Linear relationships are presented with straight lines.

Some linear relationships are illustrated below in Fig. 3.3

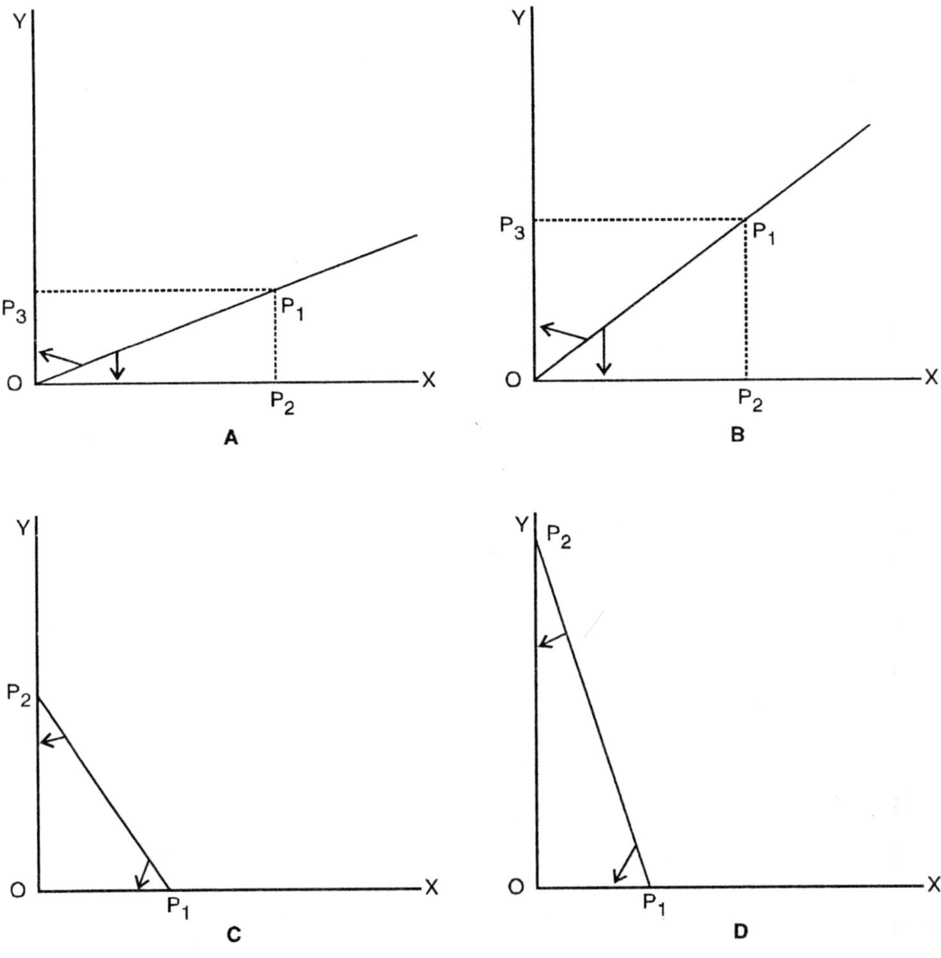

Fig. 3.3 Some straight line graphs

The lines in figures A and B show positive association of relationship between X & Y, while the lines in figures C and D show negative relationships. Each line forms an angle with each of the two axes as shown by the arrows.

Slope of the line

We define slope of the line with respect to each of the axis as the tangent of this angle. By this definition the slopes of the lines in the Fig. 3.3 A-D are :

Figures	*Slope of the line with respect to*	
	X-axis	*Y-axis*
3.3 A	$\frac{P_1P_2}{OP_2}$	$\frac{P_1P_3}{OP_3} = \frac{OP_2}{P_1P_2}$
3.3 B	$\frac{P_1P_2}{OP_2}$	$\frac{P_1P_3}{OP_3} = \frac{OP_2}{P_1P_2}$
3.3 C	$\frac{-OP_2}{OP_1}$	$\frac{-OP_1}{OP_2}$
3.3 D	$\frac{-OP_2}{OP_1}$	$\frac{-OP_1}{OP_2}$

It may be noted that for a given line, the two slopes, *i.e.*, with respect to *X*-axis and with respect to Y-axis, are the reciprocals of each other.

The slope of a line indicates the rate of change in one quantity in response to the change in the other ; *i.e.*, higher slopes (in magnitude) correspond to faster changes and lower slopes (in magnitude) correspond to lower changes. Between Figures A and B, for example, the slope of the line with respect to the X-axis is higher in the latter than in the former and it can be easily verified that rate of change in Y in response to a unit change in X is larger on line B than on line A.

Two features which make the linear relationships easy to handle are that (1) these relationships are throughout increasing or decreasing, and (2) the change is constant.

Non-linear Relationship Graphs

Here the curves are not straight lines. Since what isn't a straight line can assume a variety of different shapes, it is obvious that classification of non-linear relationships is a difficult task. We will confine our discussion to only a few classes (and within each class, to a few types) which we actually need in our farm management and production economic analysis.

Monotonic relationships. This class shows one feature in common with the linear relationships ; namely, they are throughout either increasing or decreasing. Graphs corresponding to these relationships are monotonic curves. Some of these curves are illustrated below in Fig. 3.4.

Figures 3.4 A and B indicate decreasing response relationships while figure C and D indicate increasing relationships. Unlike the linear relationships, the rate or speed with which Y changes for a given change in X does not, however, remain constant in all the ranges.

The rate of change at any point can be measured through drawing a tangent to the curve at that point as indicated by the dotted line in Fig. A. The rate of change in Y in response to change in X at this point is defined as the slope of the dotted line $\left(\frac{-OP_2}{OP_1} \text{ at } O_0 \right)$

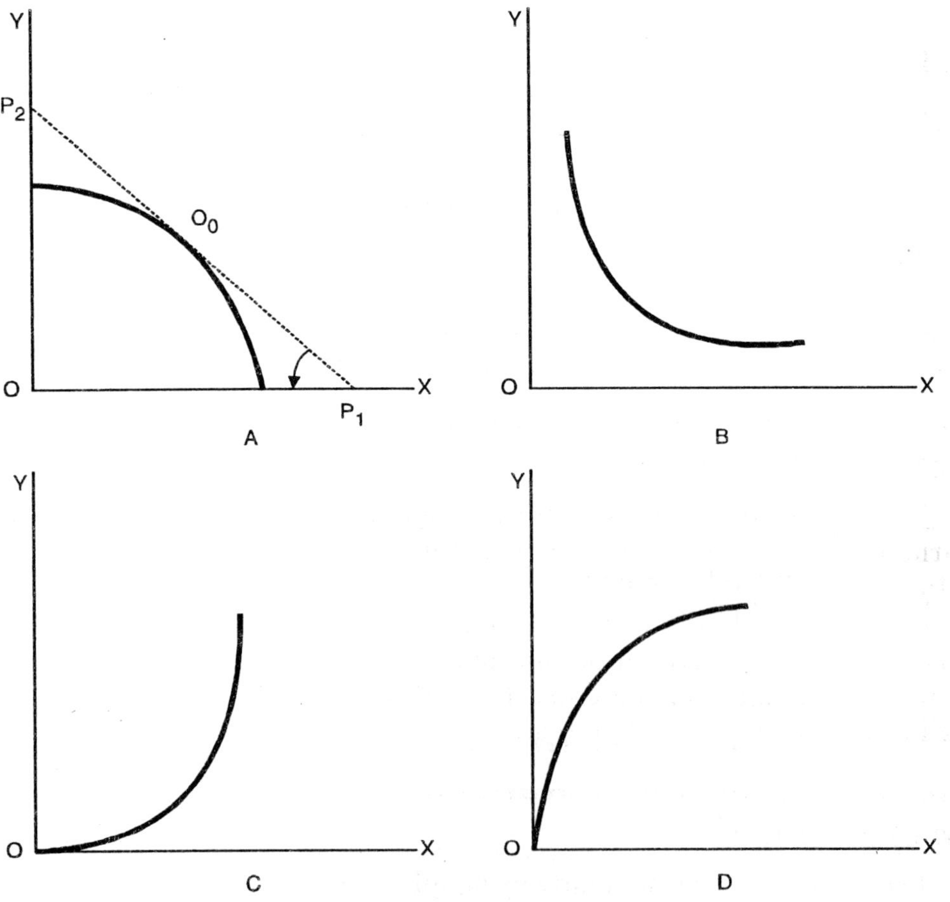

Fig. 3.4. Monotonic Curves

Non-monotonic relationships

In the non-monotonic class, the nature of relationship itself changes through the range of the curve so that this class shares neither of the two simple features of the linear relationships. Fig. 3.5 represents two types of non-monotonic relationships.

If we divide the values of X into two parts, values of X less than X_0, and values of X greater than X_0, in Fig. 3.5 A, the relationship between X and Y is of decreasing response in the first part and of increasing response in the second part. In Fig. 3.5 B exactly the reverse is true.

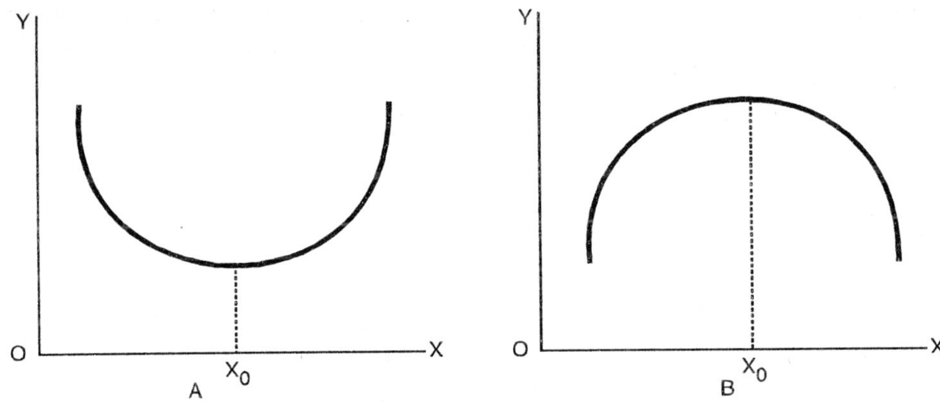

Fig. 3.5 Non-monotonic curves

Curves in Fig. 3.5 consist of a single wave. One can think of non-monotonic curves with many such waves, which are useful in discussing business cycles. For our discussion in this book, the two non-monotonic curves shown in the figures above here, are sufficient for the purpose.

Scatter Diagram

The scatter diagram gives us some approximate ideas as to how values of one variable (dependent) behaves in response to the increase or decrease in values of another variable (independent).

As shown in Fig. 3.6, the scatter diagram contains points of observed response. A curve apporoximating the values of these points (or dots) can be drawn either with a free hand or more exactly with the help of a response curve fitted through the method of least squares.

Slope of a Curve

The slope of a curve is relatively simple concept which is very much used in economic analysis. It is defined as a change in Y, or the vertical distance of a curve divided by the X or the horizontal distance. In this concept of slope, we often employ the Greek letter Δ (delta) which means "change in". Slope is thus $\pm\frac{\Delta Y}{\Delta X}$ (ratio).

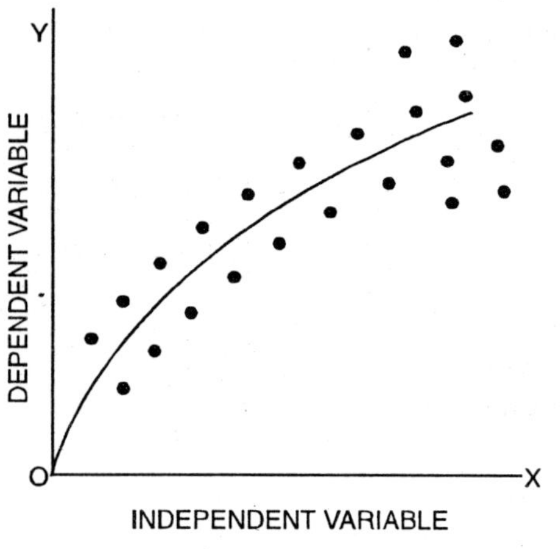

Fig. 3.6. Scatter diagram

Fig. 3.7. Slope of a curve (line)

For example, in going from K to N in the Fig. 3.7, the change in Y axis, Y is 5 in response to change of 10 in X. Thus, the slope of this curve between K and N is $\frac{5}{10}$ or 0.5. This indicates that Y increases one unit for each two units increase in X.

Total Product (TP)

A given level of total product is always associated with a particular level of input (s) use with a given production technology. Production function is often presented as total output curve because total product curve and production function are closely associated.

Average Product (AP)

The term average product refers to the average productivity of a resource. It is ratio of total product (TP) to the quantity of input used in producing that amount of product, *i.e.*, at any point on production function, it is the total output divided by the total input used.

$$AP = \frac{Y}{X}$$ where Y is product and X the input (s)

Marginal Product (MP)

The term marginal product refers to the quantity which additional (marginal) unit of factor-input adds to the total product. The marginal product (MP) at any level of the variable input can be approximated by dividing the addition to total output by the addition to total input :

$MP = \frac{\Delta Y}{\Delta X}$ (Here, Δ refers to "change in" or "addition to" the product or the input.)

It is the rate of change in total product at a given point as the quantity of input changes. This marginal analysis is a very important tool available to the economists for locating optimal points. Although average productivity provides some guidelines as to the manner in which resources are allocated, it is marginal productivity which provides the final criterion in determining optimum use of limited resources.

Average Marginal Product

The average marginal product indicates the productivity value between the two relevant input levels, *i.e.*, $\frac{20-10}{10-0}$ or $\frac{30-20}{20-10}$ and so on in Fig. 3.8.

The following two examples illustrate this concept here.

Example I		*Example II*	
Input level X	*Output level* Y	*Input level* X	*Output level* Y
0	10	0	10
5	20	5	30
10	30	10	45
15	40	15	50

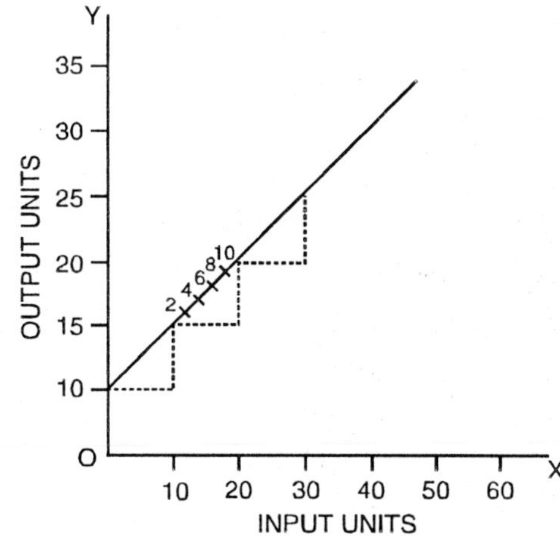

Fig. 3.8. Illustration of Average marginal product

In Example I

When $\Delta X = 5, \Delta Y = 10$

$$\frac{\Delta Y}{\Delta X} = \frac{10}{5} = 2.00$$

In Example II

When $\Delta X = 5, \Delta Y = 20$ for first dose, 15 for second and 5 for third change.

This indicates that with every change of one unit of X, there is change of two units in Y, in the first example. The MP for a unit of variable input be thus approximated by dividing addition to total output by the addition to total input.

In the second example, the first addition to input is 5 units and addition to product is 20. The average marginal product is $\frac{\Delta Y_1}{\Delta X_1} = \frac{20}{5} = 4.$

When the total level of input is 10, the total level of output is 45. At this point the 5 units have added 15 units to total product. The average marginal product is 3. The average marginal product is thus the average over all units of output (fraction of outputs) between the two levels of inputs entering the calculations.

Exact Marginal Product

Exact or point marginal product refers to the marginal product as a derivative. This indicates the marginal product at a point. The derivative gives values at a point and not an average between two points.

If the production function $Y = a + bx$, point marginal product $= \frac{\partial Y}{\partial X} = b$, which is a linear constant relationship. If the production function is non-linear, *i.e.*, $Y = a + bx + cX^2$. Exact MP will be $= \frac{\partial Y}{\partial X} = b + 2cx$.

Derivative

Derivative is a value of the change in dependent variable in response to an infinitesimally small change in independent variable.

At any point of input use on the production function, it is given by the slope of tangent on that point.

In the Fig. 3.9, for example, derivative of point marginal product at point *b* will be given by the slope of the tangent of AB, *i.e.*, $\left.\frac{\Delta Y}{\Delta X}\right|_b$.

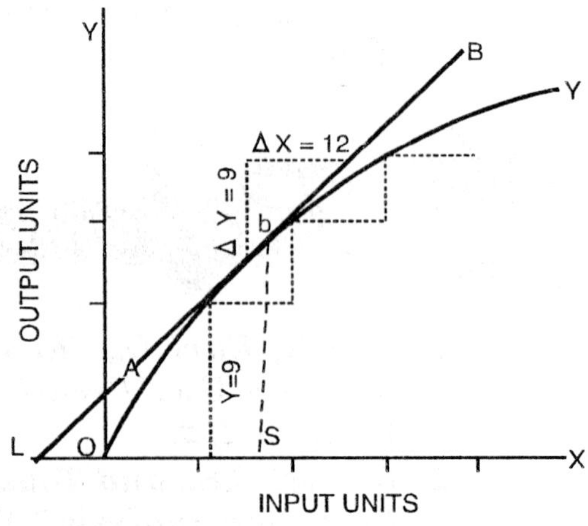

Fig. 3.9. Derivation of marginal product

1. *Define production economics and discuss its objectives.*
2. *Bring out the difference between production economics and farm management.*
3. *What is the importance of the study of production economics to a student of agriculture ?*
4. *Distinguish between the following :*
   (a) *technical unit and farm unit,*
   (b) *a farm entrepreneur, a farm manager, and a farm executive,*
   (c) *fixed costs and variable costs,*
   (d) *average marginal product and exact marginal product,*
   (e) *flow resource and stock resource*
   (f) *continuous function and discrete function,*
   (g) *average product and marginal product.*
5. *Define the following :*
   (a) *production function,*
   (b) *production period,*
   (c) *choice indicator,*
   (d) *slope of a curve.*
6. *What are different methods of presentation of economic analysis ? Discuss in detail the use of graphs in production function analysis.*

1. *Heady, Earl O., "Economics of Agricultural production and Resource Use," Prentice-Hall of India, Pvt. Ltd., New Delhi ; 1964, Chapter 1, 2.*
2. *Biship, C.E., and Toussaint, W.D. "Introduction to Agricultural Economic Analysis," New York, John Wiley & Sons, Inc., London, Toppan Company Ltd., Tokyo, Japan, 1958. Chapter 1, 2.*

Production Relationships (Factor-Product Relationships)

This chapter deals with the analysis of certain fundamental relationships involved or obtained in the production of farm products. There are numerous relationships between the resources and farm products, both simple and complex. It is necessary for a student of farm management or production economics to understand these relationships thoroughly so that he is able to analyse different problems of production or resource use for maximisation of a specific objective function. Major production relationships fall under three categories, *i.e.* ;

1. Factor-product relationship
2. Factor-factor relationship
3. Product-product relationship

These relationships are discussed here in three following chapters. In this chapter, discussions are made on factor-product relationships.

FACTOR-PRODUCT RELATIONSHIPS

For the study of economics of production (may it be in the field of agriculture or industry, intra-farm or inter-farm, regional or national level) in respect of resource allocation to optimise production, an understanding of input-output or factor-product relationships is important. First, it is essential to study the physical or technical relationships. Then, for decision making, application of economic choice indicators such as price ratios is required.

We proceed first with simple situations to understand the basic principles by confining ourselves to physical factor-product relationships of a single variable resource and single product. This situation is realistic also. Many times, resources or capacities of technical units, such as an acre of land or a cow, are fixed and choice is to vary the input of only one factor, such as fertilizer or labour. Fertilizer application to an acre of land, feed to a dairy cow or a unit of birds can, for example, be varied while other inputs such as fixed capital, buildings, implements and technical know-how remain the same. Under such a situation pertinent questions would be : how much fertilizer to apply ; how much feed to be given to a cow or a unit of birds ? Such situations involve single factor-single product relationships. They are known as single variable production functions, too.

As explained in an earlier section, the relationship that exists between inputs of a resource or resources resulting in another quantity (output) is termed a production function. In a production function, various levels of an input are involved with corresponding outputs of the product. Thus, production function refers to the quantitive aspects of the process of production. The kind of product and the amount of product depends upon or is a function of the kind and quantity of inputs used. Production functions can be expressed in three forms : *i.e.* tabular, graphic, and algebraic.

Tabular form. It can be illustrated with fertilizer response data as below :

Yields Response Data of Wheat Grains (in quintals) to Fertilizer (N) Used in kilograms per acre

Fertilizer (N) Input (X)	*Total Yield Output (Y)*
0	2
10	5
20	11
30	18
40	25
50	31

Graphic form. The same data can be presented in the form of a graph as :

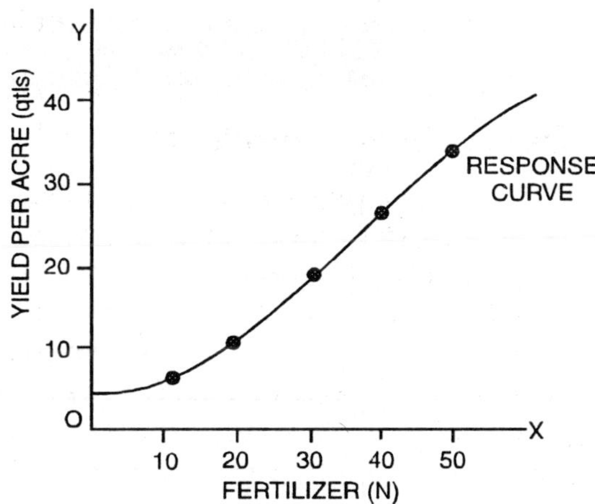

Fig. 4.1. Graphic presentation of factor-production relationships.

Algebraic form. Algebraically, production functions can be expressed as : $Y = f(X)$

Where Y represents dependent variable such as yield of a crop, egg production, milk yield and X represents independent variable such as fertilizer, labour, feed, etc. and f denoting "function of."

If the independent variables are two, the production function can be written as : $Y = f(X_1, X_2)$

For a number of independent variables (say n variables), this function can be expanded as : $Y = f(X_1, X_2, X_3, X_4, \ldots\ldots\ldots\ldots, X_{n-1}, X_n)$

Normally, there are more than one independent variables involved in the production of a commodity. In the case of a single variable production function, only one variable is allowed to vary whereas others are held constant. Such a function where one independent variable changes and others are held constant can be expressed as : $Y = f(X_1/X_2, X_3, \ldots. X_{n-1}, X_n)$.

If more than one independent variable changes and a few others are held constant, the relationships can be expressd as.

$Y = f(X_1, X_2, \ldots.. X_{n-1}, X_n/X_{n+1}, X_{n+2}, \ldots, X_{n+k})$

Here X_1 to X_n factors are variable and X_{n+1} to X_{n+k} are fixed factors.

TYPES OF PRODUCTION FUNCTIONS (RETURNS RELATIONSHIPS)

There can be three types of input-output relationships in the production of a commodity where one input is varied and the quantities of all other inputs are fixed. The nature of relationships between a single input and a single output can be either of the one or a combination of types given below ;

(*i*) constant marginal rate of returns (constant productivity),

(*ii*) increasing marginal rate of returns (increasing productivity),

(*iii*) decreasing marginal rate of returns (decreasing productivity),

Brief descriptions of these three types are given below.

1. Constant marginal returns function

In constant returns or linear relationships, each additional unit of the variable input when applied to the fixed factor(s), produces an equal amount of additional product *i.e.*, the amount of product increases by the same magnitude for each additional unit of input. This is not a very common relationship in agriculture and holds true only within a limited range. As an example, each addition of one acre of land (technology and other factors remaining the same) will add the same amount of product. Again, employment of an additional tractor plus driver will do the same amount of work as a previous tractor and driver unit did.

A hypothetical numerical example on fertilizer response data will make the relationship further clear (Table 4.1).

TABLE 4.1

Constant Relationship—Fertilizer Response Function (Hypothetical Data)

Doses of Fertilizer (Kg) X	*Marginal Dose (Kg)* X	*Total Production of Wheat (Kg)* Y	*Marginal Yield (Kg)* Y	*Marginal Rate of Returns (Kg)* Y/X
0		1300		
	10		.50	50/10 = 5
10		1350		
	10		50	50/10 = 5
20		1400		
	10		50	50/10 = 5
30		1450		
	10		50	50/10 = 5
40		1500		
	10		50	50/10 = 5
50		1550		

The relationship in Table 4.1, shows that with every increase in input, there is equal or constant increase in the level of output. It is known as a constant marginal returns function.

This constant relationship can be illustrated with a graph as in Fig. 4.2 below.

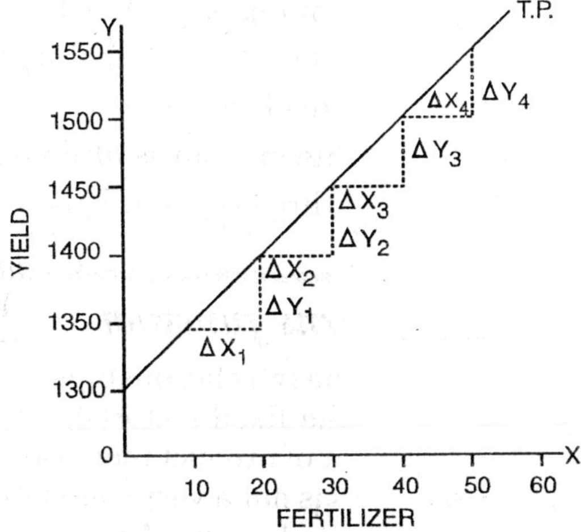

Fig. 4.2. Constant returns relationship

The production function in Fig. 4.2 is a straight line, having the same slope throughout its entire range. This relationship can also be expressed as :

$$\frac{\Delta Y_1}{\Delta X_1} = \frac{\Delta Y_2}{\Delta X_2} = \ldots\ldots = \frac{\Delta Y_n}{\Delta X_n}$$

The constant returns production function can be presented by an algebraic equation of the farm $Y = a + bx$. The estimated equation of the example given above is $Y = 1300 + 5X$. This shows that 1300 Kg. of wheat are produced without applying fertilizer and wheat output (Y) increases by 5 Kg. for every increase of one kilogram of the fertilizer.

Linear production functions do not exist when inputs per acre or per animal are intensified. Such a relationship only exists where the initial doses applied per acre are very small. The additional doses applied at this stage give constant returns within such a small range. Agronomists and soil scientists sometimes make recommendations as if the production functions were linear, which, of course, is never true in real practice. Before making any recommendation, one should, therefore, carefully consider the nature of returns and economic criteria.

2. *Increasing marginal returns function*

In this case every additional or marginal unit of input adds more to the total product than the previous unit ; *i.e.*, addition to total product is at an increasing rate. In actual practice, the cases of purely increasing returns are rarely available except, again, in very limited range. This relationship is possible when the fixed factors of production are in excess capacity and addition of the small units of a variable resource makes more and more efficient use of fixed resources. For example, small quantity of wheat seed applied when other factors of production such as fertilizer, irrigation and other cultural practices can be used at high levels will give low returns and as the quantity of seed increases from a very low level, it might provide a case of increasing marginal returns as is shown in Table 4.2 on a hypothetical data.

TABLE 4.2

Response of Different Seed Rates on Wheat Yield

Wheat Seed Rate(Kg) X	*Marginal Dose (Kg.)* X	*Total Production of Wheat (Kg.)* Y	*Marginal Production* Y	*Marginal Rate* Y/X
10		1000		
	5		25	25/5 = 5
15		1025		
	5		50	50/5 = 10
20		1075		
	5		75	75/5 = 15
25		1150		
	5		100	100/5 = 20
30		1250		
	5		125	125/5 = 25
35		1375		

The production curve showing increasing marginal returns is of the shape shown in Fig. 4.3 below.

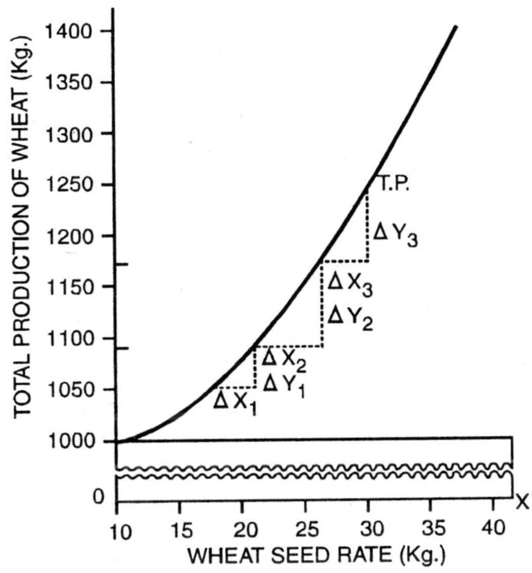

Fig. 4.3. Increasing returns to a single factor.

The shape of the curve will go steeper and steeper with the added inputs *i.e.*, slope gets convex to the origin. In this case, the following relationship holds true.

$$\frac{\Delta Y_1}{\Delta X_1} < \frac{\Delta Y_2}{\Delta X_2} < \frac{\Delta Y_3}{\Delta X_3} < \ldots\ldots < \frac{\Delta Y_n}{\Delta X_n}$$

This means that ratio $\frac{\Delta Y}{\Delta X}$ will go on increasing as more and more units of input are added.

3. Decreasing Marginal Returns Function

In this type of function, each additional unit of input adds less to the total product than the previous unit did. Diminishing marginal returns exist, for example, if the first input adds 20 units, to the total output while the second adds 15 units, the third adds 10 units, fourth adds 5 units and so on. This function exists in almost every practical situation in agriculture. Responses to fertilizers, insecticides, seeds, irrigation, feeds, etc. all show diminishing returns. A production function of a single variable nature showing diminishing returns throughout is given in Table 4.3 above :

TABLE 4.3

Application of Fertilizers and Output of Wheat

Fertilizer Input X	*Marginal Dose X*	*Total Wheat Production (Kg) Y*	*Marginal Production Y*	*Marginal Rate of Change Y/X*
0	—	500	—	—
10	10	1400	900	900/10=90
20	10	2100	700	700/10=70
30	10	2600	500	500/10=50
40	10	3000	400	400/10=40
50	10	3300	300	300/10=30
60	10	3500	200	200/10=20

This table shows that every time 10 units of fertilizer are added, the marginal addition to the total output goes on decreasing.

This fact is illustrated by the triangles in Fig. 4.4.

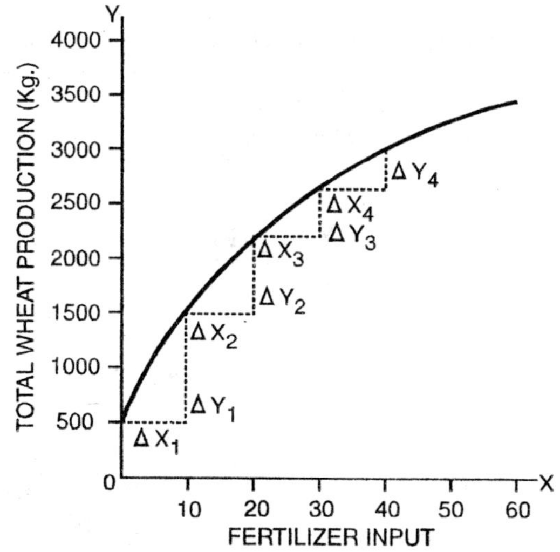

Fig. 4.4. Decreasing returns to a single factor.

The curve in the Fig. 4.4 is concave to the origin. This relationship can also be indicated as follows :

$$\frac{\Delta Y_1}{\Delta X_1} > \frac{\Delta Y_2}{\Delta X_2} > \ldots\ldots\ldots > \frac{\Delta Y_n}{\Delta X_n}$$

Since $\Delta X_1 = \Delta X_2 = \Delta X_3 = ... = \Delta X_n$ in Fig. 4.4, the ratio $\Delta Y/\Delta X$ goes on decreasing as higher and higher input level is adopted.

This is a technological law of biological responses and is applicable in almost all practical situations of agricultural production under varied farm situations. Before taking any decision, however, one needs to have an understanding of the concepts of total, average and marginal products and their relationships as well as factor-product price ratios.

RELATIONSHIPS BETWEEN TOTAL, AVERAGE AND MARGINAL PRODUCTS

Different production relationships have already been discussed in terms of total output. Here we discuss two other important physical returns or productivity relationships ; *i.e.*, average and marginal product and how these total, average and marginal products are related to each other. Since both average and marginal products are derived from total products, the average and marginal product curves are closely related to the total product curve. These curves are shown in Fig. 4.5 and correspond to the data in Table 4.4.

TABLE 4.4

Relationship Between Total, Average and Marginal Products(Hypothetical Data)

Units of Fertilizer Input X	*Total Product* T.P.(Y)	*Average Product* A.P.(Y/X)	*Marginal Product* $M.P.\frac{Y}{X}$	*Remarks*
0	0	—	—	
1	2	2	2	Increasing at
2	5	2.5	3	increasing rate
3	9	3	4	
4	14	3.5	5	Increasing at
5	19	3.8	5	constant rate
6	23	3.83	4	
7	26	3.71	3	
8	28	3.5	2	Increasing at
9	29	3.22	1	decreasing rate
10	29	2.9	0	
11	28	2.54	–1	Decreasing at
12	26	2.16	–2	increasing rate

Here we will confine our discussions to average and marginal products of a single resource, all other factors held constant. Both the average and marginal product curves or relationships can be derived once total product curve has been obtained.

Total Product (TPC) and Marginal Product (MPC)

Essential points to be noted in this relationship are ;

1. Since the marginal product (M.P.) is a measure of rate of change therefore.
   (*a*) when total product (T.P.) is increasing, the marginal product will be positive,
   (*b*) when the total product remains constant, the marginal product will be zero, and
   (*c*) If the total product decreases, the marginal product will be negative.
2. So long as marginal product moves upward or increases, the total product increases at an increasing rate.
3. When the marginal product remains constant, the total product increases at a constant rate.
4. When the marginal product starts declining or slopes downward, the total product will be increasing at a decreasing rate.
5. At the point the marginal product becomes zero or M.P. curve intersects X-axis, the total product will be at maximum.

Marginal Product and Average Product

Points to be noted in this relationship are

1. When the marginal product keeps increasing or is moving upward right from the beginning the average product (AP) curve also keeps moving upward. So long as MP curve remains above the AP curve, the average product curve keeps increasing. This means when the average product is increasing, the marginal product must be greater than the average product.
2. As soon as the MP curve goes below the AP curve, the AP curve starts decreasing ; *i.e.*, when average product is decreasing, the MP is always less than the AP.
3. When AP is equal to MP, at this point AP will be at the maximum. From here onward, MP will change from greater to being less than average product, the MP curve must therefore intersect AP curve from above at its highest point.

The relationship between average product and marginal product can be summarised as.

1. When MP > AP, AP is increasing.
2. When MP < AP, AP is decreasing.
3. When MP = AP, AP is at a maximum.

Elasticity of Production

The elasticity of production refers to the percentage change in output in response to the percentage change in input. It can be denoted by the symbol E_p and can be computed as :

$$E_p = \frac{\Delta Y/Y}{\Delta X/X} \text{ or } \Delta Y/Y.X/\Delta X \text{ or } X/Y.\frac{\Delta Y}{\Delta X}$$

The point is illustrated with an example given below :

Fertilizer Doses (X)	*Total Yield Arributable to Fertilizer (Y)*
0	0
1	103
2	174
3	223
4	257
5	281
6	298
7	308

As input increases from 1 to 2 units, total output increases from 103 to 174 units. Output thus increases by 71.9 percent in response to input increase of 100 percent. The elasticity of production (E_p) is $= \frac{71.9}{100} = 0.719$.

Similarly, between the second and third unit of input, the elasticity works out to be 0.56. Essential points to remember in elasticity analysis are ;

1. A production function with an elasticity of 1.0 $E_p = 1.0$ indicates constant returns throughout. This means a one percent increase in input is always accompained by a one percent increase in output.
2. The elasticity is more than 1.0 up to the point of maximum average product where it becomes 1.0.

3. The elasticity is less than 1.0 between the points of maximum average product and the maximum total product.
4. When it becomes less than zero, total product declines.
5. When elasticity of production is 1.0, marginal and average products are equal. This condition holds true at only one point on the classical production function as shown in Fig. 4.5.

A production function for which the elasticity is less than 1.0 throughout all ranges of input used will indicate diminishing returns.

THREE REGIONS OF PRODUCTION FUNCTION

The "classic" production function can be divided into three "parts", "stages", "regions", or "zones", each important from the standpoint of decision-making on efficient resource use. Input-output relationships showing total, average, and marginal productivity can be divided into three regions in such a manner that one can locate the portion of the production function in which production decisions are rational. The three stages or regions are shown in Fig. 4.5 *(a)*.

Region I. This region hold from the point of origin up to the point the MPP remains greater than APP. The APP increases throughout this region indicating that the efficiency of all the units of variable input keeps increasing. As soon as MPP equals APP, it is the end point of first zone.

Region II. This region obtains when MPP is decreasing and is less than APP. In this region at the starting point, MPP is equal to APP and it extends to the point where MPP becomes zero.

Region III. This region obtains where MPP crosses zero point and becomes negative. Negative MPP occurs when so much excessive quantity of the variable input is used that total output begins to decrease.

The Three Regions of Production Function and Economic decisions.

The production function can be used to determine the most profitable level of variable input(s) use. Alongside the physical input-output co-efficients, prices of the inputs and outputs of- course, must also be known for a complete economic analysis. If, however, the technical relationship between input and output, is known, some broad recommendations about input use can be made, even without the knowledge of prices. Such decisions are discussed below.

Region III. In the third region of the production function, the total product is decreasing and the MPP is negative. Since additional quantities of input reduce the total output in this region, it is not profitable zone even if the additional quantities of the resources(s) are available free of cost. It is therefore called an irrational zone of production ; *e.g.*, if a farmer operates in this region, it will be irrational because he will incur double loss; *i.e.*, (1) reduced production, and (2) unnecessary additional costs of inputs. There are several cases observed where farmers have been seen operating in the third region : on wheat Kalyan-227 unnecessarily heavy doses of fertilizer application by many farmers in the year 1967-68 resulted in lodging and this reduced yields. Another example is of excessive irrigation, often, given by the farmers, resulting in reduction of yield. Similarly heavy feeding schedules of animals have also been observed.

Region I. Once the farmer decides to produce, he must produce up to the level of input use where the APP is the highest. In other words, if the product has a value, input use once it gives profits should be continued until Stage II is reached, because the efficiency of the variable input keeps increasing throughout the region 1. It is not reasonable to stop using an input when its efficiency on all units used is increasing. In this region, average product keeps increasing and MP remains greater than the AP. If it is profitable to produce any output at all, it will always be profitable for the producer to add inputs as long as the average product keeps increasing. In other words, if a producer is interested in maximising his returns and if production is ever profitable, it will always pay him to go at least to the point of highest average product in the application of inputs.

Example. Suppose in a farm business, use of labour (man-months) earns for the farmer as below (wage remaining same) :

Units of Labour Use	*Marginal Product Worth (Rs.)*	*Average Product Worth (Rs.)*
1st unit	100	
2nd unit	120	110
3rd unit	140	120
4th unit	160	130
5th unit	170	138
6th unit	180	145
7th unit	170	148
8th unit	**150**	**149**
9th unit	135	147
10th unit	135	145

The figures show that it is economical to add 2nd man-month which will also improve the returns on the first man-months used. Likewise, additional man-months should continue to be used so long as average returns go on improving. The break-even point is reached at the eight man-month.

We have seen from the above discussion that Region I and Region III set the limits to the region in which it is profitable or economically rational to operate. Therefore, Region II is the region of rational decisions on resource use.

Region II. In the Region II, the total product is increasing. The marginal product keeps decreasing, but remains positive and less than the average product. The AP is also decreasing.

Within the boundaries of this region is the area of economic relevance. Optimum point of input-use must be somewhere in this rational region. The optimum point can, however, be located only when input and output prices are known. It needs to be emphasised that this region of rational production embodies diminishing returns phase. Both average and marginal products are decreasing in this region.

This discussion thus leads us to the point that the producers who want to maximise their profits must operate in Region II of the physical production function. In order to determine at what level in Region II one should operate, one needs to know the product as well as the input prices. Multiplying the quantities of product and inputs with the respective prices we can convert the physical production function into revenue and cost functions. The optimum level of input use, will be where the additional cost of an input is equal to the additional revenue which the input yields. In a situation where the decisions of an individual entrepreneur to use input does not influence the factor prices, optimum level of the variable factor use will be where the value of the marginal product equals the price of the factor in the market. It means that within the rational region of production function; *i.e.* Region II, it is the factor product price ratio which will be used as a choice indicator.

Take, for example, in Table 4.5 the price per unit of input to be Rs. 4/- and price per unit of product Rs. 3/-. Multiply the various quantities of product at different levels of input-use by Rs. 3/-. Assuming the producer's purchases are low enough not to cause the price of the input to rise, each input unit will cost Rs. 4/-. This is shown in 6th column of the Table 4.5 and Fig. 4.5.

We can see from the table that the highest net revenue can be obtained when 8 units of the input are used yielding net revenue at Rs. 73/-. If the producer applies less number of input units, say 7 units, the net revenue will be less. Here the returns from the last unit of input are greater than the costs, indicating a scope of further increasing the revenue by pushing up input use. On the other hand, if inputs are added to the point where the price of the input exceeds the value of the marginal product, the added costs go greater than the added returns. This will be the case in the previous example, when more than 8 units are used. By adding the 9th unit of input, the additional returns will be only Rs. 3/- where as the cost of this unit of input will be the same Rs. 4/-. This means it does not pay the producer to add more than 8 units of the input.

Optimum level of input use will thus be where the value of the additional product will be equal to the cost of additional input. So long as the returns are more than the added cost, one should go on pushing up production till marginal costs become equal to marginal returns.

TABLE 4.5

Factor-Product Relationship and Economic Decision Analysis

(Hypothetical Data)

	Physical Relationships				*Economic Relationships*				
	TP	*MI*	*MP*	*AP*	*MC*	*MR*	*TR*	*TC*	*NR*
Units of crop. Input (N) per acre	*Total Product/ yield Per acre*	*Marginal Input Unit added*	*Marginal Product Units of output*	*Average Product col. 2 ÷ col.1*	*Marginal Cost. @ Rs. 4/- Per unit*	*Marginal Returns @Rs. 3- Per unit*	*Total Returns from Production Col.2 × @ Rs. 3/-*	*Total Cost of Crop. In puts used*	*Net Revenue or Profit Col.8 – Col. 9*
1	2	3	4	5	6	7	8	9	10
0	2			—			6	0	6
1	5	1	3	5.00	4	9	15	4	9
2	9	1	4	4.50	4	12	27	8	19
3	14	1	5	4.66	4	15	42	12	30
4	21	1	7	5.25	4	21	63	16	47
5	26	1	5	5.20	4	15	78	20	58
6	30	1	4	5.00	4	12	90	24	66
7	33	1	3	4.71	4	9	99	28	71
8	35	1	2	4.37	4	6	105	32	73
9	36	1	1	4.00	4	3	108	36	72
10	36	1	0	3.60	4	0	108	40	68
11	35	1	-1	3.18	4	-3	105	44	61
12	33	1	-2	2.75	4	-6	99	48	51

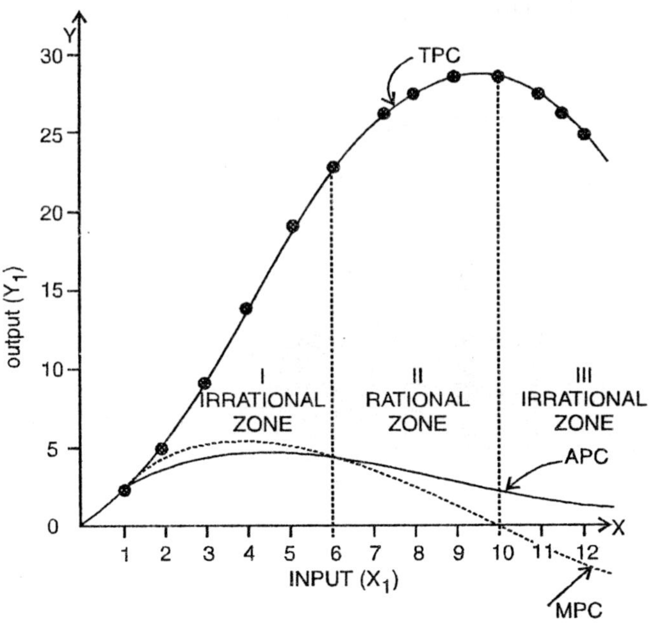

Fig. 4.5. (*a*) Relationship between total, average and marginal products (Stages of production and rational resource use)

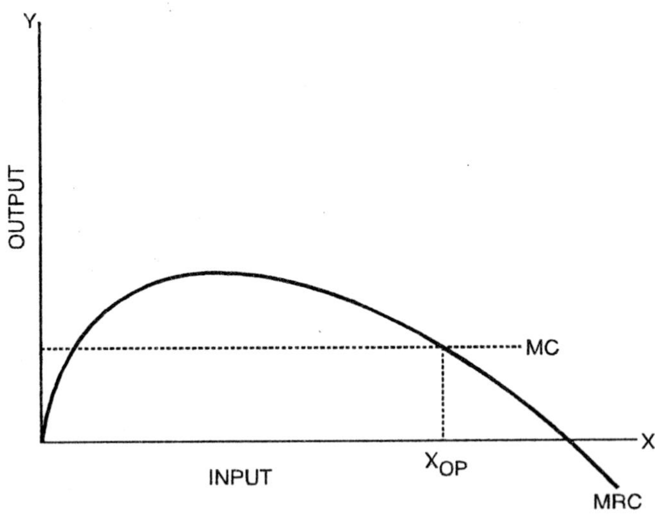

Fig. 4.5. (*b*) Marginal cost and marginal revenue curve

We can also examine this condition of profit maximisation by having the enlarged view of the Fig. 4.5 taking only marginal cost curve and marginal revenue curve. Here the profit is maximum at a point where MC is equal to MR (Point X_{OP} of input use). At this point the marginal returns curve must intersect the marginal cost curve from above.

We can also write this condition for maximization of net revenue as :

$$P_{Y1}\ \Delta Y_1 = P_{X1}\ \Delta X_1$$

where $P_{Y1}\ \Delta Y_1$ is added revenue and $P_{X1}\ \Delta X_1$ is added cost.

This can be written in ratio form as well.

$$\frac{\Delta Y_1}{\Delta X_1} = \frac{P_{X1}}{P_{Y1}}$$

IMPACT OF TECHNOLOGICAL CHANGE ON PRODUCTION FUNCTION

Technological change is one of the most important forces which alter the structure of the agricultural production process. The physical and value productivity of farm resources, for example, have been changing continuously in India and other countries in the recent past due to the constant flow of innovations in agriculture. The impact of these technical improvements is, therefore, an important area of analysis in production economics and farm management decisions.

These technological changes can (1) cause old products to be replaced by new ones, (2) create new inputs or improve old ones, and/or (3) otherwise affect the production process. Thus, technical advances may result in such developments as evolution of new crop varieties, breeds of animals and birds, invention of new fertilizers and their use methods, improved rations, new farm machinery use, etc. For a farm-firm, such technological advances can result in : (1) factor-saving technology or cost reducing technology such as development of improved tractors and machines, innovation of artificial insemination, (2) yield increasing technology, such as development, of hybrid maize and bajra, and evolution of dwarf wheat varieties, and (3) both factor-saving and yield increasing technology, such as low cost, more effective fertilizers and artificial insemination from high quality bulls. Either of these technological developments will bring about shifts in the whole body of production function and farmers will face new series of decisions to make.

So far we have discussed production functions with constant technology such as yield response to fertilizer applied in a particular way, yield response to irrigation water given in a certain manner. In such cases technology level is assumed to be given. There can be, however, different levels and grades of technology available to a farm entrepreneur. For example, application of fertilizer if possible with the broad-cast method, band application and/or spray method. Use of same quantity of the fertilizer through different methods will give different yield response. Similarly a different variety of a crop can be used such as dwarf mexican wheat (Kalyan 227, PV 18), and hybrid bajra (H-2) and hybrid maize. These new varieties will give different yield responses. With the introduction of such new techniques of production,

production functions will shift upward. If new technology turns out to be inferior to the previous one in use, production functions will shift downward.

An example in Table 4.6, based on hypothetical, figures, will clarify this concept of shift in production function

TABLE 4.6.

Total Yield of Crop 'A' by Different Methods of Fertilizer Use (Hypothetical Data)

	Total Yield Per Acre (Y) by Different Methods of Fertilizer Application		
Units of Input (X)	*Broadcast I*	*Hand placement II*	*Spray method III*
0	0	0	0
1	2	3	4
2	5	7	9
3	9	12	15
4	14	18	22
5	19	25	30
6	23	31	39
7	26	37	48
8	28	41	53
9	29	45	57
10	29	48	60
11	28	49	63
12	26	49	61

The figures in the T00able 4.6 can be depicted in the form of a curve in Fig. 4.6.

Without even considering costs and prices in this analysis, one can figure out from these production functions which technology is more efficient with respect to the use of a particular input. If one is to make a choice, highest of the production functions should be selected because at all the levels of input, use of this production function will be the most efficient one. It will give the highest physical and value returns with the input use remaining the same.

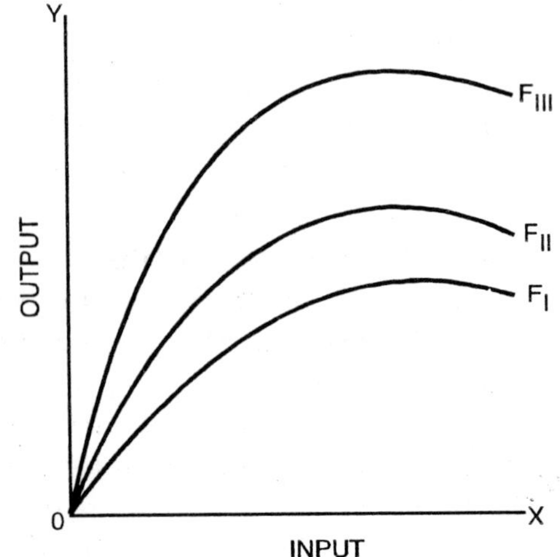

Fig. 4.6. Shifts in production function.

1. *List three major production relationships and discuss meanings of factor-product relationships in detail.*
2. *What do you understand by production functions ? Briefly describe the different types of production functions.*
3. *Discuss the relationships between the following ;*
   (a) *Total product curve and marginal product curve.*
   (b) *Average product curve and marginal product curve.*
   (c) *Total Product curve and average product curve.*
4. *What are the three zones of a production function ? How can one decide the optimum level of production ?*
5. *Why do we call Zones I and III of a production function irrational ? Why do some farmers operate in the third zone ?*
6. *What is meant by a shift in production function ? Explain, with the help of a suitable example, how farmer's decision change with a change in technology.*

1. ***Heady, Earl O., "Economics of Agricultural Production and Resource Use," Prentice-Hall of India Pvt. Ltd., New Delhi, 1964.***
2. ***Bishop, C.E., & W.D., Toussaint, "Introduction to Agricultural Economics Analysis," New York, John Wiley & Sons, Inc., London, Toppan Company Ltd., Tokyo, Japan, 1958.***
3. ***Doll, John, P., V. James Rhodes and Jerry G. West, "Economics of Agricultural Production, Markets & Policy", Homewood, U.S., Irwin 1968.***

5 Production and Costs

Up to this point, we have discussed factor-product relationships. This chapter treats the costs in a somewhat different manner. Instead of relating costs to units of factor services, we now relate costs to units of output. This chapter centres around the fundamentals of costs as they are related to problems in agriculture production.

Production costs play an important role in the decisions of the farmers. Explicity or implicity, most of the producers keep in mind the cost of producing additional units of output. In general, at given level of prices, a farmer can increase his farm income in two ways, *i.e.* (*i*) by increasing production, and/or (*ii*) by reducing the cost of production. In a competitive market, prices are not in the control of an individual farmer because there are large number of farmers who are individually producing very small proportions of total production of a commodity. His additional production must, therefore, sell at the same or even lower prices, even though additional production might involve higher costs. The second alternative is to reduce the cost of production through relationalisation of resource-use with low cost production factors. Since cost minimisation is an individual skill, degree of success in this direction, directly adds to the profits of the farmer.

The cost of production of different commodities relative to their prices is an important topic for discussion. Cost of production often becomes a policy issue when producers complain that the prices they receive for their products do not cover the cost of production. Cost of production, here, means the expenses incurred per unit of output. The items of cost that go into the cost of production are both fixed and variable costs. These expenses are always calculated with relation to a particular amount of product and in a particular time period.

THE CONCEPT OF COST

The cost here refers to the total amount of funds used in production. These funds or cost outlays for productive services are directly related to the laws of production. The nature of production function and the prices thus determine the cost structure. Cost of production exists because the supply of productive resources are scarce relative to their demand. These costs have relevance to a specific time period. The costs in any production period include the value of the resource services transformed into product in this single period rather than the value of the resources itself. The resources used in the production may be. (1)*Poly-period resources*, which represent stock of services (tractor service) and only a part of these stock of services is transformed into product in each distinct production period, and (2) *Mono-period resources* which also represent a stock of services (seed, fertilizer) but here the entire stock of services is transformed into product in a single period. In the production of one quintal of wheat, for example, there are different costs involved. Some cost items such as fertilizer, seeds, etc., are transformed into product during the production period, whereas there are other cost items such as productive services of a tractor, family labour, land etc. of which only a part goes into production process. In order to make rational choice from amongst alternatives, costs should, therefore, be considered with relation to a specified time period.

Cash Costs and Non-cash Costs.

In common usage the term "cost of production" is used in the sense of money costs or expenses of production. In economics, however, cost means the total efforts, sacrifices and exertion involved in the production of a commodity while expenses of production signify only money costs. So the cost of production involves both cash-cost items and not, cash items. Cash costs are incurred when resources are purchased and used immediately in the production process. For the most, cash costs result from purchases of non-durable inputs such as fertilizers, fuel oil, casual labour, which do not last more than one production period. Non-cash costs consist of depreciation and payments to resources owned by the farmer *e.g.*, depreciation on tractor, equipment, buildings, payments made to the farmer himself or family labour, management and owned capital.

PLANNING PERIOD

For proper understanding the process of decisions about costs, it is important to consider the planning period over which the decisions are made. On the basis of length of period for different inputs to get transformed into products, planning period can be divided into two categories. (1) Short period or short-run-planning period and (2) Long period or long-run- planning period.

Short Period

It is a period of time which is long enough to permit desired changes in output without altering or changing the size of the plant. Suppose there is a farm-firm which produces milk with 12 cows. Further, suppose that with the rise in demand for milk, prices rise and in turn margins of profit increase. The firm is encouraged to increase its production. But how can it do this ? There can be two ways. (1) Purchase and start maintaining more cows, which may not be possible immediately, (2) bring about changes in feed-mix and level of feeding which do not require change in the size of the plant (number of cows) but increases production. Short period will be different for different enterprises. Suppose a farmer has sown 10 acres of wheat in November with the expectation of a price at Rs. 80/- per quintal. Further suppose in February the expectations revise to Rs. 100 per quintal. At this stage he can not increase acreage under this crop. Alternative for him will be to add more fertilizer and get increased yields. This short period is not long enough to change size of the plant.

Long Period

The long period is generally the period which is sufficiently long for output level to be altered or changed by varying even the size of the plant. Suppose the same farmer expects that wheat production is going to be more renumerative in future years. He may try to increase land by purchasing or leasing in and improve the productive capacity by installing new tubewells etc. In other words, sufficient time period will be needed to change the size of the holding. This time period, enough to allow the change in size of plant or holding, is known as long period or long-run planning period.

CATEGORIES OF COST

Several kinds of costs are involved in even the most simple production process. Corresponding to two lengths of planning periods, there are two major categories of costs namely. (*i*) fixed costs or sunk costs or supplementary costs and, (*ii*) variable costs or prime costs. A resource or input is called a fixed resource if its quantity cannot be varied during the production period. These costs do not vary with the level of output. A resource is a variable resource if its quantity can be varied during the production period. These costs vary with the level of enterprise. In general, costs associated with fixed inputs are called fixed costs and costs associated with variable inputs are called variable costs.

Fixed Costs

Fixed costs are those which do not change in magnitude as the amount of output of the production process changes and are incurred even when production is not undertaken. These are sunk costs. These costs can be cash or non-cash fixed costs.

Fixed cash costs include land taxes, interest, insurance premia, annually hired labour etc. Non-cash fixed costs include depreciation on buildings, machinery equipment, interest on capital investment, cost of family labour and costs of management. It should be emphasised that costs do not become fixed until they have been incurred or committed After these costs get incurred they do not vary with change in output and have no bearing upon decisions to increase or decrease production. In the very long-run, however, all costs become variable.

Variable Costs

Variable costs are the costs of using the variable inputs. These costs vary with the level of production. Higher the production, more will be the variable costs : lower the production, lower will be the variable costs. These costs include items such as fertilizers, insecticides, fuel consumption etc.

Total Costs

Fixed costs plus variable costs equal total costs. Total costs are required for computing net revenue. Net revenue is equal to total revenue less total costs. Whether a particular cost item will be considered as a fixed cost or a variable one depends upon whether the input concerned is fixed or variable for the problem under consideration. During long-run planning period, all inputs are variable. Thus in the long run, there are no fixed costs. The costs which are relevant for a particular decision, therefore, depend upon the nature of the decision.

Opportunity Cost

The farm resources normally have a number of alternative uses. If they are not paid as much as they can earn in other fields, a particular farmer will find that the productive factors tend to shift to the lines of production in which they are better paid. We refer to the price that will be required to prevent the transference of factors to other uses as "opportunity cost" or "alternative costs.".

The price which should be put on any input is, therefore, the return which must be given up in the next best alternative use. Every resource used in the productive process thus, has but one true cost : opportunity cost, the next best alternative forgone.

Suppose, a farmer has 2 qtls. of fertilizer ; it adds Rs. 250 to the total revenue from wheat and Rs. 200 revenue from barley. If he fertilizes barley, his opportunity cost is Rs. 250/- which he has foregone on wheat. If he fertilises wheat, his opportunity cost is Rs. 200 foregone on barley. Thus once purchased, the market price of an input becomes irrelevant to the problem of its allocation among alternative uses. It becomes a sunk cost whether its price is high or low.

Farmers own many durable resources such as machninery or land which are used in the production process. These resources are used over several production periods. Even though they may not have a purchase price each year, these resources do have their opportunity cost *i.e.*, the money they would earn from their best alternative use. The alternative uses of many of the items on a farm, such as ploughs, thrashers, tractors, etc., may be difficult to evaluate. Their opportunity costs can be, however evaluated directly. Often rupee value is put on all resources owned by the farmer, that is the total amount of his investment in land, machinery, buildings etc. The opportunity cost of these items is then defined to be the amount that total capital investment could earn if invested in its best alternative use. If best alternative is only to deposit the money in the bank, the opportunity cost will equal interest on investment.

Family labour represents another non-cash cost. Budgeted charges can be made of family labour used on the farm. These charges represent wages the farm operator and his family could earn of employment off the farm. Just as with interest on investment these off-farm wages represent an opportunity cost of family labour.

If the opportunity cost of family labour is zero, *i.e.*, if there is no alternative opportunity of employment of family labour, no cost for these items should be charged against the business. However, the value a farmer puts on his hand and his family's leisure, becomes the opportunity cost in this case.

COST FUNCTION

As in the case of other functional relationships, the total cost curve or cost function represents the functional relationship between output and total cost. Here the discussions will relate to how costs are related to levels of output *i.e.*, what will happen to cost structure when we produce different quantities of a commodity.

These cost functions or curves can also be presented in three ways : (*i*) arithmetically (in tabular form), (*ii*) geometrically (in graphic form) or, (*iii*) algebraically (in equation form).

The Total Cost Function

The exact nature (curvature) of the total cost function depends on the nature of the corresponding production function *i.e.* the shape of the total cost curve is determined by the production function, provided that the price which the producer pays for inputs does not change as the quantity of inputs purchased changes.

Relationship Between Production Function and Total Cost Function

In order to understand how production function and total cost function are related with each other, refer to Fig. 5.1 (A) and Fig. 5.1 (B).

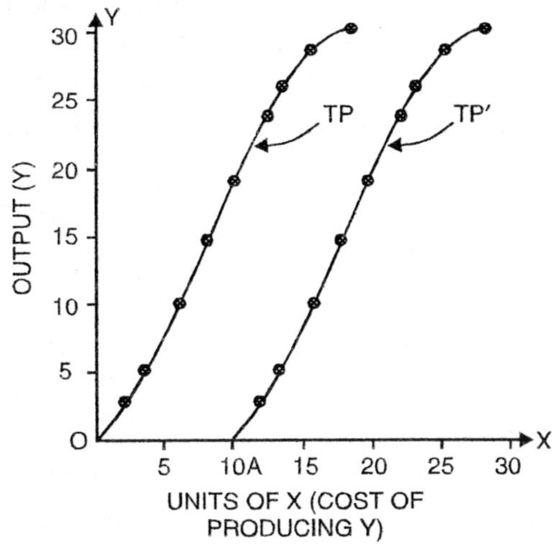

Fig. 5.1. (A) Output related to cost. (Production functions)

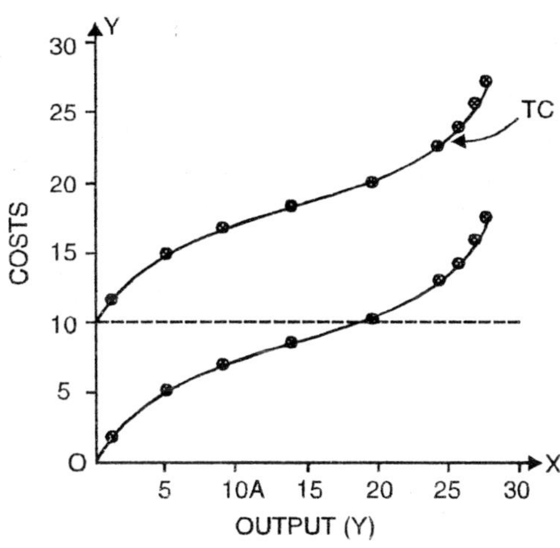

Fig. 5.1. (B) Cost related to output. (Cost-functions)

The curve TP in Fig. 5.1 (A) shows the relationship between output and use as well as cost of input at constant prices. Since each unit of input costs the same amount, this curve is identical to the production function in which 'Y' is a function of the variable input 'X' in physical terms.

There are also fixed costs involved in the production of 'Y'. Fixed costs can be shown by moving the production function to the right on X-axis by a distance equal to the fixed costs. In this case, the amount of fixed cost is represented by the distance OA. Note that fixed costs do not change the shape of the curve, only the position is affected.

When, cost is thought of as related to output, cost curves are portrayed with cost on the vertical axis and output on the horizontal axis as shown in Fig. 5.1 (B). The total cost curve in figure (B) is the same curve as TP in Fig. 5.1 (B) only the graph is turned sideways and backward. Total product curve and total cost curve are thus related in the reverse order.

There are logical reasons for expecting the total cost curve to have the general form as shown in Fig. 5.1 (A). Since each additional unit of input has a cost, we would expect the total cost curve to rise throughout its entire range. Only if the variable inputs were free, would the total cost curve go horizontal, that is the cost will be independent of output. We would expect the average cost to fall as output increases because fixed cost will spread on more and more number of units as the output expands. Under such conditions it would cost less per-unit to produce more, and consequently, the rational producer would continue to expand his production. In doing so, he would continue increasing his net revenue.

On a production function of classical type (Fig. 5.2) we would not expect the farmer operating in a region in which total cost will increase as production decreases (Region III). Hence, from the viewpoint of a firm, one would expect the total cost curve to lie between the limits of a horizontal and a vertical line as does the total cost curve in figure 'B'.

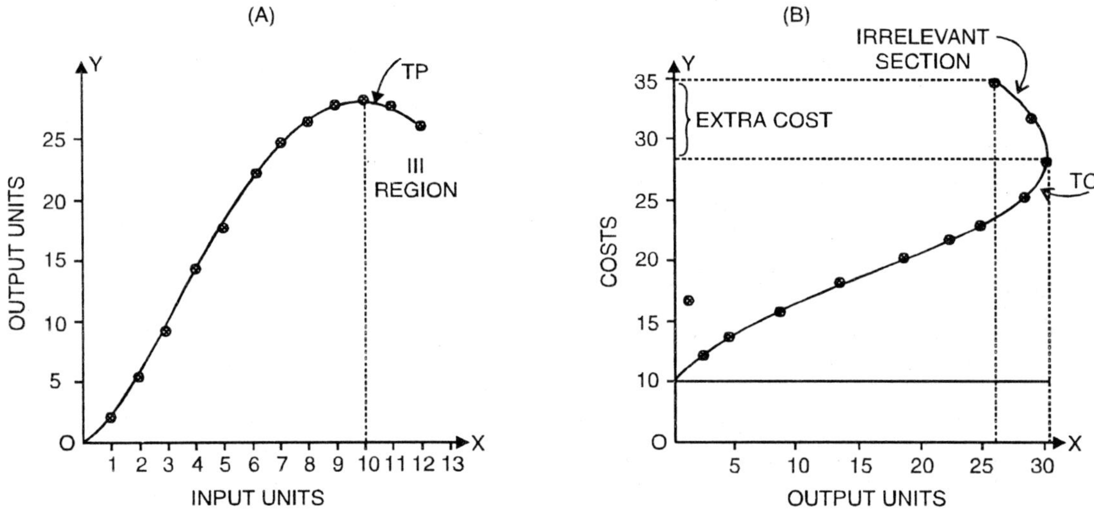

Fig. 5.2. Relationship between different production regions of production function and total cost function.

Relationship Between Total Fixed Costs, Total Variable Costs and Total Costs

For studying the relationship between fixed, variable and total costs, computation of these costs for a classic production function have been given in Table 5.1. The production function is presented in columns 1 and 2 of this table. The total cost function is given in columns 5 and 7. For simplicity sake, Rs. 10 is assumed to be the cost associated with the fixed inputs used in the production process and the variable cost is that which is incurred in purchasing the variable input(s).

TABLE 5.1

Product and Cost Relationships

Input Units	*Total Output Units*	*Average Product Units*	*Marginal Product Units Y*	*Total Variable Cost at Rs. 2/- per unit (TVC)*	*Total Fixed Cost (TFC)*	*Total Cost (TVC + TFC)*	*Average Variable Cost (VC/Y)*	*Average Fixed Cost (FC/Y)*	*Average Total Cost (TC/Y)*	*VC Change in Cost (TC/Y)*	*Marginal Cost VC / Y*
1	2	3	4	5	6	7	8	9	10		
0	0	0	0	0	10	10	0	—	—		
1	2	2	2	2	10	12	1	5	6	2	1
2	5	2.5	3	4	10	14	.8	2	2.8	2	.67
3	9	3	4	6	10	16	.67	1.11	1.78	2	.5
4	14	3.5	5	8	10	18	.57	.71	1.38	2	.4
5	19	3.8	5	10	10	20	.53	.53	1.06	2	.4
6	23	3.83	4	12	10	22	.52	.43	.95	2	.5
7	26	3.71	3	14	10	24	.54	.38	.92	2	.67
8	28	3.5	2	16	10	26	.58	.36	.94	2	1
9	29	3.22	1	18	10	28	.62	.34	.96	2	2
10	29	2.9	0	20	10	30	.69	.34	1.03	2	—
11	28	2.54	–1	22	10	32	.79	.36	1.15	2	—
12	26	2.16	–2	24	10	34	.92	.38	1.30	2	—

Note that production function has single total product curve but in cost function, the total cost curve represents two categories of cost *i.e.,* fixed costs and variable costs.

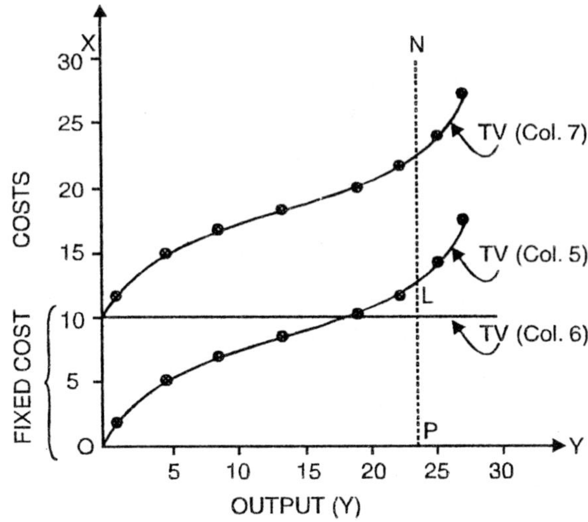

Fig. 5.3. Total cost curves related to classic production function.

***Total Fixed Costs* (TFC).** The TFC is shown in 6th column of Table 5.1. These costs are the same for all output levels. Thus, once computed from the farm or enterprise budget, TFC is known to be unchanging. TFC is graphed in Fig. 5.3. Here TFC is at level 10 for all output levels. This is represented by a straight line parallel to the horizontal or 'X' axis and located 10 units up the vertical scale.

***Total Variable Costs* (TVC).** Total variable costs are computed by multiplying the amount of variable input used by the price per unit of input. In symbolic notation, 'X' is the amount of variable input used and P_x is the price or cost per unit of input, then TVC = P_x (X). A graph of TVC computed in column 5 of Table 5.1 is shown in Fig. 5.3. TVC is zero when output and consequently the input is zero. It increases as output increases. The shape of the TVC curve depends upon the shape of the production function.

***Total Costs* (TC).** Total costs are the sum of total variable costs and total fixed costs. They are presented in column 7 of Table 5.1 and are obtained by adding TVC and TFC for different output levels. When no variable input is used, TC = TFC (see Fig. 5.3). The TC curve is equal to the vertical addition of TFC and TVC on this graph. It is shaped exactly like the TVC curve but is always higher by units of TFC on vertical axis. The shape of the TC curve, like that of the TVC curve, depends upon the production function. In symbolic notation, TC can be written as ;

$$\text{TC} = \text{TFC} + \text{TVC} \quad \text{or} \quad \text{TC} = \text{TFC} + P_x (X)$$

Relationships Between Average Fixed Cost, Average Variable Cost, Average Total Cost

The averages of the various costs are calculated in columns 8, 9 and 10 of Table 5.1. The definitions and relationships of these costs are given below ;

Average Fixed Cost (AFC). It is worked out by dividing total fixed costs by the amount of output. (Col. 6 ÷ Col.2 in Table 5.1). It is fixed cost per unit of output. AFC will vary for each level of output. As output increases, AFC decreases. Thus, when economists refer to increasing output as a method of "spreading fixed costs" they mean increasing production to divide total fixed costs among more and more units of output thereby reducing cost per unit. AFC is presented in column 9 of the Table 5.1 and shown graphically in Fig. 5.4. Here the input level changes but fixed costs remain the same ; thus decreasing fixed cost per unit of output. When output is zero, AFC = TFC, AFC always slopes downwards regardless of production function. Its general location on the graph depends upon the magnitude of total fixed costs.

Average Variable Costs (AVC). AVC is worked out by the dividing total variable costs by the amount of output. AVC varies with the level of production; the shape of the AVC curve depends upon the shape of the production function. The height of the AVC depends upon the unit cost of the variable input. AVC as computed in column 8 of Table 5.1 are graphed in the Fig. 5.4.; like AFC, AVC cannot be computed when output is zero. Average variable cost is inversely related to average physical product, *i.e.*, when APP is increasing, AVC is decreasing. When APP is maximum, AVC attains minimum (is at its lowest point). When APP is decreasing, AVC is increasing. AVC first falls due to economies of large scale production and then rises due to diseconomies of scale in production.

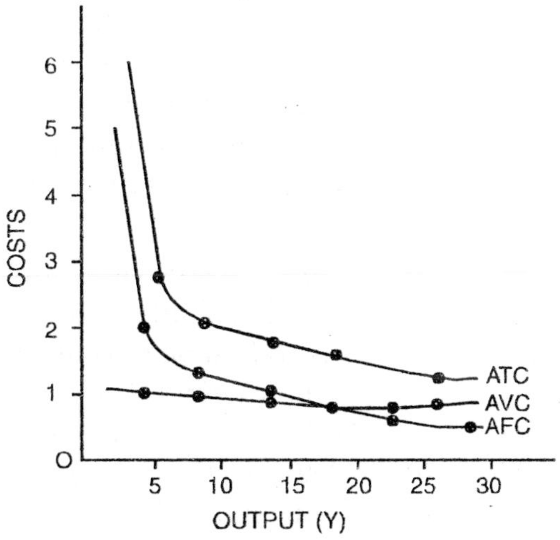

Fig. 5.4. Average Cost Curves

Thus, as on a production function APP measures the efficiency of the variable input, for cost curves AVC provides the same measure *i.e.*, (*i*) when AVC is decreasing, the efficiency of the variable input is increasing, (*ii*) It is at a maximum when AVC is at a minimum and (*iii*) it is decreasing when AVC is increasing.

Average Total Costs (ATC). ATC can be computed in two ways. (*a*) By dividing total costs by output, or (*b*) by adding AFC and AVC. ATC is presented in column 10, of Table 5.1 and is also shown in Fig. 5.4. The shape of the ATC curve depends upon the shape of the production function. In Fig. 5.4, ATC decreases as output increases, attains a minimum and increases thereafter. ATC is often referred to as the "unit cost" of production *i.e.* the cost of producing one unit of output. The initial decrease in ATC is caused by the spreading of fixed costs among an increasing number of units of output and the increasing efficiency with which the variable input is used. As output increases futher, ATC attains a minimum and begins to increase, as increase in AVC can no longer be offset by decrease in AFC.

Characteristics of Average Cost Curves

(*i*) Average fixed cost curve will continue to decline and never show upward movement because after maximum product is achieved, inputs beyond this become irrational.

(*ii*) As the production expands, the AVC keeps on declining. It reaches the lowest point and then bends upwards. At this point APP is the highest.

(*iii*) Average total cost curve has the same shape as AVC. Difference is that the lowest point in case of AVC reaches earlier as compared to ATC.

Marginal Cost

Marginal cost (MC) is the change in total cost in response to a unit increase in output at the margin. It is the change in cost associated with an increase or decrease of an additional unit of output. It is in the other words the cost of producing an additional unit of output and is computed by dividing the change in total cost (Δ TC) by the corresponding change in output (Δ Y) *i.e.*, $\Delta TC/\Delta Y$. MC is given in last column of Table 5.1 and presented in Fig. 5.6.

Actually a change in total cost is always equal to the change in variable cost at a given level of fixed cost. MC could also be, therefore, worked out by dividing the change in variable cost by the change in output.

Characteristics of Marginal Cost (MC)

As output increases, MC first falls due to more efficient use of the variable factor (s) of production and then it slopes upwards due to less efficient use of the variable factor (s). Marginal cost is related to marginal product in the same manner as AVC is related to AP.

$$MC = \frac{\Delta \text{ cost}}{\Delta Y}$$

but $\Delta\text{cost} = P_x \, \Delta X$

$\therefore$ $MC = P_x \dfrac{\Delta X}{\Delta Y}$ or $MC = \dfrac{P_x}{\Delta Y/\Delta X}$

But $\Delta Y/\Delta X = MP$

Thus, $MC = \dfrac{P_x}{MP}$

Inverse relationship between MP and MC can be seen in Fig. 5.5. (A) and Fig.5.5. (B).

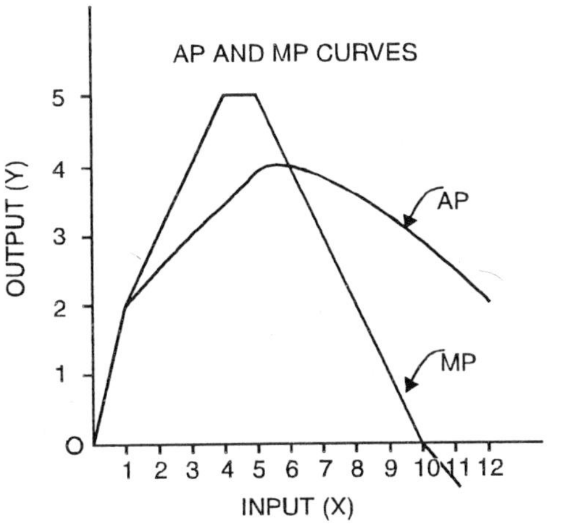

Fig.5.5. (A) AP and MP curves

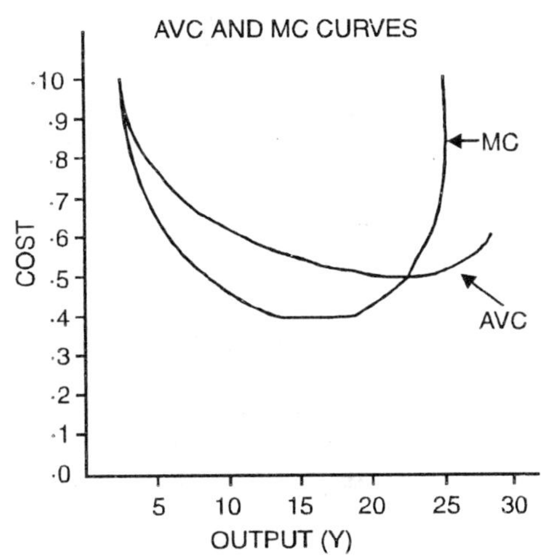

Fig. 5.5. (B) AVC and MC curves

From these figures, following relationships can be deciphered :

(*i*) When MP is at the maximum, MC is at the lowest point.

(*ii*) When MP is increasing, MC is decreasing, and

(*iii*) When MP is decreasing, MC is increasing.

Relationship Between Average and Marginal Cost

Marginal cost has a definite relationship with ATC and AVC ; (1) AVC and ATC curves will slope downwards and keep falling as long as MC curve is below them. Conversely, AVC & ATC curves will move up when MC curve is above them. (2) MC curve will intersect the AVC curve at the lowest point from below : As MC curve moves on, it intesects the ATC curve from below at the lowest point. The only difference is that MC curve intersects the AVC curve earlier than ATC curve.

DETERMINATION OF NET REVENUE AS A FUNCTION OF OUTPUT

The principle of profit maximization can be discussed in two ways :

1. as a relationship between marginal costs and marginal revenue, and

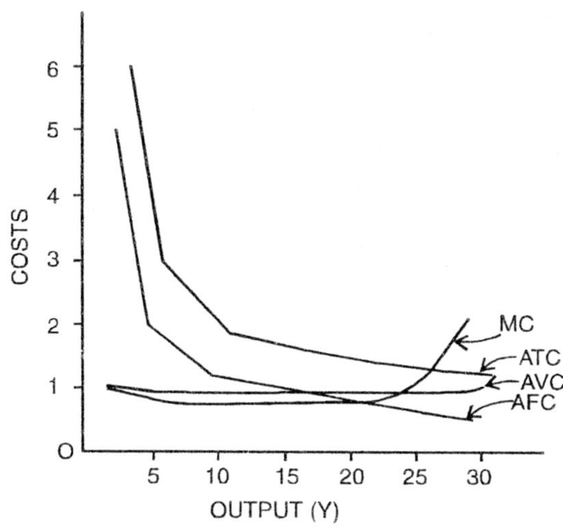

Fig. 5.6. Average, total and marginal cost curves.

2. as a marginal product ratio ($\Delta Y/\Delta X$) in relation to factor-product price ratio (P_x/P_y). MC = MR approach is presented in Fig. 5.7 and $\Delta Y/\Delta X = P_x/P_y$ approach is presented in Fig. 5.8.

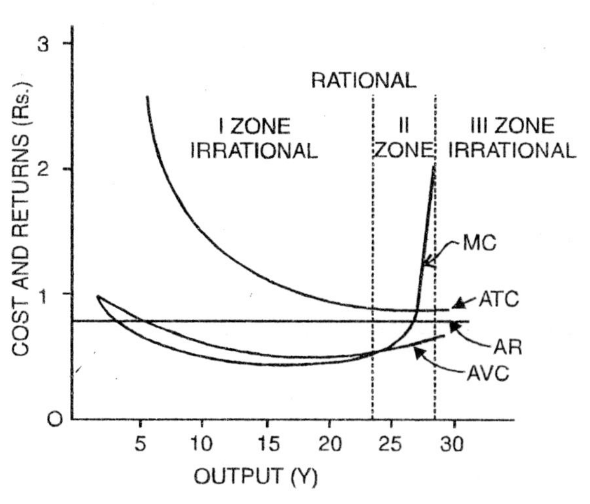

Fig. 5.7.

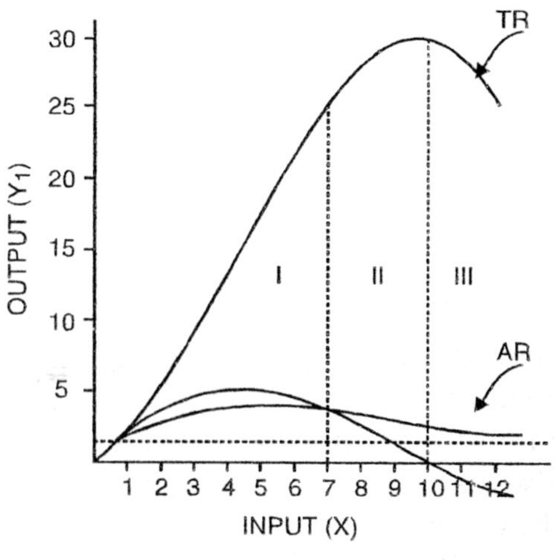

Fig. 5.8

Both these methods reach the some point on resource use attempting to maximise profit in a given time period. These two methods are in fact only two different manners of stating the same condition.

Net Revenue as related to Output

Working out of an optimum production point requires two quantities, marginal cost and marginal revenue, to be equated. Under the competitive product-market conditions which characterise agriculture, the amount of product which one farmer sells has no significant influence on market price. A farmer will receive the same price per unit whether he sells 10 quintals or 1000 quintals of maize or any other product. In other words, each unit of product sold adds the same amount to the total revenue or the gross income. Accordingly, the total revenue or gross income curve for an individual farm is linear in shape at different levels of product sold (Figure 5.9). Price curve in this case will be horizontal to the 'X' axis and MR will be equal to AR.

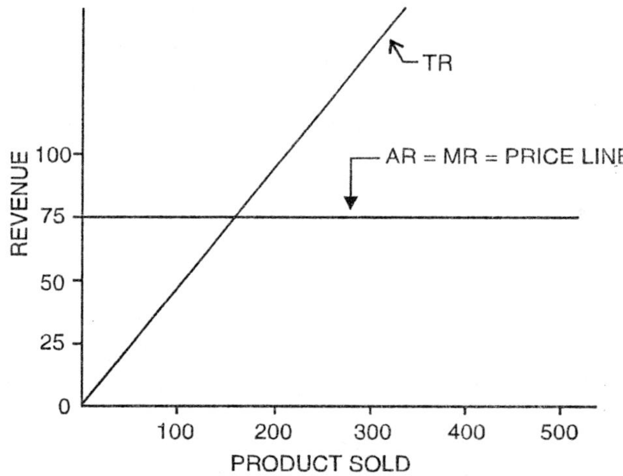

Fig. 5.9. Relationship between price and units of output sold.

If the price of a commodity does not vary with quantity sold, total revenue increases in proportion to the increase in output. Profits are at the maximum for a farm business when output (or factor input) is at a level where marginal cost is equal to the marginal revenue (MC = MR). Hence, an additional unit of output is always profitable as long as MC is less than MR because less is added to total costs than is added to total revenue. Production of an additional unit is always unprofitable, if MC is greater than MR, since more is added to the total costs than is added to the total revenue.

THREE ZONES OF COST-FUNCTION AND PROFIT MAXIMISATION

Like output function, the cost function has also three zones of production relationships. (Fig. 5.10).

In terms of the cost, Zone-III starts when output cannot increase further. This is the point of maximum production. Incurring cost beyond this point is not logical because production will not increase any further. Maybe, it decreases after this. Production beyond this point falls in an irrational zone. Zone-I starts from the origin and ends up at the point where MC cuts the AC from below.

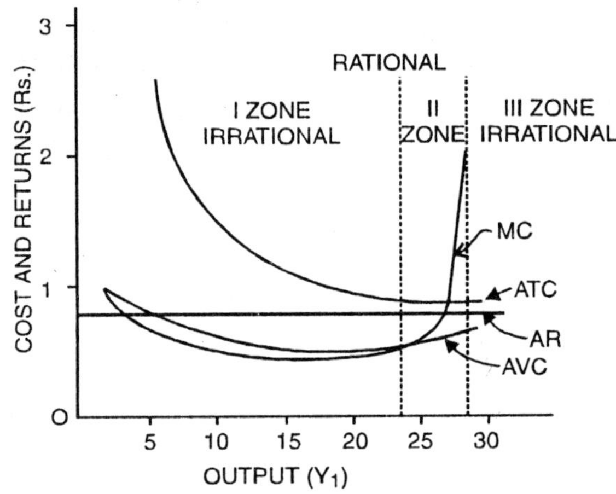

Fig. 5.10. Three zones of total cost function and profit determination

At this point, AC is the least. This point corresponds to the AP on production function when it is intersected by MP from above. This is again irrational zone because if production starts it should continue till AC goes on decreasing.

Zone-II is in between zone I and zone III, which are irrational zones. Zone II is rational zone of production. Profit will be maximum if a producer produces within the limits of zone II where MC = MR.

At this point, three conditions must be fulfilled : (1) MC must be equal to price of the product *i.e.*, MC = MR = P_Y, (2) MC curve must be still rising, and (3) Total revenue must be greater than the total variable cost.

Optimum Production Decisions Based on Total Cost and Total Revenue

Total revenue minus total costs gives profit which is also called net returns or net returns *e.g.* : when input is zero, output is zero and the profit is minus 10 (the amount of fixed cost). As output increases, profits increase, and reach a maximum of 30 at 28 units of input and 26 units of output (Table 5.2).

Maximum profit from enterprises does not necessarily occur where output is at the maximum. Output reaches a maximum of 29 at 9 units of input. Profit at this point is 30. Therefore, the point of maximum yield such as wheat per acre and litres of milk per cow, is not always compatible with the point of maximum per unit of fixed input.

TABLE 5.2.

Determination of Optimum Point of Production using TC & TR approach

Input *X*	*Output* *Y*	*Total Costs* *@ Rs. 2/-* *(TFC = Rs. 10)*	*Total Revenue* *TR* = P_y *(Y)* *@ Rs. 2/-unit*	*Profit* *(TR – TC)*
0	0	10	0	–10
1	2	12	4	–8
2	5	14	10	–4
3	9	16	18	2
4	14	18	28	10
5	19	20	38	16
6	23	22	46	24
7	26	24	52	26
8	28	26	56	30
9	29	28	58	30
10	29	30	58	28
11	28	32	56	24
12	26	34	52	22

The reason, of course, is that the efficiency of production decreases through stage II of the production function. Beyond the maximum profit point, the added inputs cost more than they are able to earn. Thus the quest for maximum yield, is not always consistent with income maximisation.

MINIMUM LOSS PRINCIPLE

There can be two decision situations (1) when selling prices cover total costs, and (2) when selling prices are less than total costs but more than average variable costs. In short run, only variable costs are important in decision-making. Once commitments for fixed costs have been made, thereafter, they are a *fact accomplished*. Fixed costs do establish the level of total costs out only variable costs affect the rate at which total costs change. Variable costs must, therefore, by covered by the selling price if production is to be profitable in the short-run. Even if the selling price or MR does not cover total average costs, production in the short-run is economical as long as marginal return is above the Average Variable cost. In this situation losses do occur, yet they are minimised by continued production. Only if selling price or MR is below the Average variable or operating cost, loss can be minimised by ceasing production, Figure 5.11 illustrates minimum loss condition ; when the selling price is OL (vertical axis) and the output is OP (horizontal axis), the average total cost is PM (or ON) as is indicated on the curve ATC and the loss per unit is RM or LN. Since the selling price OL exceeds the average variable cost OK, losses are reduced as output is extended to OP. Total returns here are more than total variable costs. Some fixed costs are still not covered.

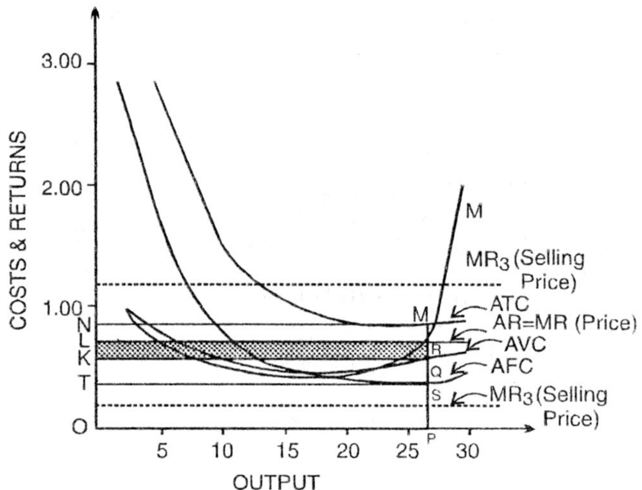

Fig. 5.11. Graphic illustration of loss minimisation condition.

At this point : total revenue = OPRL, total cost = OPMN, net loss = LRMN, variable costs = OPQK and fixed costs = OPST. Here OPMN (total costs) = OPQK + OPST or = OPQK + KQMN. Returns to fixed factors (cash Returns over variable expenses) = Total returns—variable costs = OPRL—OPQK = KQRL. If the farm-entrepreneur decides not to produce at all, loss will be equal to fixed cost (OPST). Since loss at production point P is LRMN, reduction in loss over a decision not to produce will be OPST (or KQMN)—LRMN = KQRL. Thus whatever gain we make over variable costs, is the amount by which loss on fixed costs is reduced.

While production should be maintained in the short-run if selling price is above variable cost, it cannot be continued indefinitely unless selling price exceeds average total costs. The resources and costs which are fixed in the short-run become variable in the long-run and all costs must, therefore, be covered in the long-run. Unless all fixed costs are returned over long period, the farmer must either switch over to other occupations or experience a continuous decline, in living standards.

Thus, if the total returns are more than the total costs, the objective of the producer is to maximise the profit. If however, the total returns are less than the total cost but more than variable cost, the objective of the producer is to maximise the loss in the short run.

There are number of practical cases or situations where farmers continue in operation even though total revenue does not cover total costs.

In depression period, for example, prices go down but farmers do not quit the business of farming. They continue in the business with a hope to recover the loss in the long-run. Dairy men have large investments in fixed assets, such as land, buildings etc. If for some period milk prices go down, they continue producing milk. As another example, suppose wheat production costs Rs. 800 per acre. But the prices decline and total returns are expected to be Rs. 500 only. If the farmer has already planted wheat and has incurred a cost of Rs. 400/-, by spending additional Rs. 400/- on harvest etc. he can get Rs. 500 as total returns. If he does not spend Rs. 400 on harvesting, etc., he will lose Rs. 500. So, to minimise his losses, he must spend Rs. 400 at this stage.

FACTOR-PRODUCT PRICE CHANGES AND PRODUCTION DECISIONS

It is logical to expect changes in the optimum output if either the price of the output (P) or the price of factor (P_x) changes. The following examples demonstrate the effect of changes in factor-product prices on production decisions.

Effects of Changes in Output Prices

A decrease in product price means lowering of the price line. The marginal revenue, therefore, will decrease for each level of output. If there is a fall in the prices of product (say from Rs. 1.00 to Rs. 0.75 in Fig. 5.12), the optimum output level will shift down. On the other hand, a rise in product price (from Rs. 1.00 to Rs. 1.25 in Fig. 5.12) will increase the marginal revenue and the most profitable level of output.

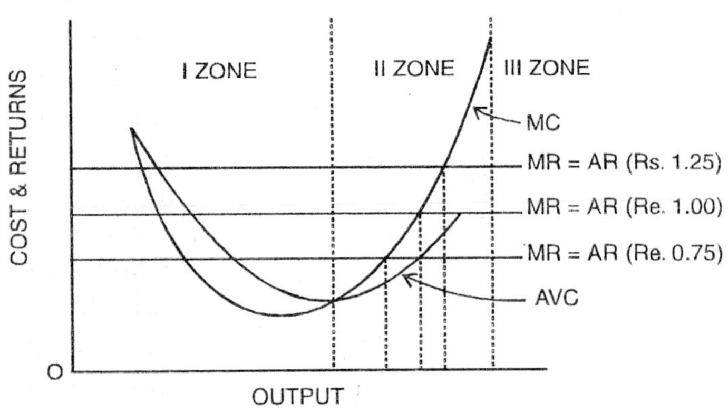

Fig. 5.12. Relationship of average and marginal cost or revenue of output with shifts in prices of output.

There is thus a direct relationship between product price changes and optimum output levels ; higher the price, higher will be the level of production; lower the price, lower the level of output.

Effects of Changes in Input Prices

Changes in input prices cause changes in production in the opposite direction from those brought about by changes in product prices (Fig. 5.13). An increase in the price of variable input causes the cost curves to move upwards. The intersection of MC with MR (selling price of product) will be at a lower output point and production will be reduced in order to maximise the net revenue.

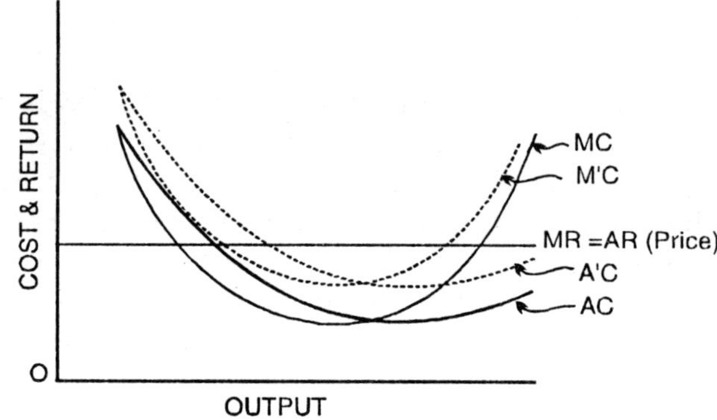

Fig. 5.13. Input price changes and production decisions.

As there occurs a shift in the MC curve with the change in the price of input, similarly there will be a shift in the AC curve also as shown in Table 5.3 and Fig. 5.13.

TABLE 5.3

Changes in the Input-Prices and Production Decision

Units of Output	*Marginal Cost*		*Average Total Cost when FC = Rs. 10 and*	
	@ Rs. 2.00	*@ Rs. 2.50*	*Input cost Rs. 2.00 per unit*	*Input cost Rs. 2.50 per unit*
0	—	—	—	—
2	1.00	1.25	6.00	6.25
5	0.67	0.83	2.80	3.00
9	0.50	0.61	1.78	1.93
14	0.40	0.50	1.38	1.42
19	0.40	0.50	1.06	1.13
23	0.50	0.61	0.95	1.08
26	0.67	0.83	0.92	1.05
28	1.00	1.25	0.94	1.03
29	2.00	2.50	0.96	1.12

This means when price of input increases, the level of output should be decreased, because in this case, cost curves will shift upwards and intersection of MC with MR will be at the point of lower output. If the price of input decreases, the cost of producing any given output will decrease and the most profitable level of production will increase. With the decrease in the price of the input, the cost-curve will shift down and the intersection of the MC and MR curves will be at a higher level of output.

1. *Discuss the importance of cost functions analysis.*
2. *Define the following :*
   (a) *Short and long-run-planning periods.*
   (b) *Fixed costs and variable costs.*
   (c) *Cash costs and non-cash costs.*
   (d) *Opportunity cost.*
3. *Discuss the relationships between :*
   (a) *Production function and total cost function.*
   (b) *Total fixed costs, total variable costs and total costs.*
   (c) *Average fixed costs, average variable costs and average total costs.*
   (d) *Average costs and marginal costs.*
4. *Name three zones of a cost function and discuss the process of profit maximisation with the help of cost curves.*
5. *Discuss how factor and product price changes affect production decisions.*
6. *Demonstrate with the help of a suitable diagram, the application of minimum loss principle.*
7. *Assignment :*
   Every student should draw neat and labelled diagrams on graph papers to show the following concepts used in cost function analysis.
   (a) *Total cost function*

Relationship between total fixed cost, total variable cost and total cost :

Units of Output	*Total Variable Cost (T.V.C.)*	*Total Fixed Cost (T.F.C.),*	*Total Cost (T.C.)*
0	*0*	*10*	*10*
2	*2*	*10*	*12*
5	*4*	*10*	*14*
9	*6*	*10*	*16*
14	*8*	*10*	*18*
19	*10*	*10*	*20*
23	*12*	*10*	*22*
26	*14*	*10*	*24*
28	*16*	*10*	*26*
29	*18*	*10*	*28*

(b) ***Average and Marginal Cost curves***

Relationship between average fixed costs, average variable costs, average total and marginal costs.

Units of Output	Average variable Costs (AVC)	Average fixed cost (AFC)	Average total cost (ATC)	Marginal Cost C	Y	$MC = \frac{\Delta C}{\Delta V}$
0	*0.00*	—	—	*0*		
2	*1.00*	*5.00*	*6.00*	*2*	*2*	*1.00*
5	*0.8*	*2.00*	*2.80*	*2*	*3*	*0.67*
9	*0.67*	*1.11*	*1.78*	*2*	*4*	*0.50*
14	*0.57*	*0.71*	*1.38*	*2*	*5*	*0.40*
19	*0.53*	*0.53*	*1.06*	*2*	*5*	*0.40*
23	*0.52*	*0.43*	*0.95*	*2*	*4*	*0.50*
26	*0.54*	*0.38*	*0.92*	*2*	*3*	*0.67*
28	*0.58*	*0.36*	*0.94*	*2*	*2*	*1.00*
29	*0.62*	*0.34*	*0.96*	*2*	*1*	*2.00*

(c) ***Net revenue as a function of output***

Detail three regions of cost function for profit maximisation. Use the data on AC and MC as given in the table above, but use enlarged scale. Assume MR = AR = Rs. 0.75.

(*d*) ***Effect of price changes of output on the production decisions***

Use the data in the table above on an enlarged scale. Assume the prices of output change from **(*i*)** ***Re. 1.00 to Rs. 1.25,*** **(*ii*)** ***Re. 1.00 to Re. 0.75.***

(*e*) ***Effect of changes in price inputs on the production decisions***

Use the data as in the table on an enlarged scale. Assume the prices of input change from : **(*i*)** ***Rs. 2.00 to Rs. 2.50,*** **(*ii*)** ***Rs. 2.00 to Re. 1.00.***

1. ***Indian Society of Agril. Economics : "Seminar on Cost studies in Agriculture", 1961.***
2. ***Bishop, CE. and W.D. Tousaint, "Introduction of Agricultural Economics Analysis.", New York John Wiley & Sons, Inc. London. 1958, Chapter 7.***
3. ***Dua, R.C. "A text book of Advanced Economic Theory". Lyall Book Depot, Meerut, 1970, Chapter 13.***
4. ***Board of Economic Enquiry, Punjab, "Economics of Farm Management in Punjab", 1954.***

Factor-Factor Relationships

The production relationships we discussed in the previous chapter dealt only with one output and one variable input; all other inputs were considered fixed. In actual situations, there are large number of inputs which are used to produce a farm commodity. The main advantage of previous production function analysis lies in its simplicity. The farmers are, however, often faced with the problem of deciding about the use of more than one resource or set of resources in substitution of other resources or set of resources. For example, it is a common problem with the farmers to decide on how much of N, P & K fertilizer to use with a view to getting a certain level of a crop output or how much of concentrates and green fodders to feed to a milch animal to get certain amount of milk or how much different ingredients of poultry feed to use for getting a particular level of poultry production. The question here is of finding out optimum or least cost combination of two or more resources in producing a given amount of output.

Our particular concern in this section is with the possibilities of substituting one factor (X_1) for another factor (X_2) as product level (Y) is held constant. Thus the objective of this analysis of factor-factor relationships is two-fold : (*i*) Minimisation of cost at a given level of output, and (*ii*) Optimisation of output to the fixed factors through alternative resource-use combinations. Conceptually, this production function does not differ from that with one variable input. Each combination of the two inputs produces a unique amount of output. If the level of either input is changed the resulting output will also change.

In order to understand the basic concepts of factor-factor substitution, we confine here at the start to only two factors and one output and start our analysis with a functional relationship : $Y = (X_1, X_2, / X_3, X_4 \dots X_n)$. Here Y is a function of X_1 and X_2 while other inputs are kept constant. This expression shows that the amount of output (Y) depends in a unique way upon the amount of the two inputs X_1 and X_2 used in the production process along with the other fixed inputs.

These relationships can also be presented in a tabular form as given in Table 6.1.

TABLE 6.1

Estimated Yields in Quintals for Various Combinations of Nitrogen and Phosphorus for Kalyan 227 Variety of Wheat in Punjab[1]

P/N	*40*	*60*	*80*	*100*	*120*	*140*
40	40.21	43.09	44.74	45.15	44.32	44.02
60	41.87	45.51	47.90	49.06	48.98	48.32
80	40.89	45.28	48.43	50.35	51.02	50.54

In this case, at each level of one factor, there is a production function for the other factor. The relationship between two factors and one product cannot be presented with two dimensional graphs. This involves three variables and involves three dimensional diagram giving a production surface. When quantities of X_1 and X_2 are increased and all other inputs are held constant, a production surface can be traced. The shape of the production surface will, of course, vary for different types of production situations.

For the sake of illustrating the concept of production surface, Table 6.2 shows the amounts of products which can be obtained with different amounts of X_1 and X_2, all other inputs being held constant. The different levels of X_1 are listed along the left side and levels of X_2 along the bottom of the table. As more of the two inputs are used, the general result is to get larger quantities of the product such as from zero output with no inputs used to 25 units of output resulting from one unit each of X_1 and X_2, 70 units of output from three units of each input and so on. There are a large number of such combinations of the two inputs which produce different levels of output. There will be, of course, only one combination which will give the maximum output. It should be noted that this box type table is simply a collection of many single-variable production functions. We can estimate effect of each input on output by keeping the other variable constant.

TABLE 6.2

Input-Output Relationships with Two Variable Inputs

	10	75	86	94	112	130	120	118	113	108	105	94
	9	82	98	108	125	138	[140]	130	117	115	113	95
Input	8	80	95	106	122	132	138	120	119	110	115	110
(X_1)	7	75	90	105	118	125	132	130	128	120	118	115
	6	67	84	96	108	115	118	125	130	125	115	110

1. Kahlon, A.S. and J.L. Kaul : "Comparative study of Economics of High Yielding Varieties of wheat-Punjab State." . Ind. Jr. Ag. Econ. XXIII (4) : P 79 Oct.-Dec. 1968.

	5	58	80	84	90	108	102	106	110	115	110	108
Input	4	45	50	60	72	86	92	100	108	98	85	81
(X_1)	3	38	45	58	70	80	82	85	90	86	80	75
	2	25	40	50	60	72	75	80	78	76	70	68
	1	12	25	31	41	57	65	65	57	65	63	55
	0	0	10	17	25	35	42	49	50	47	44	40
		0	1	2	3	4	5	6	7	8	9	10

Input (X_2)

Isoquants or Iso-product Curve

An isoquant is a convenient device for compressing the three- dimensional picture of a production function, into two dimensions. Each isoquant (or Iso-product curve) represents the various input combinations that can be used to produce a given output. Each point on an isoquants is the maximum output than can be achieved with these input combinations. In the production of most commodities, the same output can be obtained by various combinations of inputs. With the exception of the minimum output-zero and the maximum output-140 units in this case, all other output levels can be produced using several different input-combinations.

For example 80, 108 and 120 units of output can be produced using the following input combinations :

Product = 80 units		*Product = 108 units*		Product = 120 units	
X_1	X_2	X_1	X_2	X_1	X_2
units	units	units	units	units	units
8	0	9	2	10	3.5
5	1	6	3	9	3.6
3	4	5	4	6	5.5
2	6	4	7	—	—
3	9	5	10		

This table presents a few possible input-output combinations which produce the same output. There is possibility of numerous combinations which are not being presented here because of space limitations. There must, thus, exist many other input combinations that also produce 80, 108 or 120 units of output. The curve representing all combinations of X_1 and X_2 inputs that produce a given level of output is called an "iso-quant" ("*iso*" meaning equal and "*quant*" meaning quantity).

The isoquants as shown in table 6.2 trace out all input combinations that produce 80, 108 and 120 units for output. These isoquants can be drawn in two dimensions in the form of a curve which is simple as compared to production surface discussed in the last section. For example, iso-quant for 108 units of output can be located on the graph in Fig. 6.1.

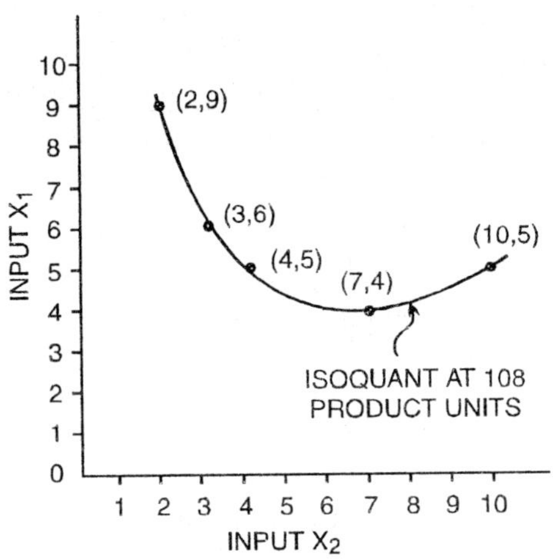

Fig. 6.1. Iso-quant or Iso-product curve for 108 units of output.

Similarly isoquants can be traced for different levels of output. We can imagine that there is an isoquant for every output level between and including 0 and 140 units. It means several isoquants can be shown in a single figure which show different levels of output with different combinations of inputs, *i.e.* every output level has an isoquant. If a number of isoquants are drawn on one graph, the figure is known as Iso-quant map. (Fig. 6.2)

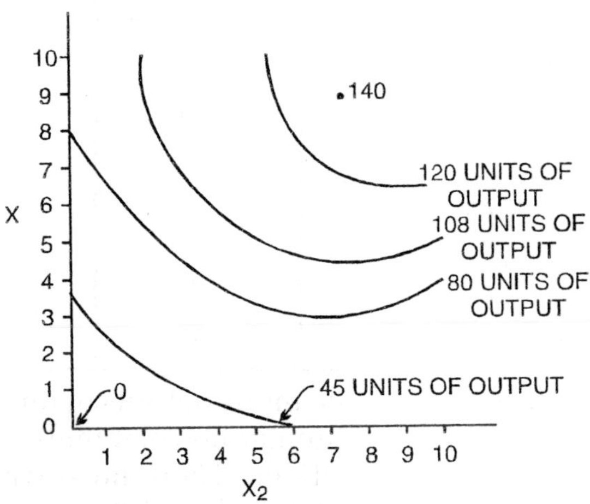

Fig. 6.2. Iso-quant map for different levels of output.

The isoquant map has the similar meaning as a contour map for topography of a countryside. On a contour map, the contour lines represent the attitude above sea level ; by following the contours, the layout of the land can be determined. Similarly iso-quant map indicates the nature of the output response to the inputs. In the Fig. 6.2, each iso-quant measures the output above zero and output increases gradually to the maximum point of 140 units. Each contour represents a given level of production. Higher contours represent higher value of production.

TYPES OF FACTOR-FACTOR RELATIONSHIPS

Many types of production surfaces are possible depending on the underlying production function. The shapes of the isoquants and production surface will depend upon the manner in which the variable inputs are combined to produce a particular level of output. There can be three categories of such combinations of inputs :

(*i*) Fixed proportion combinations of inputs,

(*ii*) Constant rate of substitution, and

(*iii*) Varying rates of substitution.

Fixed Proportion Combinations

There are certain enterprises or products which can only be produced if inputs are added in fixed proportion at all levels of production. In these cases, there is no decision-problem because the inputs combine in a fixed proportion. There is only one way of combining input which will yield a given level of product. Such inputs combine in a fixed ratio and isoquants are L—Shaped. It is difficult to find such example in agriculture. An approximation to this situation is provided by a tractor and a driver combination. To add another tractor will normally need another driver too. It is, of course, not always necessary to employ one man every time new tractor is added. It is possible that a farmer may like to keep two tractors of different sizes and capacities to perform different farm operations. In such situations, the fixed proportion analogy does not hold good.

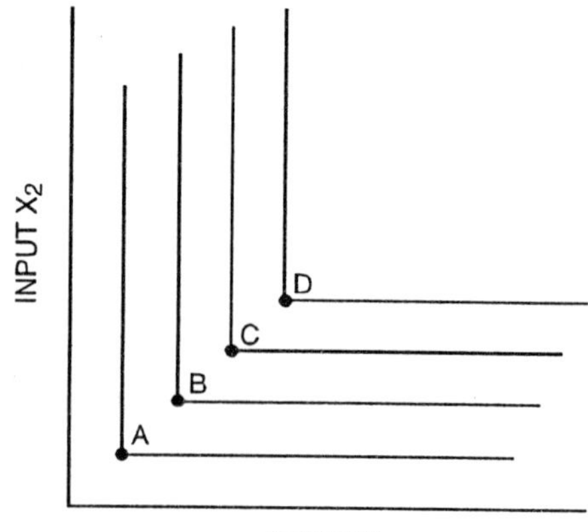

Fig. 6.3. Inputs which combine in fixed proportion.

The inputs which increase the output only when combined in a fixed proportion are known as complements. It means that only one exact combination of inputs will produce a particular level of output. Substitutes are the reverse of complements. Substitutes mean a range of input combinations which will produce a given level of output. Substitution of one input or group of inputs with other input or group of inputs can take place at different rates.

Constant Rate of Substitution

The substitution at constant rate occurs when the amount of one input replaced by the other point does not change as the added input increases in magnitude. Two inputs which substitute at constant rate are shown in Fig. 6.4 and Table 6.3. The iso-quant is a straight line in this case.

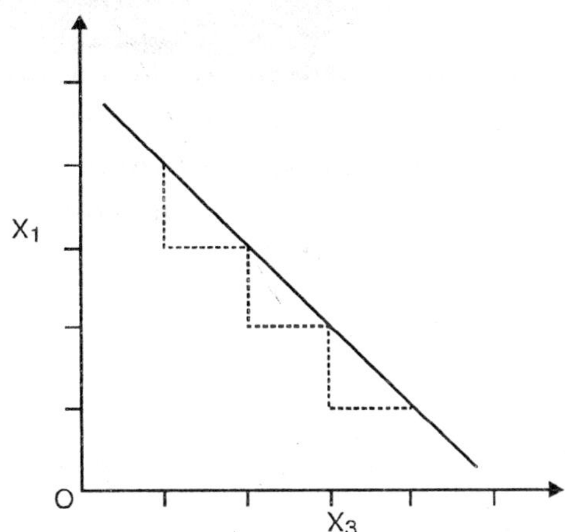

Fig. 6.4. Inputs which substitute at constant rate.

TABLE 6.3.

Constant Rate of Substitution for producing 100 units of output

X_2 (*Women labour*)	X_2 (*Men labour*)	ΔX_2	ΔX_1	$\frac{\Delta X_2}{\Delta X_1}$ (*MRS*)
10	1			
		2	1	2/1 = 2
8	2			
		2	1	2/1 = 2
6	3			
		2	1	2/1 = 2
4	4			
		2	1	2/1 = 2
2	5			

The rate at which these two inputs can be substituted at a given level of output is constant regardless of the level of the two inputs used. It is commonly called the marginal rate of substitution between the inputs and is denoted by X_2/X_1 which is the slope of the product contour at any point.

For inputs which can be exchanged at a constant rate, the slope of the product contour is constant, or in other words, substitution ratio remains the same.

$$\text{Substitution Ratio} = \frac{\Delta X_{21}}{\Delta X_{11}} = \frac{\Delta X_{22}}{\Delta X_{12}} = \ldots = \frac{\Delta X_{2n}}{\Delta X_{1n}}$$

There are many cases in agriculture where two inputs exchange or substitute each other at constant rate. Labour inputs of two workers can be exchanged at a constant rate. If two labourers do not perform equivalent amounts of work at the same time, one will perform a constant amount of work relative to the other. If two labourers perform the same amount of work, the labourer who is willing to work for lower wage will be hired. When inputs substitute at a constant rate, only one would be used ; which one to use depends upon relative prices.

Varying Rate of Substitution

There can be either increasing rate of substitution or decreasing rate of substitution.

In this case, marginal rate of substitution varies over the iso-product curve. The amount of one input (X_1) required to substitute for one unit of another input (X_2) at a given level of production increases or decreases as the amount of X_1 used increases. Substitution at an increasing rate is not commonly available. Substitution at decreasing rate is more common case in agriculture. The slope of the iso-product curve in this case becomes less steep as more X_1 is used relative to X_2.

Substitution Ratio changes as under :

$$\frac{\Delta X_{21}}{\Delta X_{11}} > \frac{\Delta X_{22}}{\Delta X_{12}} > \ldots > \frac{\Delta X_{2n}}{\Delta X_{1n}}$$

TABLE 6.4

Decreasing Rate of Substitution for Producing 100 Units of Output

X_2	X_1	X_2	X_1	$(MRS)\frac{\Delta X_2}{\Delta X_1}$
23	0			
		7	1	7
16	1			
		6	1	6
10	2			
		5	1	5
5	3			
		4	1	4
1	4			
		1	1	1
0	5			

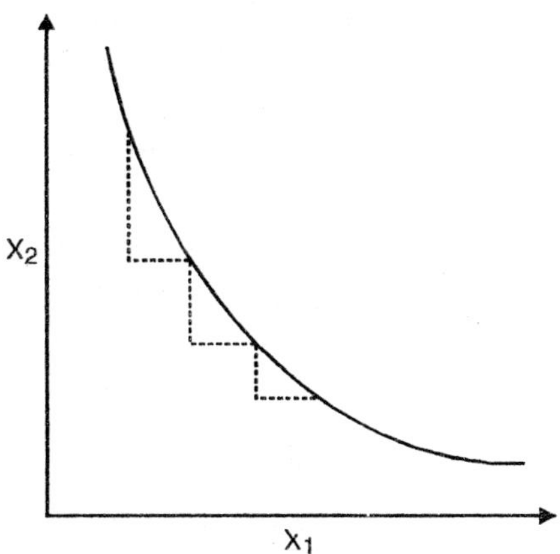

Fig. 6.5. An illustration of decreasing rate of substitution.

Thus, decreasing rate of substitution means that every subsequent increase in the use of one factor replaces less and less of the other. Examples are substitution among concentrates and green fodder, labour and capital and nitrogen and phosphorus.

Iso-cost Lines

Just as an iso-quant can be constructed to indicate all possible combinations of inputs which will produce a given quantity of output, an iso-cost can be drawn to indicate all possible combinations of two inputs which can be purchased with a given outlay of funds. Each combination of inputs has some total cost which includes the costs of two inputs (X_1 and X_2) combined. Since total outlay is a function of the amount of X_1 and X_2 used, it can be graphed in a manner similar to the production surface. Just as production surfaces are characterised by iso-quants, similarly total outlay surfaces can be described by iso-cost lines.

Suppose, for example, a farmer has Rs. 36 to spend on two variable inputs, X_1 and X_2. The cost per unit of X_1 is Rs. 3 and cost per unit of X_2 is Rs. 4. He may either purchase 12 units of X_2 or 9 units of X_2. These two points can be located at 12 units and 9 units on vertical and horizontal axes of graph as shown in Fig. 6.6. If these two points are connected by a straight line, it will be iso-cost line for total outlay of Rs. 36/- in this case. On this line, he can trace any number of combinations of the two inputs which will cost the same.

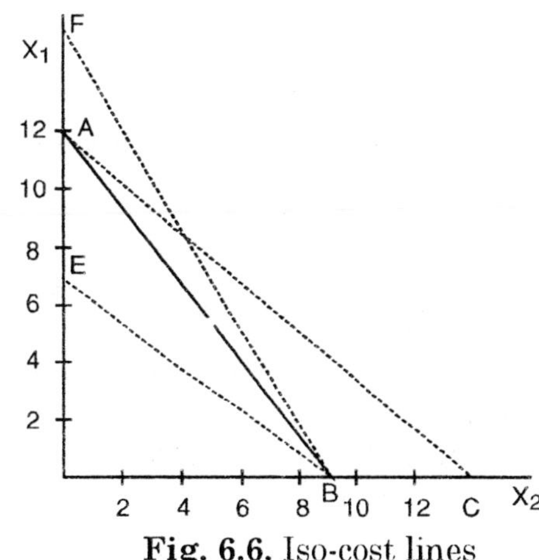

Fig. 6.6. Iso-cost lines

Similarly iso-cost can be drawn for total outlays of Rs. 18, Rs. 27 and Rs. 48. In fact, iso-cost lines can be drawn at any level of outlay. To avoid confusion, only a few iso-cost lines are drawn. This is a simple method of drawing iso-cost lines. To have detailed view of the whole span of iso-cost lines, total outlay surface should be drawn.

Mathematical equation of the iso-cost line can be obtained by solving

$T = Px_1 . X_1 + P_{x1} . X_2$ for X_1as an explicit function of X_2.

For example, $P_x . X_1 = T - P_{x2} . X_2$

and $$X_1 = \frac{T}{P_{x1}} - \frac{T_{x2}}{P_{x1}} X_2$$

In this expression, slope of the iso-cost line is $\frac{P_{x2}}{P_{x1}}$ while the intercept on the X_1-axis is given by $\frac{T}{P_{x1}}$. For a given outlay of Rs. 36/- and prices as above, iso-cost line equation in Fig. 6.6 is $X_1 = 12 - 4/3. X_2$. The iso-cost lines are linear and can be determined by their end- points. The reason for this is that the inputs are purchased by the farmers in a competitive market and prices do not change with the quantity purchased.

Characteristics of Iso-Cost Lines

The following two points need to be considered regarding the iso- cost lines.

1. Distance of Iso-cost line from the Origin

Under constant price situation each possible total outlay has a different iso-cost line. As total outlay increases, the iso-cost line moves higher and higher, further away from the origin. For example, an iso-cost line for Rs. 100 will be half way between the origin and Rs. 200/- outlay line. Both lines will have the same slope.

2. Slope of the Iso-cost lines

Changes in the input-price will change the slope of the iso-cost line. For example, when price of an input decreases, more units of it can be purchased with the same total outlay and conversely when input price increases, lesser units can be purchased. This changes the slope of the iso-cost line. In Fig. 6.6, when price of X_2 decreases, line AB will change to AC. The lines BE and BF represent similar changes in the prices of X_1, price of X_2 remaining the same. What matters here is the relative level of prices. The slope of the iso-cost line, therefore, indicates the ratio of factor prices.

LEAST-COST COMBINATION

The different concepts discussed above can be used to determine the combination of inputs which will produce a given output at a minimum cost. A given level of output can be produced using many different combinations of the two variable inputs. Here the problem is to find out a combination of inputs which should cost the least ; a cost minimisation problem.

There are three methods to find solution to cost minimisation problems.

Simple Arithmetical Calculations

One possible way to determine the least-cost combination is to compute the cost of all possible combinations and then select the one with the minimum cost. This method is suitable where only a few combinations produce a given output and calculations involved are a few and simple. Suppose there are five combinations of inputs which can produce 85 units of output as given in Table 6.5. The price per unit of X_1 is Rs. 3 and of X_2 Rs. 4. The total outlay of each combination can be determined by simple multiplications.

TABLE 6.5.

Computation of Least-cost Combination of Two Inputs for Producing an Output of 85 Units

Units of X_1	*Units of* X_2	*Cost of* X_1 *@ Rs.3.00*	*Cost of* X_2 @ Rs.4/-	*Total Outlay for* X_1 and X_2 (Rs.)
8.0	2	24.00	8	32.0
6.0	3	18.00	12	30.0
5.0	4	15.00	16	31.0
4.5	5	13.50	20	33.5
3.5	7	10.50	28	38.5

Out of five combinations calculated in Table 6.5 above, 3 units of X_2 and 6 units of X_1 is the least cost combination of inputs *i.e.* Rs. 30. Through this method, it is possible that the true least cost combination is not located because we do not consider many combination which may be there on the iso-quant to the right or to the left of the point.

Algebraic Method

Procedure for finding out least cost combination is as under

Step (*i*) Compute marginal substitution ratio = $\left(\frac{\Delta X_2}{\Delta X_1}\right)^1$

Step (*ii*) Compute price ratio = $\left(\frac{P_{x1}}{P_{x2}}\right)$

Step (*iii*) Work out least cost combination by equating

$$\frac{\Delta X_2}{\Delta X_1} = \frac{P_{x2}}{P_{x1}}$$

The least cost criterion is that MRS of X_2 for X_1 should be equal to P_{x2}/P_{x1}. By definition :

$\frac{\Delta X_1}{\Delta X_2}$ should be equal to $\frac{P_{x2}}{P_{x1}}$

This criterion can also be written as

P_{x1} (ΔX_1) = P_{x2} (ΔX_2). If at any point on the iso-quant P_{x1}. ΔX_1 is greater than P_{x2} ΔX_2 then the cost of producing the given output could be produced by increasing the use of X_2 and decreasing X_1, because the cost of added unit of X_2 is lesser than the cost of the replaced units of X_1. On the other hand, if at any point on the iso-quant, P_{x1}, ΔX_1 is less than P_{x2}. ΔX_2 the cost of producing the specified quantity of input can be reduced by using less of X_2 and more of X_1. This equality criterion signifies that any change in the input combination from this point would increase cost of producing the output.

GRAPHIC METHOD

Since slope of the iso-cost line indicates the ratio of factor prices and slope of the iso-product curve represents the marginal rate of substitution, minimum costs for a given output will be indicated by the tangency of these iso-lines. For this purpose iso-quants and iso-cost lines are drawn on the same graph for different levels of production and total outlay. The least cost criterion on a graph will be :

(Slope of iso-quant) = (Slope of iso-cost line)

Given that iso-quant is convex, the least cost combination of inputs will be at the point where the iso-cost line is tangent to the iso-quant. The least-cost solution

1. This ratio is always negative. It is, therefore, always assumed to be so and (–) is dropped in the analysis.

with the help of iso-cost line and iso-quant is illustrated in Fig. 6.7. The results obtained by this method are more exact than those obtained with arithmetic method.

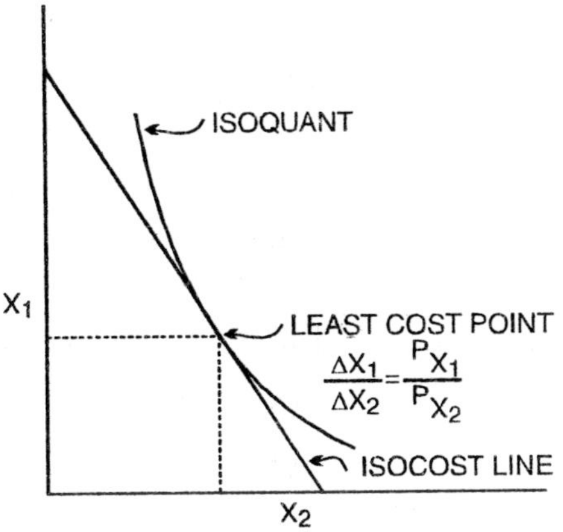

Fig. 6.7. Least cost combination of inputs at 110 units of output.

Isoclines

There can be a number of possible output levels as shown in figure 6.2 of iso-quant map, and least cost combination can be found out for these various output levels. A line or curve connecting the least cost combination of inputs for all output levels is known as isocline. This isocline passes through all the iso-quants at points where they have same slope.

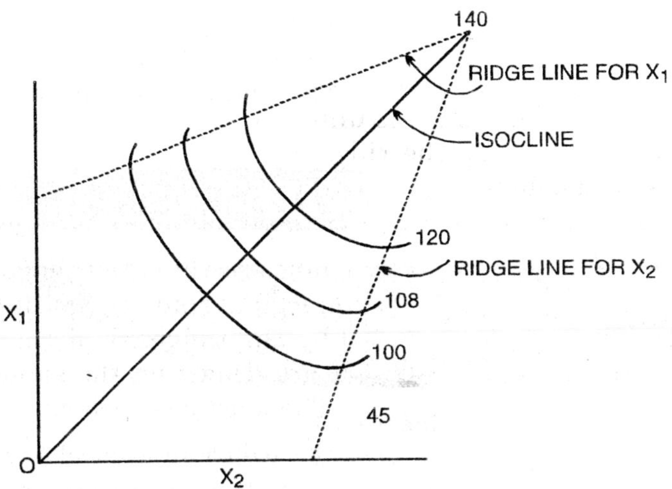

Fig. 6.8. Isoclines for various iso-quants and input price ratios.

Suppose the inputs can be supplied in divisible units. Given the iso-product contours, and slope of iso-cost lines, the minimum cost for each output is represented by their tangency points. A line passing through these least-cost combination points will show how the relative proportion of the factors changes as output is increased. This line or isocline shows that resources should be used along this line as long as the marginal value of the product is greater than the marginal cost of the resources used. Isoclines can be drawn at different sets of price ratios. Here for the sake of clarity, only two additional isoclines have been drawn and corresponding isocost lines have been omitted to avoid confusion. We will see here that as the price of X_1 drops relative to the price of X_2 increasing amounts of X_2 are included in the least cost combinations. All isoclines, of course, converge at the point of maximum output if the maximum exists.

Expansion Path

As has been explained above, there can be numerous isoclines for different possible combinations of input prices. All these sets of prices of inputs do not prevail at any particular given time. A farm manager has to consider only one set of input prices which he may think to be the most appropriate for the planning period. The isocline dependent upon this set of prices is called "expansion path". Of many isoclines, the isocline which is considered to be the most appropriate over a production period is known as expansion path. At any particular time, only one expansion path is possible.

Ridge Lines (Boundary lines)

Ridge lines represent often points of maximum output from each input, given a fixed amount of the other input. For example, in Fig. 6.8, the dashed lines represent special type of isoclines called ridge-lines. As an example, when $X_1 = 1$, output can be increased by adding X_2 upto 7 units as denoted on the ridge line. At the point, output from X_2 is maximum given one unit of X_1. Here MPP of X_2 will be zero. Past $X_2 = 7$, MPP will be negative. The ridge lines denote the limits of substitution. These lines represent the limits of economic relevance, the boundaries beyond which isocline and isoquant maps cease to have any economic meanings.

CHOOSING THE OPTIMUM LEVEL OF OUTPUT

The isocline traces out the least-cost combination of inputs for every possible output level. The farmer is, however, generally interested in the amount of product which he should produce to maximise his profits. Each least-cost combination has a cost corresponding to a particular return level and a farmer would select an output level where total returns minus total cost is the largest. On expansion path, the farmer should go on increasing output, so long as the resources allow. If we look at this from input side, it means the MVP of an input must be equal to the unit price of the input. If we see from output side, it means MC must be equal to MR. Although all points on an isocline represent least cost combinations, only one point represents the maximum profit output. In order to find out the optimum level of output for maximizing profit, the following methods can be used.

Tabular Method

Suppose different levels of output Y can be produced by different least-cost combinations of two inputs X_1 and X_2. Table 6.6 shows two least cost combinations for two levels of output (Y = 10 and Y = 20).

TABLE 6.6

Determination of Optimum Level of Output through Selecting Least Cost Combination of Two Inputs X_1 & X_2

Output Y = 10 units @ Rs. 20 per unit					Output Y = 20 units @ Rs. 20 per unit				
Input X_1 @ Rs. 5/- per unit	Input X_2 @ Rs. 2.50 per unit	$\frac{\Delta X_1}{\Delta X_2}$	Total Cost (Rs.)	Net Profit	Input X_1 @ Rs. 5 per unit	Input X_2 @ Rs. 2.5 per unit	$\frac{\Delta X_2}{\Delta X_1}$	Total Cost (Rs.)	Net Profit
0	30	—	75	125	0	60	—	150.0	250.0
2	20	5	60	140	5	40	4	125.0	275.0
4	12	4	50	150	10	25	3	112.5	287.5
6	6	3	45	155	15	15	2	112.5	287.5
8	2	2	45	155	20	7	1.6	117.5	282.5
10	0	1	50	150	25	3	0.8	132.5	267.5

Table 6.6 shows that highest net profit from producing 10 units and 20 units of product Y at least cost input combinations are Rs. 155 and Rs. 287.5 respectively. In this case farmer would receive more net profit from producing 20 units than from 10 units of the product. We can compare such other combinations and choose a level of output which may promise highest net profit.

Graphic Method

We can trace the various input-output combinations on the isocline and treat them as a separate production function. This production function can be graphed with output on the vertical axis and the two inputs in least-cost combinations along the horizontal axis such that for each amount of one input, the corresponding least-cost amount of the second input is listed. The marginal value product of the two inputs can then be derived and equated to the added cost of the two inputs.

Algebraic Method

The optimum level of output can be determined by solving the following profit maximising criterion equation :

$$\frac{MVP_{x1}}{P_{x1}} = \frac{MVP_{x2}}{P_{x2}} = 1$$

Rational and Irrational Zones of Production on Substitution Curves

Figure 6.9 shows that BC iso-quant of 85 units of output lies in rational zone of production. In this zone, positive change in one tractor must be associated with a negative change in the other.

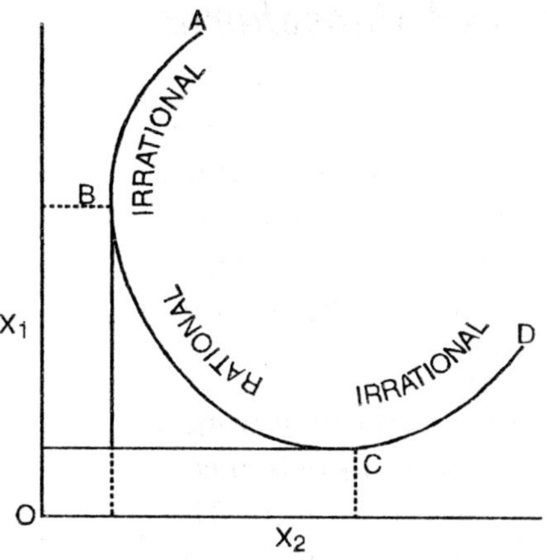

Fig. 6.9. Areas of irrational resource substitution.

The cost minimisation decisions are taken in this zone, because beyond these points towards A & D resource substitution is not possible and increased amounts of both the inputs will be needed to produce same quantity of output.

Input Price Changes and Least Cost Combination

As discussed in earlier sections, least-cost combination of inputs can be determined by equating $\frac{\Delta X_2}{\Delta X_1}$ with $\frac{x1}{x2}$. Any change brought about in the relative prices of X_1 or X_2 will vary the least-cost combination. If a farmer wants to produce at the least cost in a situation in which prices are changing, it becomes necessary for him to change the combination of inputs with every change in prices. By changing the amount of an input in relation to another, a farmer can find a combination of inputs where the rate of substitution becomes equal to the new ratio of input-prices. Shape of isoclines will also change with changes in input price ratios, which will affect cost combination in a similar way.

APPLICATION OF FACTOR-FACTOR ANALYSIS IN COST-MINIMIZATION PROBLEMS

There are many practical situations where a farmer has to choose from among kinds and quantities of inputs to determine least-cost combinations. A few illustrations are given below :

How Much Nitrogen and Phosphorus should be Added For C 273-Wheat[1]?

Whereas fertilizer is a nutrient to that plan, it is an input that becomes a cost to the farmer. To be an economically sound proposition, an input must yield returns equal to or greater than its cost to the cultivator. It is, therefore, essential that fertilizer use recommendations which promise the highest income to the farmer rather than the highest yield.

Often the farmer and the extension agency is faced with a question "what doses of fertilizers should a farmer apply to a certain crop ?" This analysis presented here provides the answer for wheat crop (C-273) in Punjab, based on experimental data of the Cereal Breeding Sub-station, Gurdaspur, for three years from 1962-63 through 1964-65.

Two charts are presented whereby a simple technique is made available for deciding upon doses of nitrogen and phosphorus application to the wheat crop, keeping in mind the relative prices of fertilizers, nitrogen, phosphorus and wheat.

Chart I is prepared at zero level of potash and Chart II at 25 pounds of K. (Potash)

HOW TO USE THE CHART ? [FIG. 6.10 & 6.11]

1. First, work out the price of nitrogen and phosphorus per pound and of wheat per kg. For example, nitrogen price will work out to be Re. 0.81 per pound if calcium ammonium nitrate with a 20.5 per cent nitrogen content is priced Rs. 36.50 per qunital. Similarly, phosphorus price will be Re. 0.86 per pound if super-

---

1. Reproduced from Gupta B.C. and S.S. Johl "How much Nitrogen and Phosphorus for C 273" Progressive farming, Sept., 1966 ?

phosphate with 16 per cent phosphorus is priced at Rs. 30.40 per quintal. Assuming the price of wheat at Rs. 60.00 per quintal, price per kg. will be Re. 0.60.

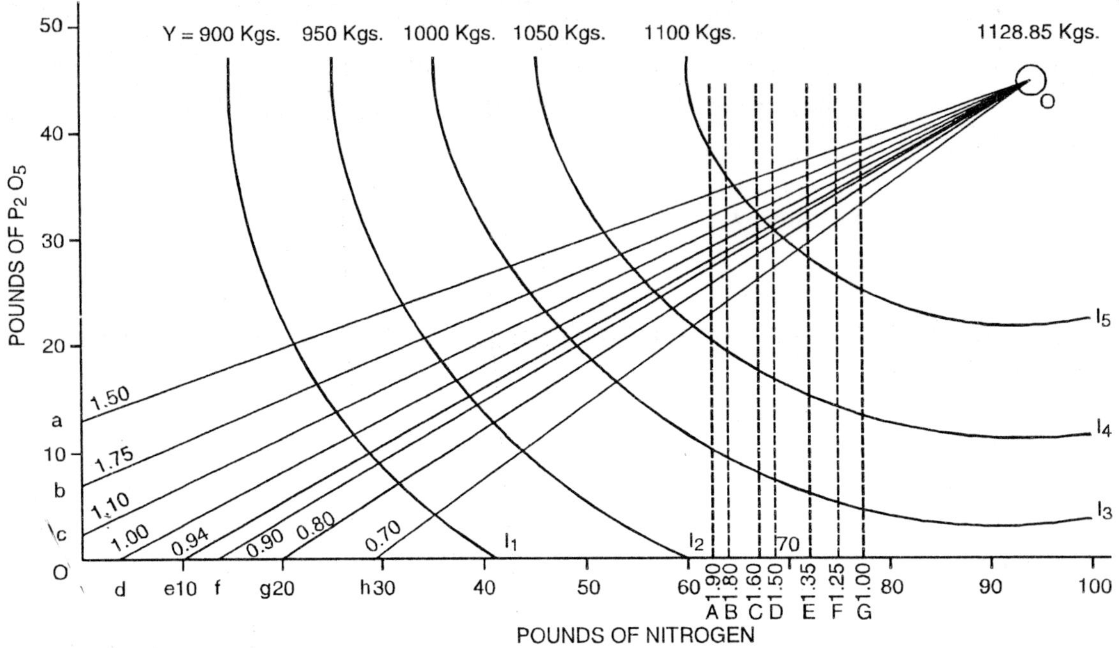

Fig. 6.10. Optimum doses N & P at K = 0 lb. level.

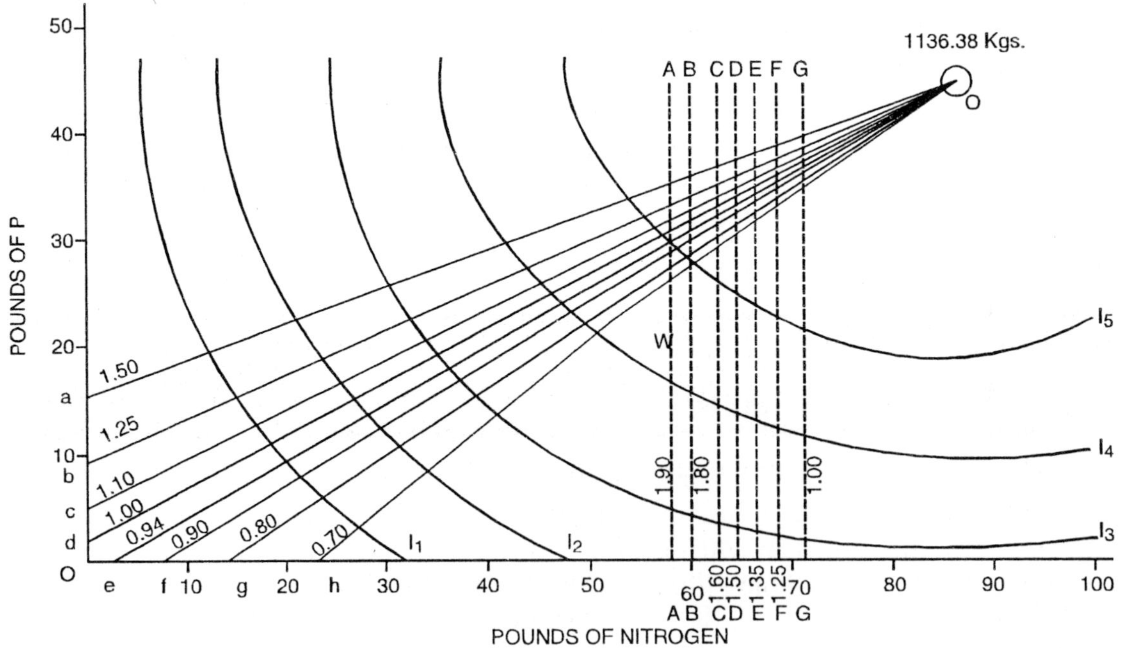

Fig. 6.11. Optimum doses N & P at K = 25 lb. level.

2. Work out the nitrogen-phosphorus and nitrogen-wheat price ratios, *i.e.* :

$$\frac{\text{Price of Nitrogen}}{\text{Price of Phosphorus}} \text{ and } \frac{\text{Price of Nitrogen}}{\text{Price of wheat}}$$

In this example : $$\frac{\text{Nitrogen Price}}{\text{Phosphorus Price}} = \frac{0.81}{0.86} = 0.94$$

$$\frac{\text{Nitrogen Price}}{\text{Wheat Price}} = \frac{0.81}{0.60} = 1.35$$

3. In the chart now, locate the line 0.94 and dotted line 1.35 corresponding to the values worked above. In this example, these lines will be 'Oe' and 'EE', respectively.

4. From the point of intersection of these two lines, draw two perpendiculars to both axes and read the corresponding values for nitrogen on horizontal axis and phosphorus on vertical axis. In this example point of intersection is 'P' and the corresponding values are 73 lb. N and 35 lb. of P in Fig. 6.10 and 67 lb. of N and 36 lb. of P in Fig. 6.11. This means if potash is applied at zero level, 73 lb. of nitrogen and 35 lb. of phosphorus will be the optimum dose; if K (potash) is applied at 25 pounds, 67 lb. of N and 36 lb. of P will be the optimum dose.

These combinations of N and P will vary with the changes in price ratios. If, for example, price of wheat changes to Rs. 37.00 per quintal, of CAN (Cal. Ammonium Nitrate) to Rs. 31.55 per quintal and super-phosphate to Rs.35.35 per quintal ; relevant price ratios will be :

$$\frac{\text{Nitrogen Price}}{\text{Phosphorus}} = 0.70 \text{ and } \frac{\text{Nitrogen Price}}{\text{Wheat Price}} = 1.90.$$

With these price ratios, point of intesection will be W and optimum doses will be 65 lb. Nitrogen and 26 lb. Phosphorus at zero level of K and 60 lb. Nitrogen and 26 lb. Phosphorus at 25 lb. of K.

5. For these combinations of nitrogen and phosphorus, expected yield of wheat can be located. These yields are predicted from the curves marked I_1, I_2, I_3.... I_n. The value of 'I' which passes through the point of intersection located in step 4 will indicate the expected yield from these inputs. If the point lies between two curves, yield can be approximated through interpolation. In the first example, the point P lies in between I_5 and the maximum point 'O'. In between these two values *i.e.* 1,100 kg. and 1,129 kg. the approximated value comes to be 1,107 kg. in Fig. 6.10 and 1,115 kg. in Fig. 6.11.

Minimisation of Costs on Fertilizer Application on Kharif Crops[1]

Here, cost of different combinations of fertilizers for kharif crops in the plains of Punjab and Haryana has been worked out based on the latest recommendations of Punjab Agricultural University. The comparative costs of fertilizers are obtained on the basis of assumptions detailed below :

Sr. No.	Name of Fertilizer	Nutrient Content percent		Price per qunital	Price per kg. of (Rs.)	
		N	P_2O_5	*(Rs.)*	*N*	P_2O_5
1	2	3	4	5	6	7
1.	Urea	46	—	84.00	1.83	—
2.	Cal. Amm. Nitrate (25%) CAN.	25	—	51.00	2.04	—
3.	Cal. Amm. Nitrate (20%) CAN.	20	—	43.70	2.18	—
4.	Amm. Sulphate (AS).	20	—	50.00	2.50	—
5.	Diammonium Phosphate (DAP).,	16	46	109.50	1.76	1.76
6.	Amm. Phosphate (AP).	20	20	81.80	2.05	2.05
7.	Super-phosphate (SP)	—	16	41.53	—	2.58

In case of mixed fertilizers, the cost was apportioned between N & P_2O_5 according to the percentage availability of respective nutrients. The Table 6.7 shows the comparative costs of different possible fertilizer combinations for kharif crops in the plains of Punjab and Haryana States. The figures within brackets indicate the cost (in rupees) of each particular combination.

Table shows that in case of all the crops Urea plus Diammonium Phosphate gives lowest cost whereas Ammonium Sulphate plus Super- phosphate gives the highest cost per acre. The difference between these two fertilizer combinations is Rs. 51.62 per acre in case of Maize hybrid and Bajra hybrid and Rs. 46.84 in case of Sugarcane. Between the highest and lowest cost combinations there are many combinations which provide opportunity to the farmers on deciding the combination best suited to their particular situations. In the event of non-availability of some fertilizer or non-practicability of a combination, the next best alternative can be selected.

In case of sugarcane, *bajra* local and *bajra* hybrid only Nitrogen is needed for the areas not mentioned in the above table. Suitable source of nitrogen can be selected keeping in view the cost of nitrogen. In case of cotton and *bajra* unirrigated

1. Gupta, V.K; and M.S. Aulakh : "You can decrease your fertiliser costs on kharif crops" *Punjab Cooperative Journal, V* (3) : 1968.

only nitrogen is needed and cheapest source can be selected as mentioned above. Groundnut requires only phosphorus and there is no other alternative to Superphosphate.

TABLE 6.7

Comparative Costs of Fertilizers for Some Kharif Crops in Plains of Punjab and Haryana

Quantity of fertilizer in kilogram per acre

Name of fertilizer combination	*Maize*		*Sugarcane*	*Paddy*		*Bajra*	
	Desi	*Hybrid*	*(Karnal, Sangrur, Hoshiarpur and Jagadhari)*	*Local*	*High yield-ing*	*Local (Feroze-pur, Sangrur and Rohtak)*	*Hybrid (FZR., Sangrur, Rohtak and Jind)*
1	2	3	4	5	6	7	8
Urea + DAP	41 + 24 (60.72)	79 + 50 (121.11)	84 + 38 (112.17)	32 + 20 (48.78)	95 +59 (144.40)	32 + 20 (48.78)	79 + 50 (121.11)
Urea + AP	27 + 55 (67.67)	45 + 115 (131.87)	60 + 90 (124.02)	20 + 45 (53.61)	59 + 135 (159.99)	20 +45 (53.61)	45 + 115 (131.87)
Urea + SP	50 +70 (71.07)	99 + 145 (143.38)	99 + 112 (129.67)	38 + 55 (54.76)	119 + 170 (170.56)	38 + 55 (54.76)	99 + 145 (143.38)
CAN 25% + DAP	74 + 24 (64.02)	144 + 50 (128.19)	153 + 38 (119.64)	58 + 20 (51.48)	174 + 59 (153.34)	58 + 20 (51.48)	144 + 50 (128.19)
CAN 25% + AP	48 + 55 (69.47)	88 + 115 (138.95)	108 + 90 (128.70)	36 + 45 (55.16)	108 + 135 (165.51)	36 + 45 (55.16)	88 + 115 (138.95)
CAN 25% + SP	92 + 70 (75.99)	180 + 145 (152.02)	180 + 112 (138.31)	72 + 55 (59.56)	216 + 170 (180.76)	72 + 55 (58.56)	180 + 145 (152.02)
CAN 20% + DAP	93 + 24 (66.92)	180 + 50 (133.41)	191 + 38 (125.08)	72 +20 (53.36)	217 + 59 (159.43)	72 + 20 (53.36)	180 + 50 (133.41)
CAN 20% + AP	60 + 55 (71.21)	110 + 115 (142.14)	135 + 90 (132.62)	45 + 45 (56.47)	135 + 135 (169.43)	45 + 45 (56.47)	110 + 115 (142.14)
CAN 20% + SP	115 + 70 (79.32)	225 +145 (158.55)	225 +112 (144.84)	90 + 55 (62.17)	270 + 170 (188.60)	90 + 55 (62.17)	225 + 145 (158.55)
AS +DAP	93 + 24 (72.28)	180 + 50 (144.75)	191 + 38 (137.11)	72 + 20 (57.90)	217 + 59 (173.10)	72 + 20 (57.90)	180 + 50 (144.75)
AS + AP	60 + 55 (74.99)	110 + 115 (149.07)	135 +90 (141.12)	45 + 45 (59.31)	135 + 135 (177.93)	45 + 45 (59.31)	110 + 115 (149.07)
AS + SP	115 + 70 (86.57)	225 + 145 (172.72)	225 + 112 (159.01)	90 + 55 (67.84)	270 + 170 (205.60)	90 + 55 (67.84)	225 + 145 (172.72)

Figure in parentheses are Rupees.

In case of those crops where top dressing of nitrogenous fertilizer is a must, major part of the nitrogen nutrient can be obtained from urea before sowing. CAN 25% can be used for application to standing crop in order to lower the cost.

1. *What is the importance of analysis of factor-factor relationships ?*
2. *State four practical examples in agriculture where factor- factor analysis can be applied.*
3. *Explain the meaning of the following concepts :*
   (*a*) *Iso-product curve or iso-quant.*
   (*b*) *Iso-cost line.*
   (*c*) *Iso-cline.*
   (*d*) *Expansion path.*
   (*e*) *Ridge line.*
4. *Explain the method of determining least-cost combination of two inputs X_1 and X_2 at given level of output with the help of a suitable diagram and data.*
5. *How will you determine the optimum level of output for maximising profit, through analysis of factor-factor relationships ?*
6. *Assignment : Draw two suitable diagrams on a graph paper using the data given below.*
   (*a*) **Output Iso-quant** *: 100 units of output can be produced using the following input combinations.*

X_1	X_2
9	2
6	3
5	4
4	7
5	10

   (*b*) *Determination of least-cost combination of two inputs X_1 & X_2 which substitute at diminishing rate for producing 90 units of output.*

X_1 input	X_2 input
1	9.50
2	7.50
3	6.00
4	5.00
5	4.50
6	4.25
7	4.15
8	4.00
9	4.50
10	5.25

1. Bishop, C.E. and W.D. Toussaint "Introduction to Agricultural Economic Analysis" New York, John Wiley & Sons, Inc. London. Chapter 9.
2. Gupta B.C. "Multi-factor Analysis of Fertilizer use on Wheat in Punjab" M.Sc. Thesis, Punjab Agril, University, Ludhiana, 1966.
3. Kahlon, A.S. & J.L. Kaul ; "Comparative Study of economics of High-yielding varieties of Wheat - Punjab state." Ind. Jr. Agr. Econ. XXIII (4) : p. 79-86 Oct-Dec. 1968.
4. Gupta B.C. and S.S. Johl, "How much Nitrogen and Phosphorus for C-273 Wheat." Progressive Farming, Sept. 1966.

7 Product-Product Relationships

In the last three chapters production process has been considered largely from the input side. First we discussed production function describing the relationships that can exist between input(s) and output, *i.e.*, factor-product relationships. Then we discussed the determination of combinations of two or more variable inputs in the production of one output, *i.e.* factor-factor relationships. In this chapter, a different view of the production process is taken. Instead of considering the allocation of inputs to an enterprise or among enterprises, we discuss enterprise combination of product-mix involving product-product relationships. Algebraically, the relationship can be written as :

$$Y_2 = f(Y_2)$$

or

$$Y_1 = f(Y_2, Y_3, Y_4 .... Y_n)$$

Suppose a farmer has 10 acres of land and he wants to grow wheat along with other competitive crops like gram, barley, sugarcane, fodders etc. In this case, acreage under wheat will be a function of acreage under gram, barley, sugarcane and fodders.

Although problems of the use of inputs are important in decision making process in agriculture, yet more common problems revolve around decisions on enterprise combinations.

As the farm resources available with the cultivators are limited and there are various alternative farm enterprises such as crops and livestock, the cultivator is generally faced with the question : How much of what to produce and with what technology ?

The question asked here is not 'How should the inputs be allocated among given enterprises ?' The problem is 'what combination of enterprises should be produced ?' The two questions ultimately arrive at the same answer ; only the vantage point differs. On a macro level, these decisions have to be made as to how much of, what to produce in respect of food, cotton, sugar, commercial products and other farm products with given national resources. It is a problem of allocation of the scarce resources among different enterprises.

BASIC RELATIONSHIPS

Before we attempt to understand the mechanics of resource allocation (budgeting or linear programming), it is essential to understand the possible relationships that can exist between different enterprises. The basic product relationships can be : Joint products, Complementarity, Supplementarity and Competitiveness.

Joint Products

Joint products result from the same production process. As a rule, the two are combined products and production of one without the other is not possible. Examples are cotton lint and cotton seed, beef and hides, wheat and straw ; mutton and wool, cattle and manure etc. In such cases, quantity of one product produced decides the quantity of the other product. Graphically, quantities of Y_1 and Y_2 that can be produced at different levels of given resources will be shown as points, A, B, C & D as given in figure 7.1.

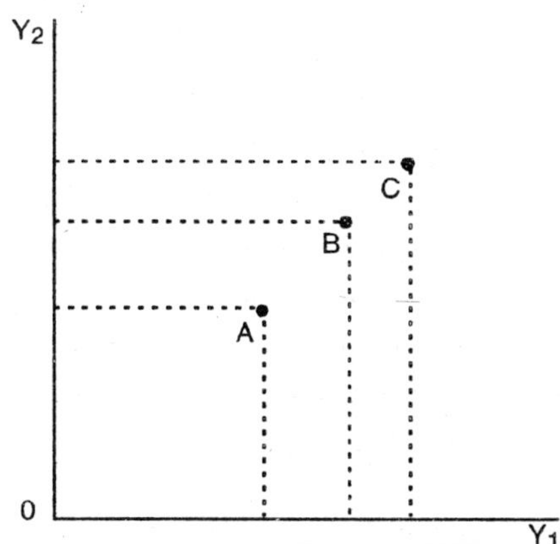

Fig. 7.1. Production possibilities of joint products.

For production decisions, joint products can be treated as one product. In the long run, however, change in the product combination is possible through research directed at changing the ratio of products. For example, a continuous increase in the price of wool compared to the price of mutton may necessitate a change in the breeds to produce a higher proportion of wool. Once this happens again in the short-run, proportions of the two products become fixed.

Complementarity

Complementarity among two enterprises exists when with a change in the level of one, the other also changes in the same direction. For example, if maize is grown after berseem crop, the yield of maize increases because berseem crop fixes nitrogen and makes the soil more fertile for the next crop.

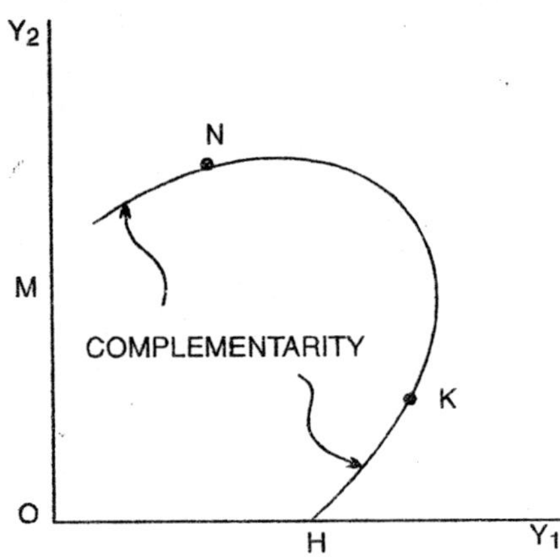

Fig. 7.2. Production possibility curve showing complementary relationships.

As shown in Fig. 7.2, the range of complementarity is from point M to Point N when production of Y_1 expands beyond zero point. The marginal rate of substitution between these two products (Y_1 and Y_2) is positive in the range of this complementarity. This is a case of double complementarity. On the other end of the curve the products are again complementary as production of Y_2 expands beyond zero. This means Y_1 must be produced at least up to point H and Y_2 up to point K, because up to these points increase in one product increases the production of the other too. Only after these two points on curve NK the decision has to be made based on relative prices of these two products.

An Example of Complementary and Competitive Relationships

An actual case of a farm in Punjab is presented in Table 7.1. When rotation WMBM is substituted for WM rotation, forage and maize relationship turns out to be complementary. Forage (Berseem) substitutes wheat $\frac{\Delta W}{\Delta B}$ at a ratio of .033. The price ratio, Pb/Pw = (0.046), is higher than the substitution ratio. It will, therefore, be profitable to introduce the forage crop, because $Pb \times B$ will be greater

TABLE 7.1
Substitution Ratio for Forage and Non-forage Rotations (one acre basis) in District Ludhiana, Punjab—1971-72

Rotations	*Acreage under different crops over rotation period of 4 seasons*					*Yield per acre (Quintals)*					*Total Production (Quintals)*					*Rate of Substitution in*		
	W	*M*	*S*	*B*	*C*	*W*	*M*	*S*	*B*	*C*	*W*	*M*	*S*	*B*	*C*	*F for M*	*Forage for W*	*Forage for C*
WM	2	2	—	—	—	6.69	7.64	—	—	—	(13.39)	(15.28)	—	—	—	—	—	—
WMBM	1	2	—	1	—	6.69	7.64 & 9.39	—	(200.00)	—	(6.69)	(17.03)	—	(200.00)		Complementary	.033	—
SMBM	—	2	1	1	—	—	9.39	(107.46)	(200.00)	—	—	(18.78)	(107.46)	(200.00)	—	—do—	.062	—
WC	2	—	—	—	2	6.69	—	—	—	(3.50)	(13.39)	—	—	—	(7.00)	—	—	—
WCBC	1	—	—	1	2	6.69	—	—	(200.00)	(3.50) & (4.16)	(6.69)	—	—	(200.00)	(7.66)	—	0.033	complementary
SCBC	—	—	1	1	2	—	—	(107.46)	(200.00)	(4.16)	—	—	(107.46)	(200.00)	(8.33)	—	0.062	—do—

Note. 1. 'W' stands for wheat, 'M' for maize, 'C' for American cotton, 'B' for Berseem forage, 'S' for Senji forage and 'F' for forage (Senji & Berseem).

2. (Rs. per quintal)

Price of wheat	=	76.00
Price of maize	=	55.00
Price of cotton	=	150.00
Price of Berseem	=	3.50
Price of Senji	=	4.00

3. Pb./Pw ratio = 0.461

Ps/Pw ratio = 0.0526

than $Pb \times \Delta W$. Further if SMBM is introduced in place of WMBM, forage and maize relationship is again complementary but forage (Senji) substitutes wheat $\frac{\Delta W}{\Delta S}$ at a ratio of .062. The price ratio (P *s*/ *P* w) is .053. Price ratio here is lower than substitution ratio. *i.e.*, $\frac{P_s}{P_w} < \frac{\Delta W}{\Delta S}$. It seems, the introduction of two forage crops (Berseem and Senji) in this rotation does not pay. But, the maize crop has shown complementarity with forage. The analysis of the rotation SMBM is therefore, incomplete. This rotation should be introduced if $Ps \times \Delta S + Pm \times \Delta M$ is greater than $\Delta W \times Pw$. In this case, these values are :

$4 \times 107.46 + 55 \times 1.75 > 76 \times 6.69$

or $429.86 + 96.25 > 508.44$

or $526.09 > 508.44$

Over all, it is profitable to introduce the double forage crop rotation.

Supplementarity

This relationship exists when increase or decrease in the level of one product does not affect the production level of the other product. Example is of wheat and maize crops in relation to land[1].

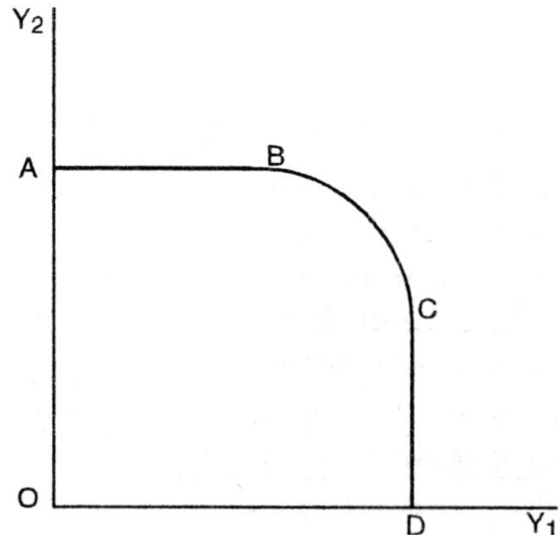

Fig. 7.3. Supplementary enterprises.

All supplementary relationships should be taken advantage of by producing both products to the point where the products become competitive.

1. Crop relationships in this book are described as in North-west India in general and Punjab state in particular. Seasonal, climatic, soil and other such differences may not make these particular crop cases applicable elsewhere.

Competitiveness

This relationship holds when increase or decrease in the production of one product affects the production of the other commodity inversely. Competitive enterprises compete for farm resources and substitute for each other. It means that when two products are competitive, some of one product must be given up to increase the level of the other product. Marginal rate of substitution between the products is, therefore, negative. Most of the decisions regarding the choice of products involve competing products. When two products are competitive, they may substitute at constant rate, increasing rate or decreasing rate.

Constant Rate of Substitution

It means that unit change in one product is throughout accompained by the same unit opposite change in the other product. There are a number of examples in agriculture where products substitute at constant rate, Gram and wheat, for example, substitute for land at constant rate. Similarly maize and cotton substitute for land. The constant rate of substitution is illustrated in Fig. 7.4.

In algebraic form, this relationship can be expressed as.

$$\frac{\Delta Y_{11}}{\Delta Y_{21}} = \frac{\Delta Y_{12}}{\Delta Y_{22}} = \ldots\ldots = \frac{\Delta Y_1}{\Delta Y_2}$$

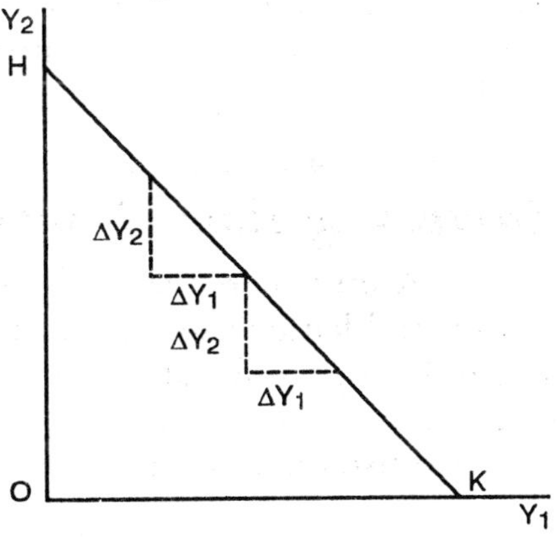

Fig. 7.4. Competitive products substituting at constant rate.

This is normally a short-run relationship. Over a longer period of time, a constant marginal rate of substitution between two products may not hold. When two products substitute at constant rate, only one of the two products will be economical to produce, depending upon their relative prices (profitability). If price-ratio is in favour of Y_2, price line will intersect the production-possibility line at point H (Fig. 7.4). If price ratio goes in favour of Y_1, the intersection point will be at K. If, however, price line is parallel to H K (production possibility line), any combination of products on line H K will be equally profitable.

Increasing Rate of Substitution

If this relationship holds true, each unit increases in level of one product is accompanied by larger and larger decrease in the level of the other product. For example, wheat and gram will substitute at increasing rate for capital and labour. When wheat acreage is increased, there would be greater and greater need to decrease gram acreage in order to release capital and labour. This relationship is shown in Fig. 7.5. As Y_1 increases, ΔY_1 remaining the same every time, Y_2 decreases by larger and larger amounts (ΔY_2 keeps increasing).

The increasing rate of marginal substitution between two products can also be expressed as under :

$$\frac{\Delta Y_{11}}{\Delta Y_{21}} < \frac{\Delta Y_{12}}{\Delta Y_{22}} < .... < \frac{\Delta Y_{1n}}{\Delta Y_{2n}}$$

In this case, maximum profits are made where physical rate of substitution between two products is equal to their price ratio, *i.e.* where slope of the production-possibility curve is equal to the slope of the price line.

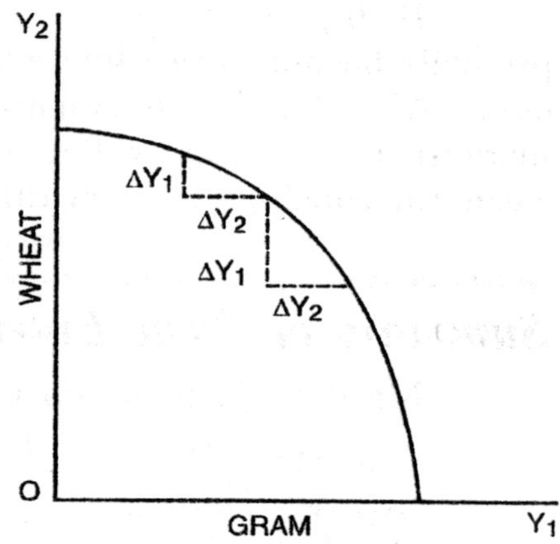

Fig. 7.5. Two competitive products substituting at increasing rate.

Decreasing Rate of Substitution

A unit increase in the level of one product in this case is accompanied by lesser and lesser decrease in the level of other product. Dairy and crops within a limited range may substitute at decreasing rate. This relationship is illustrated in Fig. 7.6. Here magnitude of ΔY_1 remaining the same, ΔY_2 keeps decreasing with every subsequent addition of ΔY_1.

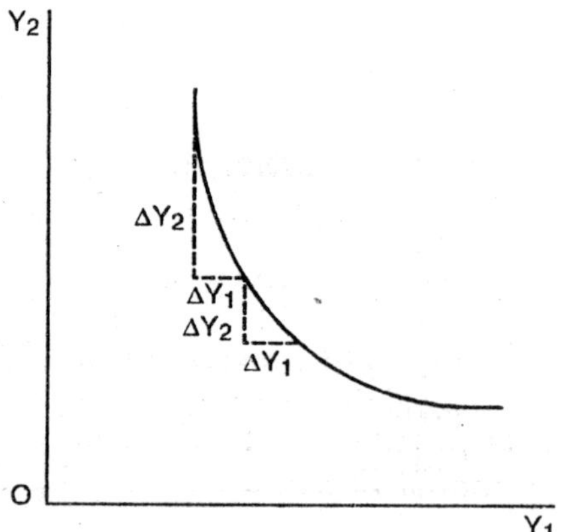

Fig. 7.6. Two competitive products substituting at decreasing rate.

The decreasing rate of substitution between two products (Y_1 & Y_2) can be algebraically expressed as under :

$$\frac{\Delta Y_{1}}{\Delta Y_{2}} > \frac{\Delta Y_{21}}{\Delta Y_{22}} > .... > \frac{\Delta Y_{1n}}{\Delta Y_{2n}}$$

If this relationship holds, it will be economical to produce only one of the products because price line will be tangent at only one of the end points of the curve. A combination of two products will never give highest returns, as each unit increase in one product will require sacrifice of smaller quantity of the other product. Such relationships are very rare in agricultural business.

Summary of Basic Enterprise Relationship

Marginal Rate of Substitution	Enterprise Relationship
$\Delta y_2/\Delta y_1 >$ zero.........	Complementary
$\Delta y_2/\Delta y_1 <$ zero.........	Competitive
$\Delta y_2/\Delta y_1 =$ zero.........	Supplementary

PRODUCTION POSSIBILITY CURVES

(Transformation Functions)

The production possibility curve presents all possible combinations of two products that could be produced with given amounts of inputs. The production possibility curve is thus a convenient device for depicting two production functions on one graph.

Production possibility curves are sometimes called opportunity curves or iso-resource curves. Term 'opportunity curve' is used because the curve presents all possible production opportunities. It is known as iso-resource curve because each output combination on this curve has the same resource requirements.

How to Draw Production Possibility Curve ?

Production possibility curve can be drawn either directly from production function or from total cost curve. The two methods are discussed below :

From Production Function

The production possibility curve can be derived from a production function as in example below :

Suppose for example 10 acres of land (X) can be used to produce two products Am. cotton (Y_1) and/or maize (Y_2) ; assuming all other inputs used to produce Y_2 Or Y_1 are highly specialised and fixed. The farm entrepreneur has to decide, how much of input X to use on each product.

The amount of land (X) that can be used to produce Am. cotton (Y_1) depends upon the amount of land (X) used in producing maize (Y_2), *i.e.*, $Y_1 = f(Y_2)$. Suppose production functions for two products using the same input are as shown :

Input (Acres)	*Product* Y_1 *Am. Cotton (Qtls)*	*Or* *Product* Y_2 *Maize (Qtls).*
1	8	12
2	15	24
3	21	36
4	26	48
5	30	60
6	33	72
7	35	84
8	36	96
9	36.50	108
10	36.75	120

Two separate production functions as given above show effects of adding the input on production of Y_1 or Y_2. A graphic presentation of these data can be shown in Fig. 7.7 and 7.8. The input X (land acreage in this case) can be used to produce either Y_2 or Y_1 or a combination of them.

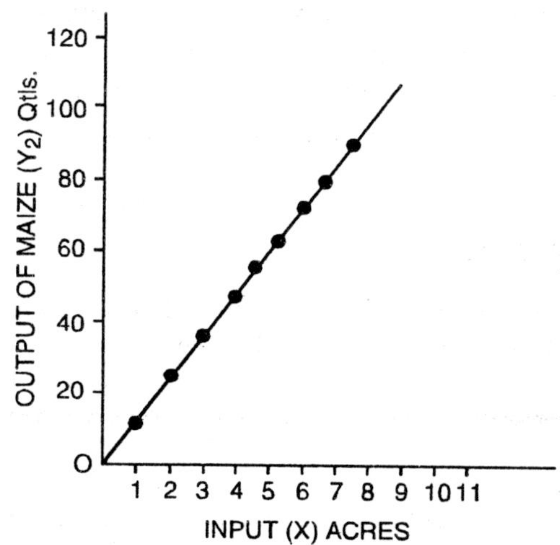

Fig. 7.7. Relationship between X and Y_2

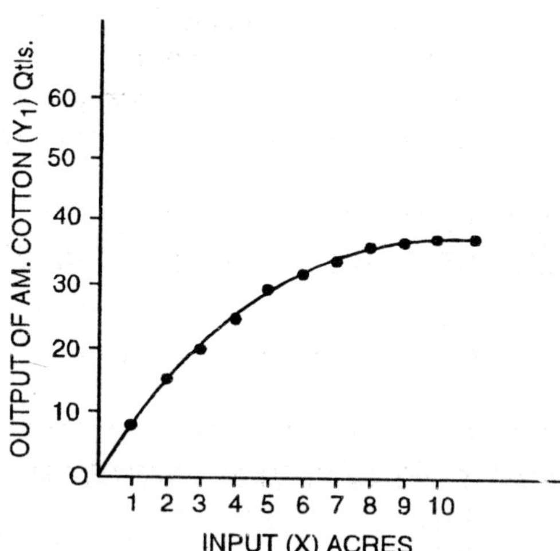

Fig. 7.8. Relationship between X and Y_1

If only 10 acres of land are available to the producer for the production of Am. Cotton and/or maize we can determine various combinations of the two products in such a manner that a maximum of one is obtained for any level of the other. Such combinations are given in Table 7.2.

TABLE 7.2
Possible Product Combinations for 10 Acres of Land

Production Possibilities for X = 10 acres		Physical output of	
Maize acreage (Y_2)	Am. Cotton acreage (Y_1)	*Maize in Qtls.* (Y_2)	Am. Cotton in Qtls. (Y_1)
10	0	120	0
9	1	108	8
8	2	96	15
7	3	84	21
6	4	72	26
5	5	60	30
4	6	48	33
3	7	36	35
2	8	24	36
1	9	12	36.50
0	10	0	36.75

If all 10 acres of land are used in the production of maize, we obtain 120 qtls. of maize and do not get any cotton. We can shift one acre of land to the production of cotton. In doing so, we get 8 qtls. of cotton and only 9 acres of land are left to produce maize which will produce only 108 qtls. In this manner we can produce other combinations of cotton and maize as shown in Table 7.2.

Plotting these two functions on a graph will give the required production possibility curve. From the various production possibility combination given in Table 7.2, a production possibility curve can be drawn in Fig. 7.9. The production possibility curve in Fig. 7.9, thus, presents all possible combinations of the two products (Cotton & Maize), with 10 units of input (10 acres of land).

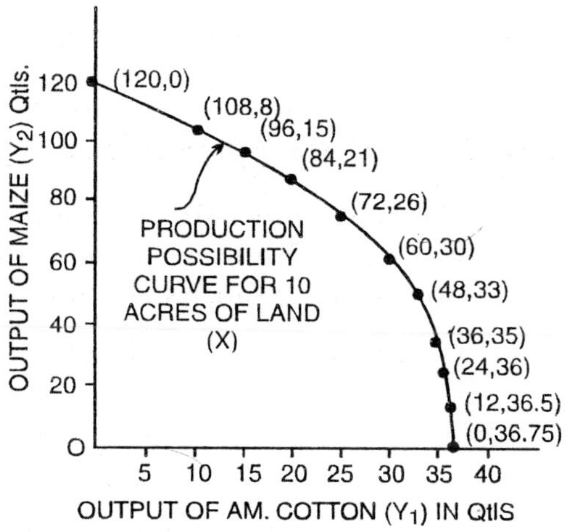

Fig. 7.9. Production possibility curve for two competing products substituting at increasing rate.

Shifts in Production Possibility Curve

Production possibility curve is affected by all the same factors that affect the production function. A change in technology or in the level of fixed inputs will cause a shift in the production function and also a shift in the production possibility curve.

As stated earlier, the production possibility curve is a convenient method of comparing two production functions simultaneously within the limits determined by the availability of the inputs). For example, a production possibility curve for 10 acres of land compares the production functions of Y_1 and Y_2 only within the limits allowed by these 10 units of input. If more or less than 10 units of input are available it will give a different production possibility curve.

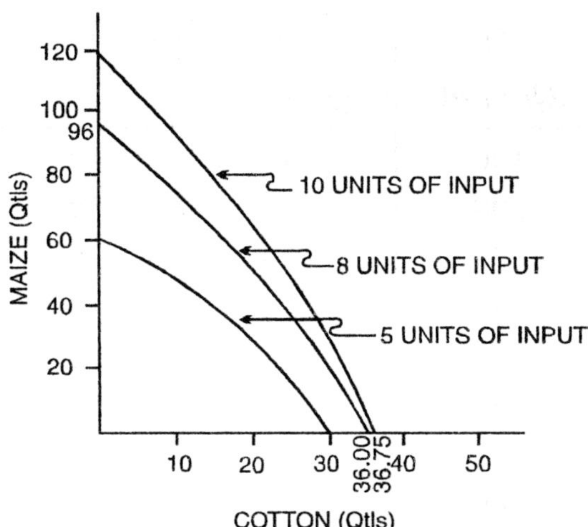

Fig. 7.10. Production possibility curves for different levels of input.

A production possibility curve for 15 units of input will represent a higher level of production of both products and will be located farther from the origin than the curve for 10 units of input. It may have a somewhat different shape from the curve for 10 units of input.

A production possibility curve for less than 10 units of input (say 5 units) would be located closer to the origin.

Marginal Rate of Product Substitution

The marginal rate of product substitution means the rate of change in quantity of one output as a result of unit increase in the other output, given that the amount of the input used remains constant.

The marginal rate of product substitution (MRPS) of Y_1 for Y_2 will be :

$$MRPS = \frac{\Delta Y_2}{\Delta Y_1}$$

The marginal rate of product substitution with 10 units of input are presented in table 7.3. Computations are similar to marginal product and marginal rates of input substitution and are not repeated here.

TABLE 7.3.

Marginal Rate of Product Substitution

Production Possibilities for 10 acres		*Marginal Change in Output*		*Marginal Rate of Product Substitution*	
Y_2 (*Quintal*)	Y_1 (*Quintal*)	Y_2	Y_1	$\frac{\Delta Y_2}{\Delta Y_1}$	$\frac{\Delta Y_1}{\Delta Y_2}$
120	0	12	—	—	—
108	8	12	8	1.50	0.67
96	15	12	7	1.70	0.58
84	21	12	6	2.00	0.50
72	26	12	5	2.40	0.42
60	30	12	4	3.00	0.33
48	33	12	3	4.00	0.25
36	35	12	2	6.00	0.17
24	36	12	1	12.00	0.08
12	36.50	12	0.50	24.00	0.04
0	36.75	12	0.25	48.00	0.02

As the amount of Y_1 increases, the amount of Y_2 sacrified increases. This is due to the decreasing marginal returns displayed by the production functions. The slope of the production possibility curve can be found out by drawing a tangent at a particular point on the production possibility curve. The slope will show the marginal rate of substitution.

Production Possibility Curves from Total Cost Curves

If total cost function is known for two products, we can easily draw the production possibility curve out of it. See Fig. 7.11 and 7.12.

Suppose we want to draw a production possibility curve for an expenditure of Rs. 800. Read from Fig. 7.11 how much of each product can be produced at this level. Then read for other allocations of Rs. 800 such as 700 and 100 ; 600 and 200, 500 and 300, and so on. Thus, read all combinations of output of Y_1 and Y_2 for a total outlay of Rs. 800. Plot them on a graph. This production possibility curve will also be called iso-cost curve because it indicates all possible combinations of the two commodities, expenditure remaining the same.

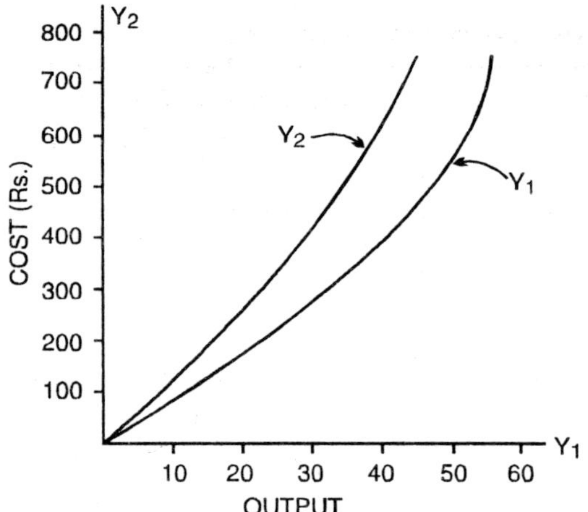

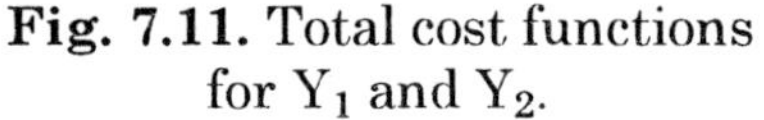

Fig. 7.11. Total cost functions for Y_1 and Y_2.

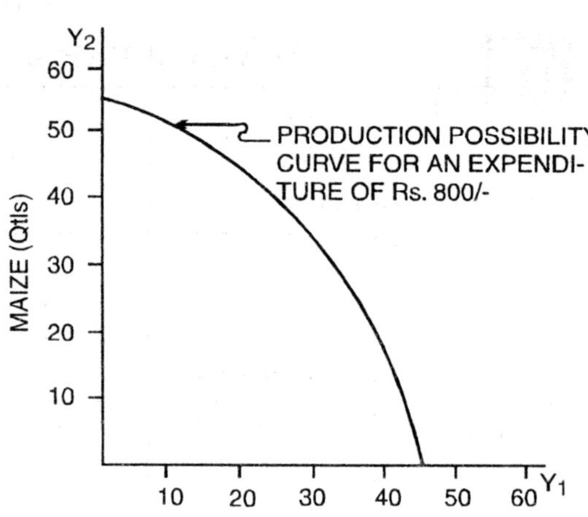

Fig. 7.12. Production possibility curve for Y_1 and Y_2.

The production possibility curves can thus be drawn either from production function or from total cost function. The shape of the production possibility curve will be quite similar in both the cases. The general shape of the production possibility curve will depend upon the basic relationships that exist between different products. Such relationships may be competitive, complementary or supplementary.

Ridge Line and Isocline for the Production Possibility Curves

We have already discussed the concept of ridge line and isocline in factor-factor analysis. Similarly ridge lines can be used to separate the range of product competition from ranges of complementarity. In the Fig. 7.13, OA & OB are two ridge lines.

These ridge lines are also called Border lines. Line OA intersects production possibility curves where they are horizontal and line OB intersects at the points where the curves go vertical.

On line, OA marginal rate of substitution of Y_2 for Y_1 is infinity and on line OB, the MR of Y_1 for Y_2 is zero.

Within the border lines production possibility curves have negative slope indicating competition. Portions outside border lines have positive slope indicating complementarity.

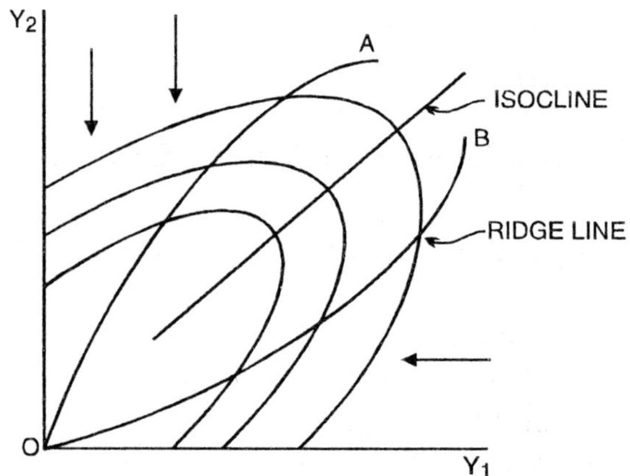

Fig. 7.13. Ridge line (boundary lines) and isoclines for production possibility curves.

ISO-REVENUE LINE OR PRICE LINE

For a farm-firm, the choice function or indicator is provided by an iso-revenue curve.

Iso-revenue line (or curve) indicates the ratio of prices for the two competing products. It is a line which defines all the possible combinations of two commodities which would yield an equal revenue or income, as illustrated in Fig. 7.14.

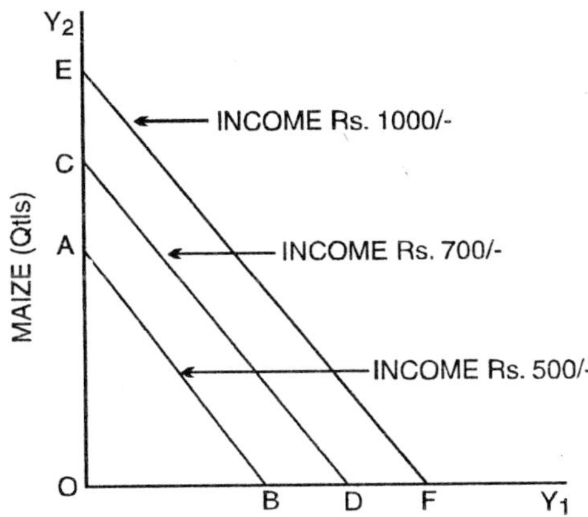

Fig. 7.14. Iso-revenue (price) lines at different levels of income.

AB, CD and EF are iso-revenue lines indicating different income levels from combinations of two products (Y_1 and Y_2). Price ratio of the products (slope of price line) remains the same so long as relative prices of the two products remain the same. So long as relative prices of the two products remain the same, the price lines will not change their slope and will run parallel to each other.

How to Draw an Iso-revenue Line ?

A line representing any given level of total revenue can be drawn on a graph. Suppose the price of cotton (Y_1) is Rs. 145/- per quintal and of Maize is Rs. 60/- per quintal. We want to draw iso-revenue line for a total income of Rs. 8090. We need to calculate : (*a*) How many units of Y_1 should be sold to earn total revenue of Rs. 8090/- ? This can be done through dividing Rs. 8090/- by Rs. 145, *i.e.*, $\frac{8090}{145} = 55.79$ units of Y_1. So $Y_1 = 55.79$ and $Y_2 = 0$ will yield an income of Rs. 8090/- (*b*) How many units of Y_2 should be sold in order to earn Rs. 8090/-?

This can be obtained as Rs. $\frac{8090}{60} = 134.83$ units of Y_1. Again, thus 134.83 units of Y_2 and zero unit of Y_1 will yield the same income. There can be many other combinations of Y_1 and Y_2 which may give the same total revenue of Rs. 8090. These points when graphed will make a straight line called an Iso-revenue line as shown in Fig. 7.15.

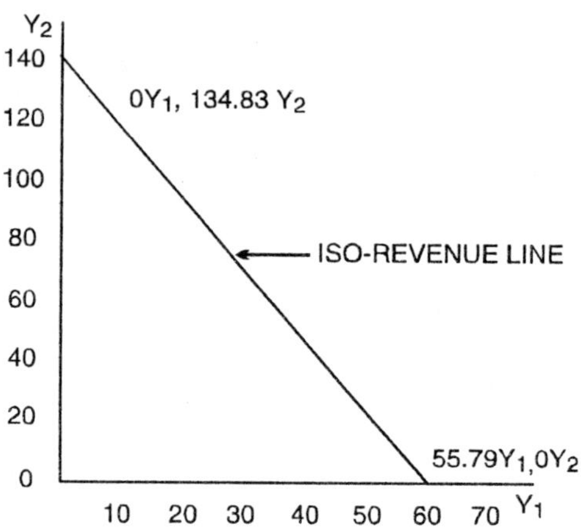

Fig. 7.15. Iso-revenue line at price Y_1 = Rs. 145 per quintal and Y_2 = Rs. 60/- per qtl. and income Rs. 8090/-

Points to be Noted regarding Iso-revenue Line

1. Iso-revenue line is a straight line, because the output prices do not change with the quantity sold. An iso-revenue line for any revenue can be determined by computing the points on the two axes and connecting these points with a straight line. Point on Y_2 axis is always equal to total revenue divided by prices of Y_2 and the points on Y_1 axis will equal total revenue divided by price of Y_1. These points indicate the amount of either Y_2 or Y_1 needed to earn that income.

2. The amount of total revenue determines the distance of the iso-revenue line from the origin. As total revenue increases, the iso-revenue line moves away from the origin. In Fig. 7.16A, the iso-revenue line A represents a higher total revenue than that represented by line B and C. B line represents a higher total revenue than C line.

3 The output prices determine the slope of the iso-revenue line.[1] When the output prices remain constant, the iso-revenue lines showing different total revenues are parallel. But a change in either price will change the slope. These effects are illustrated in Fig. 7.16B.

An increase in the price of Y_1 shifts the intersection of the iso-revenue line with the Y_1—axis closer to the origin. A decrease in the price of Y_1 shifts the

1. Iso-revenue lines and the iso-cost lines appear the same on a graph. The slopes of both are determined by the relevant price ratios. These should not be confused. They are used for different purposes.

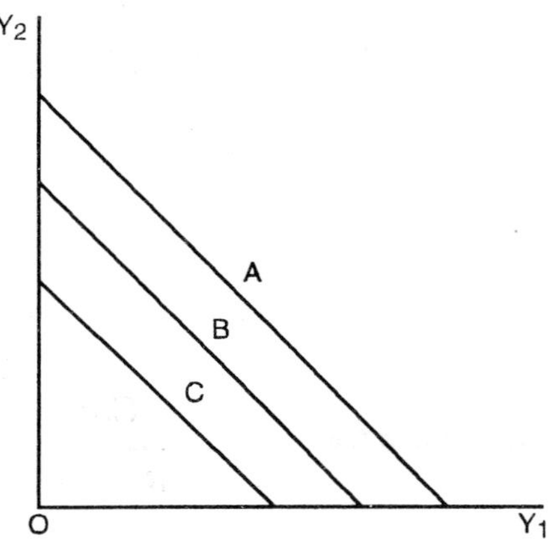

Fig. 7.16A. Iso-revenue lines for different Total revenue lines.

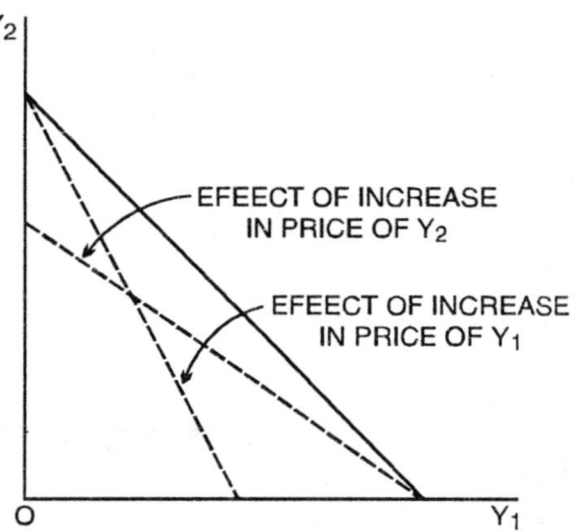

Fig. 7.16B. Effects of price changes on iso-revenue lines.

intersection of the iso-revenue line farther from the origin on the Y_1 axis. Similar changes are evidenced on the Y_2 axis in response to changes in the price of Y_2.

DETERMINATION OF OPTIMUM PRODUCT COMBINATION

For profit maximisation, a rational producer should operate in the range where two products are competitive and within this range, the choice of products should depend upon the marginal rate of product substitution and the price ratio. We have learned, the production possibility curve represents the marginal rate of substitution of two products and iso-revenue line the ratio of prices of the two products. In principle, the maximum revenue from two products using given amounts of resources will be where the physical rate of substitution between two products is equal to the rate at which the products exchange in the market or where the production possibility curve and iso-revenue line have the same slope. The other method to find out optimum level of two products is to calculate net revenue from many combinations and locate the one which promises the highest returns. Further details of these methods are given below.

Tabular Method

Probably the simpler method to understand is to compute total revenue for each possible output combination and then select the maximum revenue combination. Computations of the maximum revenue combination of two products Y_1 and Y_2 for 10 units of input are given in Table 7.4. When price of maize (Y_2) is Rs. 60/- per quintal and price of cotton Rs. 145 per quintal, the maximum revenue combination of the products is 72 units of Y_2 and 26 units of Y_1. The total returns are Rs. 8090. Every other combination of output will give lesser returns.

TABLE 7.4.

Computation of Optimum Combination of Two products (maize and cotton) for 10 units of Land input

Production Possibilities For 10 acres of land		*Gross returns from*		*Total returns from various combinations of Maize and Cotton*
Yield of Maize in Qtls.	*Yield of Cotton in Qtls.*	*Maize @ Rs. 60/- Qtls.*	*Cotton @ Rs. 145/- Qtls.*	
120	0	Rs. 7200	Rs. 0	Rs. 7200
108	8	Rs. 6480	Rs. 1160	Rs. 7640
96	15	Rs. 5760	Rs. 2175	Rs. 7935
84	21	Rs. 5040	Rs. 3040	Rs. 8080
72	26	Rs. 4320	Rs. 3770	Rs. 8090
—	—			
60	30	Rs. 3600	Rs. 4350	Rs. 7950
48	33	Rs. 2880	Rs. 4785	Rs. 7665
36	35	Rs. 2160	Rs. 5075	Rs. 7235
24	36	Rs. 1440	Rs. 5120	Rs. 6580
12	36.50	Rs. 720	Rs. 5292.50	Rs. 6012.50
0	36.75	Rs. 0	Rs. 5328.75	Rs. 5328.75

Calculation of total returns from each combination of products and selecting the maximum revenue combination this way is feasible only for a small number of combinations. Because there are numerous combinations of the output that exist along the production possibility curve, computation of total revenue resulting from all combinations would be very difficult, rather impossible. Graphic analysis is more helpful in such cases where many combinations on continuous curve are involved.

Graphic Presentation

We can determine the maximum returns combination of output with the help of production possibility curve and iso-revenue line already discussed. The optimum point is determined by using the following criterion equation :

$$\frac{\Delta Y_2}{\Delta Y_1} = \frac{P_{Y1}}{P_{Y2}}$$

The left side of this criterion equation represents the slope of the production possibility curve whereas the right side represents the slope of the iso-revenue line.

As already explained, the optimum point of product combination will be where the iso-revenue line is tangent to the production possibility curve. At this point, the slope of the production possible curve and iso-revenue will be the same. In other words, at this point, the marginal rate of product substitution will be equal to the inverse of their price ratios. This optimum combination, on the production posibility curve for maize and cotton at 10 acres of land-use is, illustrated in Figure 7.17.

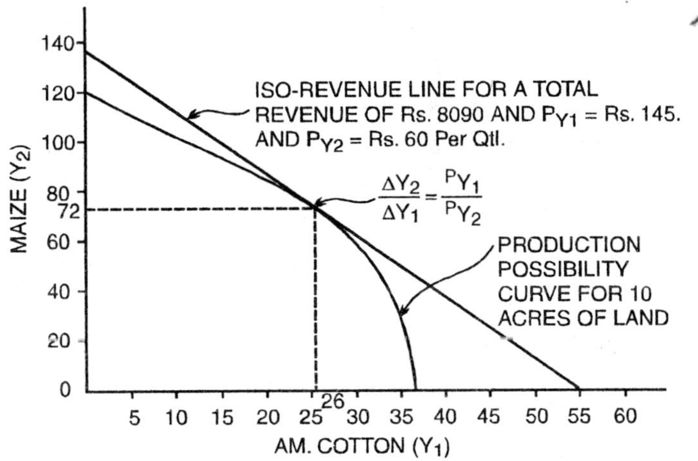

Fig. 7.17. Selection of optimum combination of two competing products on a production possibility curve.

Iso-revenue line has a slope of 2.41 $\left(\text{because } \frac{P_{Y1}}{P_{Y2}} = \frac{145}{60} = 2.41\right)$. Its tangency point on production possibility curve is K. At the point of tangency, perpendiculars on Y_2-axis and Y_1-axis show 72 quintals of maize (Y_2) and 26 quintals of cotton (Y_1) which will give the total returns of Rs. 8090.

It should be noted that the farther the iso-revenue line is located from the origin, the higher will be the total returns. In Fig. 7.16, for example, any other iso-revenue line drawn farther from the origin would not touch the production possibility curve and would, therefore, represent returns unattainable with 10 units of input. Any iso-revenue line drawn closer to the origin would represent a lower total return. Thus, the optimum combination of two products, maize 72 qunitals and cotton 26 quintals will give maximum return and any other combination will yield lesser returns than Rs. 8090. For illustration, calculation of gross returns at different prices have been made in table 7.5.

Product Price Changes and Optimum Combination of Output

Just as we have studied the effect of changes in prices of inputs in Chapters 5 and 6, changes in prices of the products will bring about changes in the optimum combination of the products. The effects of product price changes are illustrated in Figs. 7.18 and 7.19.

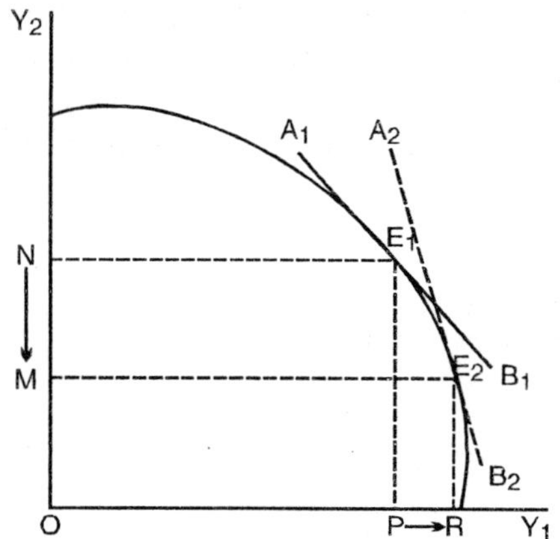

Fig. 7.18. Shift in product-combination when price of product Y_2 falls.

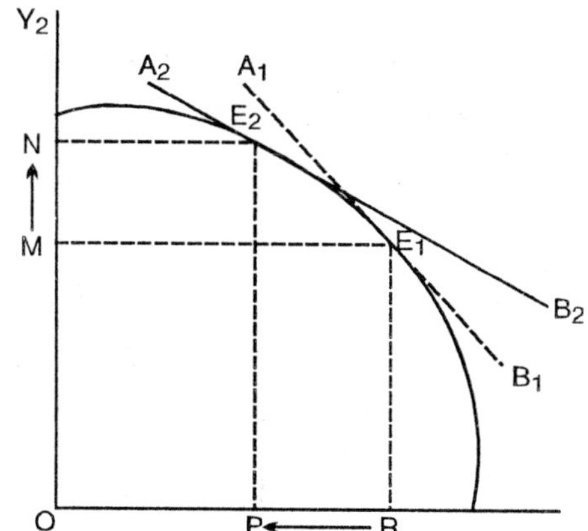

Fig. 7.19. Shift in product-combination when price of Y_1 falls.

In Fig. 7.18 AB is iso-revenue line and optimum product combination is ON units of Y_2 and OP units of Y_1. When the price of Y_2 falls, the iso-revenue line AB takes the shape of A_2 B_2 and new optimum point is at E_2 . With this shift of iso-revenue line, it will be profitable to produce less of Y_2 and more of Y_1 .

In Fig. 7.18, with optimum point at E_1 the output combination is OM units of Y_2 and OR units of Y_1 and with the shift in iso-revenue line, ON units of Y_2 and OP units of Y_1 will be produced to get the maximum returns. Thus with a shift in iso-revenue line, the optimum combination of two products also changes.

EXPANSION PATH IN PRODUCT-PRODUCT ANALYSIS

As in case of input combinations, there are iso-clines in output combination analysis also. In Fig. 7.20 several iso- revenue lines are shown each indicating a different level of revenue. Prices are assumed constant and the slope of the lines are the same.

All these iso-revenue lines are tangent to the production possibility curve at different points *m*, *o* and *p*. The line connecting these equilibrium points is the expansion path.

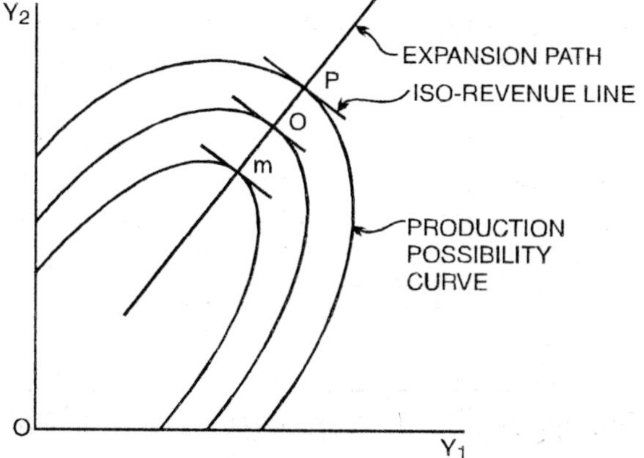

Fig. 7.20. Expansion path with iso-revenue lines and production possibility curve tangency points.

TABLE 7.5

Product-Product Relationship

Some Possible Product Combinations and Gross Returns from 10 Acres of Land, assuming Cost of Production of Two Competing Products remaining the Same

Production Possibilities combinations for 10 acres		*Physical output in quintals*		*Marginal change in production*		*Marginal rate of substitution*	*Gross Returns (Rs.) at Prices*			
Maize acreage (Y_2)	*Cotton acreage* (Y_1)	Y_2	Y_1	Y_2	Y_1	$\frac{\Delta Y_2}{\Delta Y_1}$	*Maize @ Rs. 60/- Qtl.*	*Cotton @ Rs. 145/- Qtl.*	*Total Returns PR = 2.4*	*Maize @ 50/- per qtl. and Cotton @ 200/- per qtl. PR = 4.00*
1	*2*	*3*	*4*	*5*	*6*	*7*	*8*	*9*	*10*	*11*
10	0	120	0	—	—	—	7200	0	7200	Rs. 6000
9	1	108	8	12	8	1.50	6480	1160	7640	Rs. 7000
8	2	96	15	12	7	1.70	5760	2175	7935	Rs. 7800
7	3	84	21	12	6	2.00	5040	3030	8080	Rs. 8400
6	4	72	26	12	5	2.40	4320	3770	8090	Rs. 8800
5	5	60	30	12	4	3.00	3600	4350	7950	Rs. 9000
4	6	48	33	12	3	4.00	2880	4785	7665	Rs. 9000
3	7	36	35	12	2	6.00	2160	5075	7235	Rs. 8800
2	8	24	36	12	1	12.00	1440	5120	6580	Rs. 8400
1	9	12	36.50	12	0.50	24.00	720	5292.50	6012.50	Rs. 7900
0	10	0	36.75	12	0.25	48.00	0	5328.75	5328.75	Rs. 7350

* It is assumed that cotton requires more care and better plant protection measures etc. and thus gives diminishing rate of returns in terms of yield per acre as more and more acres are added.

The points of tangency specify the most profitable enterprise combination for different production possibility curves with the prices indicated by the iso-revenue lines. As one moves up the expansion path, total revenue increases but total costs also increase.

Production Possibility Curve for More Than one Input

Normally a number of inputs are used by the farmer to produce a number of products. He has various resources such as land, labour, irrigation, building etc. to produce different products such as maize, cotton, sugarcane, groundnut, wheat, meat, milk, eggs etc. He is interested in a combination of these product which would give him the maximum returns. For understanding the process of decision making under such a situation we take two competing products and three inputs and construct a production possibility curve and then find out an optimum combination of two products. Suppose a farmer has 5 acres of land, 64 man-days of human labour and Rs. 1600 as working capital. Suppose further alternative activities available to him are maize and cotton crops. Decision matrix for him can be laid down as in Table 7.6.

TABLE 7.6.

Resource Levels and Input-output Matrix for Maize and Cotton on the Case Farm Situation

	Farm Resources	*Resource levels availability*	*Per acre input requirements*	
			Maize	Cotton
1	Kharif land fit for maize and cotton	5	1	1
2.	Labour maximum (man-days)	64	8	16
3.	Cash in Kharif season (Rs.)	1600	400	200
Returns to fixed farm resources (Rs.)		—	200	400

Based on these data, production possibility lines or curve can be drawn as in Fig. 7.21.

He can either grow 5 acres of maize or cotton or some combinations of both. A line joining the 5 acres points on both the axis will show land maximum (or P.P.C. with respect to land). With respect to labour, he can either produce 8 acres of maize $\left(\frac{64}{8}=8\right)$ or 4 acres of cotton $\left(\frac{64}{16}=4 \text{ acres}\right)$ or any combination within these limits. The line joining these two points will show labour maximum. The 3rd restriction is of capital Rs. 1600/- are sufficient to grow either 4 acres of maize or 8 acres of cotton or some combination of the two within these limits. If these three production possibility curves are drawn as shown in Fig. 7.21, intersecting each other a production possibility curve would emerge as shown by ABCE. Any combination of cotton and maize on this curve is feasible. For finding out the optimum point, however, we need the price ratio. Based on returns to fixed resources figure we, therefore, draw a iso-revenue line. The point of tangency between production possibility curve and iso-revenue line will indicate the optimum combination of maize and cotton acreage. In this particular case (Fig. 7.21), the farmer should grow 2 acres of maize and 3 acres of cotton to get the maximum revenue.

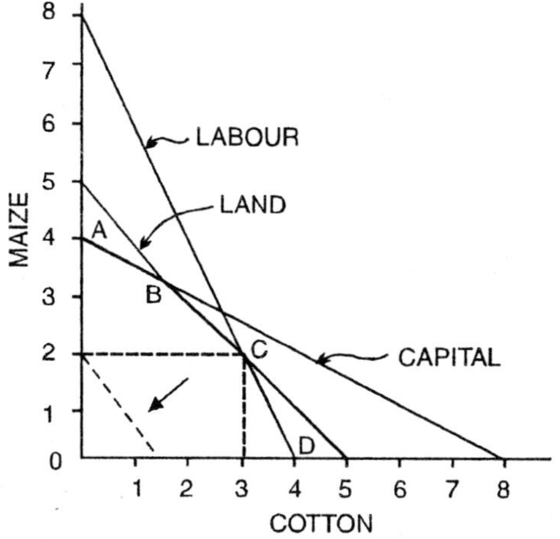

Fig. 7.21. Production possibility curve with more than one input.

Specialisation and Diversification

Different types of farming areas and various farmers within a particular type of farming area adopt a particular production pattern. Some farmers or areas specialise and some others diversify their production by having several major enterprises. Specialization means the farmer specialize in one enterprise, such as dairy farm, poultry or tea farm etc. Diversification means adopting more than one enterprise or combination of enterprises (normally each yielding less than 50% of the total income). There are many physical, economic and social factors which influence these patterns of production. Some of the important factors are discussed below.

Product Relationships. Where complementarity or supplementarity among products exist, general pattern of production will be diversified. The farmers would take advantage of complementary and supplementary enterprises and will try to grow all such crops. Where the products have competitive relationships, diversification or specialisation will depend upon the marginal rate or substitution. If the products substitute at increasing rate, diversification will predominate and if products substitute at decreasing rate, there would be a tendency towards specialisation. If products are competitive and have a constant marginal rate of substitution, specialisation will be the most profitable.

One Crop Season. In most parts of India (mainly in the Central and Northern India) farming is mostly diversified because of two distinct seasons *i.e. Kharif* and *Rabi*. Farmers grow maize, paddy, cotton, groundnut, etc. in *kharif* season and wheat, gram, barley, barseem in *rabi* season. In some countries such as U.S.A., there is only one crop season. Farmers generally specialise in one or a few crops only.

Length of Sowing Season. If sowing period for a particular crop is short, diversification goes favourable. On the other hand, if the sowing period is longer, specialisation may result.

Risk and Uncertainty. There are many risks and uncertainties in farming and the farmers try to reduce them. Diversification is one of the methods used. Farming may be diversified even though producing of only one commodity would promise the greatest net revenue. Many farmers grow mixed crops like wheat and gram, to avoid the probable chances of failure of one crop. Also the farmers spread their risk on many crops. It is particularly true of vegetables growers.

Large Investment and Size Economy. Recent technological developments have put forth many new machines and equipment which may require heavy investment. In order to reap size economy on these equipments, farmers expand production of one or a few commodities (specialisation), as is happening to wheat production in Punjab. But the same factor might necessitate growing of more than one crop in a year to get the machines engaged throughout the year.

Business Skill. With the advancement of technology, business of agriculture is becoming more complex and farmers need to update themselves with the new information pouring in from time to time. It is difficult to keep informed on new developments in numerous enterprises and some farmers can do a better job by concentrating on one or two main enterprises. Modern business requires better business skill for each enterprise and no farmer can become expert of all operations on many enterprises in farming. Progressive farmers, therefore, sometimes prefer to master the techniques of production on a few important crops to make best use of their skills.

1. ***What is the importance of product-product relationships analysis ? State 5 practical examples in farming where analysis is applicable.***
2. ***Name the various basic relationships that exist between products under different farming situations and discuss their meanings.***
3. ***Explain the meanings of the following with suitable diagrams and data :***
   (a) Production possibilities curve
   (b) Iso-revenue line.
   (c) Specialised and diversified farming.

4. *Complete the following by using the most appropriate words in the blanks :*
   (a) *As the total revenue increases, the iso-revenue lines moves......... the origin, a production possibility curve moves.....the origin as the level of output decreases. (towards, away from).*
   (b) *The use of product-product relationship analysis mainly lies in............and of factor-factor analysis in............(minimising the costs, maximising the returns)*
   (c) *The optimum product combination at the given level of resources will be where M.R.S. is equal to.........*
5. *With the help of a suitable example, illustrate the method of determination of the maximum revenue combination of two products (Y_1 and Y_2), with given units of an input (X).*
6. *How will you draw a production possibility curve for two for more inputs for producing two competing products Y_1 and Y_2 ? How will you determine maximum-income-giving combination of these two products ?*
7. *Why do most of the farmers grow combination of crop enterprises, even if a particular crop enterprise may give the highest returns?*
8. *Discuss the various factors which influence the determination of product combination.*
9. *What are the main differences between factor-factor and product-product analysis ?*
10. *Assignment : Show with the help of a diagram maximum revenue combination of products on production possibility curve ; given the following information :*

Units of Input = 7 acres

P_{Y1} = *Rs. 4 per unit*

P_{Y2} = *Rs. 2 per unit*

Production possibilities Y_2	and Y_1	Revenue from Y_2	Revenue from Y_1
43	0	86	0
42	7	84	28
40	13	80	52
36	18	72	72
30	22	60	88
22	25	44	100
12	27	24	108
0	28	0	112

1. *Heady, Earl, O., "Economics of Agricultural Production and Resource Use." Chapter 7, 8 & 9. Englewood Cliffs, N.J., Prentice-Hall, Inc., 1952.*
2. *Kahlon, A.S. and S.S. Johl, "Requisties of Crop Planning", The Indian Journal of Agronomy : X (4) Dec. 1965.*
3. *Bishop, C.E. and W.D. Toussaint, "Introduction to Agricultural Economic Analaysis", Chapter 11, New York, John Wiley and Sons, Inc., London.*
4. *Kapur, T.R. and A.S. Kahlon, "Optimum Cropping Patterns for Upper Dhaia Region for I.A.D.P. District Ludhiana (Punjab)." Ind. Jr. Agr. Econ. XXII (2) April-June 1967.*
5. *Bradford, L.A. and Johnson, G.L., "Farm Management Analysis", Chapter 11, New York : John Wiley & Sons Inc; 1953.*

8 Principles Involved in Farm Management Decisions

Basically, farm management is an application of agricultural sciences and economic principles to the organisation and operation of a farm business. There are no separate principles or rules for each part of the business; rather each principle applies to all parts. The purpose of this chapter is to help understand some commonly used economic principles in managing a farm business.

Farm management principles serve as a guideline for collecting and using requisite information for rational decision-making. They also provide a set of tools for the preparation of farm budgets and production programmes. These principles help provide answers to various farm problems and save time and energy otherwise lost in trials and errors to arrive at appropriate decisions. Knowledge of these principles enhances entrepreneurs' sense of judgement, a pre-requisite for meeting the demands of a business, especially under odd situations requiring a discriminating intellect.

The following are the six basic principles involved in making rational farm management decisions :

(*i*) Principle of variable proportions or laws of returns.

(*ii*) Cost principle

(*iii*) Principle of substitution between inputs.

(*iv*) Equi-marginal returns principle or Opportunity cost principle.

(*v*) Principle of substitution between products.

(*vi*) Principle underlying decisions involving time and uncertainty

These farm management principles are briefly discussed below :

PRINCIPLE OF VARIABLE PROPORTION

It has three phases : (*a*) diminishing returns, (*b*) constant returns and (*c*) increasing returns.

(*a*) Diminishing returns. It is basic natural law affecting many phases of management of a farm business. It is a law of fundamental importance in agriculture. This law describes the relationship between output and a variable input when other inputs are held constant. The law can be stated as follows : "If increasing amounts of one input are added to a production process while all other inputs are held constant, the amount of output added per unit of variable input will eventually start decreasing." It states that if the quantity of one factor is increased with quantities of other factors held constant, the marginal increment to the total product may increase or remain constant at first but will eventually decrease after a certain point. The operation of this law can, however, be delayed by improvements in technology and/or improvement in managerial ability. Ultimately this law must operate in the practical world. The levels to which yields per acre, milk per cow or weight per poultry bird should be pushed are the kind of questions which involve the law of diminishing returns. It is, thus, an important point in farming to decide the level to which a farmer should push his output per acre or per cow, etc. to secure the maximum possible profit. This principle of returns is also important in specifying how large a farm should be or how much labour and/or machinery be added. In this context, resources can be classified as variable resources and fixed resources. For example, an acre of land would be a fixed resource with the farmer, but fertilizer would be a variable resource. As additional quantities of fertilizer are given to an acre of crop, the return to each additional dose will eventually become lesser and lesser. When diminishing returns hold true, it is seldom profitable to produce a maximum yield per acre or milk or meat per animal, although exception might exist.

It can be said that the added quantity of a variable resource applied to a fixed acre of land or given head(s) of livestock adds less and less to the yield or output. Examples are application of seeds, fertilizers, irrigation etc. which have a characteristic of diminishing marginal productivity. There are some farmers who lose sight of diminishing returns to variable factor-use and consider the highest yield per acre, the highest milk yield per cow etc. always to be the best level in terms of profit. This way they think only in terms of physical yields and not in terms of costs and profit. True, many farmers would need to raise their production levels in order to increase their profits, but they must consider cost also at some point. One can easily decide the level of resource use or level of production by using the following profit rule under the conditions of diminishing returns.

Keep adding variable resource(s) to the fixed resource(s) as long as the added return is more than the added cost. For example, a farmer might want to know how much fertilizer should be added to one acre of paddy to maximise his profits, the price of paddy being Rs. 50/- per quintal and price of fertilizer Rs. 30/- per unit and physical input-output data on paddy yield response to fertilizer given as in Table 8.1.

TABLE 8.1

Marginal Cost and Marginal Returns Analysis of Paddy Yield Response to Application of Fertilizers

Fertilizer Units per Acre (50 kgs CAN)	*Yield of Paddy (Qtls.)*	*Total Cost @ (Rs. 30 per Unit)*	*Marginal Cost (Rs.)*	*Marginal Product (Qtls.)*	*Marginal Returns (Rs.)*	*Total Returns (Rs.)*	Profit *(Rs.)*
	(T.P.)	(T.C.)	(M.C.)	(M.P.)	(M.R.)	(T.R.)	
0	2	0	0	0	0	100	100
1	6	30	30	4	200	300	270
2	9	60	30	3	150	450	390
3	10.5	90	30	1.5	75	525	435
4	11.5	120	30	1.0	50	575	455
5	12.0	150	30	0.5	25	600	450
6	11.5	180	30	— 0.5	— 25	575	395
7	10.5	210	30	— 0.1	— 50	525	315

Analysis begins by comparing marginal or added costs and added returns. One should stop applying additional doses of fertilizer where the fertilizer is just balanced by the added returns.

As shown in Table 8.1, the optimum level of fertilizer to be used in this case is 4 units. Beyond this level, the marginal return is lesser than the marginal cost. If we calculate total profit at each unit of fertilizer, as given in last column, we observe that the net returns/profits per acre are the highest (Rs. 455) at four units of fertilizer use. One may not go up to the last profitable unit because apart from the cost of the input (fertilizer units) there may be some indirect costs such as costs of spreading of the fertilizer and extra cost on bigger harvest etc. In practice, therefore, even an economic farmer would apply fertilizer a little below this break-even point. Such simple exercises for taking day to day operational farm decisions can save the farmer from many losses and increase his net returns from the farm business. This principle should therefore be helpful in making decisions such as :

(*i*) The level to which yield per acre, milk per cow, etc. should be pushed to secure maximum profit.

(*ii*) The size of the farm one should operate with given resources of capital, labour and management.

(*iii*) The amount of fertilizer, labour or type of machinery one should use.

(*b*) ***Constant returns.*** It means each marginal unit of a variable resource adds the same amount of the output to the total production. Though 'diminishing marginal productivity' is the rule, constant productivity is frequently observed when no resource is fixed and all are increased together in the same proportion. For example, another acre may be as productive as the first with same inputs. If one acre of wheat requires 20 manhours of labour, 30 kgs. of seed and 13 inches of irrigation water and yields 10 quintals of wheat, the second acre will require an additional 20 man-hours of labour,30 kgs. of seed and 13 inches of irrigation water and will also yield 10 quintals of wheat. The second acre is just as productive. The marginal or added production from each increase in resource input is the same ; this is a case of constant productivity.

Another case is when one or more resources are fixed but have excess capacity. For example, family labour or a farmer may not be fully employed. A storage godown may have surplus capacity. A tractor may be big enough to control 50 acres holding but the farmer may have only 27 acres. If variable input is added to such a resource-mix situation, constant returns may result.

Under constant productivity, each unit input increase is just as profitable as another. Under such conditions the profit rule is : If production is profitable on first unit, keep producing till the constant returns hold. Do not produce at all, if production is not profitable on first unit. In a sense, follow the same principle, *i.e.* continue adding the variable resource to the fixed resource(s) as long as the return is greater than the added costs.

Limits on constant returns are reached as some of the factors become fixed. If nothing else becomes fixed, management becomes a fixed resource. The productivity of one resource depends on the amount of the other(s) with which it is used. For example, if capital is fixed at a low level for the farm as a whole, labour productivity will be lower. Since the productivity of one resource depends on the amount of other resource(s) with which it is combined, farmers having different quantities of land, capital, labour and management will have different programmes. What is best for one farm is, therefore, seldom best for the other(s). Each farmer must get the right balance of resources and a unique optimum farm organisation consistent with the resources he has.

(*c*) ***Increasing returns.*** There are few cases in farming business where increasing productivity may be found. Increasing productivity means added resources give increasing returns. This relationship may hold only over a very limited range of production and is applicable when all resources are increased together and not when some resources are fixed. For example, a cattle shed constructed for 30 cows may cost more per cow than if one is constructed for 60 cows, the cost involved in the latter case may not be doubled because of some economies on account of joint walls etc. but the gross returns per cow might be the same. Use of added resource(s) thus, will give increasing returns in such cases. In this case each additional unit gives higher and higher returns. So long as this relationship holds, production should keep expanding.

COST PRINCIPLE

Most of the producers give considerable importance to the cost of production while taking production decisions. When we speak of cost of producing a commodity. we generally refer to the expenses incurred in producing a unit of a product in a particular time period. Without specifying the amount and the time period, any reference to cost will be meaningless.

Accounting Periods

There can be two accounting or planning periods : short run and long-run. Short run is a period of time which is sufficient enough to permit desired changes in output without altering the size of the plant. The long run is generally considered to be the period which is sufficiently long for output to be altered by varying either the size of the plant or by making a more or less intensive utilisation of the existing plant.* During the short-run it may be possible, for example, to increase production through increased use of labour and/or by increasing the quantities of other inputs. In the long run, size of the holding can be varied either by increasing the acreage or by increasing the number of permanent workers. Thus, the manner in which production can be varied depends upon the length of the planning period under consideration.

Types of Costs

The relationship of costs to the income is very important in farming. Just as there are two categories of planning periods, there are two corresponding categories of costs also viz. fixed costs and variable costs. Fixed costs are sunk costs or overhead charges. They do not change with the level of production. These costs are fixed such as, taxes, rent, electricity meter charges, insurance, depreciation, family labour etc. These are the expenses on farm which must be paid even if nothing is produced. For example, if you hire a man on a year round basis, his wage is a fixed cost. Costs do not become fixed until they have been incurred, they do not vary with the change in output and can have no bearing upon management decisions with respect to using less or more of these inputs. In the short-run some costs are fixed and others can be varied. In the long run, however, all costs become variable and influence long run decisions to stop, decrease or increase the size of the farm.

Variable costs are those which vary with the level of production. These include the costs of adding the variable inputs. They do not occur if we produce nothing ; amount depends on what we produce. For example, if we use more fertilizer to

---

* J. Viner, "Cost Curves and Supply Curves", Zeits Chrift fur Nationalokononrie, III, 1932.pp.32-46.

produce more grains, the fertilizer costs go up. In making production decisions in the short-run to decrease or expand production, only variable costs need to be considered. Seed, tractor fuel, repairs, feed, fertilizer cost, other such items represent variable costs. Labour if hired on daily basis is also included in variable costs. If harvesting is done on custom basis, it is a variable cost.

Fixed costs plus variable costs are equal to total costs. Net revenue is equal to total revenue minus total costs. A farmer may have to quit farming if total revenue is not greater than total costs in the long run.

The costs relevant for a particular decision depend upon the nature of the decision under consideration.

Application of the Fixed & Variable Cost Principle

In order to maximise net revenue, variable (or added) costs are the relevant costs to be considered. In this context, profit rules for decisions in the long-run and short-run planning period can be described as under.

In the short run, gross return must cover the variable costs. The maximum net revenue is obtained when marginal cost (MC) equals the price of the product (MR).

If gross returns are less than total costs (variable costs + fixed costs) but are still larger than the variable costs, guiding principle should be to keep increasing production as long as added returns (MR) are greater than added costs (MC).

In the short run, MC = MR point may be at a level of input use which may involve a loss instead of profit. Yet, at this point loss will be minimised. In such a situation, objective should be to minimise losses in the short run. This situation of operating the farms when price or MR is greater than average variable cost but lesser than average total costs is common in agriculture. This explains why the farmers do as they do; why they keep on farming, even when they run into losses.

In the long run, gross return should be more than variable plus fixed costs (total costs). For taking production decisions in such a situation one should go on using resources as long as the added returns remain greater than added total costs. Here the objective is to maximise profit instead of minimising the losses.

Take, for example, an actual farm situation as given in the Table 8.2. In column 2, Rs. 6000 are shown as gross returns against a total costs of Rs. 1200 (variable costs Rs. 480 + fixed costs Rs. 720), giving net returns of Rs. 4800. Suppose the prices of maize decline to 1/6th of prices during the year 1971—72, gross return would be Rs. 1000. If costs remain the same at Rs. 1200, there would be a loss of Rs. 200; but it will be still profitable to keep operating the farm because if farm is not operating, the fixed costs of Rs. 720 will be the loss. If farm is operated, gross income of Rs. 1000 exceeds the variable costs of Rs. 480 by Rs. 520. By this much amount, the loss of Rs. 720/- on account of fixed costs gets reduced. Here the farmer will be minimising his loss.

TABLE 8.2

An Illustration of Maximizing Profits and Minimising Losses on a 10 Acre Maize Farm Situation in I.A.D.P. District, Ludhiana 1971–72.

Particulars	*10 kgs. N per acre (Existing)* (Rs.)	*75 kg* of N per acre on maize desi (budgeted)* (Rs.)	*100 kgs. N per acre on hybrid maize (budgeted)* (Rs.)
1	*2*	*3*	*4*
(*a*) **Fixed Cost**			
(*i*) Land revenue	50.00	50.00	50.00
(*ii*) Building and equipment depreciation and repairs	145.00	145.00	145.00
(*iii*) Interest on average capital investment	225.00	225.00	225.00
(*iv*) Other fixed costs	300.00	300.00	300.00
Total Fixed Costs :	720.00	720.00	720.00
(*b*) **Variable Costs**			
(*i*) Hired labour charges	270.00	285.00	295.00
(*ii*) Seeds	50.00	50.00	150.000
(*iii*) Fertilizers (*a*) C.A.N.	50.00	375.00	500.00
(*b*) others	—	—	—
(*iv*) Custom work	15.00	15.00	15.00
(*v*) Irrigation water charges	60.00	60.00	60.00
(*vi*) Insecticides	15.00	15.00	15.00
(*vii*) Others	20.00	20.00	20.00
Total variable costs	480.00	820.00	1055.00
(*c*) **Total Costs**			
(Fixed + Variable Cost)	1200.00	1540.00	1775.00
Gross return	6000.00	7000.00	7065.00
Net return	4800.00	5460.00	5290.00
Added Costs	—	340.00	235.00
Added Returns (Gross)	—	1000.00	65.00
		Profit 660.00	Loss of Rs.170

* CAN @ Rs. 50/- per quintal .

The added or marginal quantities are more important than total costs or fixed costs. For example, in columns 3 and 4 of Table 8.2 all the other costs are the same except for fertilizer, seeds and labour. With the addition of 75 kgs. of Nitrogen per acre, gross returns increase by Rs. 1000 against marginal cost of Rs. 340, giving an additional net profit of Rs. 660/-. When 100 kgs. of Nitrogen per acre are applied compared to 75 kgs. Nitrogen marginal income increases by Rs. 65, costs go up by Rs. 235, giving a net loss of Rs. 170.

Certain variable costs when incurred or committed become fixed costs. Suppose there is a farmer who has sown one acre of wheat crop. He has already invested Rs. 200 on account of the cost of seed, fertilizer, labour, irrigation and machine-use which cannot be withdrawn at this stage. If the crop gets damaged due to hail storm etc., during its growth period, costs incurred up to this point even though variable, cannot be retrieved. Suppose harvesting costs at this stage are estimated at Rs. 50/- and total returns are Rs. 75/-. In this situation the farmer should consider only the added cost of harvesting. Since the returns are more than these costs, it will be profitable to harvest the crop even though total income per acre may be less than total per-acre costs. In this particular case, the farmer should spend Rs. 50/- to gain Rs. 75/- and minimise his loss by Rs. 25/-. The sum of Rs. 200/ - already spent has become fixed cost and by spending additional Rs. 50/-, the loss of Rs. 200/- will be reduced to Rs. 175/-.

The selling price must therefore be greater than the variable cost of producing each unit of product in the short-run if farming is to be carried on. Over the long period, however, selling price must be greater than the variable cost and fixed cost per unit. Once these costs are covered, farm entrepreneur will not be interested in the average or per unit of cost of production. The marginal or added cost of each increase in production will be then important in determining how far he should go. It will be seldom economical to produce with the lowest per unit cost. The point of lowest average cost is not necessarily, the point of lowest marginal cost and even lowest marginal cost is not the optimum point. The optimum point will be where added returns are equal to the added cost. However, the optimum point can be at the point of lowest per unit cost only in a case where the minimum cost coincides with the maximum profit output. This is the case when selling price or marginal revenue is equal to minimum cost.

PRINCIPLE OF FACTOR-SUBSTITUTION

(Least-cost Combination)

In agriculture, various inputs or practices can be substituted in varying degrees for producing a given output. A producer has to choose a particular combination of inputs which would be most profitable.

At a given level of output, he has to decide upon the least cost-combination of practices or inputs. There are large number of alternatives for performing different farm operations and obtaining output through different combinations of inputs. A few of such alternatives can be (1) use of bullocks vs. tractor for a given size of a farm, (2) harvesting of crops by machines vs. manual labour, (3) milking machines vs. hand milking for a given herd of cows, (4) wheat bhusa, green fodder and grains-mix in dairy feeds, (5) combinations of potash, phosphate and nitrogen in fertilizers for crops.

A number of combinations of concentrates and green fodder, for example, can be used in producing a given amount of milk. Forage usually substitute at diminishing rate for gain. Problem here is to find the least cost combination of green fodders and grains, milk production remaining the same a combination of fodders and grains which, cost remaining the same, will yield maximum output of milk.

Cost minimisation will depend not only upon the cost of inputs and prices of products but also upon the rate of substitution. For example, if hand labour costs less relative to cost of performing the operations by machines, costs may be lowered by substituting labour for machinery. If machine costs are low relative to labour, labour should get substituted with machine operations.

Procedure for Working Out the Least-Cost Combination

Step 1. Compute the substitution ratio (marginal rate of substitution) by dividing the number of units of the replaced resource by the number of units of the added resource :

$$\text{MRS} = \frac{\text{No. of units of replaced resource}}{\text{No. of units of added resource}} = \frac{\Delta X_1}{\Delta X_2}$$

Step 2. Compute the price ratio by dividing the price of the "added" resource by the price of the "replaced" resource :

$$\text{PR} = \frac{\text{Cost per unit of added resource}}{\text{Cost per unit of replaced resource}} = \frac{Px_2}{Px_1}$$

Step 3. Find the point where the substitution ratios and price ratios are equal.

$$\frac{\Delta X_1}{\Delta X_2} = \frac{Px_2}{Px_1} \text{ OR } \Delta X_1 . Px_1 = \Delta X_2 . Px_2$$

Profit Rules.

(*i*) If the substitution ratio is greater than the price ratio, one can reduce the costs by using more of "added" resource.

(*ii*) If the substitution ratio is lesser than the price ratio, costs can be reduced by using more of "replaced" resource.

(*iii*) If the substitution ratio equals the price ratio, it is the point of the least cost.

APPLICATION OF THE PRINCIPLE OF FACTOR-SUBSTITUTION

The rate at which the inputs can be exchanged to maintain a given level of output may be either constant or varying. Given the technical or physical rate of substitution, the least cost combination of resources will differ with different prices. As an example, we consider a simple case of substitution with two variable inputs substitution at either constant or diminishing rate.

Constant Rate of Substitution

Suppose men and women labour substitute at constant rate in 1 : 2 ratio. At different price levels, the cost of hoeing of one acre of crop will be given as in Table 8.3.

In case of wage rate of women labour at Rs. 2/- per day and that of men at Rs. 6/- per day, the price ratio of 3.00 is more than the substitution ratio of 2.00. This means that men labour (costing Rs. 6/- per day) should not replace women labour (costing Rs. 2/- per day) and use of women labour alone will give the lower cost.

In the second case, substitution ratio of 2.00 is greater than price ratio of 1.33. In this case, the farmer should employ men labour alone.

In the third case, Rs. 2.00 value of men labour replaces Rs. 2.00 value of women labour and therefore any combination will cost the same. These three situations are illustrated in Fig. 8.1.

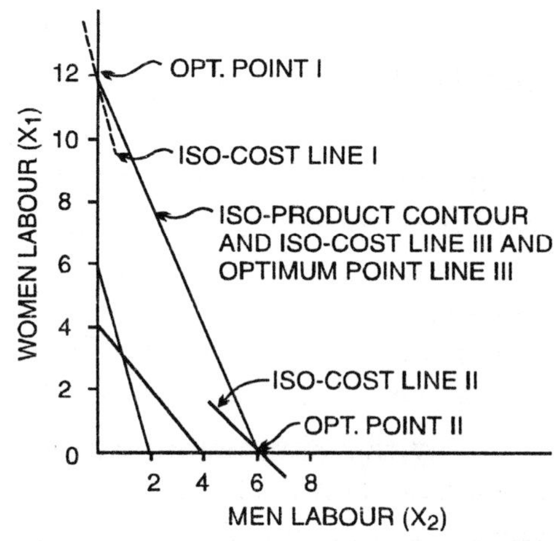

Fig. 8.1 An illustration of substitution of Two variables at constant rate.

TABLE 8.3

Least-Cost Combination of Farm Labour-Use for Hoeing of one Acre of Wheat—Men and Women Labour substituting at a Constant Rate

Combination of labour days for hoeing one acre of wheat		*Added doses of inputs*		*Marginal rate of substitution*	*Cost of hoeing of one acre with different levels of wages for men (Px_2) and women (Px_1)*		
Women Labour (X_1)	*Men Labour (X_2)*	X_1	X_2	$\frac{X_1}{X_2}$	Px_2 @ Rs. 6/- / Px_1 @ Rs. 2/- *(PR = 3.00)*	Px_2 @ Rs. 4/- / Px_1 @ Rs. 3/- *(PR =1.33)*	Px_2 @ Rs. 6/- / Px_1 @ Rs. 3/- *(PR = 2.00)*
(1)	(2)	(3)	(4)	(5)	(6)	(7)	(8)
12	0				24	36	36
10	1	2	1	2	26	34	36
8	2	2	1	2	28	32	36
6	3	2	1	2	30	30	36
4	4	2	1	2	32	28	36
2	5	2	1	2	34	26	36
0	6	2	2	2	36	24	36

PR = Price Ratio

Diminishing Rate of Substitution

Suppose a farmer wants to compute maintenance feed ratio for a two-year old calf from two feed stuffs namely green fodder and wheat 'bhusa'. Price of green fodder and wheat 'bhusa' differs in different seasons and the two fodders substitute for each other at diminishing rate as detailed in the Table 8.4.

With a diminishing rate of substitution, least-cost combination is less often realised by using only one input. Here again, costs are at the minimum, when the substitution ratio is equal to price ratio.

In Table 8.4, under the first set of prices, cost is the lowest at the 5th combination when

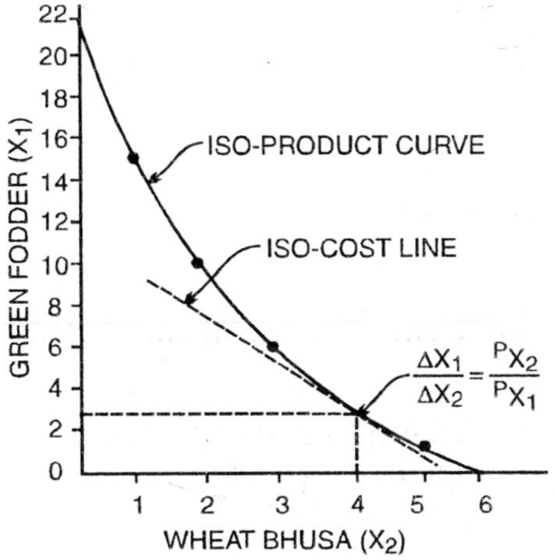

Fig. 8.2. An illustration of substitution of two variables at Diminishing rate.

the price ratio is 2.66 and substitution ratio 3.00. The 4th combination is more costly than the 5th because Re. 0.08 value of wheat bhusa replaces Re. 0.12 value of green fodder. Bhusa, therefore, should be added further. Sixth combination is more costly than the 5th, because Rs. 0.08 value of bhusa replaces only Re. 0.06 value of fodder and it pays not to replace fodder by bhusa. Therefore, 5th combination gives us the least cost combination of fodder and bhusa.

TABLE 8.4

Least Cost Combination of Green Fodder and Wheat 'bhusa' for a Two-year old calf—Two products substituting at Diminishing Rate

Combination of fodders		*Marginal Changes*		*Marginal rate of substi-tution*	*Cost of maintenance of the calf with prices*		
Green fodder (kgs.) X_1	*Wheat bhusa (Kgs.)* X_2	X_1	X_2	$\frac{\Delta X_1}{\Delta X_2}$	*Bhusa @ 8P/kg. Fodder @ 3 P/kg. (Price Ratio = 2.66)*	*Bhusa @ 7P/kg. Fodder @ 4P/kg. (Price Ratio = 1.75)*	*Bhusa 8P/kg. Fodder 2P/kg. (Price Ratio = 4.00)*
(1)	*(2)*	*(3)*	*(4)*	*(5)*	*(6)*	*(7)*	(8)
21	0				63	84	42
15	1	6	1	6	53	67	38
10	2	5	1	5	46	54	36
4	3	4	1	4	42	45	36
5	4	3	1	3	41	40	38
1	5	2	1	2	43	39	42
0	6	1	1	1	48	42	48

Under the second set of prices, the 6th combination gives the lowest cost when price ratio is 1.75 and substitution ratio 2.00. All other combinations are more costly.

Special Cases of Substitution

There are certain practices which substitute for others and also add to the output at the same time. An example is of hybrid maize seed replacing 'desi' maize seed. Hybrid maize uses about the same quantity of seed but produces more yield per acre. Here it may increase the cost but it adds more to the value of the production than it adds to the cost. The superiority of the substitute practice is established not only by the cost of the new practices but also by the value of the added yield. In estimating the profitability of such practices, budgeting technique becomes more useful. It is a case of shift in the production function.

LAW OF EQUI-MARGINAL RETURNS

If the farmer had access to any amount of working capital and labour and could expand his acreage and building facilities etc., as far as he wished, he would not have any difficulty in deciding which commodities to produce ; he would not even compare one enterprise with another. Instead he would produce all crops and livestock products physically possible in his locality, considering weather, climate, soil and other physical factors. The decision rule would be simple ; select all products which can be produced and expand output as long as the added returns are greater than added costs. But choice on the number and size of enterprises in this manner cannot be made because resources are limited. Expansion of one enterprise or practice generally requires an equivalent contraction in another. The question is 'which enterprise or combination of enterprises will give the highest income ?' Such an optimum choice of enterprises is made based on the principle of equi-marginal returns or the principle of opportunity cost. Profits will be the greatest if each unit of labour, capital and land is used where it adds the most of the returns. In other words, this principle lays down : the best combination of enterprises or practices will be where limited resources are allocated in a manner that one cannot change the use of a single unit without reducing the income. This principle, thus, states that resources should be used where they bring not only the greatest average returns, but also the greatest marginal returns. For an illustration of this principle, suppose a farmer has Rs. 5000; he can grow crops, raise dairy or poultry. His problem will be : what amount of capital he should invest on each enterprise to get highest profit. The problem is illustrated in Table 8.5.

TABLE 8.5

Marginal Returns to Capital on Three Enterprises

Amount of capital used (Rs.)	*Marginal Returns (Rs.)*		
	Crops	*Dairy*	*Poultry*
1000	1300	1400	1500
2000	1300	1200	1250
3000	1200	1100	1100
4000	1200	900	1000
5000	1100	.800	900
Total returns from Rs. 5000/-	6100	5400	5750
Net Profit	1100	400	750
Average returns per rupee invested	1.21	1.08	1.15

Average returns will be the highest if the whole amount is spent on crops with gross returns at Rs. 6100/- and profits Rs. 1100/-. The marginal returns will, however, dictate spending of this money as under.

Amount	Enterprise	Added Returns
First Rs. 1000/-	Poultry	1500
Second Rs. 1000/-	Dairy	1400
Third Rs. 1000/-	Crops	1300
Fourth Rs. 1000/-	Crops	1300
Fifth Rs. 1000/-	Poultry	1250
Total Returns from Rs. 5000/-	—	6750
Net Profit	—	1750/-

So this principle dictates that the resources should be used not where they bring the highest average returns, but where they yield the highest marginal returns. The best combination of enterprises is attained not when we select profitable crops, but when we select the most profitable crops. The profitability of an enterprise depends on the price of the product the direct costs attached to the enterprise and the amount of product sacrificed as one enterprise gets replaced with the other.

For the application of this principle, one needs data on prices of products, direct costs attached to each enterprise and also amount of production sacrificed when one enterprise is replaced with the other. Budgeting or programming techniques take this principle into consideration for working out an optimum production plan.

OPPORTUNITY COST PRINCIPLE

The farm resources are always limited and there are more than one alternative to use these resources. When resources are used in one product, some alternative is always foregone. The opportunity cost is the value of the next best alternative foregone. The value of one enterprise (sacrificed) is the cost of producing another enterprise.

The opportunity cost principle, thus, refers to advantages (returns) which might have been obtained from any factor if it had not been used in producing that commodity, but would have been used for other next best purpose. If a cultivator, for example, has Rs. 800/- for investment in his farm business, he will make a choice from various alternative uses to which this money could be put. He might have the following alternatives.

(*i*) Purchase of a buffalo giving net returns Rs. 80/- *i.e.* 10% returns on the funds invested (after making the allowances of interest and depreciation and up-keep etc.)

(*ii*) Purchase of a water lift on 5-acres farm ; net return Rs. 100/- (12.5% returns on investment).

(*iii*) Invest on a bullock cart for transporting his produce to the market, thereby increasing share in the consumers' rupee—a net return of Rs. 60/- (7·5% returns).

The farmer gets the highest return of Rs. 100/- from use in water lift as compared to Rs. 80/- on the purchase of a buffalo and Rs. 60/- from investment on the cart. Opportunity cost of choosing one alternative, is to surrender the next best alternative. In simple terms it is the cost equivalent to the returns from next best alternative foregone.

PRINCIPLE OF COMBINING ENTERPRISES

A farm manager is often confronted with the problem as to what enterprise to select, and the level at which each enterprise should be taken up. How far he can go or should go in combining one enterprise with another enterprise or replacing one enterprise with another, depends partly on the interrelationships between different enterprises and the prices of products and inputs.

Types of Product Relationships

The enterprises can have any one or combinations of the following relationships.

1. Independent enterprises
2. Competitive enterprises.
3. Supplementary enterprises.
4. Complementary enterprises.
5. Joint enterprises.

Independent enterprise are those which have no direct bearing on each other ; an increase in the level of one neither helps nor hinders the level of the other. Such a relationships is rare and is possible with practically unlimited supplies of inputs. In such cases, each product should be treated separately.

Joint products are those which are produced together *e.g.*, cotton and cotton seed, beef and hides, wheat and straw, mutton and wool, cattle and manure, etc. The quantity of one product produced decides the quantity of the other product.

In case of joint products there is no economic decision to make with respect to the combination of products and the two products can be treated as one. In the long run, however, changes in the relative prices of the two products may necessitate a change in the product combination. For instance, a continued increase in the price of wool compared to the price of mutton may necessitate a change in the quality of the breeds which would produce a higher proportion of wool. Once this happens the proportions of the two products become fixed.

Competitive Enterprise

Competitive enterprises are those which compete for use of the farmer's limited resources. Use of a resource to produce more of one necessitates a sacrifice in the quantity of the other product.

When enterprises are competitive, three things determine the exact combination of the products which would be the most profitable.

(*i*) The rate at which one enterprise substitutes for the other,

(*ii*) The prices of the products, and

(*iii*) The cost of producing the products.

The rate at which one product substitutes for another is known as the marginal rate of substitution. Two products can substitute for each other at :

(*i*) Constant rates of substitution

(*ii*) Decreasing rates of substitution, and

(*iii*) Increasing rates of substitution.

Constant Rate of Substitution between Products

The production possibility curve in this case would be a straight line. It means that unit change in one product is accompanied by the opposite change in the other product at the same rate throughout. For example, two crops (gram and wheat) substitute at constant rate for land. This relationships can be expressed as :

$$\frac{\Delta Y_{12}}{\Delta Y_{11}} = \frac{\Delta Y_{22}}{\Delta Y_{21}} = \ldots\ldots \frac{\Delta Y_{n2}}{\Delta Y_{n1}}$$

For diagrammatic presentation, see Figure 7.4. For finding out an optimum combination of two products, we need to work out the following :

(*i*) Substitution ratio $= \frac{\text{Amount of replaced product}}{\text{Amount of added product}} = \frac{\Delta Y_2}{\Delta Y_1}$

(*ii*) Price ratio $= \frac{\text{Price of added product}}{\text{Price of replaced product}} = \frac{P_{Y1}}{P_{Y2}}$

Optimum point of the combination of the two products will be located where :

$$\frac{\Delta Y_2}{\Delta Y_1} = \frac{P_{Y1}}{P_{Y2}}$$

Rule. In this situation of constant rate of substitution, profit can be maximised by producing only one product or otherwise maximum profit will be indifferent to the combination of enterprises.

Example. Suppose a farmer has two competing crops to produce, *i.e.* maize and cotton on a 10 acre farm. For simplicity we assume the cost of production per acre of these two crops to be the same. With the help of the following data in Table 8.6., we can find out optimum combination of these two products.

TABLE 8.6

Determination of Maximum Revenue giving Combination of Two products with Constant Rate of Substitution

Production Possibility combinations		*Marginal rate of product substitution*	*Returns*	
Maize (Y_2- Yield 12 qtls) (acres)	*Cotton (Y_1- Yield 6 qtls) (acres)*	$\frac{\Delta Y_2}{\Delta Y_1}$	*Maize @ Rs. 70/- Qtl. Cotton @ Rs. 150/Qtl.* $\left(\frac{P_{Y1}}{P_{Y2}} = 2.14\right)$	*Maize @ Rs. 80/- Qtl. Cotton @ Rs. 150/Qtl.* $\left(\frac{P_{Y1}}{P_{Y2}} = 1.87\right)$
4	0		3360	3840
3	1	2	3420	3780
2	2	2	3480	3720
1	3	2	3540	3660
0	4	2	3600	3600

From this table, we can easily find out the optimum combination of two products by comparing the marginal rate of substitution with the price ratio.

If marginal rate of substitution is greater than price ratio; $\frac{\Delta Y_2}{\Delta Y_1} > \frac{P_{Y1}}{P_{Y2}}$ (last column), Y_2 will be profitable.

If marginal rate of substitution is less than price ratio $\left(\frac{\Delta Y_2}{\Delta Y_1} < \frac{P_{Y1}}{P_{Y2}}\right)$ will be more profitable.

If marginal rate of substitution equals price ratio, any combination of the enterprises will give the same profit.

Decreasing Rate of Substitution between Products

When two products are substituting at a decreasing rate, the production possibility curve is convex to the origin. It means a unit increase in one product is accompanied by less and less decrease in the level of other product. Such conditions are seldom found in agriculture. This relationships can be expressed as under :

$$\frac{\Delta_{12}}{\Delta_{11}} > \frac{\Delta Y_{22}}{\Delta Y_{21}} > ..... > \frac{\Delta Y_{n2}}{\Delta Y_{n1}}$$

Rule. Under such conditions, maximum profits can be obtained by producing only one of the two products. A combination of the two products will not yield maximum profits since successive increases of one unit in the production of one product requires the sacrifice of smaller and smaller quantities of the other product. One reason for the production possibility curve to be convex is that the cost limits the use of variable input in such small quantities that both products are produced in state I. *i.e.* the area of increasing marginal physical productivity.

Increasing Rates of Substitution between Two Products

Where two products are substituting at an increasing rate, the production possibility curve is concave to the origin. It means that each unit increase in level of one product accompanied by more and more decrease in the level of another product. For example, wheat and gram substitute at increasing rate for capital or labour which means when wheat acreage is increased, gram acreage will have to be decreased more and more for the purpose of releasing capital. The increasing marginal rate of substitution can be expressed as :

$$\frac{\Delta Y_{12}}{\Delta Y_{11}} < \frac{\Delta Y_{22}}{\Delta Y_{21}} < ..... < \frac{\Delta Y_{n2}}{\Delta Y_{n1}}$$

Rule. In such a situation, profits are maximised by producing a combination of the two products where substitution ratio equals the price ratio.

Example. Suppose a farmer can grow paddy and cotton on his 10 acre farm. For simplicity, we assume the cost of production per acre of these two crops to be the same, and work out gross returns of the different production combinations as in Table 8.7. Even without calculating the gross returns, we can find out the optimum combination of two products by comparing their physical substitution ratio with their price ratio. At the point, they are equal, the combination of the two products will give the maximum revenue.

TABLE 8.7

Determination of the Optimum Combination of Two Competing Products assuming Same Costs per Acre for Each Crop and Increasing Rate of Substitution

Production possibilities				*Marginal rate of product substitution*	*Gross Returns*
Paddy Y_2		*Cotton Y_1*			*Paddy @ Rs. 60 per qunital*
Acres	*Yield qtls.*	*Acres*	*Yield qtls.*	$MRS = \frac{\Delta Y_2}{\Delta Y_1}$	*Cotton @ Rs. 150 per quintal* $\left(\frac{P_{Y1}}{P_{Y2}} = 2.5\right)$
5	60	0	0		3600
4	48	1	6	2.0	3780
3	36	2	11	2.4	3810
2	24	3	15	3.0	3690
1	12	4	18.5	3.4	3495
0	0	5	21.5	4.0	3225

Maximum returns are realised where the physical rate of product substitution between two products is equal to their inverse price ratio. In this case, the gross returns of Rs. 3810 will be the maximum, with a combination of 3 acres of paddy and 2 acres of cotton.

Note.

(*i*) If the two crops have different costs, the ratio of net prices should be compared with the substitution ratio.

(*ii*) The combination of enterprise which is profitable in one year need not be the most profitable next year because of changes in the price relationships.

Supplementary Enterprises

Two products are said to be supplementary when an increase in the level of one does not adversely affect the production of the other but adds to the total income of the farm. *i.e.* enterprises which do not compete with each other but add to the total income. For example on many small farms, a small dairy enterprise, a poultry enterprise or a small bee-keeping enterprise may be supplementary to the main crop enterprise, because they utilise surplus family labour and shelter available and perhaps even some feeds which would otherwise go to waste. In the beginning, such enterprises are added in order to fully utilise the available resources but when they are expanded far, they become competitive for the inputs. When two products are supplementary, both the products should be produced upto the end of the supplementary stage. As long as the returns added by each enterprise is greater than its costs, the relative prices of two products are not important.

Sometimes enterprises are supplementary for one resource competitive for another. In such cases, the relationship should be treated as one of competitive even though they are supplementary to one another in respect of other resource (s).

Complementary Enterprises

Complementary enterprises are those which add to the production of each other, *e.g.* Berseem and Maize crops. Two products are complementary when the transfer of a variable input from the production of one product to the production of the other results in an increase in the production of both products. When two crops are complementary enterprises, the use of resources for the two crops results in the increased production of both the crops.

This relationship exists only when one enterprise produces an element which is required in the production of another enterprises *e.g.* legumes and grasses become complementary to grain crops when the former (1) furnish nitrogen, (2) control soil erosion, and/or (3) maintain or improve soil tilth to the extent that greater production of grain crops become possible over time on the same acreage.

Two enterprise do not remain complementary over all possible combinations. They become competitive at some stage. When both complementary and competitive relationships occur, the complementary relationships occurs first and then is followed by the competitive relationship.

When two products are complementary, both the enterprises should be produced upto the end of the complementarity stage without reference to the prices of the two products. When they enter the competitive stage, the substitution ratio and the price ratio of the two products should be considered and the optimum combination determined as in the case of competitive enterprises.

Principle of Comparative Advantage

According to this well known principle, different areas will tend to produce those products for which they have the greatest comparative, and not just absolute advantage. This leads to the establishment of different types of farming existing in a particular area.

TIME COMPARISON PRINCIPLE

Farm management involves dynamic adjustment of the farm organisation and operations. Such an adjustment relates to taking account of (*a*) time element in the calculation of present value of future incomes and (*b*) the risks and uncertainties involved in farm operations over time.

The first adjustment involves a method of discounting the future returns. The rate of discounting will perhaps be lower for a farmer with unlimited capital than for a farmer with limited capital.

The risks and uncertainties are a general rule in agriculture. While some risks are insurable, the others are not. The most important risks and uncertainties occur due to natural calamities, fluctutions in prices of inputs and outputs and changes brought about by innovations and other technological improvements. Producers tend to discount returns to adjust for these uncertainties. Some farmers are security minded and are averse of taking risks. Such farmers will be reluctant to adopt new practices or enterprises. Thus, they discount for the uncertainties at a very high rate.

Time has a very siginificant influence on costs and returns and as a result involves considerations which should be recognised in managerial decisions. There are many decision situations where this principle finds application, such as : soil conservation programmes which bear fruit over a long time; use of land for growing crops or putting it under an orchard which may not give returns for 5-10 years ; purchasing of dairy cows in milk by paying more or purchasing heifers and raising them till they begin to produce etc.

Two aspects of the problem are considered under such situations . (*a*) growth of a cash outlay over time, and (*b*) discounting of future income.

Growth of a Cash Outlay

The cash outlay grows over time due to the compounding of interest charges or opportunity costs involved in using the capital : If Rs. 100 are put in a savings-account with annual interest at 5% compounded, it will increase or grow to Rs. 127.63 by the end of five years. A cash outlay or investment made in a farm business grows over time in a similar manner. Farm improvements, machinery, breeding stock, milk cows are examples. While such items depreciate over time, growth of the remaining capital invested has to be considered in the analysis whether the investment will be profitable. For example, it costs Rs. 30/- per acre to grow nepier grass which would be in production for three years, with one-third of the capital outlay charged off each year. Thus, one third of the Rs. 30/- (Rs. 10/-) would be invested for one year, another Rs. 10/- for two years and Rs. 10/- for three years. The value of this investment would grow to Rs. 33.10 by the end of the three-year period. Thus Rs. 33.10 would be the appropriate cost to use in determining whether it would pay to plant nepier grass.

Since costs grow as a result of interest or opportunity cost accumulations, the equation for compounding interest may be used to show growth in the cash outlay :

$$S = s\,(1 + i)^n$$

'S' represents the sum at the end of 'n' periods ; 's' the amount which is invested for 'n' periods ; 'i' the interest rate.

Discounting Income

Discounting income is the procedure whereby the present value of the future income is determined. The concept is the reverse of "growth in value" due to accrued interest. Thus, with interest rate at 5%, Re. 1.00 today grows to Rs. 1.05 in a year and conversely, Rs. 1.05 a year from now is worth only Re. 1.00 today.

Formula : $$PV=\frac{q}{(1+r)^n}$$

PV = Present value of the future amount,

q = future amount

r = rate of interest

n = No. of years in the future.

Example. A farmer wants to purchase a Tractor. The alternatives are,

1. Purchase a new tractor for Rs. 25000/- that will last 10 years.
2. Purchase an old tractor for Rs. 15000/- and replace it after 5 years with another old tractor worth Rs. 15000/-. This means that he shall have to invest Rs. 15000/- now and lay aside an amount which will become Rs. 15000/- within 5 years to replace the old tractor.

(A) Farmer with unlimited capital has the opportunity of lending the money at usual interest rate, say 5%.

$$PV = \frac{15,000}{(1.05)^5} = \text{Rs. } 11,760/-$$

His comparison is Rs. 25000/- for new tractor and Rs. 15000/- plus Rs. 11760/– (Rs. 26760) for old tractor. The new tractor is profitable for the farmer with unlimited capital.

(B) Farmer with limited capital has an opportunity of investing money in poultry and can make a return of 15 percent within the year. His discounting rate will be 15 per cent *i.e.* opportunity cost of not using money for poultry.

$$PV = \frac{15,000}{(1.15)^5} = \text{Rs. } 7455/-$$

His comparison is Rs. 25000/- for new tractor and Rs. 15000/- plus Rs. 7455/- (Rs. 22455/-) for old tractor. The old tractor is profitable for farmer with limited capital.

Example 2. A farmer wants to purchase one power thresher. He has the following alternatives to follow ;

1. Purchase a new power thresher for Rs. 3000/- which will last for 10 years.

2. Purchase an old thresher for Rs. 1800/- and replace it after 5 years with another old thresher worth Rs. 1800/-

Suggest him the appropriate course of action :

(*i*) If the farmer has unlimited capital— only opportunity of lending the money at usual interest rate, of say 5%.

(*ii*) If the farmer has limited capital—has opportunity of investing money in dairy and may make return of 20 percent within the year.

We can easily calculate the present value of future incomes using the Table 8.8 and make quick comparison of the two alternative methods of investments.

TABLE 8.8

Present Value of Rupee One of Cost or Income for Years and Discount Rates Indicated.

	Interest or Discount Rate									
Year	2.0	3.00	5.00	6.00	8.00	10.00	15.00	20.00	25.00	30.00
1	.980	.971	.952	.943	.926	.909	.870	.833	.800	.769
2	.961	.943	.907	.890	.857	.826	.756	.694	.640	.592
3	.942	.915	.864	.840	.794	.751	.751	.658	.579	.512
4	.924	.888	.823	.792	.735	.683	.572	.482	.410	.350
5	.906	.863	.784	.747	.681	.621	.497	.402	.328	.269
10	.820	.744	.614	.658	.463	.386	.247	.162	.107	.073
15	.743	.642	.481	.417	.315	.239	.123	.065	.035	.020
20	.673	.554	.377	.312	.258	.148	.061	.026	.012	.005

(*a*) Farmer with unlimited capital.

Alternative I	(*i*)	Purchase an old thresher @	Rs. 1800.00
	(*ii*)	Purchase another old thresher by depositing Rs. 1800 $\times .747 = 1344.60$ in bank @ 6% rate of interest	Rs. 1344.60
		Total amount	Rs. 3144.60

Alternative II Purchase of a new power thresher for Rs. 3000.

In this case, second alternative is superior.

(*b*) Farmer with limited capital and has opportunity of investing money in dairy enterprise and earn 20%. For him,

Alternative I.	(*i*)	Purchase an old thresher	Rs. 1800.00
	(*ii*)	Purchase another old thresher after 5 years by (Rs. 1800 × .402 = Rs. 723.60) in Dairy to 20%	Rs. 723.60
		Total Amount	Rs. 2523.60
Alternative II		Purchase of a new thresher.....	Rs. 3000.00

In this case, it is profitable to purchase two old threshers instead of one new thresher. There are numerous such examples where this analysis can be applied.

Limitations of the Principles of Farm Management

An important assumption underlying the economics of farm management is that the producers aim at maximising net income. In India, a large number of farmers have small operational holdings. One of the most important objective behind the farm plan of most of the small farmers remains consumption. The small farmers generally take a long term decision on what to produce, how to produce or how much to produce. With little to buy and sell in the market, they have not to make such decisions as 'when to buy and sell and where to buy and sell'. Further, the resources at the command of small farmers are extremely limited. This sets a limit to their capacity to produce. Hence, they try to concentrate their resource on the production of food required for family consumption. The only resource available in plenty is generally the family labour, but there is a limit of its utilisation without the availability of complementary capital The small farmers, therefore, continue to adopt traditional methods of production which involve no new investment. Thus, the range of technological or economic alternatives open to these farmers is very small. Consequently, the possibility of improving the farm organisation through the application of the principles of farm management remains limited.

Despite the above limitations, farm management has an important role to play under Indian conditions. Even though majority of the farmers produce mainly for subsistence, they can aim at maximisation of the gross production rather than of net income. Through time as the supply of scarce resources like improved seeds, fertilizers, pesticides, credit, etc. development of communication and market facilities, dissemination of information on market intelligence, better techniques, better combination of crops, better rotation of crops, etc., improve, the farmers would become more and more commercial minded, and they would be able to effect technological and economic adjustments aimed at stepping up production and net income. Farm management principles are, therefore, likely to gain greater applicational value in the near future.

The general environment for decision making can be speedily improved on the following lines :

(*i*) Research and extension efforts directed towards supplying needed economic and technical information to the farmer- decision maker.

(*ii*) Investing in education for better decision making, and

(*iii*) Reducing the uncertainty and expanding the planning horizon.

Some decision making functions can be specialised by institutions or organisations such as Farm Management Consultancy Service. Examples of U.K., U.S.A. and Yugoslavia are worth noting in this direction.

1. ***Discuss the difference between diminishing physical and diminishing economic returns.***
2. ***Is fixity of a factor or factors necessary in diminishing economic returns ?***
3. ***Why is the emphasis placed on additional economic returns ?***
4. ***Do the lowest average costs and highest marginal returns occur at the same point ? Discuss.***
5. ***Explain what is meant by the point of marginal returns. Can you determine the point by knowing the cost of the factors but not the price of the product ?***
6. ***What economic principles are involved in determining the combination of resources ?***
7. ***How do farmers obtain flexibility in fixed costs ?***
8. ***Why is added or marginal cost rather than average cost so important in making decisions ?***
9. ***Explain how the opportunity cost or equi-marginal returns principle involve the farm organisation as a whole.***
10. ***Demonstrate with the help of a suitable example, the application of the principle of substitution of resources or practices where they substitute at constant rate.***
11. ***Define the following :***

    (a) Complementary enterprises, (b) Supplementary enterprises,

    (c) Competitive enterprises, (d) Joint products.
12. ***Explain with the help of a suitable example, how to determine the optimum combination of two competing products to maximise the net returns.***

13. *State four examples where principle of time comparison can be applied. Demonstrate the application of this principle for a farmer who wants to purchase one combine harvester for his farm business. Take hypothetical data for illustration.*

Assignment

14. *Find out how one should utilise Rs. 1500/- among different crop-enterprises to get greatest profit, given the following data.*

Amount of money spent		*Added returns from using different amounts of capital for three enterprises*		
Marginal	*Total*	*Hybrid Maize*	*Paddy*	*Cotton*
250	(250)	425	375	325
250	(500)	350	325	280
250	(750)	325	290	275
250	(1000)	320	270	255
250	(1250)	315	260	252
250	(1500)	302	255	250
—	—	—	—	—
Total Returns		—	—	—
Average return per Re. invested		—	—	—
Net Profit		—	—	—

Decision.

15. *Complete/delete/correct/use the most appropriate words in the following :*
    (i) *In the short run, the objective in farming should be to cover fixd costs/ variable costs/total costs.*
    (ii) *Profit rule for taking decisions regarding the level of production under the law of diminishing returns is...................................*
    (iii) *The constant productivity resources is found under the following two situations.*
        (1) ....
        (2) ....
    (iv) *The following threee factors can delay the operation of the diminishing returns in agriculture.*
        (1) ....
        (2) ....
        (3) ....

(v) *When one enterprise neither adds nor hinders the production of another enterprise, the production relationship is known as supplementary/independent/complementary/competitive.*

(vi) *When two resources substitute at diminishing rates, the least cost combination will be obtained normally, by using a combination of two resources/only one resource/where MRS = PR.*

(vii) *Marginal product refers to...*

(viii) *When two resources substitute at constant rate, the following three rules guide us to find out the least cost combination of factors of production.*

(1) ....

(2) ....

(3) ....

(ix) *The increasing productivity holds true mainly where...........*

(x) *The principle of "equi-marginal returns" states that the profits will be greatest, if each unit of labour, capital and land is used where it.........................*

1. *Forster, G.W., "Farm Organisation and Management". New York Prentice-Hall Inc. ; 1953.*
2. *Heady, E.O., "Economics of Agricultural Production and Resources Use". New York : Prentice-Hall, Inc., 1952.*
3. *Heady, Earl O. and Harald R. Jenson, "Farm Management Economics". Englewood Cliffs, N.J., Prentice-Hall, Inc., 1954, Chapter 4.*
4. *Bradford, Lawerence A. and Glenn L. Johnson, "Farm Management Analysis", New York, John Wiley & Sons, Inc., 1953, Chapter 8 and 9.*
5. *Indian Society of Agril. Economics "Seminar on Farm Production Planning and Programming", Indian Society of Agril. Economics, Bombay, 1965.*
6. *Indian Journal of Agril, Economics : Conference Number 1963.*

9 Tools of Farm Management Analysis

In the light of the economic factors and farm management principles outlined in the preceding chapter, it is possible to re-organise the farm business so as to produce a more efficient and profitable system. The objective of this chapter is to demonstrate the application of some common techniques or tools used in the farm planning process, to maximise the farm income under various sets of farm situations.

FARM PLANNING

All business undertakings, ranging from a few rupee corner shop to the large commercial firms, plan their production and marketing operations consciously with a discriminating intellect in respect of what, how much and how to produce, and when and where to buy and sell. The planning of the operations and their execution is the secret of their economic success. Unfortunately our farmers are not that business-minded. If, however, agriculture is to play a real role in the development of the economy, the farmers have got to consider farming as a business undertaking.

With the recent technological development in agriculture, farming has become more complex business and requires careful planning for successful operations. Most farmers probably have some kinds of plans about the organisation and operation of their farms. Perhaps, in most cases, they are not very systematically worked out, they may be based largely on habits or customs. The farm boy learns the cropping pattern followed by his father and his neighbours and tends to follow more or less the same pattern himself. But here we are interested in scientific planning—planning that is systematic, written and based on the best information available and aimed at achieving the maximum of satisfaction for the farmer and his family out of their resources. It is the deliberate and conscious effort on the part of the farmer to think about the farm programmes in advance and adjust them according to new knowledge on technological developments, changes in physical and economic situations, price structures, etc. Farm planning process, thus, introduces a measure of economic content into farming business. Those who cannot make rational decisions and need adjustments will find the farming not a profitable proposition for them. The various advantages of farm planning can be grouped under the following heads :

1. Income improvements

Farm planning approach is an integrated, coordinated and advance programme of actions which seek to present an opportunity to cultivators to improve his level of income. It is his opportunity of income maximisation which induces farmers to adopt desirable changes. Such income maximisations could be achieved from a given bundle of resources by re-organising present type of production as well as introduction of changes in technology.

Many studies conducted in India have shown that farm incomes can be appreciably increased through careful planning of production programmes of the farms even with the existing production techniques available to the cultivators. Some of the studies conducted in the department of Economics and Sociology, Punjab Agricultural University, Ludhiana have shown big potential of increasing income through farm planning (see Table 1.1)

2. Educational process

Farm planning is an educational tool to bring a change in the outlook of the cultivators and the extension workers. Knowledge of the latest technological advances in agriculture is a pre- requisite for better farm planning ; so farmers keep their information up-to-date through this forced action situation of farm planning process. This acts as a self-educating tool for the farmers. The farmers can closely study their own business and see more clearly their opportunities and limitations, thus, improving their managerial ability.

3. Desirable organisational changes

Farm planning is an approach which introduces desirable changes in farm organisation and operations and makes the farm a viable unit. In its broad sense, it may mean any contemplated change in the method or practices followed on the farm; or it may mean the complete re-organisation of the farm business. The advantage of farm planning approach lies in its treating the farm as an operational unit and tailoring the recommendations to fit into the individual farmers' opportunities, limitations, problems and resource position.

How Farm Planning Helps

Basically, farm planning helps the cultivator to do the following things in an organised, systematic and effective way :

1. It helps the farmer to think about him and gather ideas on the alternative methods and practices which might be useful to him in his farming business.
2. It helps him to examine carefully his existing resource situation and past experiences as a basis for deciding which of the new alternative enterprises and methods fit his situation the best.
3. Within the framework of new ideas and opportunities and his own resource position, it helps him make rational decisions on what to do.
4. It helps him to identify clearly the various supply needs for his alternative improved plan, *i.e.*, estimation of the requirements of seeds, fertilizer, plant protection materials etc.
5. It helps him to find out the credit needs, if any, of the new plan.
6. It gives him an idea of the expected income after paying off his loans, etc. The increased income from the new plan might act as an incentive for better future planning.

Farm planning is thus a process of making decisions regarding the organisation and operation of a farm business so that it results in a continuous maximisation of net returns of a farm business.

Objectives of Farm Planning

The ultimate objective of farm planning is the improvement in the standard of living of the farmer and immediate goal is to maximise the net income of the farmer through improved resource use planning.

It is generally assumed in farm planning that a farmer is primarily interested in maximising his net income. This is probably valid for most farmers, as a higher net income provides him the means for satisfying many of his wants. It is a convenient convention, therefore, to evaluate a plan on the basis of the net income that can be derived from it. This can be easily estimated by budgeting. But while this is convenient, we are by no means restricted to this objective. We could just as well direct economic analysis at maximising security, minimising risk or minimising labour requirements. We will, however, for convenience in the short time, confine ourselves largely to planning for maximum net income. By working out several alternative plans the farmer can, of course, make his choice on the basis of several objectives.

When the objective is maximisation of net income, it involves commonly called “the planning horizon”. The length of the planning period on the basis of the farmers situation has to be, therefore, decided. The main objective is to maximise the annual net income sustained over a long period of time.

Why is a written plan needed ?

"The improved farm planning is a process of observation, appraisal and analysis of weighing the merits of new and old ideas and then deciding which ideas to use in the period ahead."[1] This process is learnt much better if the results of the thinking and reasoning are written down in a simple but organised way. This is the main reason for using various farm planning proforma (written forms). The proforma are not, however, a substitute for logical thinking and reasoning but are an aid to it.

We generally observe that every farmer whether progressive or backward, literate or illiterate, decides about his whole farm every year in the beginning of each crop season as to what crops he will sow in each field, what methods will he use to grow the chosen crops and how and where will he sell. Most farmers do not feel the necessity of writing these decisions on paper. They still do planning and budgeting, but it is mental rather than written form. The farmers with long experience and particularly having a simple and small business organisation may be able to do planing this way. But farming has now become more complex because of the rapid changes that are coming in physical, social and economic set up. It is practically impossible for farmers to simply remember all the figures necessary for setting up a complete farm budget in their minds. To be more systematic or organised in thinking and reasoning in farm planning, the farmers must have a written farm plan. A written farm plan should, therefore, show the crops to be grown, the livestock to be raised, the practices to be followed in their production, the programme for the use of labour, the investment to be made in equipment and machinery and similar other details about the use of farm-resources.

Who is to make farm plan ?

When an architect develops a blue-print for a house, he must know a great deal about the house builder. He needs to know what features will please his client, whether he is interested in appearance, functional qualities, durability or in-expensiveness. Most home builders are interested in all these features; but these objectives are often somewhat in conflict. A more durable house may be more expensive, a more functional house may be less beautiful, etc. Therefore, some of these objectives will usually have to be compromised. Since different people place different values on all these features, a good architect will plan the house with the builder rather than for him. It is much the same with farm planning.

1. Malon, Carl C., "Farm Planning..its purpose and method", Farm Management Training, Report of the First Central Training Course for District Farm Management Specialists in I.A.D.P. (New Delhi, Ministry of Food and Agriculture, 1962), pp. 76-82.

Farmers have many objectives. They want low risks, low investment, a certain amount of leisure time, security, high net income this year and in future years. It is usually not possible to maximise all these goals at once. Maximum net income 5 to 10 years from now may be achievable only by sacrificing some net income in current and the next few years. High income will usually involve greater risk than low one and will usually require heavier investments. More leisure will usually be at the cost of lower earnings, etc. Different farmers put different values on each of these and, therefore, one cannot develop a suitable plan for a farmer without knowing how he wants to compromise these objectives. One, therefore, will have to plan a farm with the farmer.

The decision-making should also rest with the farmer because it is he who will gain or lose by implementing the decisions. Moreover, the farmer would be more willing in implementing the decision made by himself than when it is made by someone else for him.

Principal Characteristics of a Good Farm Plan

Under the Indian conditions, a good typical farm plan should have the following characteristics and information :

1. It should provide for efficient use of farm resources such as, labour, power and equipment.
2. The crop plan should have balanced combinations of enterprises, *i.e.*, it should :
   (*i*) provide for given minimum production of different food, cash and fodder crops,
   (*ii*) help maintain and improve soil fertility,
   (*iii*) help raise and stabilise farm earnings, and
   (*iv*) improve distribution and use of labour, power and water requirements throughout the year.
3. Avoid excessive risks.
4. Provide flexibility.
5. Utilise the farmer's knowledge, training and experience and take account of the farmer's likes and dislikes.
6. Give considerations to efficient marketing facilities.
7. Provide programme of obtaining, using and repaying the credit.
8. Provide for the use of up-to-date modern agricultural methods and practices.

TECHNIQUES OF FARM PLANNING

There are many techniques or tools or models and aids available to a farm planner for generating answers to multifarious farm management problems either separately or simultaneously.

The various tools and aids to farm planning are depicted in the following chart :

CHART 1—TECHNIQUES OF FARM PLANNING & BUDGETING

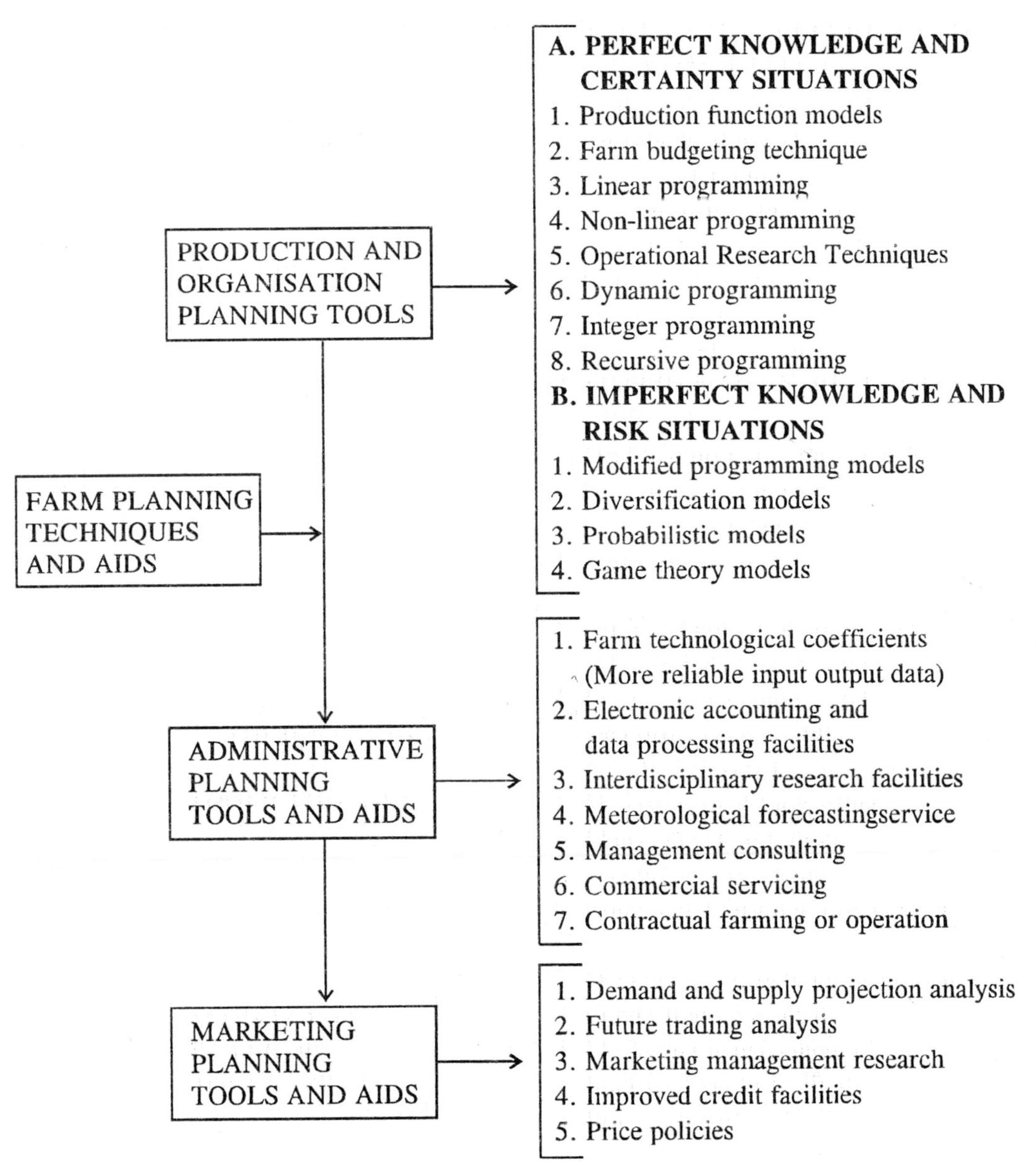

INFORMATION NEEDED FOR PLANNING AND BUDGETING

(*a*) Farm Planning under Perfect Knowledge

The information needed for farm planning can be classified into five categories :

1. Resources available on the farm-statement of resource restrictions.
   (*a*) (*i*) Topography
   (*ii*) Drainage
   (*iii*) Soil management problem-soil sample, yield history.
   (*b*) (*i*) Land holding
   (*ii*) Irrigation potential
   (*iii*) Labour on farm
   (*iv*) Working capital
   (*v*) Farm buildings.

Also the information will need to be complied on additional resources that can be acquired.

2. Outputs to be produced : List of process and farm enterprises.
3. Technical input-output coefficients organized as linear "processes' or in a functional form.
4. Expected prices of farm products and inputs.
5. Social, institutional and personal framework within which the farmer operates his farm business.

(*b*) *Farm Planning under Imperfect Knowledge*

Additional data required for farm planning under imperfect knowledge are:

1. Price and yield variability information—for modified linear programming model.
2. Time series data on yields and prices—for diversification models.
3. Information needed on probability distribution for probabilistic and game theory models.
   (*a*) possible sets of events (such as various types of possible weather conditions, various credit policies, various price levels)
   (*b*) possible action alternatives available to the farmer,

(c) specification of possible consequences either in monetary terms or in utility terms,

(c) subjective probability distribution attached to a set of events.

A brief description of the various farm planning techniques/aids is given below. Budgeting and linear programming will be dealt in some details.

*Production Function Analysis**

This method is used for the estimation of the functional relationship between farm inputs and outputs. This functional relationship along with information on product and factor prices and the available quantities of inputs is used in answering some of the farm planning questions. The usefulness of the production function model as a direct aid in farm planning is very limited. Yet, the production functions can be a potential aid in estimating response function for different farm inputs.

FARM BUDGETING

Farm budgeting is a method of analysing plans for the use of agricultural resources at the command of the decision maker. A farm plan is a programme of the total farm activity of a farmer drawn up in advance. A farm plan should show the crops to be grown; the practices to be followed in their production; the combinations of other enterprises; use of labour, the investments to be made in equipment and buildings and similar other details.

The expression of such a farm plan in monetary terms by estimation of receipts, expenses and net income is called budgeting. In other words, farm budgeting is a process of estimating costs, returns and net profit of a farm or a particular enterprise.

We will be concerned with both planning and budgeting as the budget helps us to evaluate alternative plans and select the one that is most suitable. Planning without calculating the receipts and expenses in monetary terms, is not of much use. So, farm planning and budgeting go side by side.

Three major points of application of a farm budget are as under :

Application prior to the Crop Season

The major use of a farm plan prior to the beginning of a season is to outline the programme of work, study this programme indicating planned organisation and operational practices from the standpoint of management principles. In brief, it supplies a method by which a farmer can make his major mistakes on paper

* See Heady, E.O. J.L. Dillon : "Agricultrual Production Functions", lowa State University, Ames, U.S.A., 1961.

before the season starts and then find and correct these mistakes before they affect his returns or repaying capacity.

Application during the Farm Year

A farm plan is best used during the operations as a flexible guide or yard-stick and not as a fixed rule for every operation. To the efficient farm manager a farm plan serves as a compass to keep the operator on the right track.

Application at the end of the Season

The analysis of the estimated results as compared with actual results from each of the individual enterprises and the entire farm business as a unit serve to make future plans more effective in determining the strong and weak points of the farm business and in planning for improving the efficiency and increasing net earnings.

TYPES OF FARM BUDGETING

There are two types of steps or methods of farm budgeting : (*a*) partial budgeting—enterprise budgeting, and (*b*) complete budgeting.

(*a*) *Partial Budgeting*

It refers to estimating the outcome or returns for a part of the business, *i.e.*, one or a few activities. It may be desired for example, to estimate additional cost and returns from growing one acre of hybrid maize in place of local maize. Here additional costs due to seeds, manure, irrigation, etc., need to be estimated compared with additional expected returns. Partial budgeting may be as well used as an aid in full budgeting.

Partial budgets are commonly used to estimate the effects or outcomes of possible adjustments in the farm business before such adjustments are actually made. Partial budgeting analysis is simple, quick and easy. It provides a method for deciding how far expenses and yields should be increased of a particular enterprise. Changes in organisation can be worked out without complete reworking of the whole plan. It, however, fails to consider all the relevant factors in maximising net returns to the farm as a whole. It also does not allow substitution between resources, and it overlooks complementarity and competition between different enterprises. A combination of partial budgets may not necessarily add to a total budget, and will never explain the allocation of joint costs between different enteprises.

Illustrations of a Partial Budget

Problem 1.

The digging of groundnut with manual labour may become a problem in view of the increasing shortage of labour at the harvest time. A new machine "groundnut-digger-shaker" has been developed. This machine can be mounted on the hydraulic lift of a 30 H.P. tractor and is easy to operate. Partial budget can be set up to work out the economics resulting from the introduction of this machine.

Partial Budget

Adjustment. Economics of Groundnut Harvesting per acre by Groundnut-digger-shaker v/s Manual labour

Debit		*Credit*	
(*a*) increase in costs per acre	Rs.	**(*a*) Decrease in costs per acre**	Rs.
1. Depreciation for 2 hours $\frac{2200 \times 2}{2500} = \frac{44}{25} =$	1.76	Manual labour 60—2 = 58 man hours @ Rs. 0.75 per man hour	43.50
2. Interest @ 10%	0.18		
3. Tractor (32 H.P.) cost for 2 hours @ Rs. 6.56/hr.	13.12		
(*b*) Decrease in return per acre Decrease in yield @ 2.5% *i.e.*, 0.15 qtl. @ Rs. 90/qtl.	13.50	**(*b*) Increase in returns per acre**	Nil
A. Total increased cost and reduced returns Rs.	28.56	**B.** Total reduced costs & increased returns Rs.	43.50

Net change in income (gain) B—A = Rs. 14.94.

Decision

The analysis shows that the cost of digging groundnut can be decreased by Rs. 14.94 per acre by digging with groundnut-digger- shaker rather than by manual labour.

Problem 2

It has been found by the Department of Plant Breeding in collaboration with the Agronomy Department of the PAU that application of 4.40 kgs. of Nitrogen per acre in the form of urea as foliar spray on wheat, 45 days after sowing together with 8.80 kgs. Nitrogen per acre added to the soil, increased the yield by 51.20 kgs. per acre as compared to the application of full dose (22.80 kg. N) in the soil. Here the problem is to work out the economics of these two methods.

Partial Budget

Adjustment. Soil versus Foliar Application of Nitrogen on Wheat

Debit		*Credit*	
(a) Increase in costs per acre	Rs.	**(a) Decrease in costs per acre**	Rs.
1. Cost of spraying 0.8 hour with foot sprayer	1.15	1. Fertilizer cost = 9.6 kgs. or urea @ Rs. 94.30/qtl.	9.05
2. Thrashing & Winnowing cost for 0.51 qtl. @ Rs. 3.43 per qtl.	1.75		
3. Marketing costs @ Rs. 1/-per qtl.	0.51		
(b) Decrease in returns per acre	Nil	**(b) Increase in returns per acre**	
		1.Wheat yield 0.51 qtl. @ Re. 80 per qtl.,	40.85
		2. Wheat straw 0.51 qtl. @ Rs. 5 per qtl.	2.50
A. Total of (a) + (b)	= Rs. 3.41	B. Total of (a) + (b)	= Rs. 52.40

Net gain (change in income B—A) = Rs. 48.99

Decisions

This partial budget analysis shows that the foliar application increases net returns per acre by Rs. 48.99 over the soil application.

Problem 3

Through experiments conducted by the Soil Engg. Department of PAU, it has been found that nitrogen at 48 kgs. per acre in the form of C.A.N. applied to wheat Kalyan-227 in three split doses, *viz.* 1/2 at sowing, 1/4 at crown root initiation and 1/4 at heading stage, resulted in the highest grain yield of 2181 kgs. per acre which was 1.69 qtls. higher than that obtained through single application. The problem is to find out whether it was economical to split the doses.

Partial Budget

Adjustment. Comparison of Split doses *v/s* Single dose Application of Nitrogen to Wheat.

Debit		*Credit*	
(*a*) Increase in cost per acre	Rs.	**(*a*) Increase in returns per acre**	Rs.
1. Labour for second application at crown root initiation 0.8 M.H. @Re. 0.65/M.H.	0.52	1. Wheat yield 1.69 qtls. @ Rs. 80 per qtl.	135.20
2. Labour for third application at commencement of heading 0.8 M.H. @ Rs. 0.65 per M.H.	0.52	2. Wheat straw 1.69 qtl. @ Rs. 5.00 per qtl.	8.45
3. Wheat threshing and winnowing for 1.69 qtl. @ Rs. 3.40/qtl.	5.75		
4. Marketing costs @ Rs. 1 per qtl.	1.69		
(*b*) Decrease in returns per acre	Nil	**(*b*) Decrease in costs per acre**	
		1. Labour for 1st application at sowing time 0.40 M.H. @ Re. 0.65 per M.H.	0.26
Total '*a*' and '*b*'	= Rs. 8.48	Total of '*a*' and '*b*'	= Rs. 143.91

Net gain due to split application Rs.= 135.43

Decision

This analysis show that the farmers could increase their returns from wheat Kalyan-227 by Rs. 135.43 per acre by splitting up the Nitrogen application into three doses rather than by applying Nitrogen in a single dose at the sowing time.

Enterprise Budgets

Enterprise budgets are used to estimate inputs required, costs involved, and expected returns from a particular enterprise. The purpose of budgeting an enterprise is to aid in selection of inputs and enterprises consistent with the resources available and to show combination(s) that will increase income from the farm business. Several kinds of data are necessary for budgeting an enterprise. These are :

Physical inputs data (seed, fertilizer, insecticides, etc.).

Field output data (yields per acre at different levels of inputs use).

Prices data for inputs and outputs.

Selection of data to use in enterprise budgets requires considerable judgement. Before the use of data, some adjustment to fit the conditions prevailing on a particular farm must be made.

ENTERPRISE BUDGET

Crop **Wheat** Variety **Kalyan 227**

Assumptions

(*a*) Soil Type (check)	Light — (Sandy and Loamy sand) Medium ✓ (Sandy loam, loam and Clay loam) Heavy — —(Clay)
(*b*) Internal soil drainage problem (check)	Yes —— No ✓
(*c*) Depth of water table (ft.)	Monsoon 8-10 ft. Dry period 22 ft.
(*d*) pH Value (check)	Acidic — (pH below 6.50) Normal ✓ (pH 6.5 to 8.5) Alkali — (pH above 8.5)
(*e*) Present Fertility Level (check) (based on past yield and soil tests)	Low — Medium ✓ High —

(*f*) Irrigation (Persian Wheel' Pumping Set, Tube-well, Canal)

Electric tube-well capable of irrigating one acre in 4 hours

(State with reference to capacity also)

(*g*) Rotation :

Hybrid maize-Wheat Kalyan 227

(*h*) Land is owned Yes

(*i*) All labour is hired Yes

BUDGET

I. RETURNS

Expected Normal yield per Acre

Main Product $\frac{\text{Wheat Grain (Kalyan 227)}}{\text{(Specify)}}$ = 20 quintals

Bye Product $\frac{\text{Wheat Bhusa}}{\text{(Specify)}}$ = 23 quintals

Gross Cash Value

Main Product	20 Quintals @ Rs. 76/Qtl	=	Rs. 1520.00
Bye-product	23 Quintals @ Rs. 5/Qtl	=	Rs. 115.00
	Total	:	Rs. 1635.00

II. CASH EXPENSES (Variable)

Item	*Quantity/acre*	*Rate per unit (Rs.)*	*Total value (Rs.) (2 × 3)*
1	*2*	*3*	*4*
1. **Seed**	30 kg.	1.00	30.00
2. **Seed treatment**			
(Chemical used)			
Agrosin GN	0.125 kg.	0.25/100gm.	0.31
3. **Manures and Fertilisers**			
Farmyard Manure	—Tons	——	——
Compost	—Tons	——	——
C.A.N./Am. Sulphate	2.70 Qtls.	51.00	137.70
Superphosphate	1.65 Qtls.	42.00	69.30
Muriate of Potash	0.45 Qtls.	50.20	22.59
Di. Amm. Phosphate	—kgs.	——	——
4. **Plant Protection**			
(Pesticides/fungicides used)			
Sulphos tablets	8 tablets	0.30/tablet	2.40
——	——	——	——
——	——	——	——
5. **Interculture** (Chemical used)			
——	—kgs.	——	——
6. **Irrigation**			
Electricity for 8 Irrigations	96 units	0.12/unit	11.52
Diesel, fuel and oil	—Litres	——	——
Canal water	——	——	——
Hired water charges (Govt. or private)	——	——	——

1	*2*	*3*	*4*
7. **Cash expenses on other materials**			
Electricity consumed (excluding irrigation)	—Units	——	——
Diesel, Fuel and Oil consumed (excluding irrigation)	—Litres	——	——
——	——	——	——
8. **Labour :** (Work out first, labour and power requirements as in Appendix I)	Hours	Rate (Rs.)	Amount (Rs.)
(*a*) Total Labour Requirements (take the total from column 6 of Appendix I)			
(*i*) Normal labour requirements	149	0.75	111.75
(*ii*) Peak season labour requirements	112	1.25	140.00
(*b*) **Work accomplished on contract basis**			
Threshing and winnowing of wheat on power thresher	——	——	44.00
	——	——	——
Total (1-8)			Rs. 569.57

9. Interest on operating capital (item 1-8)	
Rs. 569.57 @ 9.5% for 3 months	Rs. 13.53
10. Total cash variable expenses (1-9)	Rs. 583.10
III. CASH VALUE RETURNS OVER	
Total Cash Variable Expenses : (Returns to fixed factors) (Total of items in I minus Total of items in II above)	Rs. 1051.90

Appendix-I

ESTIMATION OF LABOUR AND POWER REQUIREMENTS (Per acre basis)

Crop :— **Wheat** Variety : **Kalyan 227** Rotation :— **Hybrid Maize—Wheat**

S. No.	*Operation*	*Types of implement*	*Time used*	*Time taken per operation*	*Men in crew*	*Man hours*	*Bullock hours*	*Tractor hours*	**Wage Rate per hour*	*Cost per acre if work done*	*Time of operation (give month)*
	1	*2*	*3*	*4*	*5*	*6*	*7*	*8*	*9*	*10*	*11*
1.	Rauni Irrigation	Elec. T. well	1	5	1	5	—	—	0.75	—	October
2.	Ploughing	1st with FT Plough + 4 with Desi Plough	5	8	1	1	80	—	0.75	—	October,
3.	Planking	Sohaga	5	1.5	1	7.5	15	—	0.75	—	October
4.	Seed Treatment	Seed drum Sowing-Kera	1	0.5	1	7	—	—	0.75	—	October
5.	Sowing and Ist Fertilizer dose	Ferti-Pora	1	8	2	16	16	—	1.25	—	Nov.
6.	Bund Making	Jandra	1	3	2	6	—	—	1.25	—	Nov.
7.	Irrigation	E.T. well	7	4	1	28	—	—			
8.	Hoeing	Khurpa	2	8	6	96	—	—	0.75	—	Dec.
9.	Fertilizing 2nd dose	With Irri.	1	4	1	4	—	—	0.75	—	Feb.
10.	Fertilizing 3rd dose	Broadcasting	1	4	1	4	—	—	0.75	—	April
11.	Harvesting	Sickle	1	8	6	48	—	—	1.25	—	May
12.	Thrashing and Winnowing	Power Thresher	1	5	6	30	—	—	1.25	Rs. 44 @ Rs. 2/- qtl. for the use of power Thresher	
13.	Transportation home	Bullock cart	1	6	2	12	12	—	1.20		
(*a*)	Total peak season labour/power requirments					112	—	—		*Work out the wage rate after taking into consideration payments in cash as well as in kind.	
(*b*)	Total normal season labour/power requirements					149	—	—			
(*c*)	Grand total of labour & power requirements					(*a* + *b*)	261	123	—		

*Work out the wage rate after taking into consideration payments in cash as well as in kind.

(b) Total or Complete Budgeting

It refers to making out a plan for the farm as a whole or for all decisions on one enterprise. In case the budgeting analysis involves complete re-organisation of the farm business, it is called Complete Budgeting. Complete Budgeting considers all the crops, livestock producing methods, and estimated costs and returns for the farm as a whole.

Farmers need to make both long-run and short-run or annual budget plans. The best thing is to prepare a tentative plan on a long-term basis and phase the programme into annual plans. The emphasis in the annual plans is on operational improvements, while the long-term plan takes care also of structural improvements which are of permanent type.

Full budgeting brings about progressive changes in income, *i.e.*, it draws attention to a variety of factors affecting farm income. It takes an entire view of the farm as a whole and resources and enterprises are considered simultaneously. It considers complementary, supplementary and competitive relationships between enterprises. It allows the substitution between resources and avoids omission of any vital part of the organisation being left out of consideration.

Disadvantages are that it requires more time and efforts and more basic data in accurate form.

STEPS IN FARM PLANNING AND BUDGETING

In developing an optimum farm plan with the budgeting technique, the following steps are generally followed :

(i) Specification of the technical co-efficients of production

Farm planner should compile all relevant information from various sources to learn some of the improved farming methods and practices and the various input-output factors which can be applied to the local conditions. This entails specifying the requirements of each resource in producing each product. This kind of information must be obtained from specialists in various fields of agriculture. The main sources of relevant information are : (1) research trials, (2) trials and demonstrations on cultivators' fields, (3) crop-cutting experiments, (4) farm management surveys, (5) farmers' own trials and practical experience and, (6) information recorded by extension workers.

It is important to recognise that a particular crop may be produced by any of the many different processes, *e.g.*, wheat may be produced with or without irrigation, with or without fertilizer and of course, with various levels of fertilizers. In general, one will prefer the most efficient technology. Therefore, the technical co-efficients of production of different enterprises need to be specified.

(ii) Specification of appropriate prices

In planning ahead, one can never be sure of the prices that will obtain for different products. In some countries, much effort is put in price forecasting and development of 'outlook' information that will permit more intelligent guessing. One simple prediction model that can be used is to assume prices next year will be the same as they are this year. As an alternative, we might take the average of the last three years. Prices will need to be specified keeping in view the last years' average prices, future expectations and nature of changing technology etc.

(iii) Preparation of enterprise profitability chart

Having decided the enterprises, what prices and input-output coefficient to use as a basis for planning, one will have to evaluate the alternative opportunities and to select those opportunities which make the best use of the farmers' resources. The enterprise budgets are prepared by deducting variable cash expenses from gross returns of each enterprise. (See more explanation of enterprise budget in the preceding section). Then profitability ranking chart is prepared on the basis of net return figures of all the possible enterprises.

(iv) Preparation of the farm map

Prepare farm map depicting all the physical features such as soil types, topographical features, drainage, roads, water channels, source of irrigation, buildings, etc.

(v) Inventory of limited resources

Prepare a complete list of the farm resources which limit the size of the different farm enterprises; such as land, labour, animals, buildings, machinery and liquid capital etc. This helps assessment of resource limitations and production capabilities of the farm. To these resources, possibilities of hiring or borrowing are added. These restrictions lay down a framework, within which a farm plan is considered.

(vi) Examine the existing farm plan

Obtain full information on how each resource is being utilised and what are the outputs obtained from various enterprises adopted on the farm. In other words, examine the present plan followed by the cultivator, for its costs and returns and resource use pattern :

(*a*) Work out the variable costs such as hired labour, seed, water charges, fertilizers, insecticides, etc., for each enterprise.

(*b*) Work out the gross income from various enterprises by multiplying physical yields by price per unit of the commodities.

(*c*) Work out the returns to fixed farm resources in respect of each enterprise through deducting variables costs from the gross income.

With the help of these returns to the fixed farm resources from various crop enterprises, the total returns to the fixed farm resources from the existing plan of the farmers are analysed. Analyse the resource-use pattern based on existing plan of the cultivator as well.

(vii) *Locate the weakness of the present plan*

A careful analysis of the resource-use in the existing plan will throw up the imbalances. The various weakneses in the existing plan will act as guidelines for bringing about improvements in the alternative plan *e.g.*, relatively more area under less profitable crops or low level of use of yield increasing technology etc.

(viii) *List out the risks to agricultural production on that farm*

Make a list of all such risks involved in the agricultural production on that particular farm and bear them in mind in developing the alternative plan. To the extent possible, provide for effective steps for eliminating or reducing such risks. This refers in particular to irrigation and drainage programmes and measures on pests and disease control.

(ix) *Prepare the alternative plans*

There may be a number of alternative plans suiting the situation of the farmer. Within the framework of resource restrictions and keeping in view the weakness of the existing plan and the possibilities of incorporating modern technology, a few alternative farm plans may be developed. Alternative plans can be worked out which may vary in the amount of risk involved, labour requirements and other features as well as probable net incomes.

(x) *Analysis of the alternative plans to check the profitability and practicability of a particular plan*

New plans are analysed for costs and returns and the optimum plan which promises the highest returns (returns to fixed resources) and is the most practicable on that farm situation is selected. Check the plan to be within resource restrictions. Ideally, we should evaluate alternative plans on various points such as probable income, amount of risk involved, labour and capital requirements, etc. The farmer should select the plan for his farm which he feels will give him and his family the highest level of satisfaction in respect of these and other variables.

(xi) *Implementing the plan*

The farm planning does not end with the preparation and selection of the final plan for adoption. The most important phase is its proper execution.

There may be certain difficulties in implementing the plan, unless all the problems are properly anticipated. Plan, for example, may call for an application of mixed fertilizers. If this is not available or if the farmer does not have the credit to purchase it, he can not follow the plan. It is not likely that one will anticipate all the problems that may arise. For example, in the long range planning, one may not be able to anticipate the important changes in the price relationships. For this reason, a good plan will usually provide for flexibility. Flexibility makes it possible to alter the plan as new problems arise or new information becomes available.

OPTIMUM FARM PLAN ADJUSTMENT PROCESS
(Trial and Error Method)

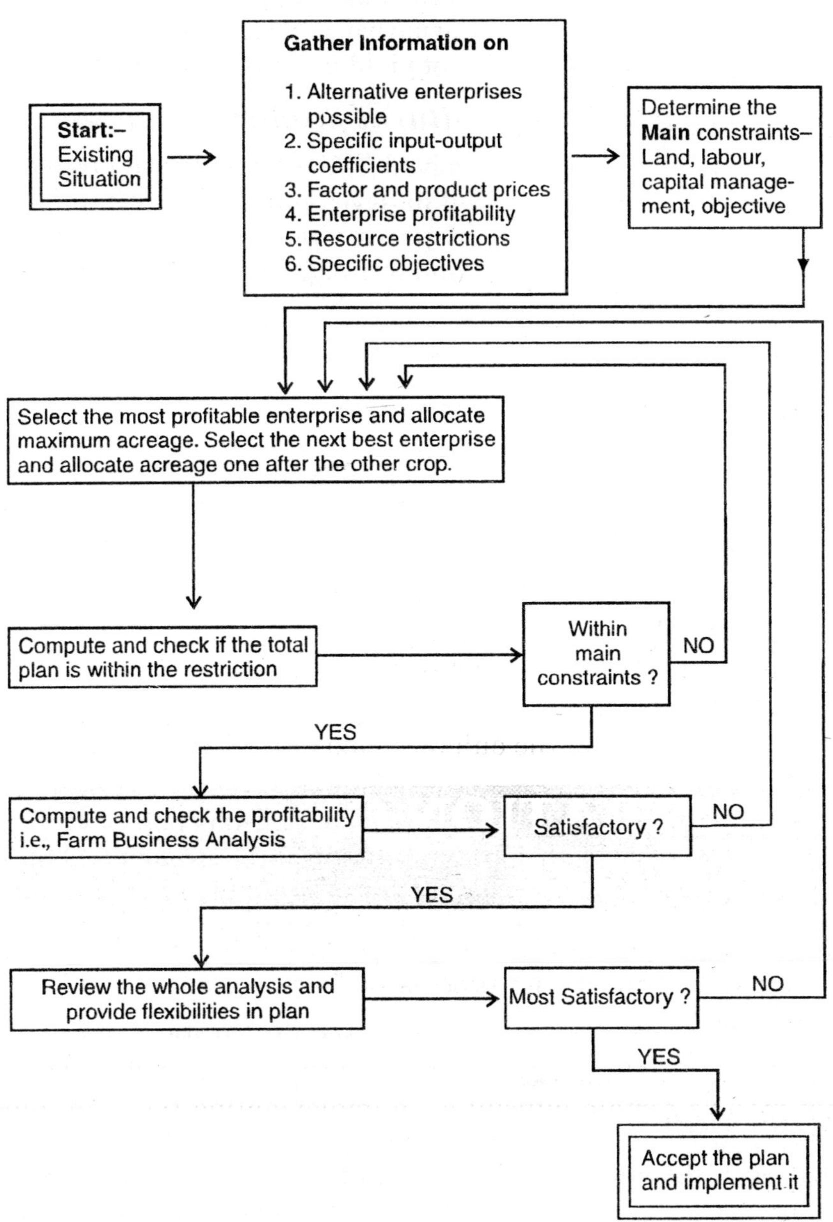

Pictorial Depiction of Farm Planning and Budgeting Process

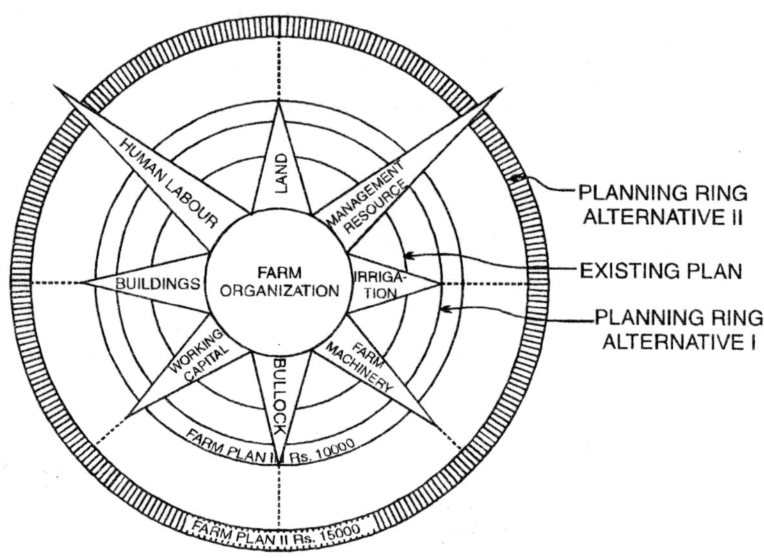

Legend

1. Each strip around the thick circle indicates the availability of different farm resources.
2. Each double line circle denotes alternative farm plans of different levels of income.
3. Dotted lines denote the enhanced amount of a particular resource.

AN ILLUSTRATION ON COMPLETE BUDGETING

Based on an actual situation in village Jaspal Banger, District Ludhiana, the various steps involved in the process of farm planning and budgeting are illustrated as under :

Step I–Farm Map

Sketch plan showing the location of different fields, wells, and irrigation channels, approach road, etc., of the holding is as under. This farm is located at a distance of about 10 kilometers from Ludhiana city.

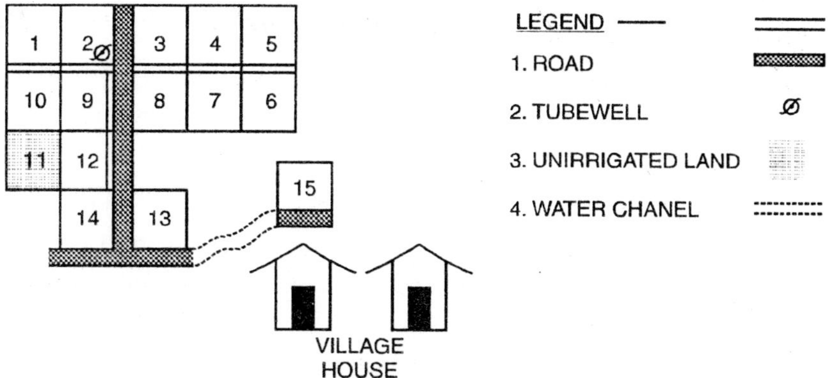

Step II–Inventory of limited resources

Details of the limited and fixed farm resources are given below :

A. Land Holding

	Irrigated	*Unirrigated*	*Total*
(*a*) Owned	12.64	...	12.64
(*b*) Rented in	2.61	0.75	3.36
(*c*) Rented out	...	...	...
Total operational holding	15.25	0.75	16.00

The soil was heavy loam with medium fertility and with 3.00 acres patch of sandy soil. Land is well levelled with one patch of higher level fields. Drainage is normal.

Land use capability classification

	Land fit for (acres)	*Remarks*
Kharif season :		
Maize-irrigated land	12.25	Remaining land was not considered to be good for these crops.
Cotton-irrigated land	8.00	
Groundnut-irrigated land	3.00	Only this much land had proper sand soil depth.
Groundnut-unirrigated land	0.75	
Sugarcane land	4.00	Remaining land was not favoured due to difficult water approach.
Kharif fodders land	5.00	...

Rabi season :

Wheat land irrigated	13.50	
Gram land irrigated	2.00	Rest of the land was heavy soil and wheat was preferred there
Gram land unirrigated	0.50	
Berseem land	3.25	Remaining land was not favoured for this crop due to difficult water approach
Other rabi fodders land	10.00	...

These land-use categories obtained were not mutually exclusive but were mostly overlapping.

B. Irrigation Capacity

The main source of irrigation was a pumpset. It took normally 5 hours to irrigate one acre with 5 H.P. Kirloskar diesel engine pump set. Irrigation was not considered a limiting factor on this farm situation.

In general cases, irrigation capacity is determined for critical periods from different sources of irrigation in the following proforma :—

Irrigation capacity during critical periods

Source of irrigation	During Summer May-July	During Winter Dec.- Feb.	Remarks
________	________	________	________
________	________	________	________
________	________	________	________

C. Permanent Farm Labour

	Peak season	Normal season
Man labour-hours/month	714	530
Woman labour-hours/month	360	360

Assuming 26 days of 8-hours during non-peak period and 28 days of 10-hours each during peak-period, the man labour hours availability was worked out.

D. Farm Animals

	Number	Condition
Draft animals :—Bullocks	3	good
Other animals :—Buffaloes	2	good
Calves	2	good

E. Farm Buildings

One shed for animals = 15' × 30'

One room for fodder and implements, etc. = 12' × 12'

One store for grains = 21' × 12'

F. Farm Machinery and Equipment

Particulars Brand/Size	*No.*	*Year when purchased (Years)*	*Original cost*	*Estimated life*	*Junk value*	*Deprecia-tion*	*Repairs*
1. Wheat drumy	1	1969	Rs. 800	6	Rs. 50	Rs. 125	—
2. Spray pump	1	1968	Rs. 250	5	Rs. 20	Rs. 46	Rs. 10
3. Bullock card	1	1965	Rs. 1500	10	Rs. 200	Rs. 130	Rs. 50
4. Others	—	—	—	—	—	—	—

G. Working Capital (Capital available for use in the farm business)

		Owned	Borrowed	Total
Kharif season	(Rs.)	1760	1000	2760
Rabi season	(Rs.)	1612	1000	2612
Total	(Rs.)	3372	2000	5372

Part of the sale proceeds of Rabi crops were available for investment in Kharif season and vice-versa.

H. Management Factor

The farmer is interested in maximising net farm income over a longer period of time. He is middle-class pass. He has experience of growing only arable crops. He has social restrictions on producing crops like tobacco. He considers growing vegetables more risky and below dignity.

I. Consumption Pattern

Commodities required (in quintals per year)

	Maize desi	Cotton	Groundnut	Sugarcane	Wheat
House use	7.50	1.00	...	4.50	12.25
Farm use	2.10	0.40	2.50	2.50	5.25

The family consumption pattern was worked out to check the provision of the minimum quantities of these commodities in the alternative plans for the purpose of home or farm requirements. The farmer was interested in growing the food articles for his consumption on his own farm even if it was not profitable to raise those products on the farm.

J. Fixed Activities

For the maintenance of the dairy and draft animals, the general pattern of land needed for Kharif and Rabi fodders was ascertained. These acreage allocations for fodders were considered as a fixed activity in each case. The acreage under fodders could, however, be reduced by producing fodders with improved techniques.

Season	Acreage	Quantity required
Kharif fodders	2.25	400 qtls.
Rabi fodders	2.34	600 qtls.

All these resource-levels (restrictions) formed the framework within which the existing and alternative cropping plans were examined.

Step III–Appraisal of the Existing Farm Plan

Full information on how each resource was being utilised and what were the incomes obtained from various enterprises adopted on the farm were examined as follows : (Table 9.1)

TABLE 9.1

Existing Farm Plan (1969-70)

Crop Enterprises	*Acreage*	*Returns to fixed farm resources*	
		Per acre	*Total*
Kharif season :			
1. Desi maize	4.00	257.74	1130.96
2. Hybrid maize	0.50	447.08	223.54
3. American cotton	2.20	480.00	1056.00
4. Desi cotton	0.45	300.00	135.00
5. Groundnut irrigated	0.70	440.00	308.00
6. Groundnut unirrigated	0.70	320.00	224.00
7. Sugarcane	1.25	1234.00	1553.00
8. Kharif fodders	2.30	For farm	livestock
Sub-total	12.60	—	4631.25
Fallow land	3.40		

Rabi season :			
1. Wheat after fallow on irrigated land	3.00	525.00	1575.00
2. Wheat after kharif crop irrigated except cotton	5.00	470.00	2350.00
3. Wheat after American cotton	2.20	450.00	990.00
4. Gram irrigated	0.50	350.00	175.00
5. Gram unirrigated	0.50	270.00	135.00
6. Barley	0.50	245.00	122.50
7. Rabi fodders	2.30	For farm	livestock
Sub-total	14.00		5347.50
Fallow land	0.75		
Total Returns to Fixed Factors (Rs.)			9978.75

Step IV–Weaknesses of the Present Plan

A careful analysis of the resource use in the existing plan showed the imbalances and a low level of resource use. Improvements in the alternative plan could be brought about in the light of the following weaknesses :

1. Some crops yielding relatively lower returns per acre, such as *desi*-maize in *kharif* and gram in *rabi*, covered comparatively larger areas than crops promising higher returns per acre such as American cotton, groundnut, sugarcane and wheat. This was mostly due to the low input requirements of these crops but this choice was inconsistent with the profit maximisation objective.
2. Enterprise budgets showed that the practice of fallowing the land in kharif season was uneconomical.
3. Existing per acre yield levels of almost all crops were much below the potential levels and could be raised through the application of improved agricultural techniques such as intensive use of chemical fertilizers, water and pesticides.
4. The restricting resources such as farm family labour and operating capital remained underutilised during various months which could be better utilised.
5. Inspite of relatively higher profitability and low input requirements, groundnut acreage was much less than the maximum permitted by the land suitability.

Step V–List of Risks to Agricultural Production on the Case Farm

On this farm, there were very low levels of risks and uncertainties involved. Risks of damage by insect pests and plant diseases were there, which could be suitably reduced through taking up preventive spraying schedules and other measures in the alternative plan.

Step VI–Preparation of Alternative Plans

Within the framework of resource restrictions and keeping in view the weaknesses of the existing plan and possibilities of incorporating modern technology, the following alternative plans were developed. (Table 9.2).

These plans reduced the acreage under fallow land and more rational use of the limited resources was planned in respect of land, labour and capital.

Step VII–Analysis of the Alternative Plans (Testing the Plan)

The alternative plans were analysed to check the profitability. The implementation of these plans was, however, ensured by working out input requirements as in Tables 9.3 and 9.4.

LINEAR PROGRAMMING ANALYSIS

Linear programming is a more systematic and accurate method of determining mathematically the optimum combination of enterprises of inputs so as to maximise the income or minimise the cost within the limits of available resources.

Linear programming is an imperical tool or a mathematical technique of activity analysis. This technique originated in World War II out of a necessity to specify ship routes for quickest and least-cost distribution of supplies on various war fronts and to allocate labour, machine tools, plant facilities and other such resources optimally so that war production is maximised.

These days linear programming techniques are utilised by all sorts of firms in making decisions about establishment of new industries and in deciding upon different methods of production, distribution and marketing and other policy decisions. The technique is being progressively utilised in finding solutions to various farm management problems and in planning the farm enterprise mix with a view of maximising the given objective functions.

TABLE 9.2

Alternative Crop Plans and their Economic Analysis (1970-71)

Crop Enterprises	*Alternative Plan I*			*Alternative Plan II*		
	Acreage	*Returns to fixed farm resources*		*Acreage*	*Returns to fixed farm resources*	
		Per acre Rs.	*Total Rs.*		*Per acre Rs.*	*Total Rs.*
Kharif Season :						
1. *Desi* maize	1.00	310.00	310.00	—	—	—
2. Hybrid maize (Ganga 5/Dekalb)	3.00	550.60	1651.80	4.00	550.60	2202.40
3. Composite maize. Vijay	1.00	595.00	595.00	2.00	595.00	1190.00
4. American Cotton 320 F	2.00	557.04	1114.08	2.00	557.04	1114.08
5. American Cotton (J-34)	0.50	808.96	404.48	0.75	808.96	606.72
6. Desi cotton (231 R)	0.25	433.67	108.42	—	—	—
7. Groundnut irrigated (M-145)	2.00	645.15	1290.30	3.00	645.15	1935.45
8. Groundnut unirrigated (Pb. 1)	0.75	520.84	390.63	0.75	520.84	390.63
9. Sugarcane (Co-1148)	1.50	1910.50	2865.75	1.50	1910.50	2865.75
10. *Kharif* fodders	2.00	consumed	by animals	2.00	consumed	by animals
Sub-total	14.00	—	8730.46	16.00	—	10305.03
Rabi Season						
1. Wheat (C 273) after Kh. crops	2.00	503.80	1007.60	1.00	503.80	503.80
2. Wheat (C 286) after Am. cotton	2.50	480.00	1200.00	2.75	480.00	1320.00
3. Wheat (P.V. 18) after Kh. crops	5.00	979.37	4896.85	5.00	979.37	4896.85
4. Wheat (Kalyan 227) after *Kharif*	2.00	949.97	1897.94	4.00	949.97	3795.88
5. Gram irrigated (Pb. 7)	0.50	411.77	209.89	—	—	—
6. Rabi fodders	1.75	consumed	by animals	1.75	consumed	by animals
Sub-total	13.75	—	9208.28	14.50	—	10516.53
Total returns to fixed factors (Rs.)	27.75	—	17938.74	30.50	—	20821.56
Increase over the existing (Rs.)	—	—	7954.49	—	—	2882.82

TABLE 9.3
Estimated Input Requirements of the Alternative Crop Plan I (1970-71)

Crop Enterprises	*Crop Plan*	*Seeds of different varieties*	*Seed treatment*		*Manures & Fertilizers*					*Irrigation Electricity*	*Plant Protection*		*Human Labour*
			Agroson Agallol GN		*FYM*	*CAN 25%*	*Super Phosphate P_2O_5*	*Muriate Potash of K_2O*	*Dia Am. Phosphate*		*BHC 10% dust*	*Endrin 20 EC*	
Acres	**Acres**	**Kgs.**	**Kgs.**	**Kgs.**	**Cart loads**	**Kgs.**	**Kgs.**	**Kgs.**	**Kgs.**	**Units**	**Kgs.**	**Litres**	**M.H.**
Kharif season													
1. *Desi* maize	1.00	8.00	0.2	—	10	100	32.50	20.00	—	96	10	—	410
2. Hybrid maize	3.00	25.00	—	—	30	600	620.00	160.00	—	64	30	—	1712
3. Composite maize	1.00	6.50	—	—	10	200	155.00	40.00	—	320	10	—	428
4. Am. Cotton (320F)	2.00	16.00	004	—	—	320	150.00	—	—	80	—	4.22	518
5. Am. Cotton (J-34)	0.50	4.00	0.01	—	—	50	37.00	—	—	224	—	1.56	130
6. Desi Cotton (231 R)	0.25	1.25	0.003	—	—	25	18.75	—	—	56	—	0.28	62
7. Groundnut Irri. (M. 145)	2.00	120.00	—	—	—	—	90.00	45.00	—	28	—	—	678
8. Groundnut Unirri. (Pb. 1)	0.75	37.50	—	—	—	—	22.50	11.00	—	192	—	—	84
9. Sugarcane C.O. 1148	1.50	4500.00	—	0.75	—	360	—	—	—	458	—	—	750
10. *Kharif* fodders	2.00	30.00	0.08	—	—	200	—	—	—	96	—	—	306
Total for *Kharif* crops	14.00	—	0.333	0.75	50	1855	1125.75	276.00	—	1614	50	6.06	5078
Rabi season													
1. Wheat (C 273)	2.00	62.00	0.250	—	—	120	—	30.00	40	128	—	—	478
2. Wheat (C 286)	2.50	87.50	0.315	—	—	150	—	37.50	50	200	—	—	595
3. Wheat (PV 18)	5.00	150.00	0.625	—	—	875	—	225.00	300	480	—	—	1335
4. Wheat (Kalyan 227)	2.00	60.00	0.250	—	—	350	—	90.00	120	192	—	—	524
5. Gram Irri. (Pb. 7)	0.50	9.00	—	—	—	—	43.00	—	—	16	5	—	68
6. Rabi fodders (Berseem)	1.75	17.50	—	—	35	87	350.00	—	—	100	—	—	200
Total for the *Rabi* crops	13.75	—	1.440	—	35	1582	393.00	382.50	510	1116	55	—	3200
Total for the year	27.75	—	1.773	0.75	85	3437	1518.75	658.50	510	2730	55	6.06	8278

TABLE 9.4

Estimated Input Requirements of the Alternative Crop Plan II (1970-71)

Crop Enterprises	*Crop Plan*	*Seeds of different varieties*	*Seed treatment*		*Manures & Fertilizers*					*Irrigation Electricity*	*Plant Protection*		*Human Labour*
			Agrosan GN	*Agallol*	*FYM*	*CAN 25%*	*Super Phosphate P_2O_2*	*Muriate of Potash of K_2O*	*Dia Am. Phosphate*		*BHC 10% dust*	*Endrin 20 EC*	
	Acres	*Kgs.*	*Kgs.*	*Kgs.*	*Cart Loads*	*Kgs.*	*Kgs.*	*Kgs.*	*Kgs.*	*Units*	*Kgs.*	*Litres*	*M.H.*
Kharif season :													
1. Hybrid maize (G. 5)	4.00	25.00	—	—	40	800	620.00	160	—	320	40.00	—	1712
2. Composite Maize (Vijay)	2.00	13.00	—	—	20	400	310.00	86	—	160	20.00	—	856
3. Am. Cotton (320 F)	2.00	16.00	0.040	—	—	320	150.00	—	—	224	—	4.22	118
4. Am. Cotton (J-34)	0.75	6.00	0.015	—	—	75	56.25	—	—	84	—	2.34	195
5. Groundnut Irri. (M 145)	3.00	180.00	—	—	—	—	90.00	45	—	192	—	—	678
6. Groundnut Unirri. (Pb. 1)	0.75	37.50	—	—	—	—	22.50	11	—	—	—	—	85
7. Sugarcane (Co. 1148)	1.50	4500.00	—	0.75	—	360	—	—	—	458	22.50	—	750
8. *Kharif* fodders	2.00	30.00	0.080	—	—	200	—	—	—	96	—	—	300
Total for *Kharif season*	16.00	—	0.135	0.75	60	2155	1248.75	302	—	1534	82.50	6.56	4694
Rabi season :													
1. Wheat (C 273)	1.00	31.00	0.125	—	—	60	—	15	20	64	—	—	239
2. Wheat (C 286)	2.75	95.00	0.331	—	—	165	—	42	55	220	—	—	660
3. Wheat (PV. 18)	5.00	120.00	0.625	—	—	875	—	225	300	480	—	—	1335
4. Wheat (Kalyan 227)	5.00	120.00	0.500	—	—	700	—	185	240	384	—	—	1068
5. *Rabi* fodders (Berseem	1.75	17.50	—	—	—	87	350.00	—	—	200	—	—	150
Total for *rabi* season	15.50	—	1.581	—	—	1887	350.00	467	615	1348	—	—	3452
Total for the year	31.50	—	1.716	0.75	60	4042	1598.75	769	615	2882	82.50	—	8146

This technique, in fact, can be used in any economic situation where there is a framework of : (*i*) resource- restrictions, (*ii*) alternative activities or processes, and (*iii*) quantifiable objective that is to be maximised, *viz.*, maximisation of profits or minimisation of costs.

Problem of farm planning arises only when there are :

(*i*) limitational resources such as land, its use capabilities, labour in peak work load periods, working capital, etc.

(*ii*) alternative activities and processes such as growing of different crops (wheat, gram, maize, cotton, sugarcane, etc.) and raising of livestock and keeping of poultry birds.

(*iii*) quantifiable objectives of maximising the returns to fixed farm resources, minimising the costs in producing a certain crop or mixing a feed, etc.

Assumptions

Although the technique has a wide field of application and can be used in any economic situation, it does not work without some basic assumptions. The assumptions are : (*i*) linearity, (*ii*) divisibility, (*iii*) additivity, (*iv*) finiteness, and (*v*) single value expectations.

Linearity

Condition of linearity has to be met in : (*i*) input-output relationships and (*ii*) prices. In input-output relationships, for example, condition of linearity is met if every unit of input adds equal increments to the output, *i.e.*, linear regression equation of the type ($Y = bx$) holds true.

Divisibility

This means the resources and activities should be capable of division into small units. In agriculture, it does not present any serious difficulty. For example, land can be divided into any fraction of an acre and capital in rupees, even *Paisas*. In case of labour, we can divide it into man-work-days and man- hours.

Additivity

This is reciprocal of divisibility. If condition of divisibility is met, there is no difficulty in meeting the assumption. This means the activities and resources must be additive in the sense when two or more activities are followed their total product must be equal to the sum of their individual products and total resources used must be equal to the sum of resources used by individual activity.

Finiteness

It means that there should be a limit to the number of alternative activities and to the resource restrictions which are considered, *e.g.*, if the farmer had an unlimited number of alternatives, he would never have them programmed because he could never finish describing additional activities and limiting resource, nor could he ever finish the computational task of determining the most profitable programme.

Single Value Expectations

Single value expectations mean that the resource availabilities and input-output coefficients as well as prices are known with certainty. The situations with input-output coefficients and resources or prices described in ranges cannot be programmed. To take care of variations in some important variables, like prices, however, techniques of variable-programming are available.

In addition to these assumptions, a definite planning period is taken into consideration while planning for optimum programmes with these techniques as with any other farm planning technique. Each enterprise is considered as an independent activity. Complementarity in crop enterprises can, of course, be taken care of through rotational planning. Also the firm or farm-firm is considered to operate within a static framework for the given period of planning.

Procedure

Collection of Data. Type and the accuracy of data needed for this analysis are of the same nature as needed for budgeting. In order to set up the problem-matrix for a farm situation, data are needed on the following aspects :

(*i*) resources limiting the farm production (fixed farm resources or resource-constraints).

(*ii*) per unit input of various fixed resources for adoption of different activities (say for growing of one acre or one quintal of wheat, gram, etc., or keeping a buffalo or a cow or a unit of 10, 50, or 1000 poultry birds).

(*iii*) per unit returns or output from various activities.

An Illustration

For illustration, the data obtained for a particular farm situation is set up in the form of a matrix as given in Table 9.5 :

TABLE 9.5

Resources Levels and Input-Output Matrix of a Simple Farm Situation*

	C	*0*	*0*	*0*	*0*	*0*	*0*	*250*	*230*	*300*	*225*	*700*	
Z	*Resource Constraints*							*Wf*	*W*	*C*	*M*	S_g	Σ
		B	P_6	P_7	P_8	P_9	P_{10}	P_1	P_2	P_3	P_4	P_5	
0	Rabi Land (P_6)	20 acres	1	0	0	0	0	1	1	0	0	1	24
0	Kharif Land (P_7)	10 acres	0	1	0	0	0	1	0	0	1	1	15
0	Irrigation Maximum (P_8)	6 acres	0	0	1	0	0	0	0	1	0	1	9
0	Labour (P_9)	1200 M.H.	0	0	0	1	0	40	40	0	0	500	1781
0	Capital (P_{10})	Rs. 450	0	0	0	0	1	30	50	60	40	120	751

In this matrix, columns P_1—P_5 are for real activities and columns P_6—P_{10} are disposal activities. A real activity column in this case indicates inputs of various fixed resources per acre of a crop that will yield an output of rupees given at the top of the column in row 'C'. A disposal activity indicates the input of fixed resources if a unit of a resource has to be kept idle or in disposal.

Solution : (Refer to simplex Solution in Table 9.6)

1. Multiply 'Z' values with corresponding column totals. This will give Z_j row.
2. From Z_j row, deduct C_j row at the top of the matrix and obtain $Z_j — C_j$ row.
3. Encircle the highest negative value in $Z_j — C_j$ row (—700 in this example). Column containing the highest negative value (P_5) will be the outgoing column.
4. Divide values of B column with the corresponding outgoing column (P_5) values. This will give 'R' column.
5. Mark the lowest 'R' value (2.4). Row containing this lowest 'R' value will be the outgoing row (P_5).
6. In this row, encircle the value contained in the outgoing column to the intersection point of the outgoing row (P_9), *i.e.*, (500).
7. Give an outgoing arrow (←) mark to this row in the Z column.

* This example has been kept simple to facilitate demonstration of the calculations in the class. On real farm situations, the resource restrictions and production alternatives (activities) are many. A more realistic farm situation is depicted in Table 9.7.

TABLE 9.6
Simplex Solution of the Linear Programming Problem

I

C	0	0	0	0	0	0	250	230	300	225	700		
Resource Restriction							*Wf*	*W*	*C*	*M*	S_g		
Z	B	P_6	P_7	P_8	P_9	P_{10}	P_1	P_2	P_3	P_4	P_5	Σ	R
0 *Rabi* Land (P_6)	20 acre	1	0	0	0	0	1	1	0	0	1	24	
0 *Kharif* Land (P_7)	10 acre	0	1	0	0	0	1	1	1	1	1	15	
0 Irrigation Maximum (P_8)	6 acre	0	0	1	0	0	0	0	1	0	1	9	
0 Labour (P_9)	1200 MH	0	0	0	1	0	40	40	0	0	500	1781	2.4
0 Capital (P_{10})	Rs. 450	0	0	0	0	1	30	50	60	40	120	751	
Z_j		0	0	0	0	0	0	0	0	0	0	0	
Z_j—C_j	0	0	0	0	0	0	–250	–230	–300	–225	–700	–1705	

II

C		0	0	0	0	0	250	230	300	225	700		
Resource Restriction							*Wf*	*W*	*C*	*M*	S_g	Σ	
Z	B	P_6	P_7	P_8	P_9	P_{10}	P_1	P_2	P_3	P_4	P_5		R
0 P_6	17.6	1	0	0	–.002	0	.92	.92	0	0	0	20.4380	
0 P_7	7.6	0	0	1	–.002	0	.92	–.08	1	1	0	11.4380	
0 P_8	3.6	0	0	1	–.002	0	–.08	.08	1	0	0	5.4380	
→ 700 P_5	2.4	0	0	0	.002	0	.08	.08	0	0	1	3.5620	
← 0 P_{10}	162	0	0	0	–.24	1	20.4	40.4	60	40	0	323.56	2.7
Z_j—C_j	1680.0	0	0	0	1.40	0	–194	–174	–300	–225	0	788.4	

III

0 P_6	17.6	1	0	0	–.002	0	.92	.92	0	0	0	20.4380	
0 P_7	4.9	0	1	0	+.002	–.0167	.58	–.7533	0	.3333	0	6.0453	
0 P_8	0.9	0	0	1	+.002	–.0167	.42	–.7533	0	–.6667	0	.0453	
← 700 P_5	2.4	0	0	0	+.002	0	.08	.08	0	0	1	3.5620	
→ 300 P_3	2.7	0	0	0	–.004	0.0167	.34	.6733	1	.6667		5.3927	7.941
Z_j—C_j	2490.00	0	0	0	.0250	5.010	–92	27.99	0	–24.99	0	2406.2100	

IV

0 P_6	10.2941	1	0	0	.0088	–.0452	0	– 0.9019	-2.7059	–1.8040	0	5.8459	
← 0 P_7	0.2941	0	1	0	.0099	–.0452	0	–1.9019	1.7050	–.8040	0	–3.1541	33.4204
0 P_8	4.2352	0	0	1	–.0029	.0039	0	–.0784	–1.2353	.1569	0	6.7069	
700 P_5	1.7647	0	0	0	+.0029	–.0039	0	– .0784	.2353	–.1569	1	2.2931	
→ 250 P_1	7.9412	0	0	0	– .0118	.0491	1	1.9803	2.9412	1.9603	0	15.8609	
Z_j—C_j	3220.5904	0	0	0	–.8856	9.5272	0	210.1176	270.1776	155.4128	0	3865.4128	

V

0 P_6	10.0000	1	–1	0	0	0	0	1	–1	–1	0	9.0000	
→ 0 P_9	33.4204	0	113.6364	0	1	–5.1364	0	–216.1250	–193.8523	–91.3636	0	–358.4305	
0 P_8	4.3322	0	0.3296	1	0	–.0110	0	–.5484	.6731	.1081	0	5.6674	
700 P_5	1.6678	0	0.3296	0	0	–.0110	0	.5484	.3269	.1081	1	3.3326	
250 P_1	8.3356	0	1.3409	0	0	–.0115	1	– .5700	.6537	.8828	0	11.6315	
Z_j—C_j	3250.1875	0	100.6364	0	0	4.9784	0	18.7773	99.9148	74.5012	0	3547.9956	

8. Divide each value of this row (P_9) by the value encircled at intersection point of outgoing column and row (500).
9. Enter these values in the second iteration, as a row introducing the outgoing column in the first iteration (P_5). This is incoming row in this iteration that substitutes outgoing row of the first iteration (P_9).
10. All other rows of the second iteration can be calculated by deducting from each figure of the row the product of the corresponding coefficient in the outgoing column of first iteration with the corresponding coefficient in the incoming row of the second iteration.

Examples. 17.6 (first figure of B column IInd iteration) = 20 (first figure of B column in Ist iteration)—1 (First figure of P_5 column Ist iteration × 2.4 (Ist figure of incoming row in B column). With this process, second iteration can be derived from the Ist iteration.

Repeat the process of obtaining Z_j row, Z_j— C_j row, finding the highest negative value (–300) in *Zj*—*Cj* row and thus locating outgoing column (P_3). Calculate R column and with the help of least 'R' value (2.7) locate outgoing row (P_{10}). Divide the row by the value at intersection point of outgoing column and row (60) and enter it as incoming row (P_3) on 3rd iteration. Work out all other values of the iteration as explained above. Go on repeating the process till all the values in the Z_j—C_j row becomes positive. This will be the final iteration (V iteration in this case).

Each iteration gives an alternative plan. First iteration gives a situation where all resources are kept at disposal. Here, the returns to the fixed farm resources are zero. Z_j—C_j row shows that by not growing one acre of 'wheat-after-fallow' the farmer is losing Rs. 250/- and for not growing one acre of 'wheat-after Kharif', the loss is Rs. 230 and so on. This is a negative programme.

The 2nd iteration gives first positive plan whereby 2.4 acres of sugarcane (4th figure column B) are planned which would give an income of Rs. 1680/-.Z_j—C_j row indicates that MVP of labour (column P_9) in this plan would be Rs. 1.40 per man-hour. Figures below the real activity columns indicate that the farmer is losing Rs. 194/- by way of not growing an acre of 'wheat-after-fallow' and Rs. 174/- for not growing 'wheat-after-kharif crop', Rs. 300/- for cotton and Rs. 225/- for maize.

3rd iteration similarly gives a farm plan wherein 2.4 acres of sugarcane and 2.7 acres of maize would be grown which would promise returns to fixed farm resources at Rs. 2490/-. Z_j—C_j row gives MVPs of labour Rs. 0.25 per man hour and of capital Rs. 5.01 per rupee. Now the cultivator is losing Re. 92 for not growing P_1 and Rs. 24.99 per acre for P_4. If on the other hand, P_2 is introduced in his production programme, he will be losing Rs. 27.99 per acre.

The fourth iteration similarly gives a crop plan of sugarcane (P_5) at 1.76 acre and 'wheat-after-fallow' 7.94 acres with an income of Rs. 3220.59. In this plan labour is not properly utilised. If the labour use is improved, lower employment labour by one unit (man hour) would add to the income by Re. 0.8856. Growing now any other crop in addition to this plan would reduce the income instead of increasing it. MVP of capital (P_{10}) in this plan has shot upto Rs. 9.53 per rupee on this farm situation.

In the fifth iteration, all values in the Z_j—C_j row are positive. This means if any further change in the plan is made, this will decrease the income. Here the analysis comes to an end and returns to the fixed farm resources are maximised. This iteration gives a farm plan of sugarcane (P_5) 1.67 acres and wheat (P_1) 8.34 acres. A slight shift from sugarcane to wheat has taken place which has released 33.42 man-hours of labour (P_9). In this plan 10 acres of Rabi land will be kept fallow, 33.42 man-hours will be unused, 4.33 acres of irrigation capacity will be unutilised, Kharif land on the other hand commands an MVP (rental value) of Rs. 100.64 on this farm and capital has the MVP of Rs. 4.98 per rupee. This means that it would pay to rent in Kharif land at any rate less than Rs. 100.64 per acre and hire out labour. Borrow capital so long as its cost is lesser than Rs. 4.98 per rupee or otherwise, it would be advantageous to rent out Rabi land up to 10 acres, hire out 33.42 man hours of labour and 4.33 acres of irrigation capacity in April-June.

A similar solution to the more comprehensive farm situation given in Table 9.7 is provided in the form of a final iteration in Table 9.8.

With this technique, we can thus develop normative optimum farm plans. By introducing hiring and purchase activities for resources limiting to farm production, we can develop plans with improved techniques of production and farm practices and at the same time find out what extra resources such as labour and capital would be required for maximising the returns.

Linear programming has, thus, tremendous potentialities in farm management research and extension. Some believe that budgeting is more useful a technique of farm management analysis than linear programming in under-developed countries, because all levels of management are brought into a planning function and we are forced to give serious consideration to this problem. It is not a question of one tool versus the other. Whether the one or the other should be used, depends upon the objective in view.

If a high degree of accuracy is to be achieved, linear programming may be preferred, because it contains more obvious guides for knowing when an optimum allocation is achieved. Algebraic signs of a set of residual values in the computational procedure show when the optimum level is reached within the alternative posed. Linear programming has, thus, an obvious advantage over budgeting in providing the objective guides. Knowledge of physical and economic setting is, of course, very necessary here for the proper formulation of the problem.

TABLE 9.7

Resource Restriction and Input-output Coefficients of an actual farm situation in Ludhiana (Punjab) during 1969-70

0	0	294	184	162	132	200	450	302	550	230	2,504
Resources	B	Wheat irri-gated P_1	Wheat unirri-gated P_2	Gram & wheat mix. on irrigated P_3	Gram on unirri-gated land P_4	Maize P_5	Amer-can cotton P_6	Desi cotton P_7	Sugar cane P_8	Grou-nd nut P_9	Σ
1. *Rabi* land for wheat irrigated	15.50 acres	1	0	1	0	0	0	0	1	0	18.50
2. *Rabi* land for wheat & gram unirrigated	3.00 acres	0	1	0	1	0	0	0	0	0	5.00
3. *Rabi* land for gram wheat mix irrig. land	13.00 acres	0	0	1	0	0	0	0	1	0	15.00
4. *Rabi* land for sugarcane	7.00 acres	0	0	0	0	0	0	0	1	0	8.00
5. *Kharif* land for cotton and maize	12.00 acres	0	0	0	0	1	1	1	1	0	16.00
6. *Kharif* land for sugarcane	8.00 acres	0	0	0	0	0	0	0	1	0	9.00
7. *Kharif* land for groundnut	6.00 acres	0	0	0	0	0	0	0	0	1	7.00
8. Labour from 15th March—15 April	554 M.H.	0	0	32	32	0	0	0	48	0	666.00
9. Labour from 15th April—15th May	251 M.H.	32	24	0	0	0	0	0	20	0	327.00
10. Labour from 15th Oct.—15th Nov.	598 M.H.	24	24	0	0	8	0	0	32	16	702.00
11. Labour from Mid Nov—Mid March	2070 M.H.	112	56	24	0	0	0	0	600	0	2862.00
12. Picking labour for cotton	2.5 acres	0	0	0	0	0	1	1	0	0	4.50
13. Irrigation capacity per week (April-June)	9.0 acres	0	0	0	0	0	1	1	1	0	12.00
14. Farmyard Manure	60 tons	0	0	0	0	10	10	8	20	0	108.00
15. Cash in *Kharif* season (Rs.)	740.00	0	0	0	0	60	60	50	70	75	1055.00
16. Cash in *Rabi* season (Rs.)	532.00	60	40	45	5	0	0	0	65	0	707.00

TABLE 9.8

Final Iteration of the Problem-matrix in Table 9.7

	C	0	0	0	0	0	0	0	0	0	0	0	0	0	0	0	0	0
Z	Resources	B	P_{10}	P_{11}	P_{12}	P_{13}	P_{14}	P_{15}	P_{16}	P_{17}	P_{18}	P_{19}	P_{20}	P_{21}	P_{22}	P_{23}	P_{24}	P_{25}
1	2	3	4	5	6	7	8	9	10	11	12	13	14	15	16	17	18	19
162	P_3	7.537756	1.973164	.973164	0	0	0	0	0	0	–.006100	0	0	0	0	0	0	–.014633
132	P_4	3.0	0	1.0	0	0	0	0	0	0	0	0	0	0	0	0	0	0
	P_{12}	5.141983	–.878450	.121425	1	0	0	0	0	0	.073004	0	0	0	0	–.000002	.000001	–.024287
	P_{13}	6.679735	0.194716	.194439	0	1	0	0	0	0	.66904	0	0	0	0	–.000002	0	–.038920
	P_{14}	6.320265	–.194716	–.194439	0	0	1	0	0	0	–.066904	0	0	0	0	–.099999	0	.038920
	P_{15}	7.679735	0.194716	.194439	0	0	0	1	0	0	.066904	0	0	0	0	–.000001	0	–.038920
230	P_9	5.28032	–.129794	–.129705	0	0	0	0	0	0	–.044596	0	0	0	0	–.079999	.013333	.025942
	P_{17}	201.4069811	–24.996079	25.002455	0	0	0	0	0	1	3.406115	0	0	0	0	–.000067	.000037	–1.399602
0	P_{16}	.719648	0.129794	.129705	0	0	0	0	1	0	0.44596	0	0	0	0	.079999	–.213333	–.025942
	P_{19}	296.971215	2.274652	2.274041	0	0	0	0	0	0	.031780	1	0	8	0	.479997	–.213335	.454830
294	P_1	7.641981	0.121550	.121425	0	0	0	0	0	0	.073004	0	0	0	0	–.000002	.000001	–024287
	P_{20}	840.865035	77.445976	101.372068	0	0	0	0	0	0	32.103780	0	1	0	0	–.000654	.000349	–20.275325
	P_{22}	6.178906	0.194439	.194489	0	0	0	0	0	0	.066872	0	0	–1	1	–.000002	.000002	–.038920
550	P_8	.320265	–.194716	–0.194439	0	0	0	0	0	0	–.066904	0	0	0	0	.000001	0	.038920
200	P_5	2.858641	0.389354	.389078	0	0	0	0	0	0	.133776	0	0	–1	0	.099997	.000002	–.077819
450	P_6	2.500000	.0	0	0	0	0	0	0	0	0	0	0	1	0	0	0	0
	Z	6951.213634	150.512972	120.593518	0	0	0	0	0	0	.175896	0	0	250	0	1.599592	3.067284	2.297832
	Z– C	6951.213634	150.512972	120.593518	0	0	0	0	0	0	.175896	0	0	250	0	1.599592	3.067284	2.297832s

TECHNIQUES FOR FARM PLANNING UNDER IMPERFECT KNOWLEDGE AND RISKS AND UNCERTAINTIES

One of the major assumptions underlying the farm planning process is that of single value expectations with respect to prices and input-output co-efficients. As farm plans are prepared for specifying a future course of action for the decision-maker, the adequacy of inferences drawn from the analysis will depend, among other things, on the correspondence between expected prices and yields with the actual situation as obtained in some future period, with respect to which the plan has been prepared. Such a correspondence, however, seldom exists in the real world.

Three types of uncertainties are faced by farmers in planning their farm business :

(*a*) *Price uncertainty*. It relates to the variability in factor and product prices from year to year.

(*b*) *Yield uncertainty*. It refers to variations in expected yield for a given production technique due to influence of weather and other natural calamities beyond the control of the farmer.

(*c*) *Innovation uncertainty*. It refers to the subjective uncertainty in the outcome from the introduction of a new farm practice.

The following is a brief description of the techniques to handle different types of uncertainty problems in farm planning.

Modified Programming Models

The modified linear programming models take account of variations in income from the processes considered in the model. Multiplication of yield by prices, where yield and price vary, gives the variability in income. The objective is to find the combination of activities with minimum increase in income variance for a given increase in income.

Diversification Models

Farmers practise diversified farming not only to take advantage of the complementary relationships between the enterprises but also as a device to reduce uncertainty. Mathematical models are available to specify the resource allocation among different farm enterprises, so as to minimise total variance in income.

Probabilistic Models

Components of a decision problem under imperfect knowledge are sets of possible events, actions, strategies and consequences; a criterion for ordering the consequences; and a function, assigning a consequence to each pair consisting of an action and an event.

The problem can also be depicted in tabular form as under :

Events, Actions and Consequences

Events Actions	E_1	E_2		E_m
A_1	Y_{11}	Y_{12}	—	Y_{1m}
A_2	Y_{21}	Y_{22}	—	Y_{2m}
—	—	—	—	—
—	—	—	—	—
—	—	—	—	—
A_n	Y_{n1}	Y_{n2}	—	Y_{nm}

Where an event is a circumstance relevant to the decision maker's welfare *viz.* price, weather and credit policy and Y_{ij} represents the consequence of the *i*th action, given the occurrence of *j*th event.

A subjective probability distribution defined over the set of possible events is postulated in probabilistic models.

Game Theory Models

In game theory models, certain events are recognised as possible but probabilities cannot usefully be applied to them. In such models, evaluation of possible strategies requires establishment of preferences among sets of possible consequences.

A detailed conceptual framework for incorporating various risk and uncertainty elements in the decision process of the farmers is provided in the last chapter of this book.

1. *What do you understand by an improved farm plan ? How does it differ from the traditional planning of the farmers ? Why is a written plan needed ?*
2. *What are the advantages of farm planning ? Name the different techniques which can be used for farm planning under Indian conditions.*
3. *Define farm budgeting. How is a farm budget useful in the successful operation of a farm business ?*
4. *With the help of a suitable example, illustrate the various steps to be followed for the complete re-organisation of a farm business.*
5. *What do you understand by partial budgeting ? What are its advantages ? Demonstrate the application of partial budgeting by taking two suitable examples from agriculture.*
6. *What type of data do you need for farm planning ? What are the different sources of data for farm planning ? Discuss weak and strong points of each source.*
7. *What is linear programming technique ? What are the basic assumptions of the linear programming analysis ?*
8. *Demonstrate the application of linear programming analysis in solving farm resource allocation problems.*
9. *Discuss the similarities and dissimilarities between farm budgeting and linear programming. Which of the two techniques is more useful and under what situations ?*

1. *Agrawal, G.D. and Randhawa, N.S. "Budgeting in Farm Planning"*, Agril. Situation in India : *XIV (1) : April 1959, pp. 11-17.*
2. *Agrawal, R.C. and Heady, E.O. "Applications of Game Theory Models in Agriculture".* Journal of Agril. Economics : *XIX (2) : 1968.*

3. *Agrawal, R.C. and Sharma, V.K. "A Case Study of Practical Utility of using conventional and relatively modern decision making tools in Farm Planning (Budgeting and Linear Programming)".* Technical Bulletin No. *2, U.P. Agril. University, Pantnagar, Distt. Nainital.*
4. *Castle, Emery N. and Manning H. Becker, "Farm Business Management" Ch. 7. The MacMillan Company, New York, London, 1965.*
5. *Dorfman, Robert; Paul A. Samuelson and Robert M. Solow, "Linear Programming and Economic Analysis" McGraw-Hill Book Co. Inc., New York, 1958.*
6. *Heady, E.O. "Application of Game Theory in Agricultural Economics"* Canadian Journal of Agril. Economics : *6(1) : 1968.*
7. *Heady, E.O. and Harold R. Jensen, "Farm Management Economics" Prentice-Hall of India (Pvt.) Ltd., New Delhi, 1964 Ch. 5.*
8. *Heady, E.O. and Wilfred Chandler, "Linear Programming Methods", The Iowa State College Press, Ames, U.S.A., 1958.*
9. *Hopkin, J.A. and William, G. Murray, "Elements of Farm Management", Ch. 8 Prentice-Hall, INC. Englewood Cliffs, N.J., U.S.A. 1960.*
10. *Indian Society of Agril. Economics, "Seminar on Farm Production Planning and Programming," July 1965.*
11. *Jai Krishna, "A Linear Programming Model for the Selection of Crop Enterprises on an Average Farm in Western Uttar Pradesh",* Ind. Jour. Agril. Economics : *XVI (4) :*
12. *Johl, S.S. and Kahlon, A.S. "Economics of Cropping Pattern (An analytical case study)",* Indian Jour. Agril. Economics, *XVIII (1).*
13. *—, Application of Programming Techniques to Indian farming Conditions, PAU, Bulletin, 1969.*
14. *Kahlon, A.S. and Karam Singh, "Application of Partial Budgeting Technique to Farm Business Problem," Punjab Agricultural University, Extension Bulletin, Sept. 1970.*
15. *Kahlon, A.S. and Acharya, S.S. "Farm Planning and Budgeting", Punjab Agril. University, Ludhiana, Extension Bulletin, May 1970.*
16. *Kahlon, A.S. and Johl, S.S. "Requisites of Crop Planning (an application of programming techniques)",* The Ind. Jour. Agronomy : *X(4) : pp. 356-61. December 1965.*

17. —, *"Resource Variable Programming with Improved Production Techniques : An Analytical Case Study"*, Journal of Research, *June 1964 Issue.*

18. *Kapur, T.R. and Kahlon, A.S. "Optimum Cropping Patterns for Upper Dhaia Region of I.A.D.P. District Ludhiana (Punjab) :* Ind. Jour. Agril. Econ : *XXII : 46-69 : April-June 1967.*

19. —, *"Making Individual Farm Adjustments through Synthetic Models of Optimum Cropping Patterns (a case study of I.A.D.P. District, Ludhiana"*, Asian Economics Review *: IX (4) : 417-34 : August 1967.*

20. *Singh, Kartar and Sharma, V.K. "Mechanics of Farm Planning and Budgeting". Farm Management, Extension Bulletin No. 1, U.P. Agril. University, Pantnagar, Distt. Nainital 1968.*

21. *Sidhu, T.S. and Kahlon, A.S. and Raghbir Singh "A Case for Standard Farm Plans"*, Agricultural Situation in India, *August 1968.*

22. *Young, W.Y., "Methods of Farm Management Investigations", F.A.O. Agril. Development Paper No. 64, Food and Agril. Organisation of the United Nations, Rome, 1958, p. 123.*

Farm Business Analysis

The basis of progress and success in business is experience. Without suitable records and accurate interpretation of them, however, much of the value of experience is lost. Accounts preserve experience and if properly analysed, brings out its real significance. No business worth of its name, is operated today without keeping accounts. The main purpose of this chapter is to make the students understand the necessity and importance of maintaining farm records; to enhance their ability to handle a set of records and accounts; to improve the analytical ability in processing the data collected in farm record books and lastly to improve the competency in interpretation of the results.

The subject of farm business analysis is dealt with under different names *viz.* Farm Accountancy, Farm Records and Accounts, or Farm Book-keeping. The objective is the same and the difference lies in the methods of treatment or approaches. Some definitions of these terms are given below :

Farm Accountancy is defined as an art as well as the science of recording in books business transactions in a regular and systematic manner so that their nature, extent and financial effects can be readily ascertained at any time of the year. Farm book-keeping is known as a system of records written to furnish a hisotry of the business transactions, with special reference to its financial side (Adams). Farm accounting thus, in the usual sense is an application of the accounting principles to the business of farming. It is an applied science requiring modifications to suit the needs of varied and less definite operations of a series of agricultural enterprises (Efferson).

It is not the purpose of this chapter to teach advanced book-keeping and accountancy but to expose the students to simple types of records and accounts that can be easily maintained and analysed on an average farm.

FARM BUSINESS ANALYSIS

The main object of farm business analysis is to examine as to : (*i*) how does the business fare at a certain time; (*ii*) where are the weaknesses; and (*iii*) what improvements are possible. There are some subsidiary objectives too, such as providing background information for farm policies and for getting credit facilities etc. The following are the three steps or stages of farm business analysis :

(*i*) Proper recording of accounts and activities,

(*ii*) Analysis and interpretation of results, and

(*iii*) Presentation of results.

Recording of Data

Proper recording of the data in the relevant columns of suitable record books is very essential. The daily transactions need to be recorded neatly and correctly in the appropriate columns meant for the purpose. Making summaries and analysing the recorded data becomes very difficult if systematic method of making the entries is not followed and sometimes all the time and effort put in a haphazard record are lost. It is, therefore, necessary to select suitable types of record books.

Analysis and Interpretation

Raw data in the farm financial records kept by farmers will have little value unless they are properly summarised, tabulated, and analysed. The second stage of farm accounting begins with the determination of the proper measures of income and the computation of management and efficiency factors for the farm.

Finally tabulations and charts are made to show the factors which affect the farm success and failure so that an individual farmer, by comparing his performance with these measures or standards, may be able to recognise his weak points and take necessary steps for improvements.

Present Position in Farm Record-Keeping

A farm record or an account is simply another farm management tool. This tool is developed and used for the same purpose like any other farm equipment is used on the farm to aid the farmer in obtaining greater profits or making larger savings in the operation of his business[1]. These records besides making the farmer plan-minded, also provide valuable facts to be used in future planning.

Even a petty shopkeeper in a village or town maintains records and accounts of his business but a farmer with much larger investments in farm assets *viz.* land, buildings, equipment, tractors, tubewells, etc. and considerable recurring expenses

1. Efferson, N. Norsman, "Farm Records and Accounts", p. I. John Wiley & Sons, Inc., New York Chapman & Hall, Limited, London.

on farming, often does not pay attention to this aspect. The result is that, unlike the shopkeeper, the farmer has no clear picture of what is really happening to his investments and efforts in farming business. For the farmers operating at average level of efficiency, the capital investments may not be yielding even the equivalent of the rate of interest on fixed deposits. Farm family labour working at the farm may not be earning even the market wage-rate. Often the farmers continue to lose money year after year in the business of farming but are not aware of it mainly because they do not maintain farm accounts. Without farm accounts, a farmer cannot exercise any effective financial control over his farm business. He is as helpless as a person who rides a blind horse without reins. The decisions that he makes are guided by vague estimates and guesses based on his past experience of farming. "Such a farm business without farm records is just like a wall-clock without hands."

Some farmers keep sale-slips from commission agents as records of their income and cash memoranda as records of important farm purchases. A still larger number of farmers enter important items of receipts and expenditure in their pocket diaries on a date folio on which such transactions take place. Such records, at their best, are only aids to memory otherwise, they are rarely drawn upon for decision making or for a year to year review of farm business because they are not kept in a readily usable form and evidently serve a very limited purpose.

If farm records are not made use of and no lessons are learnt for future operation, the records are as good or as bad as not kept. The main reason why some farms are not profitable is the lack of proper organisation and failure to follow improved methods of farming, not of course the lack of keeping records. Simply the maintenance of records will not change a farmer's loss into profit. If anything does the trick, it would be better management resulting from the lessons learnt from farm-records.

To be of a real help in running a farm business, the records need to be kept in a systematic and duly classified form so that they can be summarised to give a concise and precise picture of the farm operations over the year. Such records can serve another useful purpose of making comparison with the successful farms under the similar farming conditions.

ADVANTAGES OF FARM RECORDS & ACCOUNTS

The various advantages of keeping systematic farm records can be described as under :

1. Means to higher income

To obtain higher income, farmers must have exact knowledge about present and potential gross income and operating costs. The best way to obtain information on present results is to keep records and accounts, in order to :

(i) know the financial status at a point of time,
(ii) know gains and losses over time,
(iii) know the better sources of income and items of cost,
(iv) keep a check on unproductive expenditure,
(v) examine comparative profitability and costs involved for different enterprises,
(vi) locate weak points in the farm organisation,
(vii) compare farm efficiency with the farmers operating under comparable farming situations, and
(viii) develop rational short-term and long-term production plans.

2. *Basis for diagnosis and planning*

Diagnosis of management problems is the pre-requisite of sound planning. Records and accounts provide the basic information needed for such a diagnosis.

3. *Way to improve managerial ability of the farmer*

It helps to acquire business habits which can be of help in taking advantage of changes in the economic environment. The farmer gets a better insight into the working of his business, which helps him in finding out the defects which can be set right by exercising better control and effecting economies. The farmer can avoid mistakes and losses which would otherwise result due to dependence only on his memory for guidance.

4. *Basis for credit acquisition and management*

Properly kept records and accounts can demonstrate and authenticate the production and income potentials and credit worthiness of the farmer. Thus lending agencies can help the farmer in meeting his credit needs more readily and he can manage his credit utilisation properly.

5. *Guide to better home management*

Records and accounts provide information on farm-household economy. This is particularly important in India where farm and home management are so closely integrated. Analysis of farm records provides good guides for the allocation of resources between production improvement and immediate family welfare.

6. *Basis of conducting research in Agricultural Economics and production economics*

Research requires precise and correct data which is possible only if proper records and accounts are maintained on the farms included in the study.

7. *Basis for government policies*

The farmers need to continuously feed the facts for state and national farm policies such as land policies, price policies, and crop insurance, etc. Records and accounts are helpful in obtaining the correct data for examining and developing such policies to be sound.

PROBLEMS AND DIFFICULTIES IN FARM ACCOUNTING

Most of the Indian farmers have a distaste for maintaining farm account due to lack of education, business orientation, and time required to do this job. Some of the specific difficulties in maintaining accounts are :

1. Subsistence nature of farming

Farming as a business is, relatively speaking, a small size operation in India. Farmers cannot engage separately trained accountants for helping them in farm accounting. Subsistence nature of farming does not produce any incentive for keeping the records.

2. Farming is a laborious work

Farming requires a lot of physical labour, in addition to mental work of management. In the daily routine, the farmer usually gets exhausted in the evening and does not feel like sitting at the desk to complete records and accounts.

3. Triple role of Indian farmer

Indian farmer plays a triple role in running his business, *i.e.* that of a manager, a financier and a labourer.

He needs, therefore, to know his wages as a labourer, his returns to capital, and his returns to his management role. Complex types of records which would give such information are difficult to maintain.

4. Illiteracy and lack of business awareness

The very low level of literacy among the Indian farmers is a hindrance in developing the required level of business awareness on the part of the cultivators and they do not, therefore, realise the need for records and accounts.

5. Complicated nature of the agriculture business

It is a biological industry and is always subject to weather and other natural uncertainties. It requires an accounting system which can handle various complexities involved in the business of farming. Such complicated accounts are difficult to maintain.

6. Inadequate extension service

Sufficient number of trained specialists in farm management are not available who could help farmers maintain accounts of their business. Recently Punjab Agricultural University, Ludhiana has taken a lead in India in appointing Assistant Extension Specialist (Farm Management) at each district headquarter.

One of their function is to help farmers maintain farm records and accounts. They have started assisting farmers to maintain systematic records and accounts on demonstration centres in each district. Such a service needs to be further strengthened. Further, the farmers can be organised in farm records associations. These farm records associations will help their members-farmers in maintaining accounts, analysing the data and interpretation of results.

7. Non-availability of suitable farm record books

Lack of standardised, easy to understand and maintain account books or proforma also stand in the way of willingness of the cultivators to keep records. Standard farm record books need to be developed which may be simple and easy to understand and available in local languages. The Department of Economics and Sociology, Punjab Agricultural University, has designed a very simple record book which can meet the requirements of majority of Indian farmers.

8. Fear of taxation

Farmers are always afraid of new taxes. They fear that if they maintain records and accounts and their incomes show up high, some sort of tax may be levied on them.

Accounting Period

Different accounting periods are adopted by various businesses, suiting their needs and convenience. It may be desirable to consider an accounting period as the one that more closely fits into the production year. India has distinct seasons of production, so agricultural year may be more suitable and convenient accounting period for most parts of the country, *i.e.*, starting from 1st July and ending 30th June of next calendar year.

LEVELS OF FARM ACCOUNTANCY

No method of farm accountancy has yet been devised which will satisfy the farmers' requirements under all situations. It depends much upon the type and size of the farm. The system will vary according to the kind of information sought for and the ability and willingness of the farmer to devote the necessary time or labour for keeping the accounts. A wide variety of farm management records can be kept and they can be designed and adopted to suit the changing needs of the farmer. However, all records should contain a properly described and dated account of what is taken in and what is paid out. Beyond this, classifications are made only to suit the convenience in summarising and analysing the financial results of the business. A good recording and accounting system should be simple and accurate and should provide for consistent treatment of like items and like situations.

A good system of accounts for any farm is one that enables recording of information that the farmer needs and also permits the desired analysis of the information recorded. Farm records are usually of the following types :

(*i*) Farm Inventory.

(*ii*) Farm Financial Accounting.

(*iii*) Farm Cost Accounting.

(*a*) Full cost accounting,

(*b*) Single Enteprise Accounting.

Financial Accounting

These records and accounts relate to the operations and activities of the farm business as a whole. Records and accounts under this method set forth income, expenditure, and profit or loss of the farm business as a whole. They reveal the aggregate effect of all the farm undertakings, such as crops growing, dairy, poultry, etc. Expenditure incurred is not shown separately in their respective accounts. At the end of the year, profit and loss account and the balance sheet are prepared. It gives an over all picture of the entire business as it stands in relation to the farmer himself and to the parties involved. It is simpler than cost accounting.

Cost Accounting

(*a*) *Full cost accounting.* Under this method, accounts show income and expenditure and profit or loss of the farm business as a whole as well as of each department, enterprise or each farm- product or commodity as a separate unit. An account is kept for each enterprise or department and all income and expenditure pertaining to the individual farm enterprise is credited or debited to its respective account. Detailed records on labour, cattle feed, livestock and farm crops etc. are kept. A profit and loss account showing the net profit or net loss on the working of each enterprise as well as of the farm as a whole and balance sheet of the entire business at the end of the year are prepared. This method involves greater details. Although lengthy, it has the advantage of showing in detail how different activities stand in relation to one another. This method is useful, especially, for large farm holders who can afford the necessary labour or money for keeping such accounts.

(*b*) *Single Enterprise Accounting.* Accounts can be kept for important selected enterprises or a particular aspect of an enterprise such as production of milk, sugarcane, wool, eggs, etc. This is only a restricted form of cost accounting. It is a simpler method and takes much less time but is not so accurate or complete.

SYSTEMS OF BOOK-KEEPING

There are two systems of farm accountancy :

(i) double entry system, and

(ii) single entry system.

Double entry system. It is a method of recording each transaction in the books of accounts in its two fold aspects, *i.e.*, two entries are made for each transaction in the same set of books, one being a debit entry and the other a credit entry.

Theory of double entry. Every business transaction involves two parties-one for receiving the goods or services and the other for giving them. Every transaction, therefore, is entered at two places, for credit and for debit. The following two examples will illustrate the point :

(1) Sale of wheat for Rs. 240/-

Two accounts involved will be cash account and wheat account. The cash account will be the receiving account and hence the amount will be written on the debit side of it. The wheat account will be the giving account, hence the amount will be written on the credit side of it.

(2) Receipt of money from Mr. Singh Rs. 250/-

Here Rs. 250/- have again been received in the cash account. The cash account is therefore debtor for the sum received. Mr. Singh has paid the amount and therefore Mr. Singh's account will be the creditor. Cash account will be debited and Mr. Singh's account will be credited.

The Advantages of Double Entry System are as under

1. The system provides for complete personal and impersonal records which include assets, gains or losses. Thus nature and value of the possessions can be ascertained.
2. It furnishes ways and means for checking arithmetical accuracy because two entries are made for each transaction.
3. The system provides detailed information regarding the business, classified records of all transactions will show combined overall results of a given policy.
4. The system provides for automatic checks to prevent mistakes.
5. It affords an easy and ready reference to details of accounts.

Single entry system. This is the system which ignores the double effect of transactions. Only personal accounts of debtors and creditors are kept and impersonal accounts are ignored altogether. In fact, any method of accounting which falls short of double entry, may be called single entry system. It is therefore relatively imperfect; its results are less reliable and its accuracy cannot be tested by means of a trial balance which is possible under the double entry system alone.

In farm accounting, it is not necessary to follow the rigid systems generally followed in other businesses. We can develop many different systems of records with flexible rules and procedures according to the varying needs of the business and of the individual, keeping and using the records. In this approach, certain basic principles rather than rigid rules are outlined which can, with minor adjustments, fit into a number of different situations.

A good farm record system should : (*i*) be easy to keep, (*ii*) give needed information, (*iii*) provide the information when it is needed, and (*iv*) permit analysis of the information recorded. At times, these characteristics may be in conflict, *i.e.*, records that are easy to keep may be inadequate in terms of the last two essentials.

TYPES OF FARM RECORDS AND ACCOUNTS

(Farm Record Books)

Because of the diversity of the farm situations, not all records will be of equal use on all farms. What kinds of records to keep, will depend upon what information one wishes to have. There are many different kinds of farm records and accounts, each of which can be adopted for a given purpose on a particular farm situation. Before we discuss the various categories of farm records and accounts, it is therefore important to understand the basic principles for the preparation of forms and proforma of farm records and qualities of a good farm record system. There are no hard and fast rules for the preparation of form or proformas for farm records. They vary with the purpose, system of farming, level of understanding and capability of the farmer.

The following are the main characteristics of a good farm record book :

(*i*) simple and easy to understand,

(*ii*) suitable forms for recording the type of information the farmer wants to record,

(*iii*) provision for an itemisation and classification of all entries,

(*iv*) adequate space for itemising all entries, and the lines and spaces sufficiently wide for writing without crowding,

(*v*) ample space in each section for all the entries that are likely to be recorded, and

(*vi*) adequate instructions for recording and analysis of the recorded data.

PART OF A FARM RECORD SYSTEM

There are three parts of a farm record system : (*i*) physical farm records, (*ii*) financial farm records, and (*iii*) supplementary farm records.

Physical Farm Records

Physical records are related to the physical aspects of the operation of a farm business. They do not indicate financial position or an outcome of the farm business, but simply record the physical efficiency or performance of the farm.

Physical farm records normally include the following records :

1. Farm map, soil map and contour map,
2. Charts on physical efficiency,
3. Land utilisation record,
4. Crop production and disposal record, and
5. Livestock production and disposal record,
6. Labour records, daily work diary,
7. Machinery use records,
8. Feed records,
9. Stock/store register,
10. Poultry records,

These records are briefly discussed below :

Farm Map

It is one of the most simple and brief record of farm features. It gives a visual impression or a bird's eye view of the whole location of the farm business. It indicates relief features of the farm at a glance. The farm map does not replace the actual observation of the physical situation or location of the farm. Personal observation is necessary and the farm map is just supplementary to the physical spot observation.

1. PRODUCTION RECORDS

The importance of production records cannot be overemphasised. Production records provide standards of performance in the use of resources. They help to have plans based on facts of actual performance instead of guesses. The form and type of physical records relating to crops or livestock enterprises will depend upon the degree of specialisation and the type of farming being followed. A few simple illustration for keeping production records of farm enterprises are given on the following pages.

An Example of a Farm Layout Map (Mr. Singh's Farm)

1
2
3
4
5
6
7
14
13
12
11
10
9
8
15
16
17
18
19
24
23
22
21
20

LEGEND

1. Farm Boundary
2. Buildings
3. Tubewell
4. Water channels
5. Approach road
6. Main road

TABLE 10.1
Land Utilisation Records

Name of Farm : Singh Farm

(Area in Hectares)

Land Use	*1970-71*	*1971-72*	*1972-73*	*1973-74*	*1974-75*
Cultivated area					
Irrigated	9.00	9.00			
Unirrigated	—	—			
Building and roads	0.60	0.60			
Garden	—	—			
Idle Land	—	—			
Total	9.60	9.60			

TABLE 10.2
Cropping Pattern of the Farm

Name of farm : Singh Farm

(Area in Hectares)

Crop Enterprises	*1970-71*	*1971-72*	*1972-73*	*1973-74*	*1974-75*
Kharif season					
Maize hybrid	4.00	4.50			
Cotton American	3.00	3.00			
Sugarcane	1.00	1.00			
Groundnut	0.40	0.40			
Kharif fodders	0.40	0.60			
Sub Total	8.80	9.00			
Rabi Season					
Wheat Mexican	7.00	7.60			
Barseem	0.40	0.40			
Rabi Oilseeds	—	—			
Sub Total	7.40	8.00			
Total cropped area	16.20	17.00			

TABLE 10.3
Crop Production Records

Crop **Maize Hybrid** **Variety Ganga 5** **Total area 4.00 Hectares**

Sr. No.	*Items*	*Block/Field Nos. 1-10, Area 4 Hectares Previous Crop—Wheat*			
		Qty. No.	*Date*	*Type of implement*	*Remarks*
1.	Preparatory Tillage (Ploughing and Plankings etc.)				
	Ploughing	1	18.6.70	Tractor & Disk	Time taken 8 hrs.
	Ploughing	1	20.6.70	Tractor & Tiller	Time 5 hrs.
	Ploughing	1	21.6.70	Tractor & Tiller	Time 2 hrs.
	Planking	1	21.6.70	Tractor & Sohaga	Time 2 hrs.
	Planking	1	1.7.70	Tractor & Sohaga	Time 5 hrs.
	Ploughing	1	2.7.70	Tractor & Tiller	Time 5 hrs.
2.	Manuring (F.Y.M.)	50 Cart Load	23-27.6 70	Tractor & Trolley	160 Man hours 40 tractor hours (10 running 30 idle)
3.	Rauni Irrigation	1	4-7.7.70	Tubewell	60 hrs.
4.	Ploughing & Planking etc.				
	Ploughing	1	8-9.7.70	Tractor & Tiller	5 hours
	Ploughing	1	10.7.70	Tractor & Tiller	5 hours
	Planking	1	10.7.70	Tractor & Sohaga	2 hours
5.	Sowing/Planting	1	12.7.70	Tractor & Seed-cum-fertilizer drill	8 tractor hours. 16 man hours
6.	Seed/Plants (Kgs.)	300	12.7.70		
7.	Ridging	1	13.7.70	Jandra	40-man hours.
8.	Fertilizer at sowing time				
	(*a*) Nitrogenous				
	(*i*) C.A.N.	—	—		
	(*ii*) Urea (Kgs.)	400	12.7.70	Fertilizer drill	
	(*iii*) A.S.	—	—		
	(*iv*) Others	—	—		

	(*b*) Phosphatic				
	(*i*) Super phosphate	—	—		
	(*ii*) Di.Am. Phosphatic	500	12.7.70	Fertilizer drill	
	(*iii*) Others	—	—		
	(*c*) Potassic Muriate of Potash	400	12.7.70	Fertilizer drill	
9.	Fertilizer Second Dose				
	(*i*) Urea	250	21-25.8.70	Manual labour	
	(*ii*) —	—	—		
10.	Fertilizer Third Dose Urea	250	16-20.9.70	Manual labour	
11.	Irrigation 1.	1	24-28.7.70	Tubewell	50 hours
	2.	1	4-8.8.70	—do—	52 hours
	3.	1	14-17.8.70	—do—	51 hours
	4.	1	21-25.8.70	—do—	55 hours
	5.	heavy	4-6.9.70		
	6.	rains			
	7.	1	16-20.9.70	Tubewell	50 hours
	8.	1	10-14.10.70	—do—	47 hours
12.	Hoeing/Weeding 1.	1	26-30.8.70	Khurpa	480 hours
	2.	—	—	—	—
13.	Earthing up	—	—	—	—
14.	Spraying chemical				
	1. Thiodan (litres)	1.5	23-25.7.70	Knapsack sprayer	30 hours with 2 men in crew = 60 hrs.
	2. Sevin dust (Kg.)	4.00	12-15.8.70	—do—	40 hours with 2 men in crew = 80 hrs.
15.	Stooling	—	—	—	
16.	Picking/Plucking/ Harvesting	1	24-26.10.70	Sickles	320 man hrs.
17.	Thrashing and Winnowing	1	2-8.11.70	Manual labour and Maize sheller hand operated	760 man hrs.

18.	Total Production Brought home	165.0	—do—		
	Per Hectare yield (Qtls.)	41.25			
	Rate per quintal	50.00			
	Income from grains /Hect.	2062.50			
	Bye Product Fodder 50 Qtls/				
	Hect @ Rs. 5/- per Quintal	250.00			
	Per hectare Gross Income Rs.	2312.50			

TABLE 10.4

Summary of Production and Disposal of The Farm Produce

Name of Farm : Singh Farm

	Last years Balance		*Production*			
*Crop Enterprises**	*Qty. (Qtls.)*	*Value (Rs.)*	*Field Nos.*	*Area (Hect.)*	*Total Production*	*Yield per Hect.*
Kharif Season :						
Maize Hyb (Grains)	—	—	1-10	4.00	165.00	41.25
—do— (Stalks)	—	—		4.00	200.00	50.00
Cotton American	—	—	11-18	3.00	55.00	18.00
—do— sticks	—	—	—	3.00	120.00	40.00
Sugarcane (Gur)	—	—	18-20	1.00	65.00	650.00
Groundnut	—	—	21	0.40	6.00	15.00
Kharif Fodders	—	—	22	0.40	240.00	600.00
Rabi Season						
Wheat Kalyan 227	—	—	1-16	7.00	235.00	35.00
Wheat Bhusa	—	—	23, 24	7.00	350.00	50.00
Berseem	—	—	22	0.40	300.00	750.00
Value of milk consumed	—	—	—	—	—	—
Total						

* Details of main product and by-product of each enterprise to be entered

TABLE 10.4 (Contd.)

Year : 1970-71

Disposal										*Balance*	
Domestic Consumption		*Used as seeds*		*Fed to Cattle*		*Kind Payments*		*Sold*			
Qty. (Qtls.)	*Value (Rs.)*	*Qty. (Qtls.)*	*Value (Rs.)*	*Qty. (Qtls.)*	*Value (Rs.)*	*Qty. (Qtls.)*	*Value (Rs.)*	*Qty. (Qtls.)*	*Value (Rs.)*	*Qty.*	*Value*
10.00	500	—	—	10	500	15	750	130	6500	—	—
—	—	—	—	200	1000	—	—	—	—	—	—
—	—	—	—	—	—	4.50	900	51	10200	—	—
120.00	600	—	—	—	—	—	—	—	—	—	—
5.00	750	—	—	5	750	5.00	75	50	7500	—	—
—	—	—	—	—	—	—	—	6	600	—	—
—	—	—	—	240	1200	—	—	—	—	—	—
25.00	1900	—	—	—	—	20.00	1520	200	15200	—	—
—	—	—	—	150.00	750	—	—	200	1000	—	—
—	—	—	—	300.00	1800	—	—	—	—	—	—
—	1500	—	—	—	—	—	—	—	—	—	—
	5200								44000		

1. Total cash receipts Rs. 44,000
2. Total cash operating expenses Rs. 18,500
3. Net cash income (1-2) Rs. 25,500
4. Farm privileges Rs. 5,250
5. Net Farm Earnings Rs. 30,750

(*a*) Last year's income Rs. ....
(*b*) Present year's income Rs. ....
(*c*) Difference (*a*—*b* = *c*) Rs. ....

TABLE 10.5

Livestock Production and Disposal Record

Name of Farm : Singh Farm Year : 1970-71

	Production				*Disposal*			
Items	*Prev. Balance*	*Purch-ased*	*Produ-ced*	*Total*	*Household consumption*	*Died/ lost*	*Sold*	*Bal-ance*
(*a*) Milk animals								
Buffaloes	4	—	1	5	—	—	1	4
Cows Sahiwal	3	—	—	3	—	1	—	2
Cows Crossbred	—	1	2	3	—	—	—	3
Milk products :								
Ghee	—	—	48	48	48	—	—	—
(*b*) Poultry Birds	—	—	—	—	—	—	—	—
Eggs	—	—	—	—	—	—	—	—
(*c*) Others	—	—	—	—	—	—	—	—
________								

Labour Records

Labour records can be of two categories : (*i*) simple labour records for selected enterprises or operations, and (*ii*) complete labour records for the farm.

Simple Labour Records

It may often be useful to keep a record of the labour used on one or more enterprises where there is some special reason to study efficiency or seasonal requirements. Also, labour figures may be used to determine whether a particular enterprise with high labour requirements such as vegetables is profitable. At the end of each day enter the number of hours of labour and tractor work for each operation. Make a summary for the year by totalling the columns. These figures may be compared with rates of performance by other types of machines on the same farm (Table—10.6). To obtain a seasonal distribution of labour on the enterprise, it is necessary to make sub-total, by months or weeks, within columns.

Complete Labour Record

Some times the distribution of labour on the entire farm is required to be studied. To obtain a complete record, the amount of time each worker on the farm spent each day and on each enterprise is recorded. To find out how efficiently each of the principle operations—such as ploughing, harrowing, harvesting etc. was performed, the records must specify not only the enterprise but also the size of the machine and the implements.

Machinery Use Records (Log Book)

The use of machines on bigger farm organisations constitutes a heavy cost which needs to be economised. To have a full control over machine use and to study the performance of different machines, there is need to maintain proper machinery use record. For example a log book can be maintained for a tractor as in Table 10.7.

Store/Stock Register

For watching the store/stock position at a particular time, of different articles used at the farm, there is need to maintain Store/Stock Register for each individual farm input, see Table 10.8.

TABLE 10.6

Labour Record

Crop—Maize Hybrid Field No. 8 Area 1 acre Year 1970-71

Ploughing and Seed Bed preparation			*Sowing*			*Interculture or spraying*			*Irrigation*			*Harvesting and threshing*		
Date	*Hours*		*Date*	*Hours*		*Date*	*Hours*		*Date*	*Hours*		*Date*	*Hours*	
	Man	*Tractor*		*Man*	*Tractor*		*Man*	*Tractor*		*Man*	*Tube-well*		*Man*	*Tractor*
18.6.70	0.80	0.80	12.7.70	1.60	0.80		—	—	4.7.70	6	6	24.10.70	32	—
20.6.70	0.50	0.50	13.7.70	4.00	—	23.7.70	6	—	24.7.70	5	5	23.1.70	76	—
21.6.70	0.20	0.20				12.8.70	8	—	4.8.70	5	5			
23.6.70	16.00	4.00				26.8.70	48	—	14.8.70	5	5			
1.7.70	0.60	0.50							21.8.70	5.5	5.5			
2.7.70	0.50	0.50							16.9.70	5	5			
8.7.70	0.50	0.50							10.10.70	4.5	4.5			
10.7.70	0.70	0.70												
Total	19.70	7.70	××	5.60	0.80	××	62	—	××	36	36	××	108	

TABLE 10.7

Heavy Machinery Use Record (Log Book)

Name of Farm Machinery : Tractor Size : 35 H.P. Make : Massey Ferguson Date of purchase : May 1970

Date	*Nature of work done*	*Period used*			*Distance covered (If moving machinery)*	*Fuel oil consumed (Litres)*					*Electricity*		*Remarks*
		From	*To*	*Hours*		*Previous Balance*	*Purchased*	*Total*	*Consumed*	*Balance*	*consumed (if applicable)*	*Repair*	
18.6.70	Ploughing	8.00 A.M.	4.00 P.M.	8	—	35	10	45	24	21	—	—	
20.6.70	Ploughing	11.00 A.M.	4.00 P.M.	5	—	21	15	36	15	21	—	—	
21.6.70	Planking	8.00 A.M.	10.00 A.M.	2	—	21	—	21	18	3	—	—	
	Ploughing	10.00 A.M.	4.00 P.M.	6									
23.6.70	Transport of F.Y.M.	6.00 A.M.	6.00 P.M.	12	—	3	35	38	12	26	—		
26.6.70	Transport of wheat to market	7.00 A.M.	9.00 A.M.	2	48 Kms	26	—	26	14	12	—	Service	
		6.00 P.M.	8.00 P.M.	2									
1.7.70	Ploughing	6.00 A.M.	8.00 P.M.	14	—	12	30	42	42	—	—	—	
2.7.70	Ploughing	8.00 A.M.	1.00 P.M.	5	—	—	40	20	15	25	—	—	
8.7.70	Ploughing	2.00 A.M.	7.00 P.M.	5	—	25	20	45	15	30	—	—	
9.7.70	Ploughing	8.00 A.M.	1.00 P.M.	5	—	30	—	30	15	15	—	—	
10.7.70	Ploughing	8.00 A.M.	3.00 P.M.	7	—	15	30	45	21	24	—	—	

Table 10.8

Store/Stock Register

Name of the Article : Urea

S. No.	*Date*	*Opening Bal.*	*Receipt*	*Total*	*Issue*	*Balance*	*From whom received / To whom issued*	*Cost (Rs.)*	*Bill No. Dated*	*Remarks*
1.	1.7.70	4.00	—	4.00	—	4.00	Balance at hand	—	—	—
2.	6.7.70	4.00	20.00	24.00	—	24.00	Purchased from village Coop. Soc.	1720.00	16/ 6.7.70	—
3.	9.7.70	24.00	—	44.00	0.50	23.50	Applied to fodder Crop	—	—	—
4.	12.7.70	23.50	—	23.50	4.00	19.50	Applied to Maize Hyb.	—	—	—
5.	19.7.70	19.50	—	19.50	2.00	17.50	Applied to Sugarcane	—	—	—
6.	24.7.70	17.50	—	17.50	2.00	15.50	Applied to Cotton American	—	—	—
7.	25.8.72	15.50	—	15.50	2.50	13.00	Applied to Maize Hyb.	—	—	—
8.	28.8.72	13.00	—	13.50	1.50	11.50	Applied to Cotton American	—	—	—
9.	10.9.72	11.50	—	11.50	2.00	9.50	Applied to Sugarcane	—	—	—
10.	16.9.72	9.50	—	9.50	2.50	7.59	Applied to Maize Hybrid	—	—	—

Feed Records

These records can be maintained on the specialised livestock farms, *e.g.*, sheep rearing, dairying, donkey breeding, poultry business, etc.

The feed records may further be maintained for each separate livestock/flock unit, being fed on a separate ratio. The purpose of these records is to determine the feed efficiency. Feed records can show what quantities of feed are used for an entire enterprise, for an animal or a unit of product. They can also show the output obtained per unit of feed. With a little further analysis, they can indicate the profits per bird or animal and can help think of new feeding methods. See Tables 10.9 and 10.10.

TABLE 10.9
Feed Record

Month : July 1971

	Buffaloes : 5			*Cows : 5*			*Others*		
Date	*Bhusa (kgs.)*	*Green fodder (kgs.)*	*Concentrates (kgs.)*	*Bhusa (kgs.)*	*Green fodder (kgs.)*	*Concentrates (kgs.)*	*Feed (kgs.)*	*Green fodder (kgs.)*	*Concentrates (kgs.)*
1	25	150	5	20	125	4	—	—	—
2	25	150	5	20	125	5	—	—	—
3	25	125	5	20	100	5	—	—	—
4	20	150	5	20	150	5	—	—	—
5	25	150	5	20	125	5	—	—	—
6	—	200	5	—	150	7	—	—	—
7	—	200	5	—	150	7	—	—	—
8	—	200	5	—	150	7	—	—	—
9	—	200	5	—	150	7	—	—	—
10	—	200	5	—	150	7	—	—	—
11	—	200	5	—	150	7	—	—	—
12	—	200	5	—	175	7	—	—	—
13	—	250	5	—	175	7	—	—	—
14	—	250	10	—	175	7	—	—	—
15	—	250	10	—	175	7	—	—	—
16	—	250	10	—	175	7	—	—	—
17	—	250	10	—	175	7	—	—	—
18	—	250	—	—	175	—	—	—	—
19	—	250	—	—	175	—	—	—	—
20	—	200	—	—	150	—	—	—	—
21	—	200	—	—	150	—	—	—	—
22	—	200	—	—	150	—	—	—	—
23	—	200	—	—	150	—	—	—	—
24	—	200	—	—	150	—	—	—	—
25	—	200	—	—	150	—	—	—	—
26	—	200	—	—	150	—	—	—	—
27	—	200	—	—	150	—	—	—	—
28	—	200	—	—	150	—	—	—	—
29	—	200	—	—	150	—	—	—	—
30	—	200	—	—	150	—	—	—	—
31	—	200	—	—	150	—	—	—	—
Total	120	6275	105	100	4825	108	—	—	—

TABLE 10.10
Feed Record Summary

Name : Singh Farm | Unit : Kgs.

Month	*Buffaloes*			*Cows*			*Others*		
	Bhusa	*Green fodder*	*Concen-trates*	*Bhusa*	*Green fodder*	*Concen-trates*	*Bhusa*	*Green fodder*	*Concen-trates*
July 1970	120	6275	105	100	4825	108	—	—	—
Aug. 1970	120	6275	105	100	4825	108	20	100	—
Sept. 1970	120	6275	105	100	4825	108	25	125	—
Oct 1970	750	4500	100	600	3750	75	150	600	—
Nov. 1970	750	4500	100	600	3750	75	150	600	—
Dec 1970	750	4500	100	600	3750	75	150	600	—
Jan. 1971	750	4500	100	600	3750	75	150	600	—
Feb. 1971	1125	3750	100	600	3750	75	150	600	—
March 1971	1125	3750	100	600	3750	75	150	600	—
April 1971	1500	3000	200	900	3000	75	225	450	75
May 1971	1500	3000	200	900	3000	75	225	450	75
June 1971	2250	1500	300	1200	1200	150	300	150	75
Total	10860	51825	1715	6900	44225	1074	1695	4875	225

II. FINANCIAL RECORDS

These records are mainly related to the financial aspects of the operation of a farm business. These records are on :

(*i*) Farm Inventory.

(*ii*) Farm Cash Accounts or Farm Financial Accounts.

(*iii*) Classified Farm Cash Account and Annual farm Business Analysis.

(*iv*) Supplementary Financial Records : (1) capital assets sale register, (2) cash sale register, (3) credit sale/purchase register, (4) wage register, (5) funds borrowed, repayments register, (6) Farm expenses (paid in kind) register, (7) Non-Farm income record.

Farm Inventory

It is a list of the whole physical property of a business along with their values at a specified date. It is the complete list of farmer's assets. It is the first step in farm accounting. For an illustration, see Table 10.11.

TABLE 10.11

Farm Inventory of Singh Farm on 1st July 1970 and 30 June 1971

S. No.	Items	Beginning of the year (1.7.70)		End of the year (30.6.71)	
		Qty. Kgs.	Value Rs.	Qty. Kgs.	Value Rs.
I.	**Non-Depreciable assets**				
	(*a*) Crop Produce	—	—	—	—
	(*b*) Supplies				
	(*i*) Seeds	—	—	—	—
	(*ii*) Fertilizers :				
	Urea	4.00	344.00	2.00	172.00
	Di-Amm. Phosphate	1.00	109.50	0.50	54.75
	Muriate of Potash			0.50	25.10
	(*iii*) Insecticides/Pesticides	—	—		
	B.H.C. 10%	0.50	22.50	—	—
	Blitox	5.00	55.00	—	—
	Malathion (Litres)	10.00	146.50	5.00	73.25
	(*c*) Growing crops :				
	Cotton American (ha.)	3.00	300.00	3.00	300.00
	Sugarcane (ha.)	1.00	150.00	1.00	150.00
	(*d*) Marketable livestock	—	—	—	—
	(*e*) Others	—	—	—	—
	Sub Total	×××	1127.50	×××	775.10
II.	**Depreciable Assets :**				
	(*a*) Farm Machinery :				
	Tractor	1	21500.00	1	20000.00
	Tiller, Disc Harrow	1	5000.00	1	4500.00
	Tubewell	1	2000.00	1	1900.00
	Trolley	1	2500.00	1	2250.00
	Wheat Thrasher	1	2260.00	1	2040.00
	Seed-cum-fertilizer drill	1	2250.00		2035.00
	Other implements and Hand tools		1500.00		1200.00
	(*b*) Farm Buildings		8000.00		7840.00
	(*c*) Livestock (Buffaloes, Cows etc.)		19500.C0		17000.00
	(*d*) Land (ha)	9.60	240000.00	9.60	240000.00
	Sub Total	×××	304510.00	×××	297765.00

III.	**Cash Assets :**				
	(*a*) Cash in hand	—	1500.00	—	2200.00
	(*b*) Small Savings or Bank Deposits		12000.00		8300.00
	(*c*) Shares in Coop Soc. etc		500.00		500.00
	(*d*) Other Properties		—		—
	Sub Total	xxx	14000.00	xxx	11000.00
	Grand Total	xxx	319637.50	xxx	309540.10

	Change in Inventory	
(*a*)	Beginning Total Rs.	319637.50
(*b*)	Closing Total Rs.	309540.10
	Change (—)	10097.40

Purposes

1. A complete farm inventory, taken at the beginning of each season, will give a list of all the assets with their values : It shows what amount of capital accumulation goes back into the business. The farm inventory is a necessary step in complete farm accounting.
2. It reveals the changes in net worth through comparison of a farm inventories taken at the beginning of the year with another assembled at the end of the year. The inventory provides a basis for computing growth in net worth.
3. It enables you to work out the measures of income. Certain management of efficiency measures depend on an accurate inventory.
4. It enables to determine the depreciation costs.
5. It helps to work out the value of last year's take over of stocks and this year's left overs.
6. Basis of income statement—Except under very simple farming operations, net farm income cannot be calculated without inventories.

Time

The best time to take a farm inventory on most farms is at the beginning of the agricultural year, on or near 1st July. Usually, at this time of the year, the crop season is finished and work for the next season has not yet begun. Also, stored crops and feed supplies on hand are ordinarily low at this time, which makes the inventory jobs of physical measurement of these items and estimates of value relatively easy.

Actually, the time, the inventory is taken, is not an important factor; it can be done in any month of the year, but to be of the most value, it must be taken about the same time each year.

As regards the date for the preparation of inventory, two things should be kept in mind :

(i) **Lesser need of price estimates.** This period should be one when most of the farm produce of the year has been sold and most of the supplies and feeds on hand are exhausted, to avoid as many price estimates as possible and to save time in taking the inventory.

(ii) **Convenience.** Another important consideration is the free time available for the farmer to do the job. Although an inventory can be taken at any time of the year, it is best to take it during a period when there is little essential work to be done on the farm.

Process of Taking Farm Inventory

Taking an inventory involves two processes : (*i*) Physical counting and (*ii*) Valuation of physical assets. The farmer, with a critical eye, should walk over his farm and through the buildings to make a general inspection of the land, buildings, fences, equipment, livestock, and supplies. The physical count is necessary to verify numbers, weights and measurements. Losses, wastages or shrinkages are always occurring and can cause considerable error if the inventory is not made carefully.

Next the farmer should place value on each item using an appropriate valuation method. Valuation of farm assets presents a most perplexing problem because an error in the valuation of an inventory may render the accounting results misleading. Suppose, for example, a farmer has 200 qtls. of wheat and values Rs. 82 instead of Rs. 80 per quintal, resulting in an overvaluation by Rs. 400/-. If this is an end year inventory, it will inflate the net worth by the amount of overvaluation.

The closing inventory for a year is the opening inventory for the next year. The inflated opening inventory may reduce the income in the next year by the same amount. The inflated inventory, therefore, has the effect of shifting that amount of apparent profit from the following year to the current one. If the inventory is undervalued, it will have the opposite effect.

The errors in valuation, therefore, violate two major purposes of the records, that of showing net worth of the business and that of comparing relative profits made in different accounting periods.

METHODS OF VALUATION

There are many methods of valuation. Every method has its own merits and demerits. The use of a particular method of valuation will depend upon the purpose of the valuation and nature of the assets being valuated. As far as possible, valuation should be appropriate because inappropriate valuation can lead to unsound business decisions.

Following are the commonly used valuation methods :

1. Cost minus depreciation.
2. Cost or market price which ever is lower.
3. Net selling price.
4. Replacement cost minus depreciation.
5. Income capitalisation.

Valuation at Cost Minus Depreciation

With cost as the basis of valuation, the inventories show the total of sums actually put into the business and amount depreciated over time. This method is commonly used for such working assets as machinery and breeding livestock. This method assumes that the purchase price was an approximation of the value of the asset and its value in subsequent years can be determined by subtracting a depreciation allowance from its cost. By using a systematic method of charging depreciation to the accounting periods, financial position is reasonably well estimated and the income figure is not distorted by the market fluctuations. This method cannot be, however, applied to things produced on the farm.

Valuation at Cost or Market Price (whichever is lower)

In this method, valuation is estimated at the cost or the market price, whichever is lower. This method is commonly used for valuing purchased farm supplies. No paper profits accrue and losses due to falling prices are absorbed immediately.

Valuation at Net Selling Price

This means the price which could probably be obtained for the asset if marketed, less the cost of marketing. This conforms most closely to the present worth. This method, is used for those items that are held primarily for sale. This method, which represents the market price (less the selling costs) provides a reasonably accurate measure of the current value of the asset.

While this method may be usefully applied to crops or the livestock produced for the market, it has little meaning when applied to such things as buildings or machines for which no actual market may exist.

Valuation by Replacement Cost Minus Depreciation

This method is to valuate the assets at what it would cost to reproduce them at present prices and under present methods of production.

This method is best suited for long-lived assets such as buildings particularly where wide changes in the price level occur. This method will guard against undervaluation, but may not ensure against overvaluation.

Valuation by Income Capitalisation Method

This method is appropriate for the farm assets whose contribution to the income of the farm business can be measured and which have a long life. The capitalisation formula $V = \frac{R}{\gamma}$ can be used for this purpose, where 'V' is the value in rupees, 'R' refers to the constant income over infinite number of years in future, and 'r' is the rate of interest. This method can be used to valuate the assets like land. In practice neither the annual income nor the interest rate in future is known with accuracy. As a result, this method is generally used in combination with other methods such as the market price.

Selection of the Method of Valuation

Following are some of the suggestions which can be useful in valuation of the farm assets ;

1. All assets that will be sold within the year can be valued at the net selling price.
2. All supplies can be valued at the cost or the market price (whichever is lower).
3. Working capital assets such as machinery and equipment can be valued by use of cost minus depreciation method.
4. The farm buildings that have been constructed a long time ago can be valued by replacement cost minus depreciation method. The firm buildings that have been constructed only a short time ago may be valued at cost minus depreciation.
5. Farm land may be valued with capitalisation formula in combination with market price.

We have discussed different methods of valuation where the concept of depreciation is involved. It is, therefore, necessary to understand the various methods of calculating depreciation.

DEPRECIATION

Depreciation is a slow using up of a long lived asset. It represents the amount by which a farm resource decreases in value as a result of cause other than a change in the general price of the item. In other words, it is a decline in the value of a given asset as a result of the use, wear and tear, accidental damage and time obsolescence. Depreciation involves prorating the original cost of an asset over its useful life. The amount of depreciation charged should, therefore, correspond to the loss in the value of the asset over time. The computation of depreciation would not be necessary if all items purchased were completely worn out by the end of each year. However, the items such as buildings, equipment and livestock, etc., are used up gradually over a long period of years and an important question arises about the determination of the cost of such articles for one specific year. Depreciation occurs because of factors like ordinary wear and tear in use, complete exhaustion of the article, unusual damage or deterioration and obsolescence. The value of the asset may become completely exhausted or reduced to its junk value.

Method of Computing Depreciation

There are many methods of computation of depreciation but none of these methods can be considered the most appropriate under all circumstances. The methods of computating depreciation can be based on either of the following two assumptions :

(*i*) Assets are used on a constant rate year after year or

(*ii*) Assets are used at varying rates year after year.

The advantage in one is the disadvantage in the other method. The choice of the method mostly depends upon the rate at which the asset loses its value.

The most common methods of computing depreciation are :

1. Annual revaluation
2. Straight line method
3. Diminishing balance method
4. Sum of the year-digits method or Reducing fraction method
5. Compound Interest method

Annual Revaluation

This method implies estimating the market value of the asset in the beginning and the end year inventory and then taking the difference as depreciation.

This method has the limitation that estimation of establishing annual values for items such as machines and buildings that are not bought and sold frequently becomes difficult. Also mere changes in prices may render this method unrealistic. This method is, however, useful in case of livestock in the early years of life, *i.e.*, in the appreciating phase.

Straight Line-method

This method is easy, simple and usually very satisfactory for most purposes. This method assumes that assets are used more or less to the same extent every year and therefore equal amounts of costs on account of their use can be charged every year.

This method consists of dividing the total anticipated depreciation by the number of years the particular asset is expected to last. The total depreciation is the purchased price of the article minus junk value, salvage value, scrap value or residual value, if any. By this method, depreciation will be

$$= \frac{\text{Purchase Price of the Asset the Junk value}}{\text{No. of useful years of life (expected life)}}$$

Suppose a tractor costs Rs. 24,000 when new and expected to last 10 years. The junk value of the tractor after 10 years would be Rs. 4,000/-. Then the annual depreciation would be

$$= \frac{24{,}000 - 4000}{10} = \frac{20000}{10} = \text{Rs. 2000 per year}$$

It is advisable not to charge the Junk value of most of the farm assets because it is usually negligible. Information on the number of useful years of a particular asset can be obtained from Engineers. In case of a second hand machine, one can make personal estimates. This method does not suit where assets get used up at varying rates, *e.g.* : A tractor depreciates much more during first few years than in later years.

Diminishing Balance Method

A fixed rate of depreciation is used for every year and applied to the value of the asset at the beginning of the year.

Depreciation can be computed by establishing a constant percentage rate of depreciation and using this rate each year to the remaining depreciated value of the article. The fixed rate is applied to the balance until the salvage value is reached and no further depreciation is possible. This method results in higher depreciation charges during the earlier life of the article and lower charges in later years and provides automatically for the salvage value at the end of the period.

Suppose annual depreciation is calculated by this method at the rate of 20% for a tractor costing Rs. 24,000. These results are shown in Table 10.12.

We go on taking 20% of the remaining balance until salvage value is reached, as in this case about Rs. 4033/-.

TABLE 10.12

Computation of Annual Depreciation by Diminishing Balance Method

Value at the beginning of year	*Annual depreciation*	*Remaining balance*
1st year Rs. 24000	(20% of Rs. 24000) = Rs. 4800	(Rs. 24000 – 4800) = Rs. 19200
2nd year Rs. 19200	(20% of Rs. 19200) = Rs. 3840	(Rs. 19200 – 3840) = Rs. 15360
3rd year Rs. 15360	(20% of Rs. 15360) = Rs. 3072	(Rs. 15360 – 3072) = Rs. 12288
4th year Rs. 12288	(20% of Rs. 12288) = Rs. 2457.60	(Rs. 12288 – 2457.60) = Rs. 9830.40
5th year Rs. 9830.40	(20% of Rs. 9830.40) = Rs. 1966.08	(Rs. 9830.40 – 1966.08) = Rs. 7864.32
6th year Rs. 7864.32	(20% of Rs. 7864.32) = Rs. 1572.86	(Rs. 7864.32 – 1572.86) = Rs. 6291.46
7th year Rs. 6291.46	(20% of Rs. 6291.46) = Rs. 1258.29	(Rs. 6291.46—1258.29) = Rs. 5033.17

Reducing Fraction Method

(Sum-of-the-year-Digits Method)

If it is desired to distribute depreciation expenses more heavily in the first years of the use and more lightly in the later years, the sum-of year-digits method has some advantages over the diminishing balance method because here no undistributed balance is left over.

By this method, the annual depreciation is found out by multiplying a fraction times the amount to be depreciated (cost minus the salvage value). We can determine the fraction for any year by the above formula :

$$\text{Fraction for any year} = \frac{\text{The years of life remaining at the beginning of accounting period}}{\text{The sum of the years of life of the asset}}$$

$$\text{Fraction for 1st year} = \frac{10}{1+2+3+4+5+6+7+8+9+10} = \frac{10}{55}$$

$$\text{Fraction for 2nd year} = \frac{9}{55}$$

The other computations of the annual rate of depreciation are in Table 10.13.

TABLE 10.13

Computation of annual rate of depreciation by Reducing Fraction method

Value of beginning of the year	*Annual Depreciation*	*Remaining balance*
1st year Rs. 24000	10/55 × (24000 – 4000) = 3636.36	Rs. 24000 – 3636.36 = 20363.64
2nd year Rs. 20363.64	9/55 × (24000 – 4000) = 3272.73	Rs. 20363.64 – 3272.73 = 17090.91
3rd year Rs. 17090.91	8/55 × (24000 – 4000) = 2909.09	Rs. 17090.91 – 2909.09 = 14181.82
4th year Rs. 14181.82	7/55 × (24000 – 4000) = 2545.45	Rs.14181.82 – 2545.45 = 11636.37
—	—	—
—	—	—
10th year Rs. 363.64	1/55 × (24000 – 4000) = 363.64	Rs. 363.64 – 363.64 = 0

Just as we compute depreciation by straight line method similarly we deduct salvage value from original cost each year for finding the annual depreciation.

Selection of the Depreciation Method

Selection of a particular depreciation method will depend upon two factors : (1) the method which best approximates the loss in the value of the asset and (2) ease of computation Table 10.14 shows the rate of depreciation and undepreciation balance for three methods : straight line, diminishing balance and reducing fraction method.

Table 10.14.

Comparison of annual depreciation rate calculated by different depreciation methods for a tractor costing Rs. 24000 having expected useful life of 10 years and a salvage value of Rs. 4000

	Straight line method		Diminishing balance method		Reducing fraction method	
Year	Annual Depreciation	Remaining Values Rs.	Annual Depreciation	Remaining Values	Annual Depreciation	Remaining Values
1	Rs. 2000	Rs. 18000	Rs. 4800	Rs. 19200	Rs. 3636	Rs. 20364
2	Rs. 2000	Rs. 16,000	Rs. 3840	Rs. 15360	Rs. 3273	Rs. 17091
3	Rs. 2000	Rs. 14000	Rs. 3072	Rs. 12288	Rs. 2909	Rs. 14182
4	Rs. 2000	Rs. 12000	Rs. 2458	Rs. 9830	Rs. 2545	Rs. 11636
5	Rs. 2000	Rs. 10000	Rs. 1967	Rs. 7864	Rs. 2182	Rs. 9455
6	Rs. 2000	Rs. 8000	Rs. 1573	Rs. 6291	Rs. 1818	Rs. 7636
7	Rs. 2000	Rs. 6000	Rs. 1258	Rs. 5033	Rs. 1455	Rs. 6182
8	Rs. 2000	Rs. 4000	Rs. 1007	Rs. 4027	Rs. 1091	Rs. 5091
9	Rs. 2000	Rs. 2000	Rs. 805	Rs. 3221	Rs. 727	Rs. 4364
10	Rs. 2000	—	Rs. 644	Rs. 2577	Rs. 364	Rs. 4000
	Rs. 20000	—	Rs. 21900		Rs. 20000	

Obviously the straight line method is the easiest to compute and understand. This is the most commonly used method. The diminishing balance method and reducing fraction method give similar results. The other methods of working out depreciation are compound interest method and depreciation according to use.

Some Special Problems in Computation of Depreciation

1. The life of many machines is often longer than the normal expectations used in estimating the depreciation. The farmers need therefore, to make suitable adjustments through time by judging the actual condition of the implement or the machine.
2. In case of minor repairs, use of oil and lubrication, etc., normally no extra depreciation is charged. If, however, machines are re-conditioned or buildings are repaired or remodelled to an extent to appreciably increase their value within the accounting year, the closing inventory should recognise the change. A convenient procedure is to add the cost of the repairs to the existing value of the asset.
3. In case of small tools, they are considered to be used up within one year. Assume 100% depreciation on them.

4. If a machine is purchased second hand, the number of years it has been used and its original price may not be known, the logical procedure in this case is to estimate the remaining years of its life and begin depreciation on the purchase price.
5. When the livestock is in a breeding stage or appreciation phase—revaluation method will be more useful. But when they start depreciating, say after 3 years in case of bullocks, straight line method will be more appropriate.
6. At the initial stage of appreciation, depreciation may not be charged because expenses for feeds, etc. are already being incurred. After attainment of the adult age, depreciation must be charged.

Every method has its strong and weak points but for most of the purposes, normally straight line method is used.

NET WORTH STATEMENT

The net worth statement shows the financial condition and stability of the business at a particular point of time. Net worth is shown as an excess of assets over liabilities, *i.e.*, the liability of the business to the farmer or the farmer's claim in the business. Net worth statement is thus prepared for the farmer and not for his business. It shows whether the business is expanding or shrinking. The business is said to be solvent when the net worth or equity is greater than zero. When the total liabilities are not covered by total resources, the business is said to be insolvent or bankrupt. The difference between assets and liabilities shows the distance from insolvency position; greater the difference on positive side, the sounder will be the business. The farmer is generally more concerned about the immediate solvency than the ultimate solvency. It is, therefore, necessary to classify the assets and liabilities to know the real position of the farm business at a point of time and compare the nature of the liabilities to the assets.

The assets and liabilities can be grouped as under :

Assets

(*a*) *Fixed assets.* They are of the nature that it is difficult to convert them into cash to meet any current obligations. The examples of fixed assets are land, buildings, etc.

(*b*) *Working assets.* These are more liquid than fixed assets, such as farm machinery, equipment, etc.

(*c*) *Current assets.* They are the most liquid assets and are consumable in a year. Example are seeds, fertilizers, cash on hand, bills receivable, livestock for sale, etc.

Liabilities

(*a*) *Long duration liabilities.* These liabilities are those which do not require repayment during the current accounting period. Example is long term loans.

(b) *Intermediate liabilities.* These liabilities can be deferred or postponed for the present but fall due within the year. Examples are promissory notes and medium term loans.

(c) *Current liabilities.* Repayment of these liabilities may be demanded at once.

It will not be, thus, appropriate to buy a long-lived asset having a slow turnover with funds obtained through floating bills or short-time notes. The best policy would be to match the liabilities with the nature of assets and earnings from them in respect of time.

A model for the preparation of net worth statement of a farm situation is given in Table 10.15.

TABLE 10.15

Net Worth Statement of Mr. Singh on 1st July, 1970 and 30th June, 1971

Assets			Liabilities		
Item	Beginning 1.7.70 (Rs.)	Ending 30.6.71 (Rs.)	Item	Beginning 1.7.70 (Rs.)	Ending 30.6.71 (Rs.)
1. Current Assets			**Current Liabilities**		
Cash in Bank, shares etc.	12500.00	8800.00	Short term loans		
Cash in hand	1500.00	2200.00	Fertilizers	400.00	150.00
A/c receivable	500.00	400.00	Feeds	150.00	350.00
Feeds, grains and supplies	677.50	325.10			
Standing crops	450.00	450.00			
Sub Total	15627.50	12175.10	Sub Total	550.00	500.00
2. Medium Term Assets			**Medium Term Liabilities**		
Machinery and equipment	37010.00	32925.00	Loans on machinery and equipment	28500.00	21400.00
Livestock (Buffaloes, Cows etc.)	19500.00	17000.00	Loans for milch animals (Buffaloes and Cows)	9000.00	7000.00
Sub Total	56510.00	49925.00	Sub Total	37500.00	28400.00
3. Fixed Assets			**Fixed Liabilities**		
Land	240000.00	240000.00		—	—
Land Improvements	—	—		—	—
Farm Buildings	8000.00	7840.00		—	—
Sub total	248000.00	247840.00	Sub Total	—	—
Total All Assets	320137.50	309940.10	Total all Liabilities	38050.00	28900.00

Net Worth (Total assets minus Total Liabilities) on 1.7.70 = 282087.50
on 30.6.71 = 281040.10

Analysis of Net Worth Statement

The net worth calculated above shows only the absolute amounts by which total assets differ from the total liabilities at a point of time. This figure may not give the true picture of the financial position of the farmer. It is useful to further analyse these data to find out ratios between different categories of assets and liabilities.

Net Capital Ratio

It is a ratio between total assets and total liabilities and it is worked out to measure the degree of financial safety over a period of time by comparing the present position of the business with that on some previous date. The net capital ratios of two farmers are computed as under :

$$\text{Net capital Ratio} = \frac{\text{Total assets}}{\text{Total liabilities}}$$

$$\text{Farmer 'A'} = \frac{\text{Rs. } 40{,}000}{\text{Rs. } 30{,}000} = 1.3$$

$$\text{Farmer 'B'} = \frac{\text{Rs. } 20{,}000}{\text{Rs. } 10{,}000} = 2.0$$

Although the net worth in both the cases is the same, yet the net capital ratios indicate that the business of farmer 'B' is in much safer position than that of farmer A. For example, a decline of 25% in the prices of major assets would wipe out the margin of safety in case of the farmer 'A'. But in case of farmer 'B', it would take a decline of 50% in prices to place his business in an equally precarious position.

Working Ratio

It is derived by dividing the sum of working and current assets by the sum of medium term liabilities and current assets. It measures the financial safety of the business over an intermediate period of time.

$$\text{Working Ratio} = \frac{\text{Sum of working and current assets}}{\text{Sum of medium term liabilites and current liabilities}}$$

Current Ratio

It is obtained by dividing the current assets by the current liabilities. This ratio measures the degree of immediate solvency of the business.

$$\text{Current Ratio} = \frac{\text{Current assets}}{\text{Current liabilities}}$$

These ratios can also be compared over time. Wider these ratios are, better will be the financial position of the business.

The farmers should always try to improve the net worth of their business. Two factors can improve the net worth of the farmer : (*i*) changes in the general level of prices and (*ii*) increase in investment through efficient production and by ploughing back the enhanced profits of the business.

In advance countries such as U.S.A., the farmers remain more concerned about their net worth because they are business minded and their farming business requires heavy capital investments and they have to borrow frequently. On the other hand, Indian farming is based on tradition and farmers are not that business minded; liabilities are kept low and investments do not grow and net worth remains low.

Now farming is becoming more capital intensive requiring heavy investments in farm machinery. The farmers have to depend upon banks and other institutions for credit. For obtaining credit, the analysis of net worth statement is becoming more and more an important record. Bankers are interested in the "continuous net worth statement" in order to compare the financial stability and to estimate the management potential of the farmer. Net worth statements over time will show the equity of the farmer over different years as indicated in Table 10.16.

FARM FINANCIAL ACCOUNTS OR FARM CASH ACCOUNTS

These records relate to the annual operation of the business and the profits and losses associated with it. While the farm inventory is a record of the financial condition at a particular time, the farm cash account is a record of the results of the operation of the farm over a period of time, usually one season or one crop year.

Farm financial accounts can be as simple as just keeping a statement of the payments (expenses) and receipts. Detailed cash records will spilt up these expenses and receipts on the various enterprises as well as operations involved in the business.

TABLE 10.16

Operator's Continuous Net Worth Sttaement

	Items	*July 1, 1970 (Rs.)*	*July 1, 1971 (Rs.)*	*July 1, 1972 (Rs.)*	*July 1, 1973 (Rs.)*
	Assets				
1.	Cash in hand and banks	13500.00	10500.00	15500.00,	
2.	Accounts receivable	500.00	400.00	2500.00,	
3.	Securities and bonds etc.	500.00	500.00	1500.00	
4.	Other investments	—	—	—	
5.	Feed grain and supplies	1127.50	775.10	500.00	
6.	Livestock cattle	19500.00	17000.00	14075.00	
7.	Poultry	—	—	—	
8.	Other Current assets	—	—	—	
9.	**Total current assets (1 – 8)**	35127.50	29175.10	34125.00	
10.	Machinery and equipment	37010.00	32925.00	29500.00	
11.	Farm Buildings	8000.00	7840.00	14850.00	
12.	Farm Land	240000.00	240000.00	240000.00	
13.	Other fixed assets	—	—	—	
14.	**Total fixed assets (10 – 13)**	285010.00	280765.00	274350.00	
15.	**Total assets (10 + 17)**	320137.50	309940.10	308475.00	
	Liabilities				
16.	Short term loan	400.00	150.00	—	
17.	Bills payable	150.00	350.00	—	
18.	Other current liabilities	—	—	—	
19.	**Total current liabilities (16 – 18)**	550.00	500.00	—	
20.	Mortgage on farm land	—	—	—	
21.	Long/Medium term loan	37500.00	28400.00	21500.00,	
22.	Others				
23.	**Total medium and long term liabilities (20 + 21 + 22)**	37500.00	28400.00	21500.00	
24.	Total of liabilities (19 + 23)	38050.00	28900.00	21500.00	
	Net worth (15 – 24)	282087.50	281040.10	28975.00	

TYPES OF CASH ACCOUNTS

There can be many such records within the system of complete records for assembling facts needed in the operation of farms. Important records are discussed below :

Farm Diary. Diary is meant for daily recording of all important events on the farm. It may include weather reports, any unusual event(s) of the day, as well as cash receipts and expenses from all resources.

Farm Business Cash Record. It is a record of all cash receipts from and all cash expenses incurred on the farm business. The farm business cash record omits all personal cash expenses and all non-farm cash income. The objective of this record is to measure changes in the farm business only as far as cash transactions are concerned. The business cash record can be maintained in a simple form or a classified form.

Personal Cash Record. It is strictly a record of all personal expenses of the farm family, excluding all the farm costs and usually a recording of the cash income of the family from all sources, regardless of whether the income is from farm or non farm sources.

Complete Cash Record. It includes expenses on all items both personal and business and income from all sources recorded according to source types.

How to Maintain the Farm cash Record ?

Many kinds of farm cash account books can be used. Unfortunately, the farm accounting problems vary from farm to farm and no farm record book can be developed that will exactly meet the needs of all the farmers. Only broad outlines can be developed here which may be adjusted to suit to a particular farm situation : An example is given in Table 10.17.

CLASSIFIED FARM CASH RECORD

The classified cash record is a modified and more complicated form of the simple cash record meant to provide more detailed facts about the farm business that can be obtained from the simple cash record. It provides details of the costs on and returns from the different farm enterprises, as well as a general summary of the cash costs and returns from the entire farm business (Table—10.18).

TABLE 10.17

Simple Farm Cash Record of Singh Farm

Expenses			*Receipts*		
Date	*Particulars*	*Amount (Rs.)*	*Date*	*Particulars*	*Amount (Rs.)*
July, '71			July, 71		
July 6	Urea 20 quintals @ 86/-	1720.00			
July 9	Paid to Casual hired labour	60.00	15	Sale proceeds of milk	225.00
July 10	Purchased diesel oil 200 L.	180.00			
July 11	Purchased Potash 4 Qtls.	200.80	31	Sale proceeds of milk	369.00
July 11	Purchased Di-amm. Phosphate 10 Quintals @ 109.60	1096.00			
July 16	Labour for weeding sugarcane 8 men @ Rs. 6/-	48.00			
July 23	Endrine 1.50 litres	27.00			
July 29	Electricity charges for motor	40.00			
July 31	Feed (Concentrate for animals)	180.00			
Aug. '71			Aug. '71		
Aug. 6	Mobil oil 5 litres	17.50			
Aug. 9	Paid to casual labour	87.00			
Aug. 10	Insecticides and pesticides	145.00	12	Sale proceeds of milk	216.00
Aug. 12	Labour for G. Nut	48.00			
Aug. 18	Repair and service of Tractor	352.00	31	Sale of milk	240.30
Aug. 25	Paid to Artisians for repair of implements	25.00			
Aug. 27	Purchase of feed	210.00			
Aug. 27	Paid to labourer S. Karnail Singh	48.00			
Aug. 31	Electricity bill for the month	40.00			
Sept.'71			Sept. '71		
Sept. 6	Labour charges for hoeing maize and Ground nut	345.00	16	Sale proceeds of milk	185.40
Sept. 9	Purchased Diesel oil	186.00	30	Sale proceeds of milk	215.00
Sept. 20	Repair of tractor	26.00			
Sept. 26	Purchased insecticides/ pesticides	182.00			
Sept. 29	Labour for sugarcane	48.00			
Sept. 30	Elect. Charges	40.00			
Oct. '71			Oct. '71		
Oct. 3	Feed for Buffaloes	180.00	16	Sale of milk	216.00
Oct. 17	Labour for Groundnut harvesting	90.00	28	Sold groundnut 6 Qtls. @ 100/-	600.00
Oct. 18	Purchased chains for Cows and Buffaloes	16.00	31	Sold cotton 20 Qtls. @ Rs. 210.00	4200.00
Oct. 20	Urea 10 Q @ Rs. 86.00	86.00	31	Sold gur 5 Qtls. @ Rs. 150.00	750.00
	Di-amm. Phosphate 10 Qtls.	1096.00			
	Muriate of Potash 3 Qtls.	150.60			
	Total			Total	

Table 10.18

Classified Farm Cash Account of Singh Farm for year 1970-71

(*a*) Cash receipts (Rs.) for Year beginning July 1, 1970 and Ending June 30, 1971.

Sr. No.	*Date*	*To whom or where sold*	*Items & Price per unit*	*Quantity / No.*	*Cotton*	*Maize*	*Groundnut*	*Sugarcane*	*Wheat*	*Milk & Milk product*	*Poultry*	*Custom work*	*Cash Rent*	*Capital sales and money borrowed*		
														Livestock sales	*Machinery Sales*	*Govt. Loans and money borrowed*
1	*2*	*3*	*4*	*5*	*6*	*7*	*8*	*9*	*10*	*11*	*12*	*13*	*14*	*15*	*16*	*17*
1.	15.7.70	Milk Corpn.	0.90/kg.	250.00	—	—	—	—	—	225.00	—	—	—	—	—	—
2.	31.7	–do–	–do–	410.00	—	—	—	—	—	369.00	—	—	—	—	—	—
3.	12.8	–do–	–do–	240.00	—	—	—	—	—	216.00	—	—	—	—	—	—
4.	31.8	–do–	–do–	267.00	—	—	—	—	—	240.00	—	—	—	—	—	—
5.	16.9	–do–	–do–	206.00	—	—	—	—	—	185.00	—	—	—	—	—	—
6.	30.9	–do–	–do–	239.00	—	—	—	—	—	215.00	—	—	—	—	—	—
7.	16.10	–do–	–do–	240.00	—	—	—	—	—	216.00	—	—	—	—	—	—
8.	28.10	Coop. Mktg. Soc.	Rs. 100.00/ Qtl.	6.00	—	—	600.00	——	—	—	—	—	—	—	—	
9.	31.10	–do–	Rs. 210.00/ Qtl.	20.00	4200.00	—	—	—	—	—	—	—	—	—	—	—
10.	31.10	–do–	Rs. 150.00/ Qtl.	5.00	—	—	—	750.00	—	—	—	—	—	—	—	—
11.	31.10	Milk Corpn	0.90/kg	238.00	—	—	—	—	—	214.20	—	—	—	—	—	—
		Total	×××	—	4200.00	—	600.00	750.00	—	1880.20	—	—	—	—	—	—

Note. One or more pages for each month is required. Additional columns may be added or substitution made for more enterprises on a specific farm.

Table 10.18

Classified Farm Cash Account of Singh Farm (Contd.)

(*b*) Cash Expenses (Rs.) for the Year beginning July 1, 1970 and Ending June 30, 1971.

Date	Description of Transaction	*Cash rent & custom charge*	*Labour : permanent and temporary*	*Fuel & Oil*	*Machinery Building repair etc.*	*Artisans*	*Electricity*	*Fertilisers*	*Seeds*	*Pesticides & Insecticides*	*Feeds*	*Interest*	*Capital Cost* *Machines A*	*Capital Cost* *Bullocks B*	*Kind Payment*
1	2	3	4	5	6	7	8	9	10	11	12	13	14	15	16
July 6	Urea 20 Qtl. 86/-	—	—	—	—	—	—	1720.00	—	—	—	—	—	—	—
9	Casual labour	—	60.00	—	—	—	—	—	—	—	—	—	—	—	—
10	Diesel oil 200 L.	—	—	180.00	—	—	—	—	—	—	—	—	—	—	—
11	Muriate of Potash 4 Qt.	—	—	—	—	—	—	200.80	—	—	—	—	—	—	—
11	Di-amm. Phosphate 10 Qt.	—	—	—	—	—	—	1096.00	—	—	—	—	—	—	—
11	Maize Hybrid Seed	—	—	—	—	—	—	—	20000	—	—	—	—	—	—
16	Labour for Sugarcane	—	48.00	—	—	—	—	—	—	—	—	—	—	—	—
23	Endrine 1.5 litre	—	—	—	—	—	—	—	—	27.00	—	—	—	—	—
29	Electricity charge for motor	—	—	—	—	—	40.00	—	—	—	—	—	—	—	
31	Feeds (Concentrates)	—	—	—	—	—	—	—	—	—	18.00	—	—	—	—
	Sub Total	—	108.00	180.00	—	—	40.00	3076.80	200.00	27.00	180.00	—	—	—	—
Aug. 6	Mobil oil 5 litre	—	—	17.50	—	—	—	—	—	—	—	—	—	—	—
9	Labour for maize	—	87.00	—	—	—	—	—	—	—	—	—	—	—	—
11	Insecticides & Pesticides	—	—	—	—	—	—	—	—	145.00	—	—	—	—	—
12	Labour for groundnut	—	48.00	—	—	—	—	—	—	—	—	—	—	—	—
18	Repair and service of Tractor	—	—	—	352.00	—	—	—	—	—	—	—	—	—	—
25	Paid to Artisans	—	—	—	—	25.00	—	—	—	—	—	—	—	—	—
26	Purchase of feed	—	—	—	—	—	—	—	—	—	210.00	—	—	—	—
29	Labour	—	48.00	—	—	—	—	—	—	—	—	—	—	—	—
31	Electricity Bill	—	—	—	—	—	40.00	—	—	—	—	—	—	—	—
	Sub total	—	183.00	17.50	352.00	25.00	40.00	—	—	145.00	210.00	—	—	—	—

Limitation of the Cash Accounts

The cash account does not provide facts which will show the gain or loss or any measure of real profit for the farm as a whole for any specific year or given period of time, *e.g.*, transactions in the cash account record are restricted to those of the cash only. It does not also show gains or losses for different enterprises which make up the farm business.

INCOME STATEMENT

The objective of preparing the income statement is to summarise the data on income and expenses to present a truthful picture of the year's performance. An income statement is the list of all farm expenses or business debts on one hand and all receipts or business credits on the other. After bringing these together in a convenient form, expenses are subtracted from receipts to determine the net income for the year. A typical income statement is given in Table 10.19.

Analysis of the Year's Records

Farm records are seldom kept just for the sake of "keeping records". They represent a means to control the farm's business operations and to aid in obtaining greatest possible returns. The most important aid in obtaining records and accounts is to point out the strong and weak points in the farm business so that the business operations in the future can be adjusted to result in higher net earning to the producer. So the records should be kept and organised with great care and a reasonable degree of accuracy.

USE OF FARM FINANCIAL ACCOUNTS

The following are the uses of farm cash accounts :

1. Check on cash availability at any time

The farm cash account provides as basis for checking the total cash on hand and in the bank at any time *e.g.* : A complete cash account with one summary column for all personal expenses, can be used at the end of any month as a running check on the cash receipts and cash expenses to-date to determine the amount of cash available for future operations.

2. Provides receipts and expenses information for quick farm adjustments

The farm cash account provides a complete record of receipts and expenses at any time :

TABLE 10.19
Farm Income Statement of Singh Farm for the Year 1970-71

	Credits (Receipts)				*Debits (Expenses)*		
Sr. No.	*Particulars*	*Page/ Column*	*Amount (Rs.)*	*Sr. No.*	*Particulars*	*Page/ Column*	*Amount (Rs.)*
1.	**Crop Sales**			1.	**Operating Expenses**, ,		
	Kharif Crops				Labour hired	331	1650.00
	Cotton	304	10200.00		F.Y.Manure	-do-	600.00
	Maize	304	6500.00		Urea	-do-	2680.00
	Groundnut	304	600.00		Di-amm. Phosphate	-do-	2198.00
	Sugarcane	304	7500.00		Muriate of Potash	-do-	505.00
	Kh. Fodder	—	—		Seeds and Plants	-do-	1080.00
					Insecticides and pesticides	-do-	1250.00
	Sub Total		24800.00		Electricity	-do-	480.00
	Rabi Crops				Fuel and oil	-do-	1575.00
	Wheat Kalyan 227	304	15200.00		Feeds Purchased	-do-	1050.00
	Wheat Bhusa	-do-	1000.00		Poultry Purchased	-do-	—
	Gram	—	—		Repair of machinery	-do-	650.00
	Barley	—	—		Miscellaneous	-do-	406.00
	Sub total		16200.00		Sub Total		14025.00
2.	**Livestock Sales**			2.	**Fixed Expenses**		
	Milk	304	3000.00		Interest Paid	-do-	2750.00
	Milk Product	—	—		Cash rent	-do-	—
	Poultry	—	—		Labour Permanent	-do-	600.00
	Eggs	—	—		Land revenue	-do-	125.00
	Milch animals		—				
	Sub Total		3000.00		Sub Total		3475.00
3..	**Miscellaneous Receipts**						
	Custom work	—	—				
	Cash Rent received	—	—				
	Govt. Payments	—	—				
	Sub Total	—	—				
A.	**Gross Cash Receipt of Farm Production 1 + 2 + 3**	—	**44000.00**	**B.**	**Gross Cash Expenses on Production (1 + 2)**		**17500.00**
	Machinery Sold	—	—		Livestock Purchase	1	2500.00
	Farm Privilege	—	5250.00		New Machinery	—	—
	Livestock sold	—	1500.00		New Improvements	—	—
	Increase in Inventory	—	—		Total New Investments	—	2500.00
	Increase in liquid assets	—	—		Decrease in Inventory	—	—
					(Liquid, fixed and working assets)	—	1097.40
	Increase in fixed Assets	—	—				
	Total increase in Assets.	—	—		Total Decrease in Inventory	—	1097.40
C.	Total Receipts	—	50750.00	D.	Total Expenses	—	21097.40

Net Cash Income (A – B) 26500.00
Net Farm Income (C – D) 29652.60

e.g.—Sometimes, farm plans need to be changed immediately in order to adjust to changing physical and economic conditions. A cash account provides the facts needed to make these revisions on a sounder basis. After the consideration has been given to the expenses and receipts, it also supplies the facts needed to make an earlier and more accurate appraisal of changes that are contemplated.

A frequent check on receipts compared with expenses will save time and money.

3. Provide information on costs and returns of different enterprises

The summarised cash account of the farm business, will provide an indication of the relative importance of the receipts and expenses from different sources. The classified receipts compared with the classified expenses, will indicate major differences in enterprise costs and returns.

4. Provide the basis for a simple study and analysis of farm business

The summarised classified cash account of the farm business provides the basis for a simple analysis of the farm business. The major objective of an analysis of any business is to provide a more intelligent basis for future planning

A farm financial account is a brief, simple record of cash transactions involving the farm business as a whole and does not provide the detailed information needed for a study of all the different internal operations of the farm. Such a record, however, will supply much information of value in planning the future operations of the farm business.

5. The analysis provides farmer an opportunity to compare the years results with his expectations (*i.e.*, his budget at the start of year).
6. It helps to make comparisons of his efficiency with performance of other farmers operating under similar conditions.
7. Analysis provides facts about the rates at which the farmer is combining resources into saleable products.

TREATMENT AND CLASSIFICATION OF SPECIAL TRANSACTIONS FOR FINANCIAL ACCOUNTS

There are a number of transactions which are common to all farms and can be handled with standard procedures in farm financial accounting. However, there are numerous transactions which are not frequent but are unique in character. Another complexity is added because of the business and family household being closely related to each other. This close tie-up presents many difficulties in handling transactions. We discuss below the treatment of certain transactions or items which cannot be handled in the financial accounts in the same manner as ordinary purchases or sales. Some of them are :

1. Government payments like subsidies, etc.
2. Capital Changes,
3. Off-farm work and family labour,
4. Joint farm and household expenses,
5. Farm produce consumed in household,
6. Non-farm income and expenses,
7. Borrowed capital and interest payments,
8. Prepayments and accruals,
9. Taxes
10. Losses.

Such transactions or happenings can be classified and accounted for by :

(*i*) *Mode of Payment* :
(*a*) If received in cash (subsidy, etc.), consider as receipt.
(*b*) If paid in the form of reduced costs, consider the reduced cost as expense.
(*c*) If the cost of any asset is taken as a subsidy, it may first be shown as receipt and then as expense—to show some value of the asset in the inventory.

(*ii*) *Purpose of Analysis*. Treat the special transaction differently depending upon the purpose of analysis *e.g.*, whether for estimating net worth or for complete yearly business analysis.

(*iii*) *Capital Receipts*. These are not included in the annual business analysis but taken care of in the inventory changes.

There is, in fact, no rigid or standard rule for treating special transaction. It depends all on one's own judgement as to how much is to be taken as a receipt or expenses. Discussed below are the cases listed earlier :

Government Payments

There are a large number of Government programmes and development schemes, through which the farmers either get cash payments in the form of prizes, premiums or they get certain concessions such as land revenue remission. While they can be treated as income from non- farm sources, they go typically as farm receipts because if the farmers were not operating a particular unit, he would have not received them.

Some of the typical examples of Government payments are discussed below :

Particulars of subsidy/remission	*Nature/purpose of transaction*	*Method of treatment of the transaction*
1. Minimum price fixed for a particular agricultural product.	Government may sometimes pay difference between market price and minimum price (floor price) fixed by Government .	Direct Receipt.
2. Premium on good quality seed.	Sometimes to encourage farmers to produce improved seed for further multiplication, Government pays premium. Example : Market price of wheat may be Rs. 80 per quintal and Government may pay @ Rs. 84 per quintal, *i.e.*, Rs. 4/- as a premium	Enter Rs. 4 as receipt of the amount of premium as paid separately.
3. Subsidy on the purchase of improved seeds.	Deptt. of Agriculture may allow subsidy on purchasing improved new strains of seeds. Example : Actual Price of wheat Rs. 80 but Government gave subsidy of Rs. 5/-. The farmer got wheat @ Rs. 75/-. It is a case of lowering the cost.	Take the cost of seeds so purchased at the reduced rate as expense, *i.e.* Enter Rs. 75 expense side.
4. Subsidy on the purchase of implements. Plant Protection equipment, Superphosphate, Insecticides, fruit plants, Poultry birds, etc.	The subsidy may be paid direct to the dealer/fabricator and the farmer may have to pay only subsidised cost. Example : (*i*) Market price of plough is Rs. 30 and a farmer got at Rs. 20 after availing a subsidy of Rs. 10 from the Government. (*ii*) Government gives subsidy of Rs. 500 for the purchase of a tractor.	This subsidy may not be taken as receipt. It is just purchasing articles at a lower cost. Rs. 500 is not the income due to operation of the business. It is just a reduction in cost.
5. Subsidy on minor irrigation loans.	Suppose one gets Rs. 2500 as a loan for tubewell, with the assumption that Rs. 500 will be allowed as subsidy after the completion of the project.	The loan should be considered only that amount after deducting the subsidy. The interest and depreciation should be charged on the balance for inventory purpose.

Particulars of subsidy/remission	*Nature/purpose of transaction*	*Method of treatment of the transaction*
6. Subsidy on green manuring.	Government allows a subsidy on green manuring @ Rs. 3/- per acre.	Enter as Receipt.
7. Kharba or Remission.	(*i*) *Cash relief :* Government may pay some subsidy on account of failure of a crop.	Enter as Production Receipt.
	(*ii*) *Fodder relief :* One raises his own fodder crop but it fails. Government may give some fodder relief.	Enter this amount of relief as receipt. It is just minimising the loss.
	(*iii*) *Cloth & Food relief :* Government may give clothes & food to flood sufferers as a relief.	This amount should not be entered as receipt for business analysis. It is personal receipt.
	(*iv*) *Remission on water rates :*	
	(*a*) Due to failure of crops, the farmer got Rs. 300 as *Kharba*.	(*a*) Rs. 300 may be taken as receipt.
	(*b*) If Rs. 300 as water rate has already been paid and entered in books on a certain date and latter on kharba occurs and Government remits back Rs. 300/-.	(*b*) In this case, do not take this amount as receipt, but as remittance.
8. Crop competition prizes and awards.	Suppose one takes extra labour and spends on additional fertilizers, etc. for winning the crop competition and gets a prize.	Direct Production Receipt.

Capital Changes

Usually farm financial accounts include pages for recording business expenses and receipts for the year. They also include pages and forms for entering other costs such as depreciation which do not show up as cash expenses and for inventory accumulations which are not accounted as cash receipts during the year.

One problem in making these entries and in computing income is to distinguish between : (*i*) the income and cost flows of the year and (*ii*) the capital investments which do not relate to the particular year but will give rise to income and cost flows over a number of years. Income and cost flows of the year are entered as receipts and expenses but capital investments are not because they provide inputs and outputs or sales over a period of years. For example, if a farmer purchases poultry birds (chicks) with the idea of feeding and selling them within a year, their costs and return will be realised within the year. But, suppose a farmer purchases buffaloes for running a dairy. This cost cannot be handled like poultry since it is a capital investment to be used over a period of years. The farmer will record the purchase price but not on the pages on livestock expenses for the current year. Buffaloes are an outlay, but the full cost is not chargeable to the year in which they are purchased. One should be careful that the full value of such transactions does not affect the expenses or receipts of the year. These purchases can be entered under 'livestock-purchase account', but the undepreciated value of buffaloes will appear in the closing inventory at the end of the year and will balance the amount of expenditure incurred except for the depreciation in value that occurred during the year.

Off-farm Work

In India, the size of holdings is very small and often insufficient to provide full time work to most of the farmers and their family members. Such farmers often supplement their incomes with off-farm work. Records of such earnings from off-farm work should be recorded separately for the purpose of analysing the efficiency of the farm business.

Family Labour

If a farmer is interested only in net farm and family income and does not actually pay wages to the family members then he should not record the family labour as an expense. If a farmer employs his son or other members of his family to replace hired workers, the wage payment should be entered as an expense.

In addition to the cash wage payment, the value of board and other perquisites should also be entered in the accounts as a labour expense.

Joint Farm and Household Expenses

Many expenses on the farm are joint in the sense that they are neither entirely for the business nor entirely for family living. Examples are : radios, newspapers, magazines, etc. which may be purchased mainly for the enjoyment of the family but they also often contribute market reports, technical information or other knowledge for farming efficiency. Other examples of joint farm and household expenses include the telephone, automobile, etc. When part of the service of an asset is used in the household, it obviously cannot be charged entirely to the farm business. A portion of such expenses should be recorded in the household or personal accounts.

It is often necessary to estimate the portion of the expenses to be charged to the household. One way is to split each expense item as it occurs. Another and easier procedure is to enter the expense items in a separate set of accounts, then allocate its use at the end of the accounting period.

Farm Produce Consumed in the Household

Considerable number and quantities of farm-raised products are ordinarily consumed by the family. They are as much a part of the farm income as commodities which are sold through regular market channels. They should be, therefore, recorded as receipts in the business accounts.

If family keeps household or personal accounts, the home-consumed products may be recorded there and carried to the business accounts as a credit at the end of the year.

Quantities as well as values both should be recorded since these may be needed in computing physical production and working out efficiency measures. The quantity and value data are then carried to the corresponding enterprise and income records at the end of the year.

The Table 10.20 gives proforma that can be used for recording the household consumption of the farm produce along with relevant data of Mr. Singh Farm.

TABLE 10.20

Record of Farm Produce Used in the Household

Singh Farm Year 1970-71

Month	*Milk*		*Eggs*		*Vegetables*		*Wheat*		*Maize*		*Gur*		*Others*	
	Litres	*Value*	*No.*	*Value*	*Kgs.*	*Value*	*Qtl.*	*Value*	*Qtl.*	*Value*	*Kgs.*	*Value*	*Qtls.*	*Value*
		(Rs.)		(Rs.)		(Rs.)		(Rs.)		(Rs.)		(Rs.)		(Rs.)
July	133	119.70	—	—	—	—	2.50	190.00	—	—	30	45.00	10	50.00
Aug.	124	111.60	—	—	—	—	2.50	190.00	—	—	40	60.00	—	—
Sept.	120	108.00	—	—	—	—	2.50	190.00	—	—	40	60.00	—	—
Oct.	155	139.50	—	—	—	—	2.00	152.00	0.50	25.00	40	60.00	—	—
Nov.	186	167.40	—	—	—	—	0.50	38.00	2.50	125.00	40	60.00	10	50.00
Dec.	186	167.40	—	—	—	—	0.50	38.00	2.50	125.00	30	45.00	10	50.00
Jan.	146	131.40	—	—	—	—	0.50	38.00	2.50	125.00	30	45.00	15	75.00
Feb.	140	126.00	—	—	—	—	1.50	114.00	1.50	75.00	45	67.50	15	75.00
Mar.	124	111.60	—	—	—	—	2.50	190.00	0.50	25.00	45	67.50	15	75.00
April	120	108.00	—	—	—	—	4.00	304.00	—	—	60	90.00	15	75.00
May	124	111.60	—	—	—	—	4.00	304.00	—	—	60	90.00	15	75.00
June	109	97.80	—	—	—	—	2.00	152.00	—	—	40	60.00	15	75.00
Total	1667	1500.00	—	—	—	—	25.00	1900.00	10.00	500.00	500	750.00	120	600.00

Non Farm Enterprise Income and Expenses

Income from enterprises other than farming accrues to some farmers. A farmer, for example, might have a small industry unit in addition to his farming business. Where this is the case, transactions related to the farm should be kept separate from those of other investments or enterprises.

If the transactions are not very frequent, other incomes and expenses can be entered in a simple record as in an example below : (Table—10.21).

TABLE 10.21

Non farm or Outside Investment Incomes & Expenses

Income			Expenses		
Date	Item	Value	Date	Item	Value
25 May	Rent received of a house in the city	Rs. 100	Jan. 30	Income tax paid	Rs. 24
26 May	Interest on bonds	Rs. 80	—	Tax on house in city	Rs. 60
Total :		Rs. 180			Rs. 84
Net Income from Non farm Sources					Rs. 96

BORROWED CAPITAL AND INTEREST PAYMENTS

Sometimes it becomes difficult to distinguish between methods for handling borrowed funds and interest payments. Interest is clearly an expense to the farm business for the use of borrowed capital. It is a payment for the use of a resource owned by other person(s) and is similar to wages for labour and rent for land. It can be entered as an expense in the relevant columns of the farm accounts. When borrowed capital is repaid it is not entered as an expense to the farm business.

Most of the single-entry accounts provide a column where some payments and expenses which are not the true expenses within the year can be entered. Otherwise they can be recorded on some other pages which the farmer may reserve for the purpose.

Accruals

It is not uncommon for a farm to have an income that has had accrued but not yet realised. Income may be earned during the year but not received until the next accounting period begins. If the true income of the business is to be determined, these credits must be entered in the accounts for the year the income accrues. Otherwise, the income for the year will be underestimated while that for the following year(s) will be overestimated. These accruals may be entered in the same manner as cash receipts with an indication that they are yet receivable. At the same time, money for a produce sold or custom work performed, etc., in a previous accounting period should not be entered in the record of receipts in the year it is received.

Prepayments or Advances

Advances or prepayments must also be recognised in the accounting period. For example, a farmer may have advanced some money to a hired man just before closing the books. Such payments should not be entered as debits against current year but should be noted and entered in the following years record.

Taxes

Not all taxes paid by the farmer receive the same treatment in the accounts. Income tax is payable after net income has been computed. It should not be entered as an item of expense. If taxes like crop cess, land revenue, etc., are paid these should be considered as farm expenses.

Death and other Losses

A fairly common cost to the farm business is the loss through death of animals and poultry birds, etc. They consume feed during the year and hence expenses are incurred while no sale proceeds are realised. The accounts should automatically take care of this type of expense, if kept on an inventory basis. If, for example, the feed which were consumed by the animals that die later on was on hand in the beginning inventory, it will show up as an inventory decrease. As an inventory decrease, it will be a debit or expense against the business. If such a feed, labour and other items were purchased during the year, they will represent a direct expense while no income may be realised from the dead animal. If insurance payment is received on the asset which is lost through fire, accident or death, it should be entered as a receipt or recognised in the closing inventory. Otherwise the business will get debited with an inventory decrease even though the operator may have been fully reimbursed through the insurance payment.

FARM EFFICIENCY MEASURES

An important element in farm business management or decision making relates to the manner in which available resources are allocated vis-a-vis the objectives of the farmer.

A "measuring stick" is necessary to provide guides and standard for appraising accuracy of decisions regarding the use of resources. One method of production is said to be more efficient than the other when it yields a greater valuable output per unit of a valuable input. From an economic standpoint, efficiency is desirable and the science of farm management deals with such principles and theories of farm business organisation which are instrumental in increasing the efficiency of the business.

Efficiency can be related to (1) the operation of the farm business as a whole, (2) any individual phase of the business, line of production or enterprise (dairy, poultry, wheat, cotton, sugarcane, maize, etc.), (3) the use of various factors of production or resources (land labour, capital), or (4) to any single input (fertilizer, feeds, machine, etc.).

Various efficiency measures, therefore, need to be developed to express technical efficiency in various farm enterprises and to relate these to the financial success.

The various farm efficiency measures can be discussed as : (*i*) Physical efficiency measures (Physical Efficiency) and (*ii*) Value efficiency (Financial Efficiency). They can be further categorised as : (*i*) Ratio measures and (*ii*) Absolute for aggregate measures.

A brief description of some of the farm efficiency measures is given below :

TOTAL AREA OF THE FARM

The first measure of size is the acreage of the farm; either of total land or land under crops. This is a fairly satisfactory measure for comparing a given type of land and a given type of farming. Average area per farm varies from region to region and the combination of enterprises also varies from good to poor soil and from humid to arid climates. One can consider number of standard acres under such situations and compare the size of farms.

Land Use Efficiency

Some of the measures or indices measuring the rate of production are :

(*i*) *Yield per acre* (production efficiency). The production efficiency of a farm with respect of any particular crop enterprise can be expressed in terms of percentage as compared with average yield of the locality.

Chart of Categories of Farm Efficiency Measures

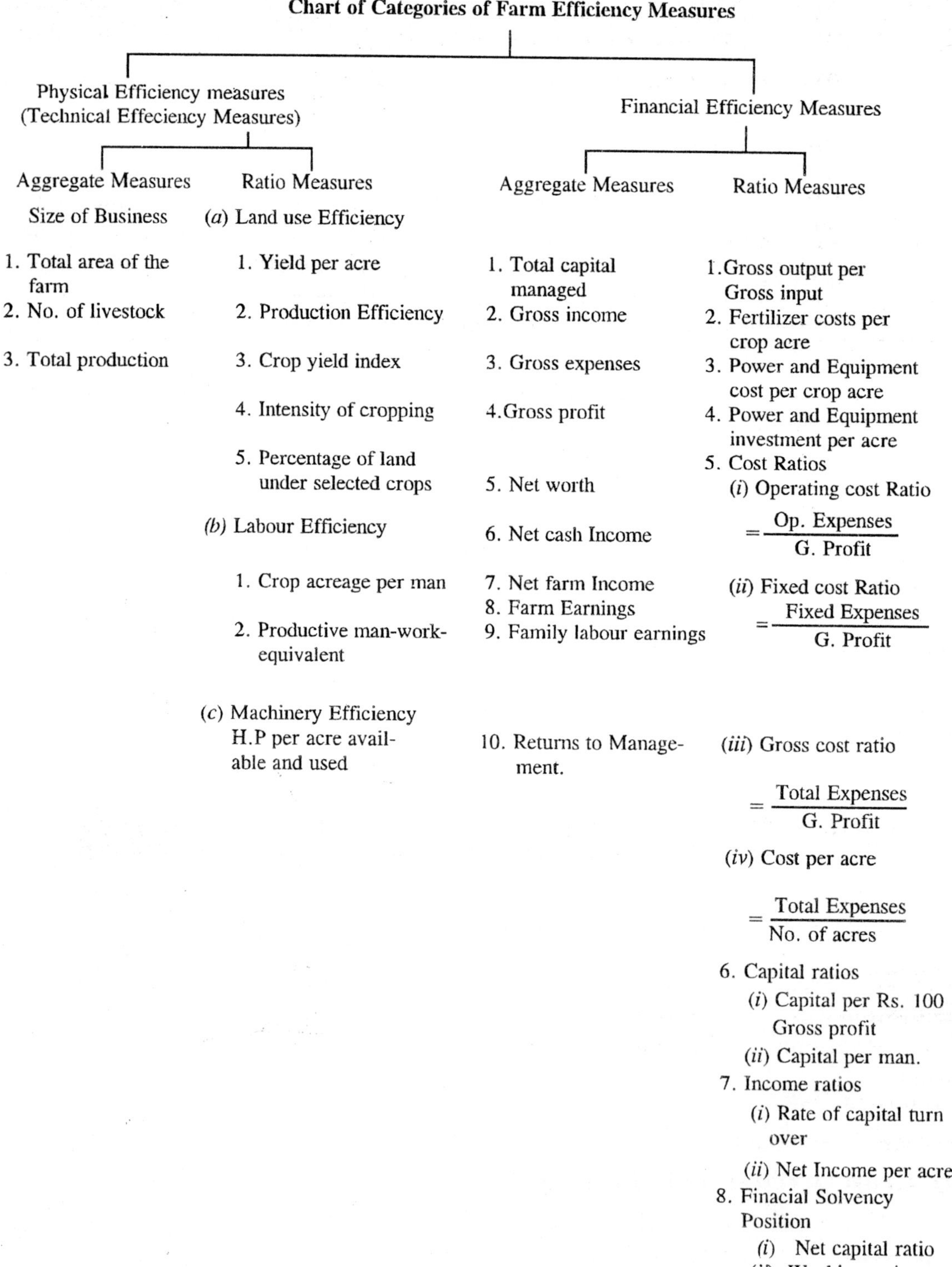

An example :

Wheat yield per acre of Farm 'A' = 13 qtls.

Average yield of the locality = 10 qtls.

$$\text{Production efficiency of farm 'A'} = \frac{13 \times 100}{10} = 130\%$$

(*ii*) *Crop yield index.* It is a measure of comparison of the yields of all crops on a given farm with the average yields of these crops in the locality. The relationship is expressed in percentage terms. This yield index is a convenient measure because it combines all the yields into a single figure.

Example :

Crop	*Acreage yield in quintals*		*Acres of crop farm 'X'*	*Crop yield on farm X as a % of locality (col. 3)/Col (2).X(100)*	*Percentage multiplied by acres*
	Locality	*Farm 'X'*			
1	2	3	4	5	6
Cotton	3 qtls.	4 qtls.	3	133	399
Wheat	10 qtls.	12 qtls.	8	120	960
Maize	10 qtls.	9 qtls.	6	90	540
Total :	—	—	17	—	1899

$$\text{Crop Yield Index} = \frac{1899}{17} = 111.7\%$$

(*iii*) *Intensity of cropping.* It measures the extent of the use of land for cropping purposes during a given year. It is expressed as a percentage.

$$\text{Cropping intensity} = \frac{\text{Area cropped}}{\text{Total cultivated area}} \times 100$$

LABOUR EFFICIENCY MEASURES

By comparing the labour efficiency we can know whether the labour on a farm is more or less than what is required. We can also find out whether the labour is relatively more or less efficient.

(i) Crop acreage per man equivalent

The significance of this measure is influenced by the varying proportion of crops with high or low labour requirements, such as potatoes compared with wheat. It is one of the simplest measures and is computed by dividing the total acres in crops by man- equivalents.

(ii) Productive man-work units per man-equivalent

It is another good and accurate general measure of labour efficiency for all types of farms. This measure is computed by dividing total productive man-work units by the number of man- equivalents on the farm. For average efficiency on most of the Indian farms a full-time worker (man equivalent) should accomplish at least 250 units per year. This measure can compare even farms in different type of farming areas with different degrees of intensity or with varying crop acreages and livestock. A productive man work unit is the average amount of work accomplished by one man in the usual 10-hour day. The total productive man work units from a given farm represent the number of 10-hour days required under average conditions and abilities to do all the work necessary on the production of crops. The P.M.W.U. are obtained by multiplying the acres of each crop and number of each kind of livestock by the average labour requirements per unit of each enterprise in a region.

$$\text{P.M.W.U. per man} = \frac{\text{Total P.M.W.U}}{\text{Man Equivalents}}$$

Capital Efficiency

This may be expressed in various ways :

Power, machinery and equipment costs per crop acre (including bullock power)

This is a useful measure and can be calculated as given in an example below (a farm of 50 acres) :

1. 10% interest on power, machinery and equipment investment (20,000)	Rs. 2000
2. Yearly repair costs (machinery & equipment)	Rs. 1000
3. Yearly depreciation allowance	Rs. 2000
4. Yearly fuel & Lubrication costs	Rs. 1000
5. Feed & fodder costs including medicine costs for bullocks and camels	Rs. 800
6. Yearly taxes	Rs. 600
7. Yearly insurance premium	Rs. 200
8. Yearly machinery hire	Rs. 800
Total :	Rs. 8400

$$\text{Machinery cost per crop acre} = \frac{\text{Total cost}}{\text{Total crop acres}}$$

$$= \frac{8400}{50} = \text{Rs. } 168/-$$

Power & Equipment Investment per crop acre :

$$= \frac{\text{Total machinery investment}}{\text{No. of crop acres}}$$

$$= \text{Rs. } \frac{20,000}{50} = \text{Rs. } 400.$$

COST RATIOS

Most of the ratios or efficiency factors discussed up to this point are needed in the process of analysis of the records. Their purpose, in general, is to indicate a strong or weak point in the organisation or operation of the business and to call attention to the specific phases or angles of the business where greater managerial attention is needed. In addition, there are other ratios that are often used in a more general analysis. They deal with the relationship between costs and returns, relationship of capital investment to income, and the rate of activity or turnover of the capital.

Cost ratios are averages and their magnitudes reflect physical production efficiency, selection of enterprises, prices received for commodities and the expense for the production elements. These cost ratios are discussed below :

(i) Operating cost ratio

The operating ratio is the percentage which operating expenes absorb out of gross profit. It shows the proportion of total income used in (1) hiring labour, (2) buying seeds, fuel and other annual supplies and (3) in keeping equipment in operation, etc.

It is computed by dividing total operating expenses by gross profit and can be expressed as a percentage or a ratio.

$$\text{Operating cost Ratio} = \frac{\text{Total operating cost}}{\text{Total profit}}$$

Improvement in operating efficiency is directly reflected in this ratio. It should be watched closely from year to year. It may also increase or decrease because income may increase or decrease due to commodity price changes.

(ii) Over-head charges (Fixed Ratio)

Fixed expenses continue in about the same amount regardless of the current operating policy. Their relative importance in production can be expressed by a ratio determined by dividing the total fixed costs by the gross profits.

The fixed costs generally include : (1) Land revenue, (2) Water taxes, (3) Other taxes, (4) Depreciation, (5) Yearly insurance premium, (6) Interest on total investment, etc.

$$\text{Over-head charges ratio} = \frac{\text{Total fixed cost per year}}{\text{Gross income}}$$

For a growing efficient business, the rate of increase in gross income should be faster than rate of increase in fixed costs. The fixed cost ratio will vary with changes both in gross profits and fixed costs. Little can be done to reduce total fixed costs within a short period but their magnitude relative to output can be reduced by expanding production while holding buildings and other such overheads *i.e.* capital, investments constant.

Costs per Acre. Both operating and fixed costs per acre can be computed as $\frac{\text{Total costs}}{\text{Number of acres}}$. These ratios do not vary with selling prices and income as does the ratio of fixed or operating costs per unit of gross profits. They are somewhat meaningless when crop and livestock are intermingled in varying proportions. Only farms with similar enterprises can be compared with these ratios.

Gross (Cost) Ratio

The gross (cost) ratio or ratio of total expenses to gross income is a combined measure of the profit making ability of the farm. While the net income expresses the amount by which income exceeds expenses; the gross ratio expresses the percentage of gross income consumed by expenses and is, therefore, independent of the absolute size of the business. Gross income and total expenses both affect the ratio. It may be large or small depending on the level of prices as well as the amount and level of expenses. It is indicative of the profit margin for the business as a whole. At any given level of costs and prices, it can be usefully employed in the analysis of the business. The percentage of gross income absorbed by expenses also varies with the type of the farm. With this ratio, comparisons between farms should be made only when the farms are of the same general organisation.

CAPITAL RATIOS

Capital ratios can also be used in the analysis of the organisation with respect to the resources of the farm.

(1) Capital per unit of Gross Income

Occasionally, a ratio is computed to measure the total amount of capital invested per unit of gross income (say thousand rupees)

$$= \frac{\text{Total capital invested}}{\text{gross income}}$$

(2) Capital per man

The ratio of capital per man indicates the combination of resources in a general way. It is, ordinarily, computed by dividing the total capital by the number of man-year equivalents employed on the farm. An optimum ratio will vary depending on the kind of farming and the availability of funds. It does not adequately reflect variations which can be possible through capital labour substitution.

(3) Rate of capital turnovers

It is the most common measure of capital efficiency. It is the ratio of the total farm income to the farm capital (total farm assets). Rate of capital turn over $= \frac{\text{Gross Income}}{\text{Total farm assets}} \times 100$. The rate of capital turnover indicates the number of years required for the farm receipts (income) to equal the average farm capital. A faster turnover rate is a sign of good farm business. A high rate of turnover is especially important for the beginning farmer who is short on capital. This rate, ordinarily, varies widely with the type of farm investments.

MEASURES OF FARM INCOME AND PROFIT EFFICIENCY

There are various measures which can be used to evaluate farm incomes and profits. The measures listed below can be useful for such an analysis.

(*i*) *Net Cash Income.* Total cash receipts from production minus total cash operating expenses.

(*ii*) *Net Farm Income.* Net cash income from production plus or minus change in inventory in non-depreciable items and depreciation on power machinery, livestock, buildings, etc.

(*iii*) *Farm Earnings.* Net farm income + value of farm privileges (farm products) used in home.

(*iv*) *Family labour earnings.* Farm earnings minus interest charges on farm capital.

(*v*) *Percent Returns to capital.* Ratio of farm earnings minus imputed value of the family labour to average capital investment, expressed in percent terms.

(*vi*) *Returns to management.* Family labour earnings minus imputed value of the family labour.

For illustration of working out these efficiency measures, see Table 10.22.

TABLE 10.22
Farm Business Analysis of a Farm Situation in Punjab

Particulars and Efficiency measure	*Present Plan 1969- 70*	*Alternative Plan 1970-71*
Net Cash Income Farm Production	Rs.	Rs.
(*i*) *Cash Receipts :*		
Sale of rabi crops	1100	1700
Sale of kharif crops	600	1200
Sale of milk	150	400
Sale of eggs	100	150
Miscellaneous sales	150	200
Sub Total	2100	3650
(*ii*) *Cash Expenses :*		
Labour rabi season	300	290
Labour kharif season	200	150
Seeds	50	200
Fertilizers	200	300
Purchase of feeds	200	385
Miscellaneous	210	150
Sub Total	1160	1475
(*iii*) *Change in Inventory :*	+ 300	+ 900
(*iv*) *Farm privileges (Farm products used at home) :*	600	1000
(*v*) *Interest Charges @ 8% on av. farm capital :*	200	375
(*vi*) *Imputed Value of Family Labour :*	450	800
A. **Net Cash Income** (*i—ii*)	940	2175
B. **Net Farm Income** (A + *iii*)	1240	3075
C. **Farm Earnings** (B + *iv*)	1860	4075
D. **Family Labour Earning** (C—*v*)	1660	3700
E. **Returns to Management** (D—*vi*)	1210	2900

Efficiency Measures and Business Decisions

The following are the common points to note in this respect :

Land use Efficiency. The intensity of cropping can be compared with established standards and necessary improvements can be made to get more production. The yield per acre and crop yield index can be compared with potentials under given conditions and the short-falls can be removed.

Labour Efficiency. By comparing the labour efficiency, it can be figured out whether labour is more or less than what is required on the farm. It can also be found out whether the labour is efficiently or inefficiently used and measures can be taken to improve the labour efficiency.

Capital Efficiency. A faster turnover rate of capital is a sign of good business. The rate of turnover on a particular farm can be compared with other farms under similar conditions.

Returns to Different Factors of Production

One can calculate the income measures to know the returns to labour, land, capital and management as all have their opportunity cost. If the actual returns are less than the opportunity cost, the farmer would need to make necessary adjustments and increase his efficiency.

Evaluation of Records and Surveys for Research

Data from the farms such as records, have one major advantage over those from survey or other sources. The records are more complete and internally consistent. It is often possible to follow the influence of a factor from one section of the business to another. If the data come from a survey and depend on the memory of the farmer some months after the event, it is difficult to trace such influences.

The records data also have some disadvantages. Most serious of these is that a group of farm record-keepers cannot be taken as representative of farmers in general.

It has been observed that those farmers who maintain records fall in the category of higher incomes. This suggests that the alert and capable farmers are more inclined to keep accounts. At the same time, farm business data from the records facilitate management and contribute to the incomes. In any case, farm records are extremely helpful to the research worker, to the extension worker, and to the teacher. Of course, they are even more valuable to the farmer who keeps them. Many of the lessons they contain can be generalised for other farmers in the same region. But, their results must be interpreted with a great deal of care. Such, records can be usefully employed in the research on the following specific aspects :

(*i*) Area variation studies to estimate the earnings and financial success of farming in different areas and under different types and systems of farming. Such an information can be helpful in taking decisions on the relative profitability of different enterprises in various areas.

(*ii*) Capital investment patterns studies to determine capital investment needed for different types and sizes of farms and for different enterprises. This information may be useful for farm financial management and to determine seasonal capital needs for different types and sizes of farms.

(*iii*) Cost of production studies to determine the cost of production per unit of various enterprises and cost of performing of various operations. With such an information, farmers can decide whether or not to shift their feed, labour, capital, etc., to other enterprises or operational activities.

(*iv*) Economies of scale studies to determine the effect of size, organisation and productive efficiency on the earnings of the farmers.

(*v*) Resource requirement studies to determine the physical input requirements in different enterprises, in different areas and in different types and sizes of farms. The information obtained through these studies can be helpful in decisions on adoption of new improved practices.

(*vi*) Historical trends to determine the general direction of the farm business earnings. These studies can indicate whether the farming in general is becoming a 'gaining' or a 'losing' business.

(*vii*) Consumption pattern studies to determine the family living costs in different areas.

1. ***Define farm accountancy. What are the objectives of the farm records ? Why and how is the study of farm accountancy important to a student of Farm Management ?***
2. ***What are the advantages of keeping farm records and accounts ?***
3. ***"A farm business without records and accounts is just like a watch without hands." Comment.***
4. ***Name three stages in keeping farm records and accounts.***
5. ***Name different types of records that can be maintained on a commercial farm.***

6. *Suggest a set of physical records that a farmer can easily maintain under Indian conditions.*
7. *What uses could you make of a map of the farm ?*
8. *What is a farm inventory ? Why is it necessary to take inventory ?*
9. (*a*) *Name different methods of valuation. State briefly some important principles governing the valuation of farm assets.*

   (*b*) *What methods should be used for inventory valuation of :*

   (*i*) *Buildings* (*ii*) *Equipment* (*iii*) *Working livestock* (*iv*) *Feeds and other farm supplies* (*v*) *Irrigation wells (original cost not known)*

   (a) *by a farmer who wants to close his farm business.*

   (b) *by a farmer who would like to continue farming.*
10. (*a*) *Define depreciation. Explain and give a few examples of each of the four most important methods of computing depreciation.*

    (*b*) *Is depreciation a genuine expense ? If so, why ?*

    (c) *What would happen to the net worth statement figure and to profit or loss figure if depreciation is ignored ?*

    (*d*) *A tractor is purchased for Rs. 15000/-. It is estimated that it will last for 10 years and that the scrap value will be Rs. 1000. Compute the annual value of depreciation by each of the four methods of depreciation.*
11. (*a*) *What do you understand by net worth statement ? Prepare a net worth statement assuming a typical farm situation.*

    (*b*) *How will a study of the asset and liability items of an inventory help to point out the direction of financing of the farm business ?*
12. (*a*) *With the data given below about assets and liabilities of a farmer, prepare net worth statement, and work out net capital ratio, working ratio and current ratio. Also comment on the financial soundness of the farm business.*

ASSETS	*July 1, 1971 (Rs.)*	*July 1, 1972 (Rs.)*
Poultry	*400*	*700*
Land	*50000*	*80000*
Cattle shed and store	*6000*	*5000*
Tubewell	*5000*	*4800*
Bullocks and buffaloes	*2500*	*3000*

Farm fences	*500*	*450*
Power equipment	*800*	*600*
Bullock driven implements	*2000*	*2500*
Seeds and feeds	*300*	*1400*
Fertilizers	*1000*	*700*
Farm Yard Manure	*250*	*300*
Cash in hand	*1000*	*2000*
Accounts receivable	*1500*	*2500*
Standing crops	*1200*	*1800*
Crops in store	*600*	*1200*
LIABILITIES		
Long term loans	*5000*	*3000*
Short term loans	*1000*	*4500*
Bills payable (short term)	*1500*	*2000*
Mortgage on land	*4000*	*25000*
Medium term loan payable	*3500*	*3000*

(b) ***Prepare a net worth statement for the following farm situation as on July 1, 1972 and make a comment on the farmer's financial position.***

He has to pay Rs. 500/- to Cooperative Society on account of fertilizer loan. He owes Rs. 100 to Mr. Singh as balance of payment due to purchase of a buffalo, Outstanding mortgage loan against land payable in yearly instalments of Rs. 10,000. He pays Rs. 500/- to Government as yearly instalment for pumping set. He has Rs. 100 as cash in hand and Rs. 500/- in bank. He expects Rs. 100 as debts receivable for sale of fodder. On annual valuation, it was found that he has one cow (Rs. 500), two bullocks (Rs. 1800), one pumping set (Rs. 3500), one cart (Rs. 600), wheat in stock (Rs. 600), 6 quintals gram (Rs. 360), gur 1 qtl. (Rs. 150), and fertilizer worth Rs. 300. He has 10 acres land valued Rs. 40,000 and farm-shed and building worth Rs. 10,000.

(c) ***With the data given below, about assets and liabilities of farm, prepare a continuous net worth statement as on July 1 each year and comment on the financial soundness of the farm business.***

ASSETS (RS.)	*July 1, 1970*	*July 1, 1971*	*July 1, 1972*
Bullocks and buffaloes	*2000*	*2700*	*3200*
Poultry	*450*	*400*	*1600*

Cattle shed and store	*5200*	*5000*	*4800*
Farm fences	*650*	*600*	*550*
Land	*50000*	*50000*	*50000*
Orchard	*5000*	*10000*	*10000*
Tubewell	*5300*	*5000*	*4800*
Power equipment	*1200*	*1000*	*1850*
Bullock driven implements	*1500*	*1600*	*1900*
Fertilizers	*180*	*200*	*350*
Farm Yard Manure	*270*	*250*	*500*
Seeds and feeds	*1500*	*1400*	*2000*
Cash in hand	*1100*	*1000*	*200*
Account receivable	*1200*	*1000*	*200*
Standing crops	*800*	*1500*	*2500*
Crop in store	*650*	*1450*	*1750*
LIABILITIES			
Long term loan	*2000*	*3000*	*4000*
Short term loan	*1500*	*2000*	*2500*
Bills payable (short term)	*1200*	*1000*	*2000*
Mortgage on land	*35000*	*30000*	*2500*

13. (a) *Draw up a proforma for an income-statement. What information will this statement contain ?*

    (b) *Discuss the various financial efficiency measures.*

14. (a) *Suppose you are required to analyse the annual financial operations of a farm business. How would you handle the following items of expenses and receipts ?*

    (i) *Loans received for purchase of fertilizer* Rs. 300/-

    (ii) *Tubewell installation expenses made during the year* Rs. 7500/-

    (iii) *Crop sold but payment not received during the year.* Rs. 3500/-

    (iv) *Loan received for the purchase of a tractor* Rs. 20000/-

    (v) *Feed expenses incurred but bill not paid during the year.* Rs. 250/-

    (b) *How are the following types of receipts and expenses accounted for in the analysis of annual income for a farm business as a whole ?*

    (i) *Unexhausted supplies of seeds and fertilizers.*

    (ii) *Government Subsidies.*

(iii) *Unsold crops.*

(iv) *Farm produced fodder fed to livestock.*

(v) *Major repairs to a tractor.*

15. *How would you handle the following items in the analysis of annual income from a farm business as a whole ?*

(i) *Cash expenses incurred on major repairs of the farm tractor.*

(ii) *20 quintals of maize raised on the farm and fed to cattle.*

(iii) *Telephone and pick-up transport expenses.*

(iv) *Received Rs. 350 as 'Kharaba' from Government on account of flood damage to the standing crops.*

(v) **Rs. 3000 received for sale of a farm machine.**

(vi) *Work hours of farm family labour.*

(vii) *Rs. 750 received as prize in tractor ploughing competition.*

(viii) *Feed expenses incurred but bill of Rs. 300/- not paid during the year.*

(ix) *Interest paid on long term loans.*

(x) *Incurred a loss of Rs. 300 in fire.*

16. *Given the following information about the business operation of a farm 'X', work out the different measures of income for this farm :*

Cash receipts from production during the year were Rs. 24,835/- and cash expenses during the year were Rs. 15,248/-. Inventory value of non-depreciable items; beginning of the year Rs. 2200/- and ending of the year Rs. 1,735/-. Depreciation Rs. 750/- capital investment : beginning of the year Rs. 75,500/- and ending of the year Rs. 35,400/-. Value of farm privileges Rs. 2000/-. Value of farm family labour Rs. 2,874/-. Rate of interest assumed at 9%. Also discuss the relative strong and weak points of each measure.

17. *Discuss the important ways in which farmers can use facts from farm records and accounts in improving the management of their farm business.*

18. *There is a farmer who has 50 acres of irrigated land on road side at a distance of about 10 miles from the city in North India. He has a tractor for cultivation and tubewell for irrigation. His major enterprises are hybrid maize and wheat seed production. He raises other crops also. Suggest him a set of suitable records and accounts which you consider he should maintain. Give reasons to support your suggestion.*

1. *Hopkins, John A. and Earl O. Heady, "Farm Records and Accounting", 5th edition. Ames, Iowa, Iowa State College, U.S.A., 1962. Chapter 1, 2, 4, 5, 6.*
2. *Efferson, J. Norman, "Farm Records and Accounts", John Wiley and Sons, Inc., New York. Chapman and Hall, Limited, London 1955. Chapters 1, 3, 4.*
3. *Castle, Emery N. and Manning H. Becker "Farm Business Management." The Macmillan Company, New York, London 1965, Chapter 4.*
4. *Yang, W.Y. "Methods of Farm Management Investigations for improving Farm Productivity", F.A.O. Agril. Development paper No. 64. Food & Agril. Organisation of United Nations, Rome 1962. Chapter 2 & 3.*
5. *Beneke, Raymond R., "Managing the Farm Business", New York, John Wiley & Sons, Inc., 1955, Chapter 20.*

11 Farm Financial Management*

A judicious management of finances of a farm business is very important for increasing the income of the farm. The subject of farm financial management deals with the study of the principles and practices of financing the farm business. It is that part of farm management which pertains to the acquisition and use of capital. The study of farm financial management thus revolves around two major problems (1) Optimum utilisation of funds within the farm business, and (2) Acquisition of funds from the lending institutions. It means that on one side, it is related to the decisions regarding utilisation of funds whether owned or borrowed and on the other hand, it concerns with the basic structure and characteristics of lending institutions as related to obtaining and using credit. The degree of success achieved in farm financial management depends to a large extent upon decisions relating to the acquisition and use of credit. The various financial management decisions are : (1) Whether to borrow or not to borrow ? (2) How much to borrow ? (3) When to borrow ? (4) From whom to borrow and at what cost ? (5) When and how best to repay the loans ? (6) What to use for security ? (7) What degree of risk should be involved ? Financing a farm for maximising the profits often requires borrowed capital. Financial risks increase as borrowings increase. Use of too little credit may reduce progress, while too much borrowing may lead to bankruptcy. Farm financial management involves the farm as a whole for taking financial decisions. The objective of farming is to maximise the returns from the farm as a whole and not increasing returns from a particular enterprise, a practice or a production unit. It is to be further recognised that no two farms are exactly alike in respect of soil, production resources, farmer's managerial ability and financial problems, etc. The financial management of a farm business is thus a micro approach. Major advantage of this approach lies in its treating the farm as an operational unit in tailoring the recommendations to fit into the individual farmer's resource-position and financial problems.

* For detailed study of the subject, refer to Johl, S.S. and C.V. Moore, "Essentials of Farm Financial Management", Today & Tomorrows Publishers, New Delhi, 1970.

It is an integrating science in the sense that the facts and findings of other sciences are coordinated for the solution of the problems of the farm to achieve the desired goals. Farm financial management specialist is a kind of "jack of all trades" yet "master of one". This means that he must know the principles of all the allied sciences in addition to the specialisation in the financial management techniques.

The study of farm financial management is important to the farmer, borrower, lending agencies and also to the farm credit advisory agencies.

Importance to the Farmer-borrower

Agricultural finance is one of the most important resource inputs. The farm entrèpreneur has to know the marginal productivity (MVP) of capital on his farm for its rational and optimal use and has to learn its judicial utilisation so that the returns to the fixed farm resources are maximised. This becomes important especially when the funds are borrowed. In order to be a good financial manager, he has to know the financing agencies, their structure and functioning so that he is able to obtain low cost credit of the right type at the right time.

A study of the subject of agricultural finance can help improve the credit acquisition and utilisation capabilities of the cultivator.

Importance of Lending Agencies

The lending agencies are interested in the profitability of the lent funds as well as in minimisation of the risks. Understanding the principles involved in financing agriculture would help them in (1) realistically appraising the credit worthiness of the cultivator so that the loans are advanced with a minimum of risk, (2) improving the repaying capacity of the borrower, and (3) participation in production planning and management in order to maximise the returns to the farm resources, which would lead to an improvement in repaying capacity of the borrower-cultivator and as a result would reduce the risks of default.

Importance to Farm Credit Advisory-service

To the farm credit advisory agency, the importance of the study of agricultural finance is self-evident. No one can guide the farmer in making rational decisions in the acquisition and use of credit unless and until he knows (*i*) the functioning of various lending agencies; what types of loans they advance, for which purpose and at what interest rate, and (*ii*) basic principles of farm financial management. Utilisation of finances is a specialised as well as crucial task. Here the credit-advisor has to provide guidance on the most efficient ways of utilisation of the scarce capital so that returns to the limited capital resources are maximised. The lending institution would need the agency in establishing the soundness of the credit proposal and efficient utilisation of funds so that the loans are advanced for rightful proposes and are utilised rationally. Unless this advisory agency is fully trained in the farm financing principles and their application to the local financing and farming situations, it cannot adequately meet the expectations of the farmers and the credit institutions.

Viewed from the position of the borrowers, lending agencies and credit advisory bodies, the study of the principles involved in farm financial management is of pivotal importance and none of them can afford to overlook its role. While awareness of these aspects is very high in the agriculturally advanced countries, there is a great need to approach the problem of financing and credit management scientifically in the developing countries as well.

ROLE OF CREDIT IN PRODUCTION AND MARKETING

Underdeveloped agriculture with vicious circle of low productivity and poverty needs no elaboration. A low level of output (and hence of income) leads to low savings and low investment that perpetuates low income. The crucial problem, therefore, is to break this vicious circle. One way is to give a considerably large injection of capital into the agricultural sector. Adoption of scientific techniques can be facilitated through adequate financing.

Funds are needed for fertilizers, improved seeds, fuel, oils, repairs, chemical sprays, hired labour, etc. Besides these operating expenses, a large investment is often required for the purchase and replacement of machines or for construction of buildings.

Modern business, agriculture being no exception, depends for its financial requirements largely on credit. With the introduction of improved techniques of production, cultivation is becoming more capital intensive. Farmer's own capital resources are turning out to be insufficient. They have to, therefore, depend to a large extent on borrowed funds. In some cases, if credit is not available, either it may not be possible for the farm operator to adopt an improved production technique or if full scale improved techniques of production are adopted without borrowing additional funds, returns to fixed resources might decline.

In traditional agriculture, technology gets adjusted to the availability of capital so that apparently additional funds are not needed. Even reorganisation of the production plan with existing state of technology may not put pressure on the capital- availability. As soon as a shift to a higher level of technology is envisaged, capital requirements shoot up. For example in Ludhiana District, studies have shown (Table 11.1) that with the introduction of optimum crop plan based on improved technology and recommended farm practices, the total capital requirements increased tremendously *i.e.*, from Rs. 2237 to Rs. 8456. Capital requirements also increased when improved production techniques were applied even on the existing cropping plan. Increase was from Rs. 2237 to Rs. 4595. The owned funds available on this farm situation were Rs. 2345. Additional capital was needed upto Rs. 2270 and Rs. 6131 when improved production techniques were introduced on existing and optimum plan respectively. This showed that credit played a major role in adoption of improved production technology.

TABLE 11.1

Farm Credit Analysis of a 16-acre Bullock Operated Farm Situation in Dehlon Development Block of Ludhiana District

Existing Farm Plans

Crop Enterprises	*Area in acres*	*Based on existing techniques* Op. Capital needs Rs. *Per acre*	*Based on existing techniques* Op. Capital needs Rs. *Total*	*Based on improved techniques* Op. Capital needs Rs. *Per acre*	*Based on improved techniques* Op. Capital needs Rs. *Total*
Kharif Season					
Desi Maize	4.07	85.50	347.98	169.40	689.46
Hybrid Maize (G. 101/De-kalb)	0.53	120.00	63.00	267.70	141.88
Composite maize (Vijay/Sona)	—	145.00	—	277.00	—
American cotton	2.19	97.50	213.52	251.00	550.13
Desi cotton	0.44	85.00	37.40	196.00	86.24
Groundnut (C-501) Irri.)	0.69	105.00	72.45	168.00	115.92
Groundnut (Pb. 1 Unirri.)	0.64	90.00	57.60	125.36	80.23
Sugarcane	1.21	255.00	308.55	426.30	515.82
Kharif fodders	2.28	45.00	102.60	86.00	195.08
Sub-total	12.05	—	1203.11	—	2374.76
Rabi Season					
Wheat C273 after fallow	2.95	85.00	250.75	125.00	369.75
Wheat (-273) after kharif	5.03	72.00	362.16	184.17	926.38
Wheat (C-286) after cotton	2.19	70.00	153.30	185.80	406.90
Wheat (PV-18) after kharif	—	210.00	—	—	—
What (Kalyan 227) after *Kharif*	—	225.00	—	—	—
Gram irrigated	0.50	65.00	32.50	111.40	55.70
Gram unirrigated	0.50	25.00	12.00	87.00	43.50
Barley	0.50	34.50	17.25	132.48	66.24
Rabi fodders	2.35	88.00	206.80	149.74	351.89
Sub-total	14.02	—	1034.76	—	2220.36
Total capital needs	—	—	2237.87	—	4595.12
Capital availability	—	—	2325.00	—	2325.00
Capital/Credit needs	—	—	+87.13	—	–2270.12
Return to the fixed farm resources			10725.40	—	13256.52

TABLE 11.1 (Contd.)
Farm Credit Analysis of a 16-acre Bullock Operated Farm Situation in Dehlon Development Block of Ludhiana District

	Improved alternative farm plans				
	Based on existing production techniques without borrowing of funds			*Based on improved prodution techniques and borrowing of funds*	
Crop Enterprises	*Area in acres*	*Op. Capital needs Rs.*		*Op. Capital needs Rs.*	
		Per acre	*Total*	*Per acre*	*Total*
Kharif Season					
Desi maize	—	—	—	—	—
Hybrid maize (G. 101/De-kalb)	5.00	120.00	600.00	267.70	1338.50
Composite maize (Vijay/Sona)	3.25	145.00	471.25	277.00	900.25
American Cotton	0.50	97.50	48.75	251.00	125.50
Desi Cotton	—	—	—	—	—
Groundnut (C-501 Irri.)	3.75	105.00	393.75	168.00	630.00
Groundnut (Pb. 1 Unirri.)	—	—	—	—	—
Sugarcane	1.50	255.00	382.50	426.30	639.45
Kharif fodders	2.00	45.00	90.00	86.00	172.00
Sub-total	16.00	—	1986.25	—	3805.70
Rabi Season					
Wheat after fallow	—	—	—	—	—
Wheat (C-273) after kharif	1.00	85.00	85.00	184.17	184.17
Wheat (C. 286) after cotton	0.75	72.00	54.00	185.80	139.35
Wheat (PV-18) after kharif	3.00	71.00	213.00	336.40	1009.20
Wheat (Kalyan 227) and kharif	8.00	210.00	1680.00	384.43	3075.44
Gram irrigated	0.50	225.00	112.50	111.40	55.70
Gram Unirrigated	—	—	—	—	—
Barley	—	—	—	—	—
Rabi fodders	1.25	34.50	43.12	149.74	187.18
Sub-total	14.50	—	2187.62	—	4651.04
Total capital needs	—	—	4173.87	—	8456.74
Capital availability	—	—	2325.00	—	2325.00
Capital/credit needs	—	—	–1848.87	—	–6131.74
Returns to fixed farm resources	—	—	—	—	29333.77

A look at the budgeted returns for a farm in Punjab will show that with borrowed funds, production plans could be reorganised so that returns after making repayments of loans would increase substantially from Rs. 13,256 to Rs. 29,333.

As in other business undertakings, agricultural firms cannot be successfully operated and expanded without borrowed funds. In India, most of the farms are capital starved. Since capital use and employment are complementary, this is one of the reasons why cultivation here has not been labour intensive. It cannot, however, be assumed that all farms without exception need credit. There are many farms which have adequate capital available and there are still others which suffer from too much credit. However, the over-all situation is that the majority of farms in India are capital starved and need credit. Marginal value productivity of capital on these farms is very high.

In many farm management studies, it has been brought out that the marginal productivity of capital is very high on Indian farms. For example, a study conducted in Ludhiana revealed the MVP of capital was 5.84 and 6.12 in *rabi* and *kharif* seasons respectively on a model farm situation. This means capital on these farms is so much a constraint that for every additional rupee invested one expects to get a return of Rs. 5.84 in *rabi* and Rs. 6.12 in *kharif* season. The credit needs on these farms were Rs. 694 and Rs. 674 in *rabi* and *kharif* seasons respectively. Through similar other studies, it has been found out that MVP of capital was very high on small, medium and large farm situations.

Often the farmers are not able to market their produce at the proper time and place because of lack of staying power and working capital for transportation. They have to sell at lower rates immediately in the post harvest period. The financing of the marketing operations is thus another dimension of farmer's needs for capital and credit.

Many farmers are, however, allergic to borrowing. They would prefer to wait with their plans till they have sufficient owned funds. Borrowing to them is bankruptcy. On the other hand, credit is instrumental in pulling the opportunities from the future to the present, *i.e.*, what may be possible for a person to achieve many years after, is made possible in the present. It cuts short the way to higher incomes and a better way of life. A qualifying condition, however, is that the credit must be used cautiously, rationally, and productively.

Thus, the trouble is not with the credit itself but with the way it has been used in areas of high risk and in times of high prices. Where farmers try to be financially independent they reduce their progress.

As Carver puts it; "There is no magic about credit. It is a powerful agency for good in the hands of those who know how to use it. So it is a buzz saw. They are about equally dangerous in the hands of those who do not understand them."

ECONOMIC FEASIBILITY TESTS OF A FARM CREDIT PROPOSAL

Before a farmer decides to borrow or a lending agency decides to advance, it is necessary to apply certain economic feasibility tests to the credit proposal with a view to determine the correct credit needs and repaying capacity of the farmer-borrower. This will help avoid excessive or inadequate financing.

There are three basic considerations which must be taken into account before a lending agency decides to advance a loan and the borrower decides to borrow : (1) returns from the Proposed Investment, (2) repaying capacity, it will generate and (3) the risk bearing ability of the borrower.

These are known as the 3 R's of credit. The main objective of this section is to demonstrate the application of these basic farm credit principles on an actual farm credit proposal.

The Situation under Analysis

A farmer (T.S. Sandhu) of village Sahenwal Kalan in I.A.D.P. District Ludhiana applied for a loan of Rs. 12,500/- for the purchase of a small tractor costing Rs. 20,000/-. He owns 19.5 acre farm. He has Rs. 7,000 owned funds. The farmer is Matriculate, served as an accountant in a foreign country and has a progressive outlook. The source of irrigation is tube-well operated by an electric motor of 7.5 H.P. He has a pair of bullocks as a power source. He considers this source of power to be insufficient to cope with the demand for power for high yielding varieties of crops. He has to hire a tractor and often the tractor is not available in peakwork periods.

Returns : The First Test

Emphasis here should be on additional returns and additional costs involved in utilising the borrowed funds. It involves working out the optimum combination of farm enterprises and the returns thereof, resulting from the additional availability of resources made possible through borrowed funds. The following points need to be kept in mind while making analysis of the returns :

1. Estimates of returns should be made on the basis of resources including borrowed funds.

2. Estimates of returns and costs should be made at the margin, not on an average.
3. Not only the MR = MC principles be kept in view while deciding the amount of credit but the law of equi-marginal returns must be fully exploited.
4. The level of other resources should also be considered before deciding upon the amount of working capital to be used. The possibilities of enhancing the level of other most limiting resources to farm production should also be examined.
5. Due care should be taken that more than the required amount of money is not advanced or obtained. At the same time, an inadequate amount of funds would not serve the purpose. Funds should, therefore, be advanced neither inadequately nor excessively, but just the amount that can be profitably used.
6. Money needed for consumption purposes should also be considered for their marginal value to the farm-family satisfaction against the marginal productivity of the production loans.

The estimated returns on the case farm-organisation with and without the use of credit, based on these principles are given in Tables 11.2 and 11.3.

Thus, the total additional capital needs will be Rs. 4683 (from Table 11.2) for current working expenses plus Rs. 12,500 for purchase of a tractor as a long term loan payable say over 10 years (= Rs. 17,183).

This gives about 34.31% returns on the investment. It is reasonably high to justify the loan to be advanced. Here the point to note is that working capital of Rs. 4683 must go along with the loan for the tractor.

The other points like adequacy of the loan, additional money needed for consumption purposes, and family's immediate obligations on marriages etc., should also be examined carefully, before a final decision is made on returns from the proposed investment.

Repaying Capacity–The Second Test

Although necessary, it is not sufficient to only analyse the productivity or the additional returns that will accrue due to the borrowed funds.

A loan may be productive but still it may not generate sufficient income to leave funds sufficient enough to repay the loan. Repaying capacity is the portion of the amount that a farm family will earn from a year's operation, which shall be available for the repayment of the loan. It should be based on an estimate of anticipated income from all sources of the borrower during the year. Repaying capacity, is therefore, worked out as a residual after meeting the requirements of the family consumption and payment of other dues, debts and repayments.

TABLE 11.2
Returns Analysis on the Credit Proposal

Sr. No.	Crop Enterprises	Crop (acres)	Existing Situation				Proposed Situation				
			Operational pattern		Gross Returns Capital needs		Crop (acre)	Operational pattern		Gross Returns Capital needs	
			Per acre Rs.	Total (Rs.)	Per acre Rs.	Total (Rs.)		Per acre Rs.	Total (Rs.)	Per acre Rs.	Total (Rs.)
	Kharif Season										
1.	Maize (Dekalb)	2.00	478.22	956.44	708.00	1416.00	3.00	663.00	1989.00	960.00	2880.00
2.	Maize *Desi*	0.50	371.13	185.56	555.00	272.50		—	—		
3.	Groundnut (M-145)	16.00	313.35	5013.60	627.30	10036.80	11.50	368.95	4241.77	1014.00	11661.00
4.	Cotton (American) J.34	—	—	—			4.00	808.96	3235.84	1200.00	4800.00
5.	Sugarcane (COJ-46)	0.50	871.50	435.75	2008.00	1004.00	0.50	1049.30	524.65	2610.00	1305.00
6.	*Chair* fodder	0.50	93.00	46.50	400.00	200.00	0.50	121.00	60.00	560.00	280.00
	Sub-Total	19.50		6637.85		12929.30	19.50		10051.76		20926.00
	Rabi Season										
1.	Wheat (Kalyan 227)	18.00	386.35	6954.30	1026.00	18468.00	18.50	443.35	8201.95	1344.00	24864.00
2.	Berseem Fodder	0.50	162.75	81.37	850.00	425.00	0.50	205.75	102.87	1125.00	562.50
3.	Sugarcane area in *Rabi*	1.00					0.50				
	Sub-Total	19.50	—	7035.67	—	18893.00	19.50	—	8304.82	—	25426.50
1.	Total operational capital requirements and gross returns	39.00	—	13673.52	—	31822.30	39.00	—	18356.58	—	46352.50
2.	Total returns over cash variable expenses	—	—	—	—	18148.78	—	—	—	—	27995.92
3.	Additional capital needs and returns over the existing situation	—	—	—	—	—	—	—	4683.06	—	+9847.14

TABLE 11.3

Marginal Analysis on the Credit Proposal

Additional Returns		*Additional Costs*	
1. Additional income over the existing plan (Table 11.2)	9847.14	1. Additional depreciation on tractor use @ 10% Rs. 12500*	1250.00
2. Saving per annum @ Rs. 10 per month per animal (Concentrate feed expenses etc.)	240	2. Interest @ 10% per annum for Rs. 12500	1250.00
3. Labour saved about 30 man days @ Rs. 4/- per day (on maintenance of bullocks)	120.00	3. Expenses on oil repair and lubricants etc.	2400.00
		4. Other expenses	300.00
Total additional returns	10207.14	Total additional costs	5200.00
Net marginal returns			5007.14

There can be two types of loans (*i*) self liquidating, (*ii*) non-liquidating or partially self-liquidating loans. The repaying capacity should be determined separately for self-liquidating and non-liquidating loans.

In case of the self-liquidating loans, the amount gets absorbed in the production process in one year or production period and the formula here is :

Repaying Capacity = Gross Income – [Living Expenses + Working Expenses (not including loan) + taxes + other loans and payments].

In case of non-liquidating or partially liquidating loans, the resources acquired with the funds are not directly consumed or are consumed over a number of years. They do not become completely a part of the first year's costs and the returns from the investment are spread over a period of several years. For non-liquidating or partially liquidating loans, the repaying capacity is worked out as :

Repaying Capacity = Gross Cash Income — (all working expenses + other loans + taxes and payments due).

---

* Money received from sale-proceeds of one pair of bullocks (Rs. 2000/-) will be needed for other contingency expenses and additional funds needed in connection with the purchase of tractor.

In this case-farm, both liquidating and partially liquidating loans are involved. The analysis will, therefore, proceed as under :

	Without Credit	*With Credit*
Gross Returns	31822.30	46352.50
Working Expenses	13673.52	13673.52
Returns over cash-expenses	18148.78	32678.98
Living expenses	7000.00	9000.00
Other loans due	3500.00	3500.00
Replacement funds	900.00	2400.00
Repaying Capacity	6748.78	17778.98

Here the balance or repaying capacity has increased from Rs. 6,748 to Rs. 17,778. The loan amount is Rs. 17,183 (Rs. 12,500 long term plus Rs. 4,683 short term). Annual payment will, therefore, be (Rs. 4,683 plus 9% interest on Rs. 4,683) + (Rs. 1,250 plus interest @ 8% on Rs. 12,500). This amounts to Rs. 7,401.36. The analysis thus shows that a loan of Rs. 12,500/- for a tractor plus Rs. 4683 as working expenses for short period will increase the repaying capacity sufficient to make repayment of the loan instalments.

Risk Bearing Ability–The Third Test

It is necessary but again not sufficient that the credit should be productive and generate sufficient repaying capacity. It is also essential that the borrower should be able to withstand the shocks of probable financial losses. This is known as the risk- bearing ability of the borrower. Assessment of risk-bearing ability is necessary because the returns and repaying capacity analysis are made on the basis of averages, *i.e.*, estimated production, prices and costs etc. But these averages seldom hold true. Agricultural business is subject to the vagaries of nature and is exposed to many other hazards such as pest attacks, diseases and price fluctuations. Variations in income occur as a rule rather than an exception. The variability in income has, therefore, to be counted for in order to arrive at a fairly stable and reliable estimate of the repaying capacity.

The overall variability in returns has been estimated to be 21% in Ludhiana district. Such variability coefficients are needed especially by the financial organisations in all parts of the country where they wish to operate. The gross income should be deflated by this coefficient and the analysis should then follow the same pattern as for repaying capacity.

Risk Bearing Ability Analysis

Deflated gross returns	= 46353 ×79/100 = 36618.08
Working Expenses	13673.52
Returns over cash expenses	22944.56
Living expenses	9000.00
Old Debt Repayments	3500.00
Replacement funds	2400.00
Deflated Repayment Capacity	8044.56

From the above table, it is shown that cultivator has good risk- bearing ability and it is safe proposition for the lending agency to advance a loan of Rs. 12,500 for the purchase of a tractor and Rs. 4,683 for working expenses. This risk bearing ability estimate is worked out at 99% level of confidence or at only 1% probability of error.

These principles have been discussed in many ways by different authors. It is sometimes discussed as 4 C's of credit which means (1) Character, (2) Capacity, (3) Capital collateral, (4) Condition and Common sense. These principles can also be discussed as 5 P's of credit which indicate (1) Purpose, (2) Person, (3) Productivity-Planning scheme or Projections, (4) Payment of instalment (Repayment), (5) Protection-security.

Repayment Plan

A well thought out repayment plan is essential for improving the repaying capacity of the borrower. A borrower might have a good repaying capacity, yet a defective repayment plan can render it insufficient. For example, if a borrower has an annual repaying capacity of Rs. 1,200 and the income accrues six monthly, but the plan of repayment provides a lumpsum repayment of Rs. 1,000 at the end of the year, it may not be possible for the cultivator to keep the money unused for six months and he might spend away part or whole of it.

Although there can be a variety of repayment plans, ranging from monthly instalment payments to a lump sum repayment after the expiry of the loan period, broadly speaking these can be classified as four types of repayment plans : (1) lumpsum repayment plan, (2) amortized even repayment plan, and (3) amortized decreasing repayment plan or quasi variable repayment plan. All these plans have, however, good and bad features.

Some Other Indicators

In addition of these analyses, scrutiny of the following documents can be of help in determining the credit-worthiness of the farmer.

1. Balance sheet, preferably overtime (Net worth statement).
2. Income statements, preferably overtime.
3. Farm Efficiency measures compared overtime and with average situations.

These aspects on the case farm are examined below :

TABLE 11.4

Balance Sheet of 'T.S.Sandhu' Farm as on 30-6-72

	Assets		*Liabilities*	
	Valuations		**Debt Payable**	
1.	Cash in hand	13000.00	Village Coop. Society	3500.00
2.	Debts receivable	1000.00		
3.	Crops :			
	Wheat in stock	2700.00		
	Soyabean	160.00		
4.	Fertilizer	115.00		
5.	Bullocks-2	2500.00		
6.	Buffaloes-2	2000.00		
7.	Buffaloes-calves-2	450.00		
8.	One cart	1000.00		
9.	T. Well & P. Wheel	3800.00		
10.	Drummy thresher	540.00		
11.	Seed drill	180.00		
12.	Spray pump	160.00		
13.	Other implements	227.00		
14.	Value of land & buildings		Net worth	258432.00
	(*a*) land 19.5 acre	230100.00		
	(*b*) farm building	4000.00		
		Rs. 261932.00		Rs. 261932.00

The balance sheet of a farm business at a point of time simply gives an indication of the capital position of the farmer. Compared over a period of time, it may indicate the trend of the business and thereby indicate the managerial skill of the farmer. Here the net-worth is quite high and farmer can afford to launch upon a programme of new investment with judgement and skill.

TABLE 11.5

Net-worth Statement of Mr. T.S. Sandhu as on 30-6-72

Assets			*Liabilities*	
	Items	*Amount Rs.*	*Items*	*Amount Rs.*
	Current Assets		**Current Liabilities**	
1.	Cash in hand	13000	Short term loan	3500
2.	Accounts receivable	1000		
3.	Supplies	115		3500
4.	Wheat	2700		
5.	Maize	—		
6.	Soyabean	160		
	Sub-total	16975		
	Working Assets			
1.	Bullocks	2500		—
2.	Machinery & equipment	2107	**Medium-term Liabilities,**	
3.	Livestock	2450		
	Sub-total	7057		
	Fixed Assets			
1.	Land	230100		—
2.	Building	4000	**Long-term Liabilities**	
3.	Tube-well	3500		
4.	P. Wheel (1/5 share)	300		
	Sub-total	237900		
	Total Assets	261932	**Total Liabilities**	3500
	New Worth	258432		

Net Capital Ratio. Net capital ratio is defined as Total Assets/Total Liabilities which is = 261932/3500 = 74.84 on this farm. It is quite high and indicates that the farm business is solvent the long run.

Working Ratio. Working ratio is defined as :

$$\frac{\text{Sum of (Working Assets + Current Assets)}}{\text{Sum of (Intermediate + Current Liabilities)}}$$

which is $\frac{24032}{3500} = 6.87$ on this farm.

The working ratio is also high enough in this case and shows that business is solvent in the medium run as well.

Current Ratio : Current ratio is = $\frac{\text{Current Assets}}{\text{Current Liabilities}}$

which is $\frac{16945}{3500} = 4.85$ on this farm. It is quite high in this case and farm business is sound enough to absorb more credit.

TABLE 11.6

Income Statement of T.S. Sandhu's Farm for the year 1969-70

	Kind	*Amount (Rs.)*
A.	**Cash Receipts**	
	1. Sale of *Rabi* Crops	18093.00
	2. Sale of *Kharif* crops	12600.00
	Total :	30693.00
B.	**Cash Expenses,**	
	1. Labour *Rabi*	4273.00
	2. Labour *Kharif*	3300.00
	3. Seed	1430.00
	4. Fertilizer	3775.32
	5. Land Revenue and Taxes	130.00
	6. Electricity charges	765.20
	Total :	13673.52
C.	**Net Cash Income** (A—B = C)	17019.48
	1. Inventory changes (+)	329.30
	2. Family consumption (+)	800.00
D.	**Net Farm Earnings**	18148.78
	1. Operator's and family labour and interest	3500.00
E.	**Returns to Management**	14648.78

Income analysis of this farm shows that the farmer has a progressive outlook and is on a good footing. A good 'Net Cash Income'. 'family consumption' and Management Returns' all indicate the soundness of the farm business. If we have income statement of the farm for a number of years, we can compare the present situation with the past.

TABLE 11.7

Crop Yield Index

Name of crop	*Average yield on the farm*	*Average yield in the locality*	*No. of acres on farm*	*Crop yield on farm as % age of locality*	*Percentage multiplied by No. of acres*
Hy. Maize	14 qtls.	12 qtls.	2.0	116.6	233.20
Desi Maize	10	8	0.5	125.0	62.50
Sugarcane	18.5	16	0.5	115.6	2200.00
Groundnut	5.5	.4	16.0	177.5	275.00
Chari fodder	110	100	0.5	110.0	55.00
Wheat	12	11	18.0	109.09	1963.62
Berseem	200	180	0.5	111.1	55.50
Total	—	—	38	—	4844.82

$$\text{Crop Yield Index} = \frac{4844.82}{38} = 12.75\%$$

Crop yield index as in table above is also quite high.

Further, cropping intensity was worked out on this farm to be 194.9% which indicates double cropping in a year on most of the acreage. Again the rate of capital turn-over for this farm works out to be 12.14% which is quite higher than the market rate. So all these tests indicate the soundness of this farm business.

USE OF FARM FINANCIAL BUDGET AND CASH FLOW CHART IN FARM FINANCIAL MANAGEMENT

A cash flow chart or map or statement is simply a month by month or quarter by quarter comparison of the expected cash income and expected cash expenses alongwith the expected cash position at the end of each month or quarter.

It is relatively easy to predict future income and expenses for each month or quarter; not to the exact paise or even the rupee, but near enough to be a valuable tool in the planning and management of the business.

CASH FLOW AS A 'MONEY MAP'

A cash flow map deals in rupees rather than kilometres and shows 'what' 'how much' and 'when'. In nearly every manner a cash flow statement is a bonafide 'map'; a map of the farms, expected cash income and cash outflow on a month to month or a quarter to quarter basis. Its purpose is to help plot the shortest and surest route from where the farmer is, to where he plans to go to alert him on possible money-saving short cuts, and to avoid costly detours. The intended destination is maximum farm profit. Just as a road map is unique to an area, so a cash flow is unique to the business. Some other farm may anticipate a similar cash flow, but the only money map of any use to a farm is the one for that farmer and only that farmer can prepare it.

A cash flow statement is thus simply a month-by-month or a quarter-by-quarter comparison of the expected cash income and expected cash expenses alongwith the cash position for each month which is the difference between total income and total expenditure. If income is predicted to exceed expenditure in a month or a quarter, the cash position is a plus amount. If expenditure will exceed income, it is a minus amount. By stringing 12 months or four quarters together into an annual cash flow statement, with a cash position for each month or quarter, it is easy to see the 'flow' of cash in and out of the business.

One point needs emphasis, *i.e.*, cash flow income and outflow projections do not replace other types of financial statements like net-worth statement, income statement etc. These records are essential to show what is accomplished in the past and where the business currently stands.

Preparation of a Cash Flow Plan

It stands to reason that the value of the cash flow statement will depend on the figures put into it. It is, therefore, important that the income and expenses estimates be realistic. While record from previous years can provide useful references, income and expenses estimates must come mainly from a "thinking out" on the production plan for the year ahead.

In some of the advanced countries like America, the cash flow charts have been used by many farmers who have found it of a great utility for full control over financial transactions. The cash flow charts are prepared on the basis of farm financial budget and family living expenditures. In most of the foreign countries such cash flow charts are prepared and used on the basis of monthwise income and expenditure estimates. Under Indian crop farming conditions, it is difficult to reckon the income and expenditure on monthly basis. Such cash flow plans, can however be prepared on monthly basis where flow of income and expenditure is more or less regular such as in poultry, dairy business. Under areable farming, there are four distinct seasonal periods during which farmers get new incomes or make new expenses over a year.

These four season—quarters are :

1. First quarter : July to September — (Expenses on sowing of Kharif crops)
2. Second quarter : October to December — (Harvesting, processing and sale of Kharif crops and expenses on sowing on rabi crops)

3. Third quarter : January to March (Growing period of Rabi crops)
4. Fourth quarter : April to June (Harvesting, processing and sale or Rabi crops)

Thus an agricultural year is divided into four quarters and for each quarter, the cash receipts, cash expenses, family's living expenditure and cash available are calculated. The steps for preparation of a cash flow chart are clear from the illustration of an actual farm situation given below :

AN ILLUSTRATION*

The case farm situation was having operational holding of 22.74 acres, tubewell irrigated and bullocks as main source of farm power. The most limiting factor on this situation was a source of power, due to which 22 per cent of the cropped area was kept as fallow in Kharif season. Some of the income prospective crops like Paddy IR-8, American Cotton J-34 were not grown.

Although these crops were agronomically suitable for the area :

(a) Alternative plan and cost and income estimates

An alternative plan was developed for this situation taking into consideration, the possibility of borrowing in activity and introduction of new farm technology. The limiting factor of farm power was removed by replacing bullocks with tractor power. (One 35 H.P. tractor of value of Rs. 22,000/-). Due to this change, more area was put under bright income crop varieties like Vijay maize, groundnut M-145, paddy IR-8, wheat PV-18 and Hira wheat. The alternative crop plan alongwith estimates on variable expenses and incomes are given as per Table 11.8.

(b) Farm financial budget

The farm financial budget was prepared by estimating the expected operating sales, capital sales, operating expenses of different crop inputs, capital expenses and the quarter in which these would occur. Estimate on the number/quantity, the cost and timings of every thing, from fixing up a building to the purchase of a new machine/crop input where capital investment was involved, was made. The anticipated expenses involved on repairs, replacements etc. quarterwise were worked out. Such estimates are indicated as per Table 11.9.

(c) Farm family living expenditure budget

Farm family living expenditure pattern depends upon the family size, standard of living, composition of family members and the existence of family

---

* Sharma, Girdhar, "Development of Standard-Financial Plans for Advancing Farm Credit for some Representative Farms in IADP District, Ludhiana" M.Sc. Thesis, Punjab Agricultural University Ludhiana 1971. (Unpublished)

TABLE 11.8
An Alternative Farm Plan and Economic Analysis of the Case Farm Organisation in Ludhiana Block of I.A.D.P. District Ludhiana

(Rupees)

	Existing farm plan (1970-71)				Alternative farm plan (1971-72)			
Crop Enterprises	*Area in Acres*	*Gross return*	*Variable expenses*	*Return to fixed factors*	*Area in Acres*	*Gross return*	*Variable expenses*	*Return to fixed factors*
Kharif Season								
1. Hybrid maize Ganga 5	2.50	1451.25	544.74	906.51	—	—	—	—
2. Maize Vijay Composite	—	—	—	—	4.00	3972.00	1720.00	2252.00
3. Desi Maize	7.50	3192.00	1039.62	2152.38	—	—	—	—
4. Groundnut M-145	3.00	1058.75	250.75	808.00	7.00	7098.00	1890.00	5208.00
5. Cotton Desi G-27	1.37	503.12	227.17	366.00	—	—	—	
6. Cotton American J-34	—	—	—	—	5.00	6000.00	1900.00	4100.00
7. Sugarcane Co J-46	0.87	1533.37	344.75	1188.82	1.00	2610.00	1280.00	1330.00
8. Paddy I.R. 8	—	—	—	—	3.00	4110.00	1515.00	2595.00
9. Soyabean No. 1	0.12	56.25	21.25	35.00	—	—	—	—
10. Maize fodder	—	—	—	—	2.00	2500.00	360.00	2140.00
11. Kharif fodder	2.38	Fed to the	farm cattle	—	0.74	Fed to the	Farm cattle	—
12. Fallow	5.00	—	—	—	—	—	—	—
Sub Total	22.74	7794.74	2428.28	5456.71	22.74	26290.00	8665.00	17625.00
Rabi Season								
1. Wheat Kalyan Sona	17.62	15447.00	3489.87	11957.13	13.00	18096.00	5395.00	12701.00
2. Wheat PV-18	1.25	1197.00	233.50	963.50	5.00	7115.00	2075.00	5040.00
3. Wheat S-308	1.50	1235.00	364.37	870.63	—	—	—	—
4. Wheat Hira (HD. 1941)	—	—	—	—	3.00	5325.00	1425.00	3900.00
5. Sugarcane in Rabi	0.87	—	—	—	1.00	—	—	—
6. Rabi fodder	1.50	Fed to the	farm cattle	—	0.74	Fed to the	farm cattle	—
Sub Total	22.74	17879.00	4087.74	13791.26	22.74	30536.00	8895.00	21641.00
Grand Total	—	25763.74	6516.02	19247.97	—	56826.00	17560.00	39266.00
Increase over existing (*i*) Kharif season						18405.25	6236.77	12168.49
(*ii*) Rabi season						12657.00	4807.26	7849.74
Total						31062.26	11044.03	20018.23

TABLE 11.9

Farm-Financial-Budget (1971-72)

Name : A case Farm, Address : Village 'X' Block Ludhiana

	Quarterwise Distribution of Receipts and Expenses				
Items	*Total Rs*	*First quarter (July – Sept.)*	*Second quarter (Oct. – Dec.)*	*Third quarter (Jan. – March)*	*Fourth quarter (April – June)*
Operating sales					
1. Sale of crops excluding domestic consumption	46061.00	5500.00	13659.00	4000.00	22902.00
2. Hired out bullocks	—	—	—	—	—
3. Hired out machine	—	—	—	—	—
4. Miscellaneous/Milk	—	—	—	—	—
A. Total operating sales	46061.00	5500.00	13659.00	4000.00	22902.00
Capital Sales					
1. Machinery	—	—	—	—	—
2. Livestock	3325.00	3325.00	—	—	—
B. Total capital sales	3325.00	3325.00	—	—	—
Operating expenses					
1. Seeds	1261.76	698.00	563.76	—	—
2. Feeds	519.00	54.75	154.75	154.75	154.75
3. Chemicals	1245.51	1178.88	14.47	51.18	—
4. Fertilizers & FYM	17295.37	3230.87	12862.28	1202.22	—
5. Irrigation charges	163.12	—	50.62	100.00	12.50
6. Hired Labour	5376.53	993.87	2080.28	1280.60	1021.78
7. Hired machinery	630.00	—	250.00	—	380.00
8. Fuel	1232.00	176.00	352.00	264.00	440.00
9. Machinery repair	100.00	—	—	100.00	—
Total variable expenses	27823.29	6332.35	16328.16	3153.75	2009.03
10. Permanent labour	1367.50	523.12	35.62	35.63	773.13
11. Flat rate of electricity	444.00	111.00	111.00	111.00	111.00
12. Cash rent	1337.50	518.75	—	—	818.75
13. Land revenue	77.50	—	38.75	—	38.75
14. Payment to artesans	132.00	—	56.00	—	76.00
Total annual charges	3358.50	1152.87	241.37	146.63	1817.63
C. Total operating expenditures	31181.79	7485.22	16569.53	3300.38	3826.66
Capital expenses					
1. Machinery	25000.00	25000.00	—	—	—
2. Livestock	—	—	—	—	—
3. Building	—	—	—	—	—
D. Total capital expenses	25000.00	25000.00	—	—	—

obligations. The family size of this farm situation was 13 members. Farm family living expenditures on various items like fuel, clothes, education, entertainment, medical, religious/social and the quarter of the year in which they are likely to incur, were worked out as in Table 11.10.

TABLE 11.10

Farm Family Living Budget

Year 1971 – 72

Total No. of family members : 13, Adult : 9 Children : 4

S. No.	Particulars	Total Rs.	*Quarterwise Distribution of Expenses (Rs.)*			
			First quarter (July—Sept.)	*Second quarter (Oct.—Dec.)*	*Third quarter (Jan.—March)*	*Fourth quarter (April—June)*
1.	Fuel	1441.87	312.50	376.25	354.37	398.75
2.	Clothes	588.75	156.25	175.00	151.25	106.25
3.	Education	555.00	138.75	138.75	138.75	138.75
4.	Entertainment	165.00	41.25	39.38	43.12	41.25
5.	Medical	249.37	58.12	76.25	88.75	26.25
6.	Religious/Social	2455.00	645.00	7.50	982.50	820.00
7.	Building and others	310.00	15.00	265.00	15.00	15.00
	Total family living expenses	5764.99	1366.87	1078.13	1773.74	1546.25

(d) Cash flow chart

Many of the estimates, needed for the cash flow statement can simply be 'lifted' from the tables mentioned earlier. After totalling projected income and expenses for the operation of plan, two final types of cash outlays must be taken into account. (*i*) cash needed for family and living expenses and (*ii*) cash needed for repayment of other loans. Subtract these from the net business incomes. This will indicate whether cash position for the quarter will be plus or minus. A negative cash position in any quarter/month indicates a need for an additional amount of credit. A positive cash position provides an opportunity to reduce the amount of outstanding credit.

For the case farm, the cash flow chart was planned as in Table 11.11 that the short-term loan (Rs. 6236.77) to meet working expenses of kharif crops alongwith the medium term loan (Rs. 22000/-) for a new tractor, would be advanced in the beginning of first quarter. During the second quarter, the kharif crop loan along with the interest (Rs. 6552.49) plus first instalment of medium term loan (Rs. 2200/-) would be recovered, when the sale proceeds of kharif crops would take place. In the end of second quarter, the short term loan of Rs. 4807.26 would be advanced to meet the additional working expenses of rabi crops and it was to be recovered in the last week of fourth quarter along with interest. In addition to this, second instalment of medium term loan plus the interest for the whole year would be recovered.

TABLE 11.11

Cash Flow Chart

(Credit Control)

Name : A Case Farm — Address Village 'X' Block Ludhiana

Items	*Quarterwise Distribution of Receipts and Expenses*				
	Total Rs.	*First quarter (July—Sept.)*	*Second quarter (Oct.—Dec.)*	*Third quarter (Jan.—March)*	*Fourth quarter (April—June)*
1. Cash balance	30509.22	9643.02	12852.70	4543.81	3469.69
2. Total operating sales	46601.00	5500.00	13659.00	4000.00	22902.00
3. Total capital sales	3325.00	3325.00	—	—	—
4. Non-farm wages	—	—	—	—	—
5. Money borrowed	33044.03	28236.77	4807.26	—	—
Total cash available	113479.25	46704.79	31318.96	8543.81	26371.69
1. Operating expenses	31181.79	7485.22	16569.53	3300.38	3826.66
2. Capital expenses	25000.00	25000.00	—	—	—
3. Family living expenses	5764.99	1366.87	1078.13	1773.74	1546.25
4. Payment on previous funds	750.00	—	375.00	—	375.00
5. Payment on current funds : (Short term)	11603.11	—	6552.49	—	5050.62
(Medium term)	6572.50	—	2200.00	—	4372.50
Total expenditure	80872.39	33852.09	26775.15	5074.12	15171.03
Cash Balance	32066.86	12852.70	4543.81	3469.69	11200.66
Balance on borrowed funds-Medium-term loan	21722.22				

Note : 1. It was assumed that the kharif crop loan would be given upto 15th July and would be recovered in the last week of December every year. Similarly rabi crop loan would be advanced during second quarter and would be recovered upto last week of June every year.

2. Instalments of medium term loan would be paid upto last week of June and last week of December every year.

(e) *Projected profit and loss statement*

Useful as a cash statement, it still does not fully answer the question : Will the borrower make a profit ? For this purpose prepare a projected profit and loss statement. Subtract total cash expenses from total cash sales to get net cash income. To determine a projected profit or loss statement, adjust the net cash income figure by : (*i*) any expected increase or decrease in the value of capital items such as breeding livestock, machinery or improvements on the farm (depreciation value), and (*ii*) any expected increase or decrease in the value of inventory items such as grains livestock or supplies. To go one step further, subtract from the projected profit or loss, the amount of the money needed for family living and to pay taxes, etc. The remaining amount will be available to retire the debt and for savings and investment.

Advantages of Cash Flow Map

Reliable cash flow projections for a farm business can be of tremendous use to the farmer in estimating (*i*) how much to borrow and when, (*ii*) developing better repayment plan, (*iii*) minimising the credit requirements and thus save on interest costs, (*iv*) combining the statements on farm and home accounts (*v*) arranging the loans in advance, (*vi*) providing a convincing proof of a financially sound production plan, (*vii*) servicing the loans better, (*viii*) arranging the input supplies efficiently, (*ix*) testing the profitability of the plan, (*x*) taking advantage of term discounts, (*xi*) checking the balance-between long and short credit. (*xii*) checking the investment plans, (*xiii*) removing financial uncertainty, (*xiv*) providing better financial control, and (*xv*) planning the tax liabilities in a better way.

METHODS AND MECHANICS OF PROCESSING FARM CREDIT PROPOSALS

A careful credit analysis is a wise approach for objective basis of accepting or declining loan requests and explaining the reasons to the farmers. Presenting objective information to the farmers whose application has been rejected may enable the bank to retain the farmer as a customer and even encourage him to request for credit at a later date. Although different individual Branch Managers and/or Farm Finance Officers may follow a particular set of procedures for processing of loan applications from agriculturists, the following steps have been found very useful.

1. Personal interview

Form an idea about the frankness, integrity, honesty, acumen, capability, temperament, progressive thinking etc. of the farmer- customer through friendly talks, when he approaches the banker for the first time for credit.

2. Proper filling of loan application

Help the farmer complete the loan application form of the Bank. The farmer should be advised to give particulars of his whole operational holding instead of giving figures regarding the land, he may be considering to give for mortgage. The estimates on cost of project, gross income, variable expenses and returns should be genuine and correct.

With the completed loan application, the following revenue papers/documents should be attached :

(*i*) Fard Jamabandi—latest holding.

(*ii*) Fard Girdawari—2-3 years possession.

(*iii*) Ex-sigara-Sketch map of the land, if available.

(*iv*) 'No Due' and 'No Objection' Certificate from village Cooperative Society.

(*v*) Non-encumbrance Certificate from Sub-Registrar.

(*vi*) Affidavit from the agriculturalist that he has not borrowed and/or charged his land elsewhere and that he would not do so during the currency of the loan.

3. Verification of revenue records

Verify the ownership of land and the acreage held by the applicant through title Deeds—Jamabandi—Girdawari, rent receipt etc., Village Patwari should be consulted to know the latest position of ownership right of the farmer.

There are many practical difficulties in verification of title of borrower to land because the revenue records are not being kept uptodate. Village Cooperative Credit Societies have the advantage of possibilities of drawing, on the intimate local knowledge of the village, in satisfying themselves about the ownership of land of borrower in the absence of clear title deed. But the Commercial Banks in the absence of such local knowledge in the initial period are seriously handicapped in accepting mortgages of lands offered to them as security. Government can assist the banks by furnishing the certified extract from the registers of holdings with upto-date information. The Branch Manager should be able to conduct preliminary examination of these titles before the loan is sanctioned and legal mortgage of land is registered through Bank's Lawyer. The following two revenue records are very important to know :

(a) Jama-bandi register

This register maintains record with respect to owners and area owned by them and cultivators and area cultivated by them. It is revised and made upto-date after every five years. Proforma of Jama-bandi is attached (Table-11.12) to have full acquaintance with the columns of this important revenue record. The original Jama-bandi is kept at the Tehsil head-quarters and a copy is kept by the Patwari concerned.

TABLE 11.12
Form of Jama-Bandi

Jama-bandi : 1967-68 Village : Kasabad Tehsil : Ludhiana District : Ludhiana

1	2	3	4	5	6	7	8	9	10	11	12	13
Khawet or Jama-bandi Number	*Khatauni No.*	*Name of Ala malik*	*Name of Patti and numberdar and amount of land revenue*	*Name of owner*	*Name of cultivator*	*Well or any other source of irrigation*	*Khasra number or Rectangle number and field No.*	*Area of each field, total area of owned holding and type of land*	*Rent paid by the cultivator and its rate*	*Details of share*	*Amount of land revenue and its rare*	*Remarks*
19	12			Gobind Ram	Gobind Ram	Tube -well	**19**				Rs. 4.50	
				S/o	S/o		4	8-0				
				Devi Chand	Devi Chand		5	8-0				
				S/o	S/o		7	7-2				
							10	6-5				
				Ram Ditta	Ram Ditta		12	4-0				
							20					
							1	3-4				
							2	5-4				

(*b*) *Register of mutations*

Next in importance of Jama-bandi is the Register of Mutations. In order to keep all the entries of Jama-bandi upto-date, the village Patwari is required to keep a register of Mutation Table 11.13 (Proforma-I). There are two facets of this Register. One is called 'Parat-sarkar' and the other 'Parat Patwar'. The detailed order with regard to the transaction is written on 'Parat Sarkar' and the summary is noted in 'Parat Patwar'. After the sanction of mutation 'Parat Sarkar' is sent to Tehsil Office and 'Parat Patwar' is retained by the Patwari.

Every month, the office of the Sub-Registrar concerned is supposed to send Parchas (Information slips—Table 11.13 Proforma—II) giving the details of the transactions of sale, gifts, mortgages, etc. affecting the titles of the land-owner to the Revenue estate which have been registered in his office. Then the Patwari is required to enter the mutations on the basis of these transactions and to produce this register before the Revenue Officer in the general gathering of the people of the Estate and the Revenue Officer in turn is required to attest entires after.

TABLE 11.13 (PROFORMA — I)
Register of Mutations

Village .... Had-bast No. .... Tehsil .... District .... Entry No. ....

1	2	3	4	5	6	7	8	9	10	11	12	13	14	15
	Particulars of Previous Jama-bandi or Mutation							*Particulars of New Entries*						
Serial No.	*Name of field in the previous Jama-bandi*	*Name of "Patti"*	*Name of owner and Particulars*	*Name of cultivator and Particulars*	*Number of field land area and its kind*	*Land revenue*	*Account number of New Jama-bandi*	*Name of owner and particulars*	*Name of cultivators and Particulars*	*Number & Name of field/land area and kind*	*Land revenue*	*Kind of mutation, date Amount of mortgage*	*Fee*	*Reports of Patwari and field Kanungo*

TABLE 11.13 (PERFORMA — II)
(Appendix III Paragraph 158 form No. 4)

Memorandum of documents by which possession of agricultural land is transferred or mortgaged which have been registered before the sub-Registrar of .... for the month of ....

Serial No.	*Name of village in which the property concerned is situated*	*Nature of transfer, area transferred with khasra and Jama-bandi No.*	*Amount of consideration entered in the document*	*Name, parentage and residence of the executant of the deed*	*Name and residence of the transferee*	*Number and date of registration*	*Remarks*
1	2	3	4	5	6	7	8

Footnote : When a deed is not to take effect immediately but after a specified period, this fact should be noted in the column of remarks.

Proforma II (Contd.)

Office of Tehsilder ....

Forwarded to the Field Kanungo of circle .... with the request that he will get the case entered in mutation register.

Dated ....

Signature of Tehsildar

Forward in original to the Patwari of circle .... for entry in mutation register, if not already entered.

Dated.........................

Signature of Field Kanungo

To

THE TEHSILDAR ....

Sir,

The case has been entered in the mutation register of Mauza .... on .... at serial no ....

Dated ....

Signature of Patwari

Dated ....

Signature of Field Kanungo

Announcing them in the above mentioned general gathering. Similarly the Patwari is required to enter mutations with regard to inheritance of the death of a particular right holder and any other transaction of transfer of rights in the land which are brought to his notice. While issuing copies of the Jama-bandi, the Patwari is required to give number and type of mutation in the column of remarks. He is required to use Pencil to give the details of those mutations which have been entered but have not yet been sanctioned, Red ink for those mutations which have been attested after the Jama-bandi and Black ink for those mutations which were attested prior to Jama-bandi, a copy of which he is issuing. At the end of the copy, he is required to give a certificate to the effect that copy has been prepared by him in acordance with the entries in the Revenue Record.

Checking of Record in the Office of Sub-Registrar

It may happen that some transactions might have not been got noted to the Patwari and the borrower may get some wrongful gain out of the non-mentioning of the transactions by the Pâtwari. To avoid this, in appropriate cases, a search of the record in the office of the sub-registrar concerned since the year of the Jama-bandi may have to be made. Further to avoid any contingency with regard to litigation etc., an affidavit of the borrower will have to be taken. If some litigation is going on with regard to the land of the borrower, that will reduce the value of the land as well as the repayment capacity of the borrower. So in all the cases, the borrower may be asked to file an affidavit saying that no transaction except those mentioned by the Patwari in the copy of Jama-bandi have been made with regard to this land and also saying that no litigation is going on with regard to this land.

(c) *Khasra Girdawari*

This register contains information with respect to the name of actual cultivator of a particlar piece of land, crops grown in different seasons. The concerned patwari makes physical inspection of the crops grown in each field of his estate every season and records the relevant entries in the appropriate columns. Proforma of Khasra Girdawari is given as per Table 11.14. This statement helps to know, the possession of the land to be mortgaged for securing the advance.

4. Pre-sanction farm inspections

If the information supplied in the application needs to be conformed and supplementary information needs to be obtained, the Branch Manager or agricultural Finance Officer or Field Officer should pay a personal visit to the farm and home of the applicant for verificiation, collection of additional information etc., so as to assess the borrower's application and arrive at a decision about the sanctioning of the loan. The decision of the bank on the loan application should,

TABLE 11.14

Form of Khasra Girdawari

Village Kasabad | Tehsil Ludhiana | District Ludhiana

Serial No.	*Owner's name alongwith Jama-bandi number*	*Name of the cultivator Khatauni No. and rent*	*Area*	*Type of land according to previous Jama-bandi*	*Kharif Crop*	*Rabi Crop*	*Change of ownership cultivation & rent*	*Kharif Crop*	*Rabi Crop*	*Change of ownership cultivation & rent*	*Kharif Crop*	*Rabi Crop*	*Change of ownership cultivation & rent*	*Kharif Crop*	*Rabi Crop*	*Change of owernship cultivation & rent*
1	*2*	*3*	*4*	*5*	*6*	*7*	*8*	*9*	*10*	*11*	*12*	*13*	*14*	*15*	16	17
1	Gobind Ram	Gobind Ram														
		19	8.0	Loamy	Maize	Wheat	—	Cotton	Wheat	—	Maize	Wheat	—	Maize	Wheat	—
		4														
		5	8.0	Sandy	G. Nut	—	—	G. Nut	—	—	G. Nut	—	—	G. Nut	—	—
		7	7.2	"	"	—	—	"	—	—	"	—	—	"	—	—
		10	6.5	"	"	—	—	"	—	—	"	—	—	"	—	—
		12	4.0	Heavy	Paddy	Wheat	—	Paddy	Wheat	—	Paddy	Wheat	—	Paddy	Wheat	—
		20														
		1	3.4	Sandy	G.nut	Wheat	—	G.nut	Wheat	—	—	Wheat	—	—	Wheat	—
		2	5.4	Sandy	G.nut	Wheat	—	G.nut	Wheat	—	—	Wheat	—	—	Wheat	—

however, be communicated to the borrower at the earliest. Usually, it should not take more than a forthnight to complete formalities. During such pre-sanction farm inspections, the following aspects of the borrower should be thoroughly investigated/ assessed :—

(a) *Identification of farmer-applicant and confidential report about the integrity and credit worthiness of the borrower.* It was the experience of Government Taccavies that large number of so called farmers were granted taccavi loans who were never located any where afterwards. This was because those applicants were not fully identified and their where-abouts were never properly investigated. It is, therefore, essential to verify, the relevant whereabouts from the knowledgeable persons of the village such as village Sarpanch, Patwari, Numberdar, Gramsevak, Secretary, Co-operative Society etc. The independent enquiries should be made from these local sources about the integrity of the borrower and the proposed guarantors, if any. The other reliable source of information is the Arhtias (Commission Agents) where the farmer sells his produce. They may also be consulted about the dealings of the concerned farmer with them.

(b) *Assessment of the Existing Situation of Farming and managerial ability of farmer-applicant.* As far as possible, the Agent/Agricultural Finance Officer/Field Officer should visit the fields of the farmer and locate the boundaries with the help of ex-siggara. While going around the farm and talking to the farmer, one can get good impressions about the existing standard of cultivation, managerial ability of the farmer and feasibility of the proposed plan.

The method used in such inspection should be one of physical verification of fixed and working assets and of their titles to be pledged to secure repayment of the loan. From the income statements, receipts and gains during a year less cost and losses with net income or net loss are taken into account.

(c) *Appraisal of the feasibility of the future crop plan/Project.* The appraisal of the expected gross income from the future crop- plan is possible by examining the feasibility of the suggested cropping scheme and the expected yield per acre multiplied by the projected price.

A technical feasibility report indicating the suitability of the soil for the proposed cropping pattern, recommended varieties of the crops to be grown, recommended package of practices for these varieties, quality of irrigation water available, availability of required inputs and managerial ability of the farmers should be prepared by the Agricultural Finance Officer-Field Officer of the Bank or be obtained from the State Department of Agriculture and/or Assistant Extension Specialist (Farm Management) of the area.

The project should also be considered from the point of view of its economic viability. The economic viability refers to cost- benefit ratio. If this ratio is 1 : 1 or higher, the project should be taken as economically viable. For all practical purposes, the net return from the proposed scheme should be equal to or more than the total investment incurred in the particular scheme.

The analysis a lender makes of a loan proposal consists primarily of determining how much credit should be extended together with security required and the repayment plan. There is, therefore, need for working out the repaying capacity of the farmer to determine the safe amount of loan to be extended. The income generated from the proposed investment must be sufficient enough to meet the production expenditure, family expenditure, liabilities if any, a margin for incentive risk and payment of the bank loan.

Repayment schedule of loans should be so stipulated that crop loans are adjusted as full after the harvest/marketing of crop and a instalment of medium term advance also paid from sale of crops every season. Seasonality is necessary in the recovery of loans and for this purpose, it will have to be ensured that the due dates are so fixed that they are not too distant from the harvesting seasons and at the same time a reasonable period is allowed for enabling the cultivators to dispose of their produce at reasonable prices.

Pre-sanction farm inspection report or an appraisal note needs to be prepared incorporating all the above mentioned points.

5. *Sanction of advance*

On the basis of rational assessment given in the appraisal note, the Branch Manager should give the final decision to sanction/recommend/reject the credit proposal. This should include considerations on (*i*) Technical and economic feasibility of the proposal, (*ii*) margin money, (*iii*) mortgage of property as security, (*iv*) Hypothecation of farm machinery.

6. *Completion/execution of security documents*

Depending upon the terms of sanction of advance, the various security documents should be got executed and/or signed.

(*i*) The following steps are taken for registration of mortgage of land/ building.

- (*a*) Prima-facie examination of title deeds and search as to encumbrance to be undertaken by the Bank's approved lawyer and certificate to be obtained saying that the title is clear, marketable and un-encumbered.
- (*b*) Mortgage Deed as per the Bank's standard form or specially drafted by the Bank's lawyer to be registered with sub-Registrar (Tehsildar) alongwith requisite fee and stamp duty.
- (*c*) Mortgage should not be effected prior to search and sanction of loan.
- (*d*) All costs including the lawyer's fee are to be paid by the loanee.

(*ii*) The bank's standard security documents need to be got signed *e.g.*,— Demand Promissory Note; Deed of hypothecation; Guarantee letter; Instalment letter etc.

7. Disbursement of loan

Loan amount should be disbursed as far as possible by paying to the supplier of inputs at the request of loanee instead of paying directly to the loanee. It will be better, if disbursement of advance is made in phases, after seeing the progress of the project financed by the bank.

8. Post-advance farm inspection

The Branch Manager and/or Agricultural Finance Officer and or/Field Officer should make periodical inspections of the farmer-borrower's farm/project financed and home in village. This will not only ensure proper utilisation of loans but also timely recovery thereof. Through the visits of Experts of Bank, the farmer will get opportunity for getting technical guidance and discussing their problem and at the same time the Bank Officers will have full supervision on the proper utilisation of loans and get an opportunity to remind the borrower about the instalment due, if any.

It is important for the Bank to associate in the production programme of the farmer as repayment depends upon the returns he receives from his agricultural production. These field visits also help to develop branch business of both agricultural advances and rural deposits.

FARM CREDIT ANALYSIS KIT

One needs to know the various tools, aids and basic information for the analysis of an individual credit proposal. The broader knowledge of the loan and service policies of lenders and of their obligations and responsibilities will aid the borrower in formulating realistic plans for utilisation of the credit. A detailed knowledge of production programmes, credit worthiness and soundness of a particular credit proposal of the farmer will be helpful to the lender for taking decisions to advance loan and minimise the credit risk. The producers that lenders follow in making loans vary with the agencies in details yet the general principles remain the same.

There is a need of a folder which may contain all such information in a condensed form. This kit for farm credit analysis should have two parts : (1) Banker's farm credit kit and (2) Borrower-farmer's credit file.

I. Banker's loan folder or farm credit kit

The bank officials should have certain forms, details of procedures, loan policies and the technical information on the agricultural business. There can be two types of information/papers in this kit : (*a*) banker's loan policies, procedures and prescribed forms, and (*b*) a manual of farm technology. Bank's loan policies, procedures and prescribed forms should contain forms, such as, inventory forms, schedule of advances, repayment agreement, mortgage deeds or abstracts of liens, etc., information on different types of loans, bank's policy regarding interest charges, repayment plans, amount available for short, medium, long term loans and list of items/operations to be financed by the particular bank.

The manual of farm technology should contain :

1. General information on the operational area including a map showing type of farming areas, roads, markets. etc., climate- temperatures, precipitation, soil characteristics, topography, farming areas delineated on the basis of physical, economic, and social factors, and crop rotations.
2. Calendar of agricultural operations of the area.
3. Technological co-efficients (per acre basis) or standards of works for different farm operations including : (*i*) manual labour requirements, (*ii*) bullock labour requirements, (*iii*) tractor/machine hour requirements, and (*iv*) other input requirements.
4. Standard farm plans for different types-of-farming areas; existing and suggested cropping patterns.
5. Profitability chart or enterprise budgets including yield levels, gross returns, input levels, variable expenses and returns to the fixed factors.
6. Operational capital requirements : (*i*) for different enterprises, *e.g.*, poultry, dairy, vegetables, and (*ii*) projects like soil conservation, levelling, etc.
7. Miscellaneous data including (*i*) product and factor prices with names of firms, (*ii*) custom rates and (*iii*) canal water rates.
8. Income variability coefficients in the areas of the bank operations.
9. Local agrarian laws and customs.
10. Other credit institutions and
11. Conversion tables.

II. Borrower-farmer's credit file

The lender-bank needs certain information concerning the applicant, his family, and the business for use in analysing a loan application. For this purpose, the bank opens up a credit file or loan folder for each borrower.

The credit file should generally include the following basic records/ information :

1. Identification-cum-credit card, if available.
2. Loan application.
3. Production programme budget with and without the use of proposed credit investment, *i.e*, marginal returns analysis of the credit proposal.
4. Estimates of repaying capacity.
5. Risk bearing ability estimates.
6. Credit control chart (proposed repayment schedule) and cash flow map.
7. Inspection report of field officers or an appraisal report on : (*a*) standard of existing farming operation and soil map. (*b*) reputation of the farmer in the community, and (*c*) the soundness of the credit proposal.
8. Miscellaneous farm records including : (*a*) net worth statement—preferably overtime, (*b*) income statements—preferably overtime, and (*c*) farm efficiency measures compared overtime and with average situation.
9. Other information or documents including : (*a*) inventory, (*b*) schedule of advances and repayment agreement, (*c*) mortgage abstracts if applicable, and (*d*) the security offered.

1. ***What do you understand by farm financial management ? Discuss the various characteristics of this subject.***
2. ***How is the study of farm financial management important to a farmer, lending agency or the farm credit advisory service ?***
3. ***Discuss in detail the role of credit in production and marketing of the agricultural produce.***
4. ***"Credit is instrumental in pulling the opportunity from the future to the present." Comment.***
5. ***What are the three tests of a farm credit proposal ? Discuss the application of each test by taking a suitable example.***
6. ***What steps possibly can be taken to strengthen the repaying capacity of a borrower ?***

7. *Why is repayment capacity important in the use of a credit ?*
8. *Distinguish between loans which are self-liquidation and those which are not. How do each of these types of loans influence repayment capacity ?*
9. *What is meant by risk bearing ability ? Why is it important in credit planning ?*
10. *What do you understand by 4 C's of credit and 5 P's of credit ?*
11. *Discuss the various steps for working out risk bearing ability of a farmer borrower.*
12. *Illustrate with a simple example how will you determine the repaying capacity of a cultivator if he decides to borrow : (i) for meeting the working costs such as fetilizers, pesticides, hired labour, etc.; (ii) for the purchase of a tractor or combine Harvester.*
13. *(a) How can the study of Agril. finance be helpful to a bank officer ?*

    (b) What are the lender's and borrowers expectations from each other ?
14. *You are asked to scrutinize an application of a cultivator for a loan to purchase a 'combine' costing Rs. 175,000/-. Outline the procedure you will adopt step by step-use reasonable hypothetical data you may need and give concrete recommendations based on your scrutiny.*
15. *(a) What is a Farm Credit Analysis Kit ? Discuss the main points of information which are needed for a farm credit analysis kit.*

    (b) Discuss the role of the repayment plan in farms credit analysis.
16. *What are the advantages of a cash flow statement in farm financial management ? How will you prepare a cash flow chart ?*
17. *Discuss in brief the problems and prospectus of agricultural finance in India.*
18. *Discuss the methods and mechanics of processing a farm credit proposal by a bank officer.*
19. *Why is pre-sanction farm inspection necessary for advancing loans by a commercial bank ? Discuss various steps for conducting effective farm inspection.*
20. *What is the importance of conducting effective post-sanction farm inspections of the project financed by a commercial bank.*

1. *Johl, S.S. and Moore, C.V. "Essentials of Farm Financial Management", Today and Tomorrow's Printers and Publishers; 22B/S Original Road, Karol Bagh, New Delhi-5, 1970.*
2. *Jain, S.C., "Management in Agricultural Finance"; Vora and Co., Publishers Pvt. Ltd., 2 Round Building, Bombay-2, 1970, pp. 164.*
3. *Sharma, B.k., "Reserve Bank of India and Rural Credit", S. Chand and Co., Delhi.*
4. *Shukla, Tara, "Capital Formation in Indian Agriculture"; Vora and Co., Bombay, 1965.*
5. *Nelson, A.G. Murray, W.G. "Agricultural Finance"; Iowa State University, Ames, U.S.A., 5th Edition.*
6. *Naidu, V. Tripathi, "Farm Credit and Cooperatives in India"; Vora & Co., Bombay, 1968.*
7. *R.B.I., "Seminar on Financing of Agriculture by Commercial Banks"—Report of a seminar held on December 6-8, 1968, Bombay, 1969.*
8. *Kahlon, A.S. and Hardev Singh, "Rationale of Agricultural Credit based on Farm Plans", Jour, of Res. P.A.U., Vol. II (1) : 1965; P.54.*
9. *Kahlon, A.S. and Kapur, T.R. "Estimation of farm credit requirements of I.A.D.P. district Ludhiana from 1968-69 to 1972-73. Jour. of Research, P.A.U., Sept. 1970.*
10. *Mudhar, M.S. "Rationale of M.C.L. based on Farm Plans in Ludhiana District in Punjab"; M.Sc. Thesis, P.A.U., Ludhiana. (unpublished)*
11. *Reserve Bank of India : "Manual on Production-oriented System of Lending for Agriculture" 1972.*

12 Management of Important Farm Resources

With the help of the basic principles and methods of farm management analysis outlined in earlier chapters, we now proceed to consider specific farm management problems. These problems can be classified according to the major factors of production land, labour, machinery, equipment, etc. Here in this chapter we discuss these problems in respect of land management including farm layout, crop rotations, crop management and soil management, the next three chapters will deal with the management of farm labour, machinery and the buildings.

LAND MANAGEMENT

Land has its characteristic importance in production process and has some unique problems. Many of these problems, however, are technological in nature and can be dealt with by agronomists and soil scientists. Here we discuss only the economic problems such as the intensity of land-use, the level at which the fertility of the soil should be maintained most advantageously and the amounts that can be economically invested in improving the land and income from the farm.

The growing plants draw out the plant nutrients and water from the soil, which must be restored in order to maintain the crop yields. In fact, the main problems of land management centre around the maintenance, rather than an improvement of soil fertiliy. Deterioration of the soil and its fertility takes place through cropping, wind and water erosion and with the growth of weeds and pests. Its fertility can be replenished by (1) proper cultivation and fallowing, (2) addition of manures and fertilizers, (3) growing leguminous crops-green manuring, (4) eradication of weeds and extermination of pests, (5) levelling and bundling, (6) drainage in water-logged soils, and (7) washing away the excess of salts from soils infested with *Kallar*, etc.

The land, if properly looked after, should not depreciate and inflow-outflow ratio of the plant nutrients can be maintained.

The quantities of plant nutrients which are removed by growing a particular crop, should be restored by adding appropriate quantities of manures and fertilizers in the soil. See Table 12.1.

TABLE 12.1

Quantities of Plant Nutrients Removed from Soil by Different Crops

Crop	*Yield (kg./ha.)*	*Quantity of nutrients removed (kg./ha.)*		
		N	P_2O_5	K_2O
Paddy	2,800	82	23	123
Wheat	2,242	59	29	67
Jowar	1,121	52	18	86
Bajra	897	30	11	101
Maize	2,690	114	47	105
Barley	2,466	54	29	125
Groundnut	1,906	78	22	45
Mustard	673	22	11	28
Linseed	1,009	19	12	33
Sugarcane	87,109	120	89	288
Potato	17,575	85	30	140
Cotton lint	104	26	20	84

Source. Fertilizer Statistics, F.A.I. (1968-69).

Besides the addition of manures and fertilizers, to restore or increase the fertility of the soil, crop-rotations are of special importance in maintaining the soil fertility.

For instance, in the rotation, *wheat-sorgum + guar-gram- cotton-senji*, three crops deplete and three improve the soil fertility. The simple rule is that the level of fertility of any plot of land should be at least maintained more or less at the normal level. As the intensity of cropping and yields go high, the land should receive heavier doses of fertilizers and manures, as is the case with vegetable crops near towns and cities. However, the optimum doses of manure and fertilizers for various crops need to be carefully worked out.

Another aspect is of a proper tillage of the soil. Its main functions are (1) to kill the weeds, (2) destroy insect pest and diseases, (3) aerate the soil to facilitate chemical and biological processes and (4) open up the soil for plant-root penetration. Tillage at the proper time for the extermination of weeds and conservation of moisture is, therefore, of great importance in successful farming especially in the rain-fed areas.

Further, the farm must be properly laid out into fields of appropriate sizes, which may be divided into sub-plots. Each plot and sub-plot must be properly levelled. In sloping or rolling lands, such practices as terracing, contour ridging, contour tillage, cover cropping, sod-cultivation, etc., become important so as to check the water run off and save the soil from erosion.

In the following sections we consider briefly the various phases of the land management problem as it faces the farm operator.

EFFICIENT FARM LAYOUT

Layout of a farm refers to the manner in which a farm is divided into fields and the location and arrangement of other fixtures such as irrigation and drainage system, buildings and sheds, roads, fencing, etc. After the location of the farm is decided, the farm would need a proper layout to obtain a high level of efficiency. Most of the Indian farms have no scientific layout worth the name. In some places there is no approach road, at others too much land is wasted along the roadsides. At some places no provision for drainage is made and at others the soil is getting eroded. Fields do not have any regular shape. Sub- division and fragmentation at some places have rendered the small pieces of land uncultivable. Layout of a farm directly affects : (*a*) costs and efficiency in the use of man power, bullock power and machinery, (*b*) costs and efficiency of irrigation, drainage and fencing, and (*c*) cropping plan and profitability of the farm business as a whole.

The following factors offer a general framework for a good farm- layout :

(*a*) Purpose of the farm : experimental, demonstration, seed multiplication, or commercial (vegetables, fruit orchards, general crop farming, dairy, etc.,)

(*b*) Topography.

(*c*) Variation in soil fertility.

(*d*) Size of the farm.

(*e*) Livestock kept.

(*f*) Cropping scheme.

(*g*) Irrigation and drainge problem.

(*h*) Building structures.

(*i*) Farm communication situation-roads and field paths. Consistent with the size and purpose of the farm, topography and system of farming, a good farm layout should ensure : (*a*) a small number of good-sized fields, (*b*) rectangular fields, (*c*) minimum area under buildings, roads and water channels, (*d*) buildings located in the centre of the farm (*e*) access to every field, (*f*) minimum fencing cost, (*g*) uniformity of the soil within a field and within major blocks, and (*h*) efficient and economical irrigation and drainage system. An efficient layout is the one which takes into consideration the topography of the land, fits in well with the enterprises and crop rotations, leads to the saving of labour and ensures efficient checks and controls on farming operations.

RECOMMENDATIONS ON A GOOD LAYOUT

Farm Buildings and Sheds

The farm buildings, sheds for livestock, stores, labour quarters, etc., should be located at the farm. They should be in the centre of the farm as far as possible, so that the approach to different fields and supervision becomes easy. If this is not possible, they may be located on the side of the farm near to the main road, but not on public roads or highways. These should be located on a high ground level to provide proper drainage. The source of water supply should be near and the drinking water should be of good quality. The farm buildings should not be very expensive. Adequate arrangements must be made for the disposal of sewage and manure. To provide shade during summer and fuel wood as well as timber for use on the farm and in the house-hold, trees should be planted at suitable places. If the farmstead is located on the farm, the living houses should be away from the cattle sheds and manure pits. In hills, the buildings should be exposed to the sunlight, but should be safe from strong winds.

Some of the standards are : Cattle = 10' × 5' space per animal and Labour—10' × 12' room space + equal size verandah per labourer.

Layout of Fields

The following points should be kept in view while planning the layout of the fields, etc.

(*i*) The size, shape and location of fields should fit in with the rotations and the layout of the land.

(*ii*) On a level land, a well-laid out farm is the one that is divided into a small number of large fields. The number of main fields or blocks should either be equal to the number of years in the rotation or a multiple thereof so that they may be easily adjusted to the cropping rotation to be followed. A field rectangular in shape is considered to be better. Ill-shaped fields waste much of labour, time and resources.

(*iii*) As far as possible, a field should be uniform in soil type and level. Recommended size of the fields are : One acre in case of a bullock operated farm and 10-15 acres in case of a tractor operated farm, depending, of course, upon the total size of the farm, irrigation source and the type of farming.

(*iv*) On a sloping land, the layout should be planned with the object of checking or reducing soil erosion and conserving the soil. The fields should extend along the contour, instead of, up and down the slope.

Roads

Each field need not be connected with a road on commercial farms. Key approach roads, of course, have to be there on the sides of the farm. Main approach road from the highway to the farmstead should be wider (15' to 20') and other linking roads may be kept narrower between 9' to 10'.

Water Channels

Layout of water channels depends upon the source of irrigation. Each field must be connected with a water channel without any duplication. A tubewell (or any other water lift) should be installed at a higher point in order to facilitate an easy flow of water to all the fields in the commanded area.

Drainage

Provision of drainage is essential in any scientific layout. It depends upon the level of the land as to where and on which side of the farm drainage channels should be provided. If the land is of high level, the low level roads and water channels can serve the purpose of drains.

Fencing

Fences are an essential investment on a farm, but their type and extent depends upon the location of the farm as well as the type of the farm. Vegetable farms near the cities and gardens essentially need a permanent and strong fencing. Ordinary arable farming in the rural areas, especially when located away from *'abadi'*, may not need any fencing. Ordinary high *kacha* bunds would suffice in such cases. High *kacha* wall, *pucca* brick wall, shrub fencing such as *sarkanda* (Reeds), *thore* (cactus), *Dhaincha, sada bahar*, etc., barbed wire with wooden, brick, concrete or iron poles, are the common types of fences used in India. Since barbed wire with angle iron poles is the most popular type of fencing, it will be appropriate to know its approximate costs.

Cost of fencing. The cost of fencing a vegetable farm of $12^1/_2$ acres with barbed wire and iron poles works out as under at 1969 prices :

Suppose the sides of the farm are in the ratio of 2 : 4

then $2x.4x = 8x^2 = 12\frac{1}{2}$ acres.

$$8x^2 = \frac{25}{2} \times 43560 \text{ sq. ft.}$$

and $x = 260.9$ (say 261 ft.)

∴ Length = 1044 ft.

and breadth = 522 ft.

Perimeter = 3132 ft.

Wire = 3132 × 3ft. (Three rounds of the wire)

(*a*) Cost of the wire $= \frac{3132 \times 3}{200 \times 3} \times 48$

@ Rs. 48/- for a 200 yards bundle = Rs. 751.68 (say Rs. 752/-)

(*b*) Cost of Iron poles $= \frac{3132}{15} = 209 + 8 \text{ extra} = 217$

(with distance of 15' between poles)

Cost of 5 ft. long 217 poles, each weighing $1^1/_2$ kg. per foot @ Rs. 30/- per 40 kgs.

$$= \frac{217 \times 5 \times 3}{2 \times 40} \times 30 = \text{Rs. } 1191.25$$

(*c*) Concrete bricks, etc., @ Re. 1/- per pole = Rs. 217/-

(*d*) Labour charges = 16 × Rs.6 + 32 × Rs.3

16 masons + 32 labourers = Rs. 96 + Rs. 96 = Rs. 192/-

(One Mason and two labourers fix 13-14 poles and wire per day).

(*e*) Gate one = Rs. 300/-

Summary of Total Costs

(*a*)	Wire	= Rs. 752.00
(*b*)	Iron poles	= Rs. 1191.00
(*c*)	Concrete, cement, etc.	= Rs. 217.00
(*d*)	Labour charges	= Rs. 192.00
(*e*)	Gate	= Rs. 300.00
	Total	= Rs. 2652.00

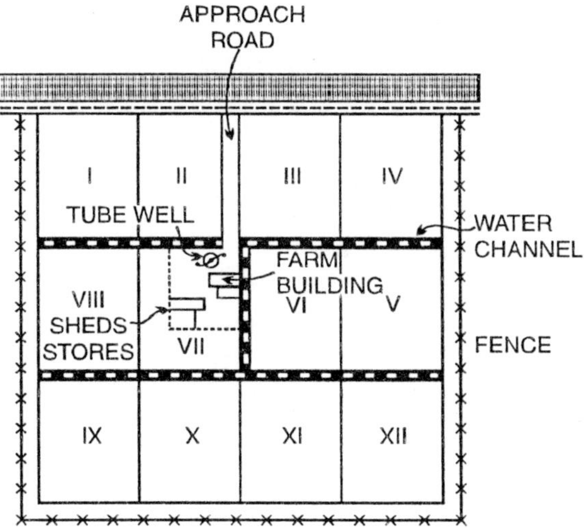

Fig. 12.1. A Model Layout of $12^1/_2$ Acre Arable Commercial Farm Canal-Well Irrigated.

Gross area	= 12.50 acres
Buildings and wells, etc.	= 0.10 acre
Roads, water channels and drainage, etc.	= 0.28 acre
Net area available for cultivation	= 12.12 acres

REMODELLING OF THE FARM LAYOUT

It is usually not easy to make changes in the farm-layout because it involves heavy investment. But with the changing techniques of production and increasing mechanisation, remodelling of the farm layout can become necessary. The compelling forces can be :

(*i*) mechanisation, replacing bullock power with tractors,

(*ii*) changing the source of irrigation, *i.e.*, replacing persian wheel with tube-well, and

(*iii*) controlling the soil erosion.

There can be many other reasons that will compel a farmer to change the layout of his farm. In this section, we will be discussing the first two factors, *i.e.*, mechanisation and irrigation, because of their importance.

In each case, we will have to consider the initial cost and also the increased cost per acre and we shall be comparing the costs with the returns and other savings which may accrue after changing the layout.

(a) Effects of mechanisation

We consider a 60 acre farm with the present layout shown in Fig. 12.2. In this case, source of power at present is bullocks. On replacing the bullocks with a tractor, a farmer will need to change the layout. The revised layout for which the farmer should go in for is shown in Fig. 12.3. The cost involved revising the layout will be due to, the cost of reorganising the farm, including the costs of removing the existing bunds and the cost of installation of new fencing. The net gains will be mainly due to the savings on labour and land.

Particulars of Existing Farm Layout

(Refer Fig. 12.2)

Total area of the farm	= 60 acres
Cropping pattern	
Wheat-Maize	= 10 acres
Wheat-Groundnut	= 15 acres
Wheat-American Cotton	= 20 acres
Sugarcane	= 8 acres
Fodders	= 5 acres
Total area under above pattern	= 45 acres
Size of the existing field	= 1 acre each (app.)
Size of the Farm-stead	= 1.4 acres
Existing fencing	= Kacha Bunds

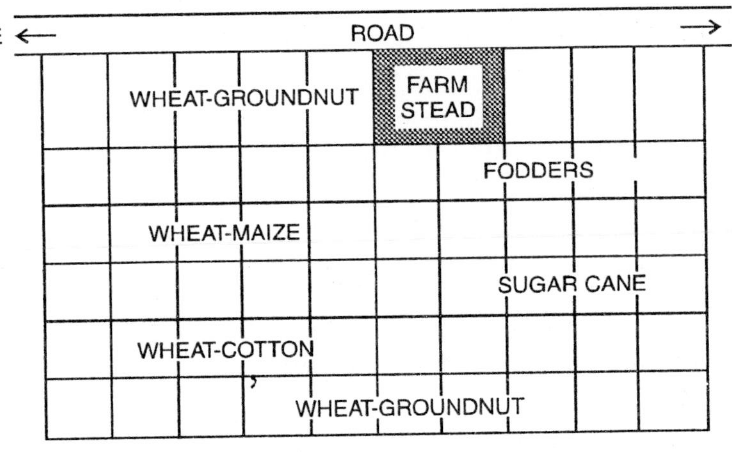

Fig. 12.2 Power Source-Bullocks.

Alternative Layout

(Refer Fig. 12.3)

If we plough with a tractor in such a small size of the field (1 = acre) then number of turns will be more and the fuel and labour costs will be high. Also the land which is occupied under the existing bunds, will go waste. For efficient utilisation of the tractor, we will have to dismantle all these bunds. The number of fields will have to be either equal to the number of years of rotations or else be a multiple of that number.

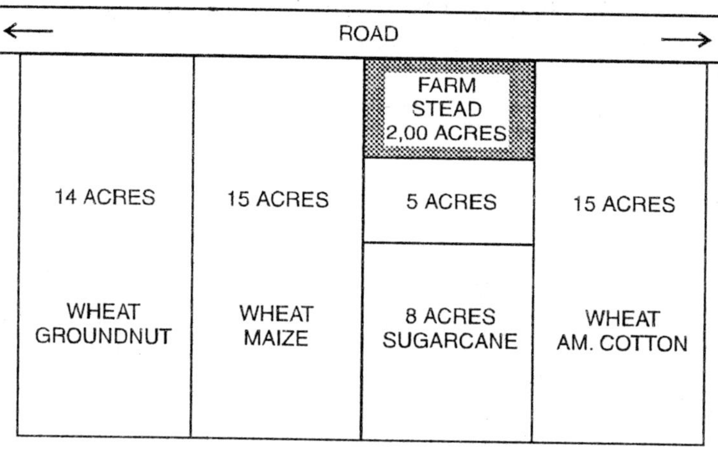

Fig. 12.3 Power Source-Tractor.

Cost Estimate for Revision of Layout

(*a*) *Cost of removing bunds.* As per field experience, the time taken by a tractor for removing bunds per acre is approximately fifteen minutes. Therefore, total hours for 60 acres will be 15 hours. This will cost Rs. 142.50 @ of Rs. 9.50 per hour.

(*i*) The additional cost of fencing within the reorganised farm will depend upon the number of additional fence poles to be installed which in this case will be equal to 270 (Fig. 12.2). The distance between different poles will be 16½ft. At the rate of Rs. 5/- per pole, cost of poles will be Rs. 1350/- . The cost of installation of these poles @ Rs. 1.50 each, will be Rs. 405/-.

(*ii*) The cost of barbed wire (having 3 rounds) with a total length of wire 270 × 16½ × 3 = 13400 ft. at the rate of Rs. 9/- per hundred feet will be equal to Rs. 1206/-.

(*iii*) Cost of stretching and fixing the wires at the rate of Rs. 10/- per 1000 feet will be Rs. 134/-.

(*iv*) Total cost on installation of new fencing, therefore, will be = 1350 + 405 + 1206 + 134 = Rs. 3240/-.

Return Estimate from Revised Layout

An investment of Rs. 3240/- on changing the layout will be beneficial in saving some land and on the efficiency of labour.

(*a*) The additional land area made available for cultivation by the revised fencing will be equal to 0.6 acre. Assuming an average net returns per acre (for 2 crops land) is equal to Rs. 1000/-, we get additional returns of Rs. 600/- per year.

(*b*) The savings in labour will be on ploughing, harrowing, and other field operations, because due to the large sized fields, time taken for turns will be reduced and the operation will become easier and quicker.

In case of the old layout, it takes 45 minutes for a three bottom 15 inches mould board plough to plough one acre. If we include the time wasted on taking turns, the total time works out to be 70 minutes. On a farm of 60 acres with 56 acres of cultivated land, total time needed for actual ploughing once will be equal to 65.5 hours approximately. On the same basis, it will take only 45.5 hours for one ploughing of 56 acres in case of remodelled farm layout. The net saving in tractor hours thus will be 65.3 – 45.3 = 20 hrs. At the rate of Rs. 9.50 per hour, total costs saved will be Rs. 190/- per ploughing of the entire farm land.

For wheat, we will need at least one ploughing, 2 harrowings, 1 seeding, and 1 harvesting. For maize also we will need at least one ploughing, 4 harrowings and planking, 1 seeding and 1 harvesting. On an average for wheat, we require at least 4 times operations by tractor, each equivalent of 1 ploughing. For maize on an average, we require tractor operations equivalent to 5 times ploughing. In one year, if wheat is followed by maize on the entire land, total money saved will be equal to Rs. 190 × (5 + 3) = Rs. 1520/–. So total savings by changing the layout will be equal to the net income due to savings on land and labour amounting to Rs. 2120/- per year. As the total cost will be Rs. 3240, it will take less than two years to return this capital.

(*b*) *Effect of change in source of irrigation*

Let us consider a 10 acre farm. Present layout is shown in Fig. 12.4. In this case, the source of irrigation is "Persian Wheel". If the farmer installs a tubewell, the efficiency of irrigation will remain low and hence he will have to change the layout accordingly. Suggested layout of water system is shwon in Fig. 12.5.

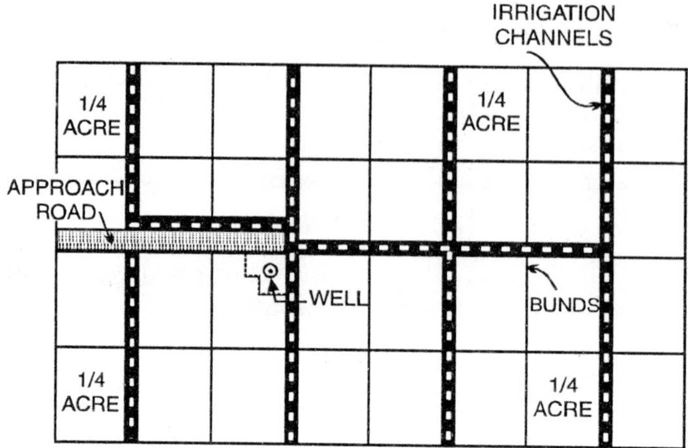

Fig. 12.4. Present Layout With a Persian Wheel

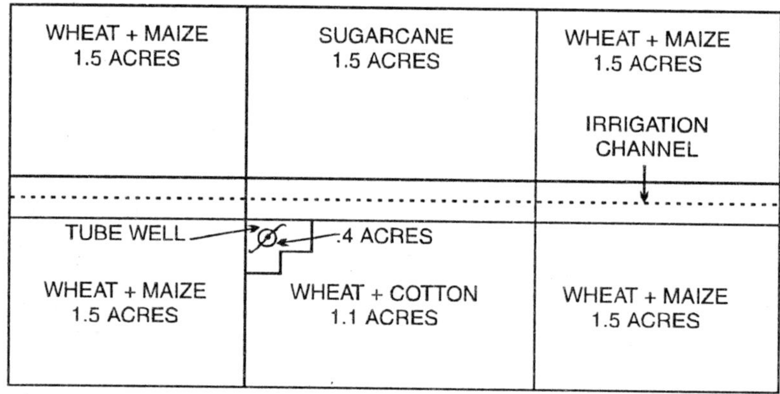

Fig. 12.5. Revised Layout with a Tubewell.

Cost Return Analysis

The costs involved in changing the farm layout are : (*i*) reorganisation cost (cost of bunding, etc.) and (*ii*) cost of channels. The returns will be from land saving, water economy, and labour saved. Time needed to level a field of 1 acre will be 25 minutes. Time needed to level the farm will be 250 minutes with a cost of Rs. 40/- approximately. The cost of changing the bunds will be approximately Rs. 5/- on 1969 wage rates. Construction of pucca channels will be the major cost. It will need 275 yards of pucca channels. At the rate of Rs. 10/- per yard of water channel, the total cost will amount to Rs. 2750. Thus, the total cost of redesigning the water channels system, will be Rs. 2800/-. On the side of returns, the new system will waste less land and will save 0.2 acres capable of yielding Rs. 200/- per year. The new system will save 80 hours of water pumping per year. At the rate of Rs. 3.50 per hour, it will save Rs. 280/- per year.

Due to this change in the layout, there will be some savings due to speed in operations. This will amount to Rs. 150 approximately. Thus, the total savings due to the new water channels layout will be Rs. 630 per year. As total investment amounts to about Rs. 2800/- it will take approximately 4 $^{1}/_{2}$ years to return the investment costs.

SOIL MANAGEMENT

The management of a soil is an integral part of land management. The central objective of soil management is to maintain, rather improve, the fertility of the soil. Soil management is closely linked with the crop management. Soil management is, the science of studying the origin, use, protection and improvement of the soil. Careful management of the soil increases the returns of the farm as a whole. In this section, an attempt is made to determine the level of fertilizer use, seeding rate, time of application of the fertilizers and the optimum method of application in order to improve the existing soil fertility, in an economic manner.

Soil Management Practices

The soil management practices include (1) maintenance of a desirable physical condition and proper water-air relationship in the soil through proper tillage practices, (2) improving the soil fertility by the addition of organic manure, following good rotations and sound cropping scheme, preventing soil erosion, removing soil barrenness through planting of tress, drainage, application of gypsum, breaking the impervious layers, deep ploughing and the adding of organic matter. The fertility can be further improved through control of soil acidity and curing the soil sickness by giving the soil good tillage, replenishing the organic matter and other plant nutrients, keeping the soil well drained, scientific dry farming, adopting scientific rotations, preventing soil erosion and using soil conservation practices.

MANAGEMENT OF SOIL RESOURCES

The soil resources can be managed properly through the following measures :

Cropping System

Cropping system refers to the sequence of crops grown to maintain the fertility status of the soil. The crop sequence of a particular soil varies with its characteristics such as the level of soil and drainage, the interest and ability of farmer and the crop alternatives available to the farmer. Many farmers will grow the crops which yield the highest net returns per acre taking into consideration the convenience of the farmer and soil conservation requirements. On high organic-matter soils, for example, one crop of legumes will maintain reasonable maize yields for two years. A second crop of maize will yield more than the previous one if some commercial nitrogen or manure is used. The cropping system which depends upon a legume crop to supply most of the nitrogen is satisfactory even though forage yields may be low. It increases the grain yield of the following crop(s), which would be possible otherwise with only a heavy fertilization. So the management problem here is whether to grow a legume with maize or maize along with a heavy fertilizer. Similarly there can be so many other crop alternatives and fertilizer combinations.

Organic Matter

Organic matter is the remains of plants, animals and microbes in all the stages of decomposition. Wheat/paddy-straw, maize stalks, grass roots and farm yard manure are some of the materials which normally decompose in the soil. Any cultivation which will cause more rapid depletion of the organic matter through aeration and sun would need to be avoided. The objective should be to balance the depletion and stabilize the inflow and outflow of the organic matter of the soil.

Crop Yields

Due to the introduction of high yielding varieties, crop yields have in many cases, more than doubled. These varieties deplete the soil of nutrients more than the earlier varieties. Here it is a question of more careful balancing of the yield levels with the plant nutrient additions into the soil.

Erosion and Soil Improvement

The control of erosion by water or by wind is one of the major problems in soil management. It has to be checked by terracing, giving appropriate contours and slopes to the cultivated fields. Improvement of soil includes the use of lime, gypsum, fertilizers, and the farm manures.

Economics of Fertilizer Use

The optimum use of fertilizer depends upon its commercial price, chemical composition and also on the type of the soil and the crops grown. Application of a unit of fertilizer is economical, if the value of the increase in crop yield due to the quantity of fertilizer added is greater than the cost of the fertilizer used. If a unit of fertilizer does not increase the yield enough to pay for its cost, its application will not be economical and will not add to the net returns even though it may increase the yield.

Selection of the fertilizer is also one of the management problems. A fertilizer should be selected based on its nutrient composition and cost.

FERTILIZATION MANAGEMENT PROGRAMMES

In deciding when and how much fertilizer to use, the following considerations have to be given :

1. The principles of diminishing marginal returns and increasing marginal costs for deciding how much fertilizer to apply, if the operator has an unlimited amount of capital.
2. The opportunity cost principle for deciding whether to use the available capital on fertilizer or to invest it in some other line of the business.
3. The substitution principle for deciding what combination of the elements to use. How far, for example, the farmer should substitute fertilizer for manure (or legumes and grasses in rotation) and vice versa.
4. The operator also needs to figure out ways to handle for risks and uncertainty involved in high yielding varieties and higher costs of fertilizers.

ILLUSTRATIONS

(*a*) *How much fertilizer to add*

A few examples on fertilizer use have been worked out on the basis of experimental data available at Punjab Agricultural University, Ludhiana and illustrated in Table 12.2.

The optimum level of nitrogen fertilizer does in this case (Table 12.2) is 80 kg. per hectare because it gives the highest net profit (7128 rupees). But if one unit more is added, the net profit goes negative.

From the first table, it is not possible to reach any decision on phosphorus use, because with the addition of every unit, the net profits go on increasing. This means doses have not been tried sufficiently high. In example-2, Table 12.2, optimum level of phosphorus application is 90 kg. per hectare, giving highest returns of Rs. 2326.3.

TABLE 12.2

Determination of Optimum Level of Fertilizer Application on Wheat in Punjab

Example 1A. Nitrogenous Fertilizer (Urea).*

S. No.	*Fertilizer dose (N) kg/ha.*	*Yield per hectare (quintals)*	*Marginal product (quintals)*	*Marginal return @ Rs. 80/- q. (Rs.)*	*Total Return (Rs.)*	*Total cost @ Rs. 130 per kg. (Rs.)*	*Marginal cost (Rs.)*	*Returns per hectare (Rs.)*
1.	0	12.65	0	0	1012	0	0	1012
2.	40	23.45	10.80	864	1876	52	52	1824
3.	80	90.40	66.95	5350	7232	104	52	7128
4.	120	35.50	– 54.90	– 4360	– 2840	156	52	2684
5.	160	34.85	– 0.65	– 52	2288	208	52	2080

Example 1B. Phosphatic Fertilizer (Bone meal) :

S. No.	*Fertilizer dose (N) kg/ha.*	*Yield per hectare (quintals)*	*Marginal product (quintals)*	*Marginal return @ Rs. 80/- q. (Rs.)*	*Total Return (Rs.)*	*Total cost @ Rs. 0.83 per kg. (Rs.)*	*Marginal cost (Rs.)*	*Returns (Rs.)*
1.	0	18.62	0	0	1489.60	0	0	1489.60
2.	50	25.23	6.61	528.80	2018.40	41.50	41.50	1976.90
3.	100	27.36	2.13	170.40	2188.80	83.00	41.50	2105.80

Example 2. Phosphatic Fertilizer (Super phosphate) :**

S. No.	*Fertilizer (Phosph-orus) dose*	*Yield (wheat) per hectare (quintals)*	*Marginal produc-tion (quintals)*	*Marginal returns @ Rs. 80/-q. (Rs.)*	*Total returns (Rs.)*	*Total cost @ Rs. 0.83 per kg. (Rs.)*	*Marginal cost (Rs.)*	*Net profit (Rs.)*
1.	0	23.92	0	0	1910.00	0	0	1910.00
2.	30	26.76	2.84	224.00	2139.00	24.9	24.9	2114.00
3.	60	28.80	2.04	163.00	2301.00	49.8	24.9	2251.20
4.	90	30.12	1.32	105.00	2401.00	74.7	24.9	2326.03
5.	120	28.78	—1.34	—107.00	2290.00	99.6	24.9	2190.04

* **Source.** Annual Reports-Department of Soil (1968-69) pp. 76, P.A.U., Ludhiana.

** **Source.** Annual Report (1966-67) Department of Soils, P.A.U., Hissar.

(b) *Optimum time of application of fertilizers*

The Table 12.3 shows that the time of application of the fertilizer has a great effect on the yield. T_3 (application of fertilizer-1/3 at sowing, 1/3 three weeks after sowing and 1/3 at heading) gave the highest yield in both the cases (80 kg. of fertilizer per hectare and 160 kg. of fertilizer per hectare). Though this application involved the use of some more labour yet on economic tests it was advisable to apply fertilizer 1/3 at sowing time, 1/3 three weeks after sowing and 1/3 at headig time.

TABLE 12.3

Optimum Time of Fertilizer Application

Time of application	*Wheat yield Q./ha. (1967)*	
	Dose of Fertilizer	
	80 kg./ha.	*160 kg./ha.*
T_1 = whole at sowing	17.60	21.54
T_2 = $^1/_2$at sowing, $^1/_2$ three weeks after sowing	21.35	35.67
T_3 = $^1/_3$ at sowing, $^1/_3$ three weeks after sowing and $^1/_3$ at heading	27.80	41.02
T_4 = $^1/_2$ at sowing and $^1/_2$ at earning stage	16.98	22.18

Source. Annual Report (1968-69) p. 40, Dept. of Agronomy, Punjab Agricultural University, Ludhiana.

(c) *Selection of method of application of fertilizers*

It has been observed through a number of experiments that the method of application of fertilizers effect the yield of crops and in turn income. Table 12.4 shows the effect of method of application of nitrogen at different levels on wheat crop.

TABLE 12.4

Effect of Placement of Nitrogen on Wheat*

S.No.	*Method of Application*	*Yield Qt./ha.*	*Cost Rs. @ 1966 prices*
1.	Broadcasting at sowing (80 kg.)	19.22	2.00
2.	Side placement 2.3" on either side (80 kg. ha.)	19.00	8.00

3.	Drilling 2 1/2" below the side (80 kg./ha.)	19.22	2.00
4.	Broadcasting at sowing (120 kg.)	21.45	2.50
5.	Side placement 2.3" on either side (120 kg./ha.)	22.20	10.00
6.	Drilling 21/2" below the side (120 kg./ha.)	22.20	2.00
7.	Broadcasting at sowing (160 kg.)	22.92	3.50
8.	Side placement 2.3" on either side (160 kg.)	25.28	13.00
9.	Drilling 21/2" below the side (160 kg./ha.)	23.72	2.00

***Source.** Annual Reports (1966-67) p.71. Dept. of Soils, P.A.U. Ludhiana.

When the dose of nitrogen was 80 kg., the yield in case of broadcasting and 2 1/2" drilled below the side was the same. In this case, broadcasting should be followed because of easiness. When dose was 120 kg., yield by drilling 21/2" below was higher whereas cost of labour remained the same.

When we increase the dose to 160 kg./ha., the yield in the case of side placement increased to the highest as compared to the other methods. Cost of labour was more, yet it was less than the increase in production. It was, therefore, advisable at higher doses to use the method of side placement.

(d) *Choice of mode of fertilizer placement*

Fertilizers can be applied by different methods and they give different response to such mode of placement. See example given in Table 12.5.

TABLE 12.5

Effect of Mode of Fertilizer Placement on Maize Grain*

	Mode of Placement	Yield Q./ha. Fertilizer kg./ha.	
		30 kg./ha.	60 kg./ha.
1.	Broadcast	26.43	27.03
2.	Placement below seeds at sowing	33.43	25.22
3.	Side placement	20.62	23.62

***Source.** Annual Reports (1968-69) p.135, Dept. of Soils, P.A.U., Ludhiana.

When the dose of fertilizer was 30 kg./ha., the yield was maximum by placing the fertilizer below the seeds at the time of sowing. Cost of labour was expected to be much lesser than the increase in production. When the dose was increased from 30 to 60 kg./ha., the yield by broadcasting method was more. It turned out to be the least cost method because same labour could broadcast it with the seeds at the sowing time.

(f) Selection of source of plant nutrient from various fertilizers

There are a variety of fertilizers which give different quantities of the same plant nutrients. Their costs per unit also vary. The farmers are interested to select the cheapest source of nutrients from fertilizers. For selection of proper source, see Table 12.6.

TABLE 12.6

Sources of N.P.K. in Fertilizer and their Costs

Name of the fertilizer	*Nutrient Content in percentage*	*Price of Fertilizer in Rs. per kg.*	*Price of the nutrient content in Rs. per kg.*
(*i*) Nitrogen (N) content			
Urea	44.46	0.610	1.30
Ammonium Sulphate	20.60	0.336	1.77
Ammonium Chloride	25.00	0.335	1.42
Ammonium Sulphate Nitrate	26.00	0.455	1.75
CAN	20.5 to 25	0.355	1.42
(*ii*) Phosphorus Content in P_2O_5 Form			
Single super phosphate	16	0.213	1.34
Diamm. Phosphate	46	0.750	1.63
Bone Meal	25.30	0.250	0.83
(*iii*) Potash (K) Content in K_2O			
Muriate of Potash	60	0.309	0.52
Potassium Sulphate	48	0.377	0.78

Decisions

Nitrogen :

Price of Nitrogen in Urea was Rs. 1.30 per kg. which was the least cost. Urea was thus the most economical source of Nitrogen.

Phosphorus :

The price of phosphorus in case of Bone-meal was Rs. 0.83 per kg. which was the cheapest source of phosphorus.

Potassium :

Price of potassium was minimum, *i.e.*, Rs. 0.52 per kg. in case of Muriate of Potash. So this was the least cost source of this nutrient.

(f) Selection of combination of fertilization and seed rate

Effects of fertilization and seed rate were very pronounced on the yield of sugarcane. When the nitrogen level is zero, the maximum net returns can be had with seed rate at 35,000 sets/acre. The optimum level of seed rate, therefore, at zero nitrogen was 35,000 sets. When the level of nitrogen was changed to 100 lb., the optimum level again works out to be 35,000 sets. At the nitrogen level of 200 lb. per acre; optimum level changes to 30,000 sets.

TABLE 12.7

Effects of Seed Rate and Nitrogen Application on the Yield of Sugarcane

Fertilizer Treatment lb./acre	*Seed Rate (Sets)*	*Yield Mds./acre*	*Marginal Seed rate*	*Marginal Yield*	*Marginal cost*	*Total cost*	*Marginal returns*	*Total returns*	*Net returns*
	S_1	169.6	—	—	—	125.00	—	508.8	383.8
N_0	S_2	207.9	5000	38.3	25.00	150.00	114.9	623.7	473.7
	S_3	227.5	5000	19.6	25.00	175.00	58.8	682.5	507.5
	S_1	446.7	—	—	—	182.00	—	134.0	1158.1
N_1	S_2	432.7	5000	– 13.8	25.00	207.00	– 40.4	1298.1	1091.0
	S_3	485.5	5000	52.6	25.00	232.00	157.8	1456.5	1224.0
	S_1	494.7	—	—	—	239.00	—	1484.1	1245.0
N_2	S_2	527.3	5000	32.6	25.00	264.00	97.8	1581.9	1318.0
	S_3	515.4	5000	– 11.9	25.00	289.00	– 35.7	1546.2	1257.0

Seed Rate: S_1 = 25000 sets, S_2 = 30000 sets, S_3 = 35000 sets

Nitrogen level: N_0 = 0 lb./acre, N_1 = 100 lb./acre, N_2 = 200 lb./acre

At Price of Sugarcane = Rs. 3/md., cost of seed = Rs. 0.50/100 sets. Cost of N_2 = Rs. 0.57/lb.

Source. M.Sc. research thesis "Effect of spacing on growth and yield of sugarcane", PAU, Ludhiana 1969.

Weather and Price Risks in Fertilizer Use

Use of fertilizer involves risks because decisions are made early in the year and the crop is harvested several months later. Decisions are made based on normal weather conditions and prices prevailing in the market. When the crop is ready for the market, prices may vary widely or climate or weather may not remain normal during the growth period and returns may vary significantly from the expectations. (A detailed theoretical construct of the effects of risk and uncertainty is given in the last chapter.)

Going back to Table 12.2, (effect on phosphorus fertilizer on wheat), 90 kg./ per hectare of fertilizer dose has been recommended under the normal conditions when the price of wheat is Rs. 80 per quintal. If the prices in the market change, the decisions on inputs-use will also change directly.

1. *What is the importance of scientific land management ?*
2. *What do you understand by an efficient farm layout ? Give its importance and discuss factors determining the good layout of a commercial farm.*
3. *Suggest a good system of farm building. Discuss the various points that should be kept in view for planning a good building and road programme.*
4. *Why is fencing necessary for a commercial farm ? How will you work out the cost of fencing a 12-acre farm situated near a city, assuming current prices.*
5. *What do you understand by a scientific soil management ? Discuss its importance and management characteristics of the soil resource.*
6. *What economic principles do help to decide the level of fertilization of a crop ? Demonstrate the application of those principles by giving suitable examples.*
7. *Evaluate the following statements :*
   (a) *The most profitable amount of a factor of production to use is that at which the production is maximum.*
   (b) *One should continue to use a resource until there is no further increase in the amount of product.*
   (c) *One should continue to use a resource to the level where the last addition just pays for itself.*
8. *The following data from a fertilizer experiment illustrates the principle of diminishing returns in the physical sense :*

Mixed fertilizer applied/acre	*Potato yield per acre*
None	*30 quintals.*
6 units	*160*
12 units	*220*
18 units	*260*
24 units	*290*
30 units	*310*
36 units	*320*

(i) What more information do you need to interpret it in the economic sense ?

(ii) How would you proceed to work out the optimum dose of fertilization ?

1. *Heady, E.O. and Jenson, H.R. "Farm Management Economics", Prentice Hall (India), Ltd., New Delhi-1961, Chap.*
2. *Annual progress reports of soils department, P.A.U., Ludhiana.*
3. *Punjab Agricultural Hand Book 1971. Punjab Agricultural University, Ludhiana.*
4. *Ray Chaudhari, S.P. "Use of Artificial Fertilizers in India". I.C.A.R. Technical Bulletin (Agric.) No. 13, 1969.*
5. *Kahlon, A.S. and Surjit Singh, "An Economic Analysis of Irrigation and Fertilizer Requirements for Sugarcane Crop", Journal of Res. V(1) March, 1966.*

Farm Labour Managment

Labour efficiency in agriculture refers to the amount of productive work accomplished per man on the farm per unit of time. In general, the higher the labour efficiency, the greater are the returns from farming. The farmer who does not introduce new methods and techniques to increase productivity can soon go out of the business because of increasing labour costs. Inefficient labour also results in low production which in turn means low wages for the labour.

On Indian farms, land is limited, *i.e.*, farms are small in size with average land holding upto 5.0 acres only; capital is extremely limited and organisational or managerial ability is low. Labour on the other hand, is abundant. Other production resources being extremely limited, labour abundance has an overcrowding effect. The resource availability on the farms is thus imbalanced leading to a low production which results in low returns to the farm business and low farm family labour earnings. The situation, thus, creates a vicious circle as under :

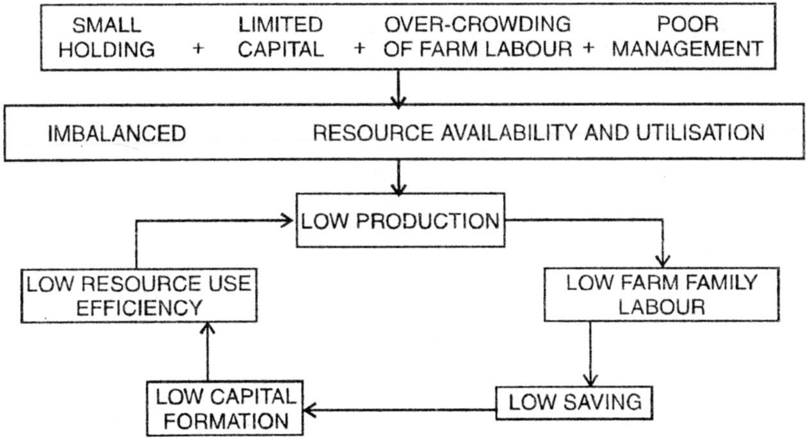

This vicious circle does not allow the farm labour a living wage and poverty conditions persist in the farm sector, especially among the agricultural labour.

Agricultural Wages and Employment

Wages of the agricultural labour in India are low and vary according to work, seasons, places, and with sex. Table 13.1 details the wage differentials in India according to skill, sex and regions. With the green-revolution, however, these wages have increased much after 1966 especially in Punjab, Western U.P. and Andhra Pradesh. There has occurred much more wage and income disparity in different groups of rural population; labourers and cultivators.

To make matters still worse, the farm labour has to face long periods of unemployment. While employed, the employment is not regular and he is under-employed for even the day he works. Agricultural work is seasonal in character; there are a few work-load-periods and a few slack seasons. In central plains of Punjab, for example, peak work load periods are :

(*i*) Mid March-Mid April—for harvest of Rabi crop other than wheat, sowing of sugarcane, cotton etc.

(*ii*) Mid April-End April—for harvest of wheat.

(*iii*) Ist July-End July—Sowing of maize.

(*iv*) Mid Oct.-Mid Nov.-for sowing of Rabi crops.

(*v*) Mid Nov.-Mid March—for sugarcane crushing and aftercare of rabi crops.

The extent of annual employment of men, according to Agricultural Labour Enquiry is reported as under :

Agricultural labour Category	*Work days in agriculture*	*Work days outside Agri.*	*Total work days*
Casual labourers	175	32	207
(*i*) with land	162	28	190
(*ii*) without land	191	34	225
Attached labourers			
(*i*) with land	280	16	296
(*ii*) without land	309	11	320
All Labourers	189	29	218

TABLE 13.1
Agricultural Wages (per day of 8 hours) in Different States of India, 1965—66

Rs.

States	*Skilled Labour (carpenters)*		*Field Labour*			
			Men		*Women***	
	*Low**	*High*	*Low*	*High*	*Low*	*High*
Andhra Pradesh	1.5	5.00	1.00	3.00	.60	2.00
Assam	3.5	10.00	2.50	4.00	1.50	2.50
Bihar	2.00	6.00	1.00	4.00	.75	4.00
Gujarat	4.00	8.00	1.00	5.00	.75	3.50
Kerala	4.00	6.00	1.75	4.00	.87	3.00
Madhya Pradesh	1.75	6.00	1.00	2.50	—	—
Chennai	1.50	5.75	1.25	3.00	—	—
Maharashtra	2.50	8.00	1.50	3.00	.50	2.50
Mysore	1.50	5.00	1.00	4.40	.75	3.50
Orissa	2.00	7.00	1.50	3.50	.75	2.50
Punjab	4.00	8.50	8.00	6.50	—	—
U.P.	2.00	5.00	1.00	3.00	—	—
W.Bengal	1.00	3.75	1.25	3.50	1.00	3.00

Source. Government of India, *Agricultural Wages in India 1965-66*, Directorate of Economics and Statistics, Ministry of Food and Agriculture, 1968.

* Wages vary according to tasks, seasons, and places within the region.

** Women do different jobs, On the same manual job their efficiency is considered to be low.

An agricultural labourer in India was thus employed as agricultural labourer for 189 days and outside of the farm for 29 days in a year. It was estimated that he remained self-employed for 48 days and unemployed for rest of the time (98 days) in a year. Agricultural Labour Enquiry report shows that only 87% of agricultural workers could secure wage-paid employment in any month and 13% remained unemployed in even peak labour load periods.

CLASSIFICATION OF FARM LABOUR

Farm labour can be classified into 4 categories : (*i*) Farm manager's labour, (*ii*) Farm family's labour, (*iii*) Permanently hired labour and (*iv*) Casual hired labour. The first three categories constitute permanent labour force available on the farm and is a fixed resource due to a general lack of mobility. Fourth category is a variable input and can be hired when needed.

Farm Manager's Labour

Except for large commercial private or government farms, which hire all the required labour and have a paid manager, Indian farmer is a manager, capitalist and a labourer. Farming with majority of the farmers is more of a subsistence type and a way of life rather than a business proposition. The farmers, therefore, do not distinguish between returns to the different factors of production owned by them. Manager's labour is, of course, the best type of available labour due to his personal interest, yet if he uses his own labour it does not permit him to be a whole-time organiser. As a capitalist, too, he is poor. As the farm incomes are not sufficient to induce capital formation, his habit of thrift too has not developed. The Indian farmer, though comparatively good labourer, remains an inefficient farm organiser and a poor capitalist.

Family Labour

Family is the main source of labour on Indian farms. Due to the limited opportunities of off-the-farm employment, family labour is a fixed resource and a cost. Family labour consists of adult males, females and children engaged in the farm work. Persons of the farm family and the period spent by them on off-the-farm employment should not be considered as farm labour.

Permanent Hired Labour

Permanent farm labour is hired on cash, kind or crop-share basis for a fixed period—(generally one year or six months). Farmer's labour + farm family labour + permanent hired labour is, thus, the total permanent farm labour which is a fixed farm resource on the Indian farms. For the purpose of management decisions and rational use of this resource, estimates of permanent labour availability have to be made for different peak-work-load periods. For example, the following estimates have been made for an average farm-family in the central Punjab :

Mid March-Mid April	51	man-hours per acre
Mid April-End April	27	man-hours per acre
Mid Oct.-Mid Nov.	55	man-hours per acre
Mid Nov.-Mid March	204	man-hours per acre

Another case study indicated that on three different sized actual holdings in one village, the labour availability during different periods varied as under :

Work-period	*Man-hours Per Acre*		
	Small farm	*Medium farm*	*Large farm*
1st period	44	23	22
2nd period	26	12	11
3rd period	45	24	22
4th period	159	71	68

Casual Labour

Casual labour is hired farm time to time and according to the demand for agricultural operations. The necessity arises mainly during the sowing and harvest periods of *rabi* and *kharif* crops. In India, 84.6% of the agricultural labour is casual and 15.4% attached (permanent) labour. Demand being seasonal only, there is always a maladjustment in the supply of and demand for the agricultural labour. Sometimes in the peak work load periods, the supply cannot meet the demand. In the slack seasons there are too many labourers seeking employment against too few jobs. Supply almost always exceeds the demand for it. Demand is generally local, specific and for a short duration.

COMPOSITION OF FARM LABOUR

Indian farm labour consists of skilled, semi-skilled and unskilled workers :

Skilled Labour

Specialised and trained labour for specific jobs is known as skilled labour, *viz.* carpenters, blacksmiths, mechanics, drivers, well-borers, etc. Some of them may not be needed too often, their ready-at-hand availability is, however, essential. Non-availability for even one hour, of a blacksmith, for example, may upset the complete programme of irrigation. Absence of a mechanic may cause a loss of the whole day of a tractor or a pumping set. Wages of the skilled workers whether engaged permanently or casually are always higher than those of the other categories of labour.

Semi-skilled Labour

Semi-skilled labour does the job which cannot be taken up by ordinary labourer, but at the same time, does not require any elaborate training. Such jobs can be performed after some experience of working with the experienced workers. The wages of such workers are a little higher than those of the ordinary unskilled labourers.

Unskilled Labour

It is ordinary labour employed for manual work, which does not need any training of specialised nature. It does not mean, however, that with experience the efficiency does not increase. Unskilled labour is generally engaged in field work as cattle attendants, cotton pickers, etc.

Special Features of Indian Farm Labour

(1) They are large in number, (2) They are mostly unskilled, (3) They lack staying power, (4) Majority of them are under debt and lack bargaining power, (5) Payments of wages are low, many times seasonal and in kind, (6) Hours of work are long and irregular and above all, employment opportunities are meagre, seasonal and uncertain. No wonder, thus, the Indian farm labour efficiency is at a very low level and large part of it is wasted by way of unemployment and underemployment.

IMPROVING THE EFFICIENCY OF FARM LABOUR

Although farm labour in India is abundant, it does not mean that the farmer should be indifferent towards improvement of its efficiency. To the farmer, increasing the efficiency of labour especially when it is hired is an important consideration. Because of variations in the system of farming, commodities produced, personal capabilities and desires of the individual farmer and the members of his family and some other differences, no two farms will have identical labour problems. There are certain general rules, however, which can be useful to a farmer in checking the strong and weak points of his labour management programme and in planning for improvement.

Some of the methods which have been found to be useful in improving the labour efficiency are : (1) enlarging the size of the farm business, (2) planning labour distribution-enterprise combination, (3) improving the field and the farm layout, (4) improving the farm building programme, and (5) improved labour management with planning of the work, incentives, and training of the workers, (6) Farm work simplification is another method to improve the efficiency of labour.

Enlarging the Farm Business

In order to utilise all available labour at maximum efficiency, sufficient work must be provided throughout the year. On many farms this can be done by enlarging the size of the farm business through (1) expansion of the land area if possible through leasing in or purchasing and, (2) adding more labour intensive enterprises to intensify the farm business. Even if no labour is hired, a waste of available manpower and a resulting inefficiency in labour use exists where the family workers are idle because of an inadequate size. Some innovations are labour intensive and lead to a higher labour employment without much increase in the stock of capital. The Japanese experience and the Indian situation indicate that the Indian agriculture can and probably will move in the direction of more labour employment in the future.

For example, a study "Impact of Yield-Increasing Technology on Farm Labour Use in I.A.D.P. District Ludhiana"* indicated that with the introduction of yield-increasing technology and crop shifts, labour input increased by 35 per cent on average farm situation. The labour utilisation can be improved by increasing the size of the farm business through improved production techniques.

PLANNING LABOUR DISTRIBUTION

Farm work should be planned so that there is employment through each working day and through each season of the year. This can be achieved through the following measures :

(i) Enteprise combination

Although Indian agriculture is fairly diversified yet the employment of labour is not regular or constant throughout the year, there are some peak work load periods and a few slack months. This leads to low level of labour efficiency. If different crop enterprises are planned such that as far as possible peak and slacks are reduced, labour efficiency will improve. For this purpose, a crop calendar can be prepared and input levels can be detailed for different crop enterprises. For example, a farmer can reduce the fallow area in *kharif* and sow such crops that need more care during the slack period of June to September and October, such as cotton, maize, rice and even sugarcane. On the other hand, reduced acreage under *Rabi* crops like wheat can decrease the harvest rush in April.

Such possibilities are different for different agricultural areas. In hills, main peak period is July-August when hoeing of maize is done. Slack periods are April—June before the rainy season sets in. If vegetables like tomatoes are planted, more work during this slack period can be created. So a shift from maize to tomatoes crop, a very high income yielding crop, will increase the farm incomes and labour efficiency.

Combining of enterprises, primarily for an even distribution of labour is not an end in itself. Substitution of different enterprises will depend upon relative

* Kahlon, A.S. and T.R. Kapur, "Impact of High yielding varieties on Farm Labour use in I.A.D.P., Ludhiana" contributions to Agril. Science and Statistics, New Delhi, 1969.

returns, other inputs required and degree of risk involved. Once the combination of major enterprises has been selected, supplementary enterprises can be adjusted until an optimum combination is reached where returns are maximised and the labour is employed optimally. Here at this point labour efficiency will be the maximum. A well adjusted diversified farming is very conducive to improving the labour efficiency on the Indian farms.

(ii) *Mixed farming*

It may not be possible to completely eliminate the peaks and the labour utilization in Indian agriculture. Mixed farming is, therefore, a better answer to the problem. Milch cattle, for example, yield high in rainy season due to availability of green fodder and grass. Addition of dairy cattle to crop farming can thus absorb surplus labour in this slack season. If lactation periods are adjusted such that maximum milk flow is in the slack season, which is quite possible through scientific methods, labour utilisation can be better rationalised throughout the year. Poultry and piggery are other enterprises that can be profitably included in the production programmes to expand employment in the slack periods.

IMPROVEMENTS IN FIELD AND FARM LAYOUT

Though a good progress has been made in India in respect of consolidation of holdings, a large number of operational holdings remain to be small and fragmented. Even at places where consolidation has been completed, owned holdings being small, land has to be rented often in more than one block. This makes the scientific layout of the farm difficult. Where the operational holdings are in one block, layout of the fields is generally defective and much labour is wasted in performing of different operations such as ploughing, planking, irrigation, etc. An efficient layout of the farm consists of straight roads, bunds and water channels with a rectangular shape. This economises the movement of labour and other equipment from field to field and increases efficiency in the performance of the operations.

Location of Farm Buildings

Generally on an average farm in India either there are no buildings or they are located remote in a village. It may not be possible and sometimes inadvisable to move from a village to a house on the farm, yet farm buildings should be as far as possible located on the farm. Much of the time is wasted in moving from village to the farm. Not only that, even the location of the farm buildings itself makes a difference. Stores, bullock sheds and other buildings should be so located on the farm that distance of individual fields from the buildings is the minimum. The buildings should be either in the centre of the farm or on one side near the main road or highway in the centre of the side.

MANAGEMENT OF LABOUR

The following specific steps can go a long way in increasing the labour efficiency :

(a) Planning the work

Farmers are not always efficient managers. Labour is wasted on many farms because of a poor management. For efficient management of labour, a farmer should (1) make a labour calender to keep down the peak labour requirements, (2) prepare a plan of work and duty list well ahead in time atleast one day earlier, (3) check implements and tools in advance for their being in working order, (4) should assign the work according to capabilities and as far as possible according to the aptitude and liking of the workers, (5) make available at hand facilities of water, etc., especially in summer, (6) keep one day's work ready for permanent labour, for rainy days and for the period when it is not possible to work outdoors and (7) set up work standards for different types of work. The following are, for example, fair standards of some of the work categories in the Central Punjab :

Ploughing	—	0.75 acres per plough
Wheat Hoeing	—	Four men per acre
Maize Hoeing	—	Four men per acre
Wheat Harvest (with sickle)	—	Five adult males per acre
Groundnut harvest	—	Ten men per acre
Rice Planting	—	Eight persons per acre

The farm manager should give new labourers a proper demonstration on different operations and keep experienced supervisors.

(b) Incentives

Work incentives are also an important part of the labour management. Labour is most efficient when incentives for work are strong. Housing, recreation, health facilities etc. should be provided to the farm workers as far as funds permit. Experienced and trained workers should be given incentives so that they prefer to stay on the farm and the farmer has not to keep employing fresh hands all the time. Incentives in the form of produce-sharing or extra bonus may be provided for better or more work. Wages should be paid in time and in full and in a willing manner. The employment of cheap or underpaid, inefficient labour is usually the most expensive practice. Good workers and permanent workers should be given better wages. Their genuine credit needs may be met. Above all the workers need to be given a human treatment. Sympathy in their difficulties and genuine interest in their affairs, makes them willing workers. Discipline by force or threats has no place in labour management on the farms.

FARM WORK SIMPLIFICATION

Farm work simplification or job analysis is a promising method of reducing the farm labour requirements which has received a good attention in recent years. Work simplification deals with work methods. Its objective is a more efficient use of labour and other resources by improving work methods so that more and higher quality of work is accomplished in less time and with less energy. Savings in time and energy are of particular importance when the time and energy saved can be applied to another productive work. However, reducing drudgery and fatigue is also important.

Farm work simplification consists of breaking each operation into its constituent parts and then examining each part carefully to determine : (1) whether that particular part of the job is really necessary or could either be omitted or combined with some other job, (2) whether the method could be simplified, so that time and money could be saved, (3) whether supplies, tools, fields, etc., are most conveniently located or could be re-arranged to avoid unnecessary trips and duplications, (4) whether tools and equipment are of the most efficient type and size, and (5) whether shifts in buildings, such as re-arrangement of doors, gates, etc., need to be made to avoid a waste of time.

Simplified approach is to break down the operation into its component parts and list all details exactly as they are done. Then question every detail : Why is it necessary ? Where should it be done ? When should it be done ? Who should do it ? What is the best way to do it ? Essentials of simplification in work methods are to : (1) reduce travel, have buildings and work areas close together, (2) eliminate back tracking, provide for circular travel, (3) move feed and supplies, using gravity, (4) provide doorways that are wide enough, level and smooth in order to facilitate use of carts, etc., (5) combine and re-arrange jobs in order to obtain a better flow of work, (6) locate tools and supplies where the work is done, (7) plan to complete one operation where another begins, and (8) avoid wasting energy and work at a reasonable speed.

An Example of Work Simplification in Poultry

A farmer had a flock of 400 birds in an old building adapted for the purpose. The house consisted of two pens with an egg and store room in the middle. A flow chart was constructed, and analysis of jobs was carried out. Based on this analysis the following improvements were made :

Original Method	*Improved Method*
(*a*) 56 lb. sacks of mash were delivered to the store across the yard, 26 feet away from the deep-litter houses.	Mash is delivered directly into the central area.
(*b*) The mash was put in two buckets and two journeys were made into each pen to fill four troughs in each.	A sack is carried into each pen every day and emptied directly into the troughs.
(*c*) The mash troughs were situated across the pens.	The troughs are arranged lengthwise.
(*d*) Gain was kept in sacks in a corner of the central area, 19 feet away from the door into each pen.	The grain is stored in a bin in the central area and a bucket is left inside this.
(*e*) The pen door opened into the central area and had to be opened and closed after each passage.	The pen door opens into the pen. The door closes automatically.
(*f*) The water troughs were cleared with a small brush carried from the table in the central area.	A brush is hung over each water trough.
(*g*) The nest-boxes consisted of two floors on either side, raised from the ground 2 feet. Wire netting prevented the birds from getting beneath the nest-boxes. Straw and litter passed there, necessitating sweeping the central area each day.	A board is placed against the wire to prevent litter from being pushed out of the pens.
(*h*) The nest-box flaps opened upwards and were kept open during egg collection by resting them on the operator's head. The egg trays were placed on the floor, and during collection the operator crouched in the most awkward position.	The nest-box flaps open downwards, controlled by a chain to allow egg trays to rest on them during collection.
(*i*) The broody crops rested on top of the nest-boxes and opened only into the central passage. When they were emptied, birds had to be carried to the pen-door and liberated.	The broody crops open into the pens as well as into the central passage to allow a quicker release of the birds.

As already stated, this was a fairly well-designed house even before these specific improvements were made. The farmer spent 25 minutes each day in tending 400 hens. With these improvements, this time was reduced by half to $12^1/_2$ minutes. In terms of costs, taking manual labour at Rs. 1.00 per hour, this amounts to a net saving of Rs. 0.20 per day, or in other words, about Rs. 75.00 per year. This, of course, does not take into account the savings in distance walked per year, which amounts to about 25 miles. The net saving in time per year is 75 hours. This is just a small example, greater savings in labour etc. can be obtained, if such techniques of work simplification are applied on bigger farms.

1. *What is farm labour efficiency ?*
2. *What are the reasons for poor efficiency of Indian farm labour ? Name the special features of Indian farm labour.*
3. *Discuss the various methods of improving the efficiency of the farm labour.*
4. *How does a crop enterprise combination affect the labour efficiency ?*
5. *How does the amount of capital influence the labour efficiency ?*
6. *Under what conditions is the labour-saving through work simplification possible in Agriculture ? Give some suitable examples where work simplification has application under Indian conditions.*
7. *List in order of importance, the jobs that can be done in a slack season on a typical farm situation in India.*
8. *Suggest some opportunities of using electricity to save a labour on the farm and estimate the margins of profit.*
9. *Describe certain specific jobs you know where labour efficiency can be improved.*
10. *Outline your idea of a successful labour policy for the hired labour. Suggest certain incentives that may be given to improve their efficiency.*

1. *Heady, E.O., Jensen, H.R. Farm Management Economics, Prentice Hall (India) Ltd., New Delhi, Chapter 13.*
2. *Kahlon, A.S. and Kapur, T.R. "Impact of High Yielding Varieties on farm Labour Use in I.A.D.P. District Ludhiana", Contributions to Agril. Sciences and Statistics, New Delhi, 1969.*
3. *Forster, G.W., Farm Organisation and Management, New York, Prentice-Hall, Inc.*
4. *Johl, S.S. and Kahlon, A.S. "Labour Utilisation Patterns and Employment Potentials of Punjab Farms : A Case Study" Indian Journal of Agril. Econ. XXI (1) Jan.-March, 1966.*
5. *Govt. of India, Agricultural Wages in India 1965-66. Directorate of Economics and Statistics, Ministry of Food and Agriculture, 1968.*

14 Farm Machinery Management

Mechanisation of selected farm operations is a key factor in the successful implementation of an intensive farming system based on intensive use of yield increasing technology and multiple cropping. Due to the seasonal nature of agricultural operations, the farmers are facing difficulty in the timely and successful performance of agricultural operations, especially during the peak labour-load periods; at the time of sowing, harvesting and threshing. To smoothen these peaks, labour saving devices can be introduced by mechanising some selected agricultural operations. This would make it possible to introduce multiple cropping on some farm organisations. Thus, switch-over to mechanical power will not only help perform the various operations in time but will also help the farmer adopt more profitable crop rotations.

Management of power and machinery is often overlooked. Recent years have seen a great change in the Indian agriculture. Machines are rapidly replacing the human and animal power. This spectacular progress in farm mechanisation has remarkably increased the farm output and the labour productivity. In changing over from manual to machine-power, a suitable set of machinery and implements for use under local conditions and relative cost-benefit relationship on various alternative types of equipment and power have to be worked out. Mechanisation increases the farmer's total investments. He has to decide how much capital he should invest in machinery and which machines he should buy, when does it pay to hire rather than buy a machine.

What Cost to Take into Account ?

Only additional costs involved should be considered when making decisions on machinery investment. Additional (marginal) costs for machines are those which occur only if the machine is purchased. Any cost which occur even if the machine is not bought are excluded from the cost of owning a machine. Cost items which are "added" and which occur irrespective of the machine purchase vary from farm to farm. However, any of the fixed costs on power units already on hand are not added costs. Such costs already have been incurred and remain the same whether or not the machine is purchased. For implements drawn by bullocks, for example, feed costs can be disregarded because bullocks have to be fed anyway. Only where the bullocks are fed more because the new implement demands that, feed costs can be added. Similar is the case of some machines. Pumping set investment does not change the depreciation or full costs of a tractor meant for ploughing. In replacing bullocks with machines, a farmer has to make repairs on machines and incur depreciation costs due to the annual use. Depreciation due to the use and time, repairs, obsolescence and taxes are all added costs.

Many machines are not insured and, thus, there is no cost in the form of premium payments. Nevertheless, the farmer carries his own risk cost. On many farms, investment in a given machine results in no added labour costs where operator and family labour is plentiful, labour is a fixed cost whether or not it is fully used. However, on farms where labour must be hired as a result of buying a machine or where operator and family labour is scarce, labour must be included as an added cost.

If a farmer borrows money to buy a machine, he pays interest. The funds he invests in machinery has other investment opportunities. Interest on the money spent in purchase of machinery is, therefore, an added cost.

Rate at which Costs are to be Charged

The farmer faces the next problem of calculating the rate at which costs are to be charged. Again, the answer varies with the individual farm situation. The physical conditions under which a machine operates and the care it is given results in a longer or a shorter life and lower or higher costs on different farms. The service life of a machine is further affected by the mechanical condition of the machine, accidental breakage of parts and possible obsolescence from replacement by more efficient machines, changes in farm power, and changes in production plans and farming practices that may eliminate the need for a particular machine.

All these factors influence the costs of owning a machine. Since the farmer purchases future services when he buys a machine, he should consider expected future costs of fuel, lubricants, repairs, taxes, insurance, interest, etc., rather than past or present costs unless these costs reflect the future. Through past experience with farm machinery and with the aid of appropriate cost studies, most farmers can fairly accurately estimate these machine costs.

The cost of having funds tied up in machinery is sometimes difficult to determine. No single answer fits all conditions. The best general statement is that the rate charged should vary with the amount of capital available. If a farmer borrows money to buy a machine, the actual interest rate paid is the appropriate charge to make. If a farmer has extra funds over and above those used in the farm business, the rate charged against the investment is the rate that he could earn on an outside loan or investment. The use of the market rate of interest is appropriate on a capital not needed to consider alternative returns on investment in additional fertilizer, livestock, buildings, etc., or other farm investments that would compete for funds. For a farmer severely tight on funds, interest cost on machinery is the rate of return his money would yield when used for other investments. This rate is particularly appropriate for the machines which require a high initial investment and whose services can be hired.

SELECTION OF SIZE OF MACHINE TO BUY

Most farm machines are now made in a range of different sizes and capacities. Farmers can adjust the quantity of service they buy through the size of the machine. More of the capital and less of labour will be required for a given job when a farmer chooses a large machine over a small one. Buying a large instead of small machine thus, substitutes capital for labour. The key points to consider while deciding upon the size of a machine are : (1) the difference in the initial cost of the large and small machines, (2) the annual use to be made of the machine, (3) the amount of additional labour saved by the large machine, and (4) the relative opportunity costs of capital and labour on the farm.

1. Initial investment

The difference in the initial cost of the large and the small machine is of an importance because the higher the investment the higher will be the total fixed costs of depreciation, interest, taxes and insurance, etc. If the large machine costs only a little more, the higher fixed costs are easily offset by the labour it saves. But if the difference in the initial cost is large, the labour and other savings may not be enough to offset the higher fixed costs.

2. Annual use

As the total fixed costs get spread over more and more units of output, the difference in the fixed unit costs between the large and the small machines lessens. For a high annual use, the fixed unit cost for the big machine may even fall below that of the small machine. Higher annual use of a large machine can be achieved through custom-hiring the services or through a joint ownership, etc.

3. Labour saved and opportunity cost of labour

The labour saved by the large machine and the relative values of labour and capital on a given farm are the key considerations because labour and capital supplies vary from farm to farm. Generally, the farmers with ample labour but limited capital and low annual use for the machines can best afford to invest in the smaller implements and equipment. These farmers generally have a high opportunity cost of capital and should invest where it brings the highest returns. On the other hand, large machines have an advantage on farms where the labour supply is limited, ample capital is available and machine have a high annual use. On these farms, labour needs to be allocated and used more efficiently. For instance, labour should be more readily available for those machine operations where timeliness is more important.

SUBSTITUTING MACHINERY FOR LABOUR

In order to lower the costs, machinery should be substituted for labour when the value of labour saved is more than the increase in machine costs. This substitution can take place when (1) changing from hand to machine methods. (2) changing types of machines and (3) increasing the size of the machines. With the help of data given below, we illustrate how the substitution principle applies to these cases.

1. Tractor Vs Bullock Power

(a) Cost of operating a tractor* :

The cost of operating a tractor (35 H.P.) is estimated as under :

Price of tractor	= Rs. 22,000
Expected life	= 10 years
Working hours per annum	= 1000
Fuel consumption	= Rs. 3.00 per hr.
Wages of operator	= Rs. 6 per day
Salvage value @ 10% of total cost	= Rs. 2200
Depreciation per hour use	= Rs. 1.98
Interest on capital per hour @ 5% per annum**	= Rs. 1.10

* Data based on survey conducted in Ludhiana District of Punjab.

** Or otherwise it can be 10% rate of interests for half this period.

Repairs and maintenance per hour @ 5%	= Rs. 1.10
Housing charges per hour @ Rs. 5 P.M.	= Rs. 0.06
Insurance per hour @ 2% per year	= Rs. 0.44
Fuel consumption per hour	= Rs. 3.00
Wages of operator per hour	= Rs. 0.75
Total costs per hour	= Rs. 8.43

(*b*) *Cost of operating with bullocks*

The cost of operating a pair of bullocks is calculated as under :

Cost of a pair of bullocks in rupees	= 1329.00
Life in years	= 10 years
Average yearly working days	= 260
Housing cost (shed cost)	= Rs. 300.00

Yearly Costs

(*i*) Interest on 1/2 investment	= Rs. 39.87
(*ii*) Depreciation (Rs. 1329 ÷ 10)	= Rs. 132.90
(*iii*) Housing cost :	
(*a*) Interest on 1/2 investment	= Rs. 9.00
(*b*) Depreciation	= Rs. 6.00
(*c*) Repair of Shed	= Rs. 5.00
(*iv*) Death loss* 5 per cent in 10 yrs	= Rs. 6.65
(*v*) Other costs	
(*a*) Medicine	= Rs . 13.82
(*b*) Shoeing cost	= Rs. 8.32
(*c*) Labour	= Rs. 135.05
(*d*) Interest on 1/2 investment on other costs	= Rs. 4.72
(*vi*) Feed and Maintenance cost :	
(*a*) *Chari* Fodder 120 days (1.00 quintal per day @ Rs. 2.50 per qtl.)	= Rs. 300.00
(*b*) Wheat bhusa 185 days (0.10 qtl. per day @ 7.00 per qtl.)	= Rs. 122.50
(*c*) *Berseem/Senji* 185 days (0.50 qtl. per day @ 2.00 per qtl.)	= Rs. 185.00
(*d*) Wheat bhusa 60 days (0.20 qtl per day)	= Rs. 48.00

* Assumption here is that farmer owns other animals also and death loss is spread on all animals equally.

(*e*) Concentrates : 2 kg. for 365 days, *i.e.*, 7.30 qtl. @ Rs. 58.0/qtl.	= Rs. 423.00
(*f*) Concentrates 2 kg. for 60 days, *i.e.*, 1.20 qtls.	= Rs. 72.00
(*g*) 1 kg. oil cakes for 60 days, *i.e.*, 0.60 qtl. @ Rs. 50.00/qtl.	= Rs. 30.00
(*h*) Salt and minerals	= Rs. 3.00
(*i*) Interest on $^1/_2$ investment on feeds	= Rs. 36.91
Total yearly costs	= Rs. 1625.04

Credit for manure produced :

Nine cart loads @ Rs. 7.00/cart load	= Rs. 63.00
Cost of maintenance of one pair of bullocks per year	= Rs. 1562.04
Average yearly working days	= 260
Fixed cost per working day (Rs.)	= Rs. 6.01
Variable cost per working day (2 kg. of concentrates @ Rs. 0.60 per kg.)	= Rs. 1.20

These costs may vary according to the hours used as under :

	Normal period 6 hours/day	*Peak period 8 hours/day*
Fixed cost per working hour	1.00	0.75
Variable cost per working hour	0.20	0.15

We can compare a pair of bullocks and a tractor best by taking an example of ploughing. We first calculate the cost per acre using a mould-board plough drawn with a pair of bullocks :

Labour required	10 man hours
Men in crew	1 man
Bullock labour	20 bullock hours
Cost of labour per acre @ Rs. 6/- per man day	Rs. 7.50
Cost of operation on bullocks	Rs. 12.00
Total cost	Rs. 19.50

Cost of ploughing with mould-board plough using a 35 H.P. tractor, based on 1.2 hours work will be = 1.2 × 8.43 = Rs.10.11. So we find that the cost of operation of a bullock pair is Rs. 19.50 whereas that of a tractor is Rs. 10.11 to plough one acre of land. A point of importance is that the time taken by the bullocks for ploughing an acre of land (with a mould-board plough) is 10 hours whereas with a tractor it takes only 1.2 hours. It is very important when timely performance of operations is required.

This comparison becomes a little difficult if we have to differentiate the quality of the work done in two cases.

(2) Economic Performance of Various Drills

Three different drills (for sowing of wheat) are analysed in this section.

(*a*) *Zora seed-cum-fertilizer drill* *

Price of the seed drill	= Rs. 700/-
No. of bullocks required for the operation	= two
No. of men required for the operation	= one
Area covered by the drill in 8 hrs.	= 2.75 acres
Expected life of the drill	= 10 years
No. of days to be used in a year	= 30 days
Annual cost of repair	= 6%
Depreciation per day	= Rs. 2.33
Interest per day	= Rs. 1.16
Cost of repair per day	= Rs. 1.40
Total fixed costs	= Rs. 4.89
Pair of bullocks on hire	= Rs. 6.00
Labour charges @ Rs. 6/- per day	= Rs. 9.60
Total operating charges	= Rs. 15.60
Total cost of operation	= Rs. 20.49
Cost of sowing and fertilizing per acre	= Rs. 7.45

(*b*) *Geeson seed drill* **

Price	= Rs. 375.00
Area covered by the drill in eight hours	= 2.7 acres
Expected life of the drill	= 10 years
No. of days to be used per year	= 30 days
Annual cost of repairs	= @ 6 per cent
Cost of labour for 8 hours	= Rs. 6/-
Depreciation per day of operation	= Rs. 1.25
Interest per day	= Rs. 0.62
Cost of repairs	= Rs. 0.75

* This is a 5-row drill designed by the Punjab Agricultural University.

** This is locally manufactured 3 row, 6 tines seed-cum-fertilizer drill.

Total fixed costs	= Rs. 2.62
Bullocks on hire	= Rs. 6.00
Labour charges	= Rs. 6.00
Total operation charges	= Rs. 12.00
Total cost of sowing per day	= Rs. 14.62
Cost of sowing and fertilization of wheat per acre	= Rs. 5.42

(c) *McCormic seed drill* *

Price	= Rs. 835.00
Area covered by the drill in 8 hours	= 4.39 acres
Estimated life of the drill	= 10 years
No. of days it will be used per year	= 30 days
Annual cost of repairs	= 6%
Cost of labour per men	= Rs. 6/- per day
Depreciation per day of the operation	= Rs. 2.78
Interest per day	= Rs. 1.39
Cost of repairs per day	= Rs. 1.67
Total fixed costs	= Rs. 5.84
Bullocks on hire	= Rs. 6.00
Labour charges per day (for two persons)	= Rs. 12.00
Total operating charges	= Rs. 18.00
Total cost of the operation	= Rs. 23.84
Cost of sowing & fertilizing per acre	= Rs. 5.43

It is clear from the analysis that the cost of sowing and fertilizing per acre of wheat crop will be Rs. 7.45, Rs. 5.42 and Rs. 5.43 by zora seed drill, geeson seed drill and McCormick seed drill respectively.

(3) *Harvesting of wheat with sickles v/s reapers*

To lower the costs, machinery is often substituted for the labour when the value of labour saved is more than the increase in machine costs.

The principle is explained with the above example of harvesting the wheat crop with sickles and reapers.

* It is a 5-row drill.

HARVESTING WITH SICKLES

(a) Daily paid labour basis

Havesting	= 40 man hours/acre
Bundling, stacking, ear-heads collection, straw-rope making	= 20 man hours/acre
Total man hours required per acre	= 60
Cost of harvesting per acre @ Rs. 7 per 8 hours	= Rs. 52.50

(b) Produce-share basis

(i) Average yield	= 1500 kg. per acre
(ii) 1/20th share value	= 70 kg.
(iii) Cost of 70 kgs @ Rs. 76/- per quintal	= Rs. 53.20

*Harvesting Cost by Animal Drawn Reaper**

Price of the reaper	= Rs. 1200/-
Life in years	= 10
Hours of use in a year	= 240
Interest rate	= 10%
Repair costs	= 40%
Animal pair hire charge without operator @ Rs. 6/- per day	= Rs. 0.75 per hour
Daily Paid Labourer Charges @ Rs. 6/- per day	= Rs. 0.75 per hour
Time taken to harvest one acre	= 6.65 hrs.

A. Fixed cost per hour

1. Depreciation @ 10 per cent	= Rs. 0.50
2. Interest, housing, taxes insurance (based at 10% of new cost)	= Rs. 0.50
3. Repairs @ Rs. 0.2 per hour per Rs. 100/-	= Rs. 0.24
Total fixed cost	= Rs. 1.24

B. Operating cost per hour

1. Animal pair hire charges for 6.65 hours @ Rs. 0.75 per hour	= Rs. 4.99

* Developed at the Punjab Agricultural University, Ludhiana.

2. Labour charges per hour :

(*i*) Harvesting	= 6.65 man hours/acre
(*ii*) Removal	= 10.80 man hours/acre
(*iii*) Bundling	= 8 man hours/acre
(*iv*) Straw rope making	= 8 man hours/acre
(*v*) Stacking	= 8 man hours/acre
(*vi*) Loose ear heads collection	= 8 man hours/acre
Total labour hours per acre	= Rs. 49.45
Labour cost per acre	= Rs. 37.09
Machine fixed cost	= Rs. 8.25
Total cost per acre	= Rs. 45.34

This shows that the substitution of sickle method with animal drawn reaper can save Rs. 7.86 per acre, and operation performed much quicker.

CHANGING THE SIZE OF MACHINE

Changing the size of the machine brings about a change in the costs of operations. A farmer, with a larger-sized machine can accomplish the job in a lesser time and may be at a lower per unit cost.

Take an example of a shift from small to bigger McCormic Seed Drill. Let us first calculate the cost of operation per acre using the 3-rows model with fertilizer attachment :

Price of the seed drill	= Rs. 600.00
Number of bullocks required	= Two
Number of men required	= Two
Area covered by the seed drill in 8 hours	= 2.80 acres
Cost of labour per man day	= Rs. 6.00
Hire charges per pair of bullock per day	= Rs. 6.00
Life of the seed drill	= 10 years
No. of days used per year	= 30 days
Annual cost of repair	= 6%
Rate of interest on capital	= 10%

Fixed Charges

Depreciation per day of operation	= Rs. 2.20
Interest per day of operation	= Rs. 2.20
Cost of repair per day of operation	= Rs. 1.32
Total fixed charges per day	= Rs. 5.42

Operating Charges

Hire charges for a pair of bullocks per day	= Rs. 6.00
Labour charges	= Rs. 12.00
Total operation charges	= Rs. 18.00
Total cost of operation per day	= Rs. 18.00 + Rs. 5.72
	= Rs. 23.72
Therefore, cost of sowing and fertilizing per acre with drill	= Rs. 8.60

Now let us work out the cost of operation per acre when the farmer switches over to the bigger model of the drill with 5 rows arrangement :

Price of seed-Drill	= Rs. 835.00
No. of bullocks required	= Two
No. of men required	= Two
Area covered by the Drill in 8 hrs.	= 4.40 acres
Cost of a labour (per man day)	= Rs. 6.00
Hire charges for bullocks/day	= Rs. 6.00
Life of the seed drill	= 10 years
No. of days it can be used	= 30 days
Annual cost of repairs	= 6%
Rate of interest on capital	= 10%

Fixed Charges

Depreciation/day of operation	= Rs. 2.78
Interest/day of operation	= Rs. 2.78
Cost of repairs/day	= Rs. 1.67
Total fixed charges	= Rs. 7.23

Operating Charges

Hire charges for a pair of bullocks per day	= Rs. 6.00
Labour charges	= Rs. 12.00
Total operating charges	= Rs. 18.00
Total cost of operation	= Rs. 18.00 + Rs. 7.23
	= Rs. 25.23
Cost of operation per acre	= Rs. 5.73

By switching over from a smaller drill to a larger one, the farmer saves on the cost of sowing and fertilization of wheat to the tune of Rs. 2.87 per acre or Rs. 8.33 per day. In thirty days (one sowing season) if he can manage custom work and can operate the machine all the thirty days, he will gain Rs. 249.90, which is more than the difference in the price (Rs. 235) of the two machines.

TIMELINESS OF OPERATIONS

Farm machinery helps the farmer perform farm operations in time. This is possible because a machine is capable of accomplishing larger amounts of work in a comparatively smaller time. If some crucial operation such as sowing or harvesting gets delayed, it affects the output and in turn costs and returns. To understand it better, we compare a timely sown crop with machine (tractor) and late-sown crop with bullocks. The crop under consideration is maize and the data are taken from the annual reports of the Agronomy Department of the PAU, on response of various maize germplasm sources to different agronomic practices for the period June 1, 1967, May 31, 1968. In a trial conducted at Kalimpong in a local variety (Kalimpong Yellow round) the dates of sowing were April 30 and May 20. April 30 is considered to be the normal period and planting operation was done with a four row seed planter (tractor operated) whereas on May 20, the operation was done with a pair of bullocks and a single row planter.

Yield of maize sown on April 30	19.30 qtls per acre
Yield of maize sown on May 20	11.10 qtls per acre

For a farm of 20 acres, we work out the cost of operation per acre with a seed planter (four row tractor planter).*

Price of the planter	Rs. 2,000/-
Power required	25 H.P. tractor
Man hour (labour) per acre	0.8
Machine hour per acre	0.8
Driver	1.0
Expected life	10 years
No. of days used/year	30
Annual cost of repair	6%

Fixed Charges

Depreciation per day	= Rs. 6.66
Interest per day	= Rs. 6.66
Cost of repair per day	= Rs. 4.00
Total fixed costs per day	= Rs. 17.32
Area covered in one day	= 10.70 acres
Cost per acre	= Rs. 1.62

Operating Charges

Labour charges	0.60
Machine costs 0.8 × 8.43	0.75
Driver	0.62
	Rs. 7.97
Total cost of operation per acre	=Rs. 9.59

* This planter is manufactured by Raikhy Enterprise, G.T. Road, Ludhiana (Punjab).

Cost of operation with bullocks and a single row planter will be as under :

Cost of labour per acre (2.66 man hrs.) = Rs. 1.98

Cost of bullocks (5.32 bullocks hrs.) = Rs. 479

Per acre cost = Rs. 6.77

The real gain, however, comes through the increase in yield and its effects on total and net returns. If changing the size of the machine helps timely performance of operations, it is worth consideration. The graph in Figure 14.1 illustrates that the maize sown on proper time gives much higher yield.

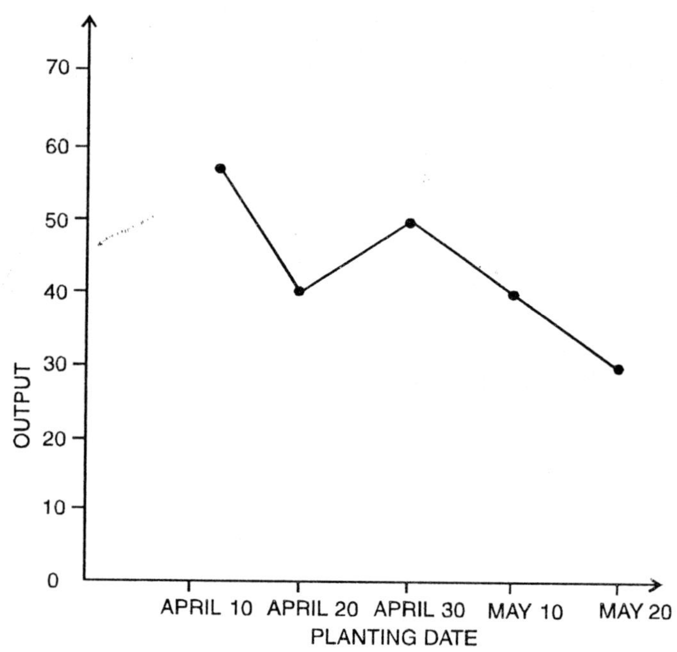

Fig. 14.1. Effect of Timeliness of Sowing on the Yield of Maize.

HIRING Vs OWING A MACHINE

In response to the change in factor costs, the level of mechanisation has been increasing in the past. It appears that many farmers cannot justify the use of capital to finance this investment in machinery; this situation frequently arises where the returns per rupee invested in other factors of production, such as fertilizer, pesticides, livestock, etc. turn out to be greater.

Source. Annual Report, Department of Agronomy, PAU, 1968.

Many farmers cannot justify certain machines such as tractors because of their small land holdings; 57.6 per cent of farms in India are less than 2.5 acres in size and 87.5% are less than 10 acres. However, custom work enables the farmer on a small unit to overcome some of these problems. He can either hire or purchase a machine and spread his costs by performing custom work for others. If he can find sufficient outlet for his services, the latter method has many advantages. It provides him with the opportunity to sell some of his own labour and the use of his other equipment. For example, along with tractor, he can get custom work for his harvesting machine.

If he hires for himself, the farmer will be hiring additional labour also while he himself may remain idle, purchase and hiring out of the services solves a very frequent economic problem on small farms of an excess capacity of the tractor and labour supply due to the indivisibility of these factors.

Trends in Custom Work

As more farms become equipped with machines, the total volume of custom work for farm operations may decline. However, custom work will become increasingly important for jobs requiring specialised equipment like earthmoving, ditching, tilling, terracing, harvesting and threshing, etc.

Such work is increasingly being done by full time commercial custom operators, while most custom work in growing and harvesting crops is done by full-time farmers.

It is, thus, suggested that factors other than the actual costs should also be considered by farmers before they decide to invest in a machine. These additional factors may include : (1) opportunity cost of the labour at harvest time, (2) alternative possible uses of the given capital that may yield a higher return, (3) timeliness of operations, (4) lack of availability of skill on the farm for operating the machine, (5) personal prestige in machine ownership. A number of farmers cannot justify the machines they own on a conventional economic analysis. A number of other factors that enter into the investment decision shed more light on this apparent economic irrationality and indicate how the conventional analysis needs to be modified.

ESTIMATION OF BREAK EVEN POINT FOR A FARM MACHINERY

Procedure for estimation of the minimum size of operations required to justify the purchase of a particular farm machinery is illustrated by the above examples :

WHEAT THRESHING AND WINNOWING MACHINE

A. Initial costs

Price of power wheat threshing and winnowing machine	= Rs. 3000.00
Sale tax @ 7%	= Rs. 210.00
Transport & forwarding charges	= Rs. 60.00
Price of 20 H.P. electric motor	= Rs. 2200.00
Sale tax @ 7% on motor	= Rs. 154.00
Total initial costs	= Rs. 5624.00
Junk value of thresher and motor	= Rs. 500.00
Useful expected life	= 10 years

B. Annual fixed cost

Annual depreciation	= Rs. 512.40
Annual interest @ 10% on $^1/_2$ of the total investment	= Rs. 281.34
Annual maintenance repair Rs. 15/- per season	= Rs. 15.00
Total annual fixed cost	= Rs. 808.74

C. Variable cost per hour

(*i*) Unskilled labour 6 persons @ Rs. 6/day	= Rs. 4.50
(*ii*) One supervisor or operator @ Rs. 8/-per day	= Rs. 1.00
(*iii*) Electricity consumed per hour 8 units @ 0.12 paise per unit	= Rs. 0.96
(*iv*) Use-repair	= Rs. 0.25
Total variable costs per hour	= Rs. 6.76

D. Break-Even-Point

Output of machine per hour	= 4 quintals
Variable cost per qtl.	= Rs. 1.69
Custom charges per qtl. @ 6 kg. grain per qtl. (at Rs. 76 per qtl.)	= Rs. 4.56

Minimum quantity of wheat to be threshed to justify the purchase of one power wheat thresher.

$$\frac{\text{Total Annual Fixed costs}}{\text{Custom charges} - \text{Variable costs}} = \frac{808.74}{4.56 - 1.69} = 282 \text{ quintals.}$$

The graphic illustration of this method is provided in Figure 14.2. As shown in the above example and in the graph, the B.E.P. = $\frac{FC}{S - VC}$ (FC = Annual fixed costs, S = Custom charges and VC = Variable costs).

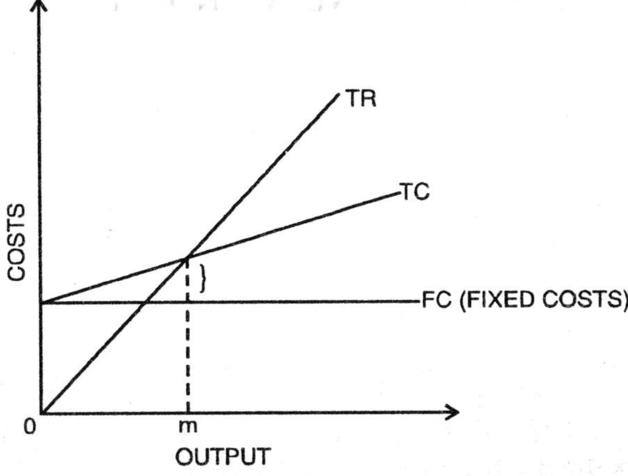

Fig. 14.2. Estimation of Break-Even-Point of a Farm Machine.

HAND OPERATED MAIZE SHELLER

In this section the break even point is calculated for a hand operated maize sheller :

A. Initial costs

Price of the sheller	= Rs. 280.00
Sales tax @ 7%	= Rs. 19.60
Transport charges	= Rs. 5.00
Total	= Rs. 294.60
Salvage value	= Rs. 50.00
Life	= 5years
Capacity per hour	= 1.2 quintals

B. Annual fixed cost

1. Depreciation	= Rs. 49.00
2. Annual interest on half investment	= Rs. 14.70
3. Annual maintenance repairs	= Rs. 5.00
Total :	= Rs. 68.70

C. Variable cost per hour

1. Unskilled labour	= Rs. 1.50
Supervision @ Rs. 8/- per day	= Rs. 1.00
Total cost per hour	= Rs. 2.50
Cost per qtl.	= Rs. 2.08
Custom charges per qtl.	= Rs. 3.00

Then break even point :

$$\frac{\text{Fixed cost}}{\text{Custom charges} - \text{Variable cost}} = \frac{68.70}{3.00 - 2.08} = 74.7 \text{ quintals.}$$

To make the costs even, a sheller must therefore shell about 75 quintals of maize every year. Similarly, break even point for "Punjab maize sheller" costing Rs. 3648 is 290 quintals. For "Punjab Drummy Wheat Thresher" costing Rs. 4363, the break even point is 103 quintals per annum. For the "Power Wheat Thresher" costing Rs. 6373, the break even point works out to be 132 quintals.

PURCHASE OF OLD Vs NEW MACHINE

While deciding upon purchasing a new or an old machinery, farmer has to make a special discrimination. Depending upon the resources available to him, he needs to make use of "Time Comparison principle". The principle, mathematically states

$$PV = Q/(1 + r)^n$$

where PV = present value of the future amount,

Q = amount to be spent at a future date,

r = rate of interest,

n = number of years in future when money is to be spent.

The principle is explained taking an example of the purchase of a small combine. The new combine costs Rs. 25,000/- and a second hand combine is available at Rs. 15,000/-. The farmer's decision rests on the basis of the capital he has is calculated on the life of new combine, say 10 years. His choice is either to buy a new machine and operate it for 10 years or buy an old one and replace it after 5 years. If he has unlimited capital, there is opportunity for this capital to be deposited in the bank to earn 6% interest.

So if he buys an old combine now and after 5 years he will have to purchase another old combine :

The present value of Rs. 15,000 will be $\frac{15000}{(1.06)^5} = \text{Rs. } 11{,}660$

The present value of total amount to be spent is Rs. 15,000 + Rs. 11,660 = Rs. 26,660. If he purchases a new combine he spends only Rs. 25,000 which is cheaper for him. So he should buy a new combine.

If the farmer has limited capital, and an alternative is available to him to invest on a poultry enterprise which can get him up to 15% p.a. net return, then the present value of Rs. 15000 will be $\frac{15000}{(1.15)^5} = \text{Rs. } 7455/\text{-}.$

The present value of total amount currently needed is = Rs. 15000 + Rs. 7455 = Rs. 22455/-. If he has to buy a new combine he has to spend Rs. 25000/-. It is, therefore, economical for him to buy an old combine worth Rs. 15000/- now, start a poultry enterprise and then after 5 years buy another old combine of the value of Rs. 15000/-. His decisions thus vary with the opportunity cost of his capital and the price of the new and old machines and the life of these machines.

BASIC INFORMATION FOR FARM MACHINERY MANAGEMENT DECISIONS

Soundness of a decision depends upon the correctness of the basic data. A farm decision maker has to, therefore, seek information and data on various aspects from as many sources as he can. The following Tables from 14.1 to 14.6 are meant to provide some basic information on various aspects related to the farm machinery in order to facilitate correct and easy decisions in this respect :

Effective field capacity of a machine is given by :

$$C = \frac{SWE}{10}$$

where C = effective field capacity, hectares per hour,

S = speed of travel km. per hour,

W = rated width of machine metres,

E = field efficiency, per cent.

For most tillage and other operations, a field efficiency of 82.5 per cent is assumed and in this situation, the effective field capacity is :

$$\text{Hectares per hour} = \frac{\text{Width in m.} \times \text{Speed in km. p.h.} \times 0.825}{10}$$

Average fuel consumption for tractors

Tractor type Av. fuel consumption, litres per hour per rated drawbar horse-power.

Wheel-type, Petrol = 0.322

Wheel-type, Diesel = 0.397

Track-type, Petrol = 0.341

Track-type, Diesel = 0.284

Rated drawbar horse-power is 75 per cent of the maximum

TABLE 14.1

Basic Technical Information about some Important Agricultural Machines and Implements

Name of the Implement	*Size (cm.)*	*Average Pull (kg.)*	*Capacity per day (Hectare)*	*Total Weight (Kg.)*	*Approx. price (Rs.)*	*Remarks*
1. Punjab Plough Junior (mould board)	14	80	0.36	21	26.00	These are general purpose light but sturdy ploughs and are suitable for all types of soils.
2. Punjab Plough Senior	17	90	0.40	23	28.00	
3. Punjab Soil Stirring Plough	25	80	0.40	21	23.00	It opens furrows like a lister.
4. Punjab Triphali adjustable with 3 tines beam.	3 tines	80	1.01	22	34.00	It is suitable for interculture of cotton and sugarcane and for the general preparation of seedbeds.
5. Disc Harrow (single action)	6 discs of 41 cm.	100	1.21	104	172.00	It should follow ploughing to prepare an ideal seedbed in the minimum time.
6. Bar Harrow	17 pegs (122)	75	1.62	40	60.00	It is suitable to take out grass, break crust and pulverise the soil.
7. Bund Former	27	100	6.44 km long bund	28	40.00	It makes low bunds economically.
8. Fertilizer Seed Drill	3 tines	91	1.21	104	370.00	It places fertilizer below the seed (wheat, oats, desi maize, millets, etc.) automatically with regulated dozes.

TABLE 14.1 (Contd.)

Basic Technical Information about some Important Agricultural Machines and Implements

Name of the Implement	*Size (cm.)*	*Average Pull (kg.)*	*Capacity per day (Hectare)*	*Total Weight (Kg.)*	*Approx. price (Rs.)*	*Remarks*
9. Maize planter (fertilizer attachment)	Single row	54	1.01	82	350.00	It places the fertilizers in a band nearly 2.54 cm. on the side and 3.81 cm. deeper than the seed. It can plant hybrid maize, groundnut and cotton.
10. Olpad Thresher	20 discs	68	70 kg./hr.	—	405.00	Where mechanically driven thresher cannot be adopted, this thresher is very suitable to replace the phala.
11. Power Wheat Thresher	107 cm. drum	20 H.P. (Electric Motor) 25 H.P. (Tractor)	350 kg./hr.	—	3000.00	The wheat grain is graded; cleaned and bagged automatically in this machine.
	91 cm. drum	15 H.P. (Electric Motor) 20 H.P. (Tractor)	220 kg./hr.	—	2000.00	The straw is beaten to make fine bhusa. Cost of threshing 45.4 kg. grains of wheat is approx. Rs. 1.00 with a tractor and 50 paise with an electric motor.

Source. Punjab Agricultural Hand Book, Punjab Agricultural University, Ludhiana, 1972.

TABLE 14.2

Draft and Power Requirements of Various Agricultural Machines

Machines	*Draft and power requirement*
Tillage implements	
Plough	Light 140-350 Grams per square cm. of furrow section
	Medium 350-630 Grams per square cm. of furrow section
	Heavy 630-845 Grams per square cm. of furrow section
	Extreme upto 1260 Grams per square cm. of furrow section
	Average 350-845 Grams per square cm. of furrow section
Ridger	600-1000 kg. for straight ridging
Disc tiller	220-520 kg/m. for tilling
Single action disc harrow	60-190 kg./m.
Tandem disc harrow	120-150 kg./m.
Tandem disc harrow heavy duty	250-340 kg./m.
Spike tooth harrow	45-90 kg./m.
Spring tooth harrow	110-270 kg./m.
Duck foot field cultivator	130-240 kg./m.
Roller	45-90 kg./m.
Planting machinery	
Grain drill	15-120 kg./m.
Row crop planter	120-180 kg./m.
Cultivation tools,	
Rotary hoe	45-90 kg./m.
Field cultivator	30-140 kg./m.
Spring tine cultivator	40-45 kg./m.
Blade harrow (bakhar)	90-150 kg./m.
Harvesting machines,	
Reaper	90-150 kg./m.
Grain binder	100-220 kg./m.
Combine Harvester PTO operated	6.8-13.7 m.h. p./m. of cutter bar
Combine self-propelled	6.8-10.2 m.h. p./m. of cutter bar width
Corn picker, 2 row	2-5 (P.T.O.), m.h. p./row
Stationary silage cutter	0.79-1.67 m.h. p. per hour per ton

Drawbar horse-power is given by :

$$\text{DBHP(Metric)} = \frac{\text{(Draft in kg.)} \times \text{(Speed in km. per hour)}}{270}$$

TABLE 14.3

Rate List of Agricultural Implements

Sl. No.	*Name of the Implement*	*Size cm.*	*Rate Rs. P.*	*Manufacturers*
1	2	3	4	5
1.	Punjab Plough (Senior) with beam	17	28.00	Govt. Engg. Workshop, Nilokheri
2.	Punjab Plough	14	26.00	M/s Thakhur Dass & Sons, G.T. Road, Khanna, Distt. Ludhiana.
3.	Punjab Plough (soil Stirring)	17	23.00	M/s International Mfg. Co., Hospital Road. Jagraon, Distt. Ludhiana
4.	Kangra Plough with beam (soil inverting)	11	21.70	M/s National Eng. Co. Spatu Road, Ambala City.
5.	Kangra Plough with beam (soil stirring)	11	22.70	
6.	Kangra Plough without beam (soil inverting)	11	16.20	
7.	Kangra Plough without beam (soil stirring)	11	17.20	
8.	Hilly Plough (soil stirring)	9	18.90	Other fabricators registered under the Quality Marking scheme and categorised for these implements.
9.	Hilly Plough (soil inverting)		19.80	
10.	Punjab Triphali adjustable with beam		34.00	Govt. Engg. Workshop, Nilokheri.
11.	Punjab Triphali adjust-able without beam		27.00	M/s International Mfg. Co., Hospital Road, Jagraon, Distt. Ludhiana.
12.	Punjab Triphali fixed with beam		32.00	M/s Pritam Singh Gurdial Singh Gardhiwala, Distt. Hoshiarpur.
13.	Punjab Triphali without beam		25.00	Other fabricators registered under the Quality Marking Scheme and categorised for these implements.

Sl. No.	*Name of the Implement*	*Size cm.*	*Rate Rs. P.*	*Manufacturers*
1	2	3	4	5
14.	Punjab Hilly Triphali with beam		25.75	
15.	Punjab Triphali without beam		20.50	
16.	Automatic Rabi Seed Drill		150.00	M/s Allied Trdg., Co., Railway Road, Ambala City.,
17.	Punjab Disc Harrow No. 1 with salwood beam		60.00	M/s National Engg. Co., Spatu Road, Ambala City.
18.	Bar Harrow (Steel frame)		58.00	Other fabricators registered under the Quality Marking Scheme and categorised for these implements.
19.	Hilly Line Bar Harrow		28.25	
20.	(*i*) Punjab Seed Grader (hand driven)		607.00	Hindsons (Patiala) Pvt. Ltd., The Lower Mall, Patiala.,
	(*ii*) Punjab Seed Grader (power driven, without motor)		637.00	Patiala Industries, Sirhindi Gate, Patiala.
	(*iii*) Punjab Seed Grader (power driven with motor)		1,175.00	Other fabricators registered under the Quality Marking Scheme, Cat. 'A'.
21.	Punjab Single Row Cotton Drill		21.50	1. M/s National Engg. Co., Ambala. 2. M/s Allied Trdg. Co., Railway Road, Ambala City. Other fabricators registered under Quality Marking Scheme Cat. 'B'.
22.	Wheel Hand Hoe		32.00	M/s Lyallpur Traders, Nabha Gate, Patiala-3.
23.	Rocker Sprayer (Sigma Brand 'A' quality)		172.00	M/s Sigma Steel Industries, A-2, Industrial Estate, Ludhiana.
24.	Rotary Hand Duster (shoulder mounting type)		105.00	—do—

Sl. No.	*Name of the Implement*	*Size cm.*	*Rate Rs. P.*	*Manufacturers*
1	2	3	4	5
25.	Seed Treating Drum		79.00	—do—
26.	Hand Compression sprayer (18 litre capacity)		165.00	—do—
27.	Knapsack-Sprayer		135.00	American Spring and Pressing Work, Marve Road, Malad, Bombay.
28.	Cynogas Foot Pump		44.00	—do—
29.	Double Barrel Stirrup Pump		87.00	—do—
30.	Maize Dibbler		11.25	Lyallpur Traders, Nabha Gate, Patiala-3.
31.	Rice Puddler		100.00	—do—
32.	Hand-cum-Power Corn Sheller		270.00	R. Reikhy Enterprises, Reikhy Building, G.T. Road, Ludhiana.
33.	Offset Disc Harrow with 8 discs and salwood beam		230.00	Allied Trading Company, Railway Road, Ambala City.
34.	Bakhar (Randa) Senior		24.18	Vishwakarma Engg., Works Rajbir Market, Charkhi Dadri.
35.	Bakhar (Randa) Junior Junior		22.46	—do—
36.	Geeson Seed Drill (3 tined)		198.00	G.S. Agril. Engg., Works, Vill. Nurpur, Dist. Jalandhar.
37.	Planter (One row)		350.00	R. Reikhy Enterprises, Reikhy Building, G.T. Road, Ludhiana.
38.	Geeson Seed-cum-Fertilizer Drill (3 tined)		370.00	G.S. Agril. Engg. Works, V.&P.O. Nurpur, District Jalandhar.
39.	Ludhiana Thrasher 106 cm. size		3200.00	M/s Friends Own Foundry, Miller Ganj. Ludhiana.
40.	Regular Wheat Thrasher		2700.00	M/s Standard Agril. Engg. Co., 825, Industrial Area, Ludhiana.

Sl. No.	*Name of the Implement*	*Size cm.*	*Rate Rs. P.*	*Manufacturers*
1	2	3	4	5
41.	Regular wheat Thrasher 106 cm. size		2250.00	(*i*) M/s Kapoor & Co., Faridkot. (*ii*) Parma Nand Ganda Singh, Kachehri Road, Ambala City. (*iii*) Surjeet Engg. Works, Kotkapura.
42.	Regular wheat thrasher 106 cm. size		2240.00	M/s Bharat Tractors, Kotkapura.
43.	Wheat Thrasher and Winnowing Machine		3000.00	M/s Friends Own Foundary, Miller Ganj, Ludhiana.
44.	(*i*) Punjab Drummy-Thresher 106 cm. size, Major, 'A' (angle iron wide box frame).		1187.00	M/s National Engg. Corporation, Sunami Gate, Sangrur.
	(*ii*) Punjab Drummy Thresher Major 'B' 106 cm. size (angle iron narrow box frame).		1050.00	M/s Bharpur Singh & Sons, Ladwa, Distt. Karnal.
	(*iii*) Punjab Drummy Thresher Minor 100 cm. size (angle iron logged frame).		770.30	M/s Amar Singh Tarlochan Singh, Jagraon, Distt. Ludhiana.
	(*iv*) Punjab Drummy Thresher Minor 90 cm. size (angle iron logged frame.)		680.00	M/s International Manufacturing Co., Hospital Road, Jagraon, Distt. Ludhiana.
45.	Punjab Drummy Thrasher Minor.		525.00	M/s Bakhtawar Singh Sagoo, Gurdwara Ludhi, Jagraon, District Ludhiana.
46.	Maize Sheller		280.00	M/s Bakhtawar Singh Sagoo, Gurdwara, Ludhi Jagraon, District Ludhiana.

TABLE 14.4
List of Manufacturers of Tractors and Power Tillers in India

Sl. No.	*Name and Address of the Firm*	*Model and Make of Tractor*	*H.P.*	*Approximate Price*
Tractors				
1.	M/s Eicher Tractors India Ltd. N.I.T. Faridabad (Haryana)	Eicher 115/8	26/27 H.P.	Rs. 17,480/-
2.	M/s Hindustan Tractors Ltd. Construction House, Ballard Estate Bombay-1	Hindustan-35	32 H.P.	Rs. 19,570/-
		Hindustan-50	50 H.P.	Rs. 22,350/-
3.	M/s International Tractor, Co., of India Ltd. Akurli Road, Kandivli East, Bombay-67	McCormick IH.-B-275	35 H.P.	Rs. 27,600/-
4.	M/s Escort Ltd. 18/4 Mathura Road, Faridabad (Haryana)	Escorts-27W	28 H.P.	Rs. 23,626/-
		Escorts-37	35 H.P.	Rs. 21,129/-
		Ford 3000	46 H.P.	Rs. 41,000/-
5.	M/s Tractors & Farm Equipment Ltd. 202, Mount Road, Chennai.	Massey Ferguson 1035	32 H.P.	Rs. 25,800/-
Power Tillers (Hand Tractors)				
1.	M/s Krishi Engines Private Ltd. Industrial Estate, Sant Nagar, Hyderabad-18	Krishi-V-500	5 H.P.	Rs. 8,000

TABLE 14.5
Constants and Conversion Factors useful in Pumping Water and Irrigation Works

Conversation factors	
Kilogram per square metre	= 0.999 cm. of water at 4°C
	= 7.3558×10^{-3} cm. of mercury at 0°C
Cm. of water at 4°C	= 10 kilogram per square metre
Cm. of mercury at 0°C	= 135.95 kilogram per square metre
G. per square cm.	= 10 kg. per square metre
U.S. Gallon (Liquid)	= 3.785×10^{-3} cubic metres
	= 3.785 litres
Imperial Gallon	= 4.5458×10^{-3} cubic metres
	= 4.546 litres
Cubic metres	= 264.2 U.S. gallons (Liquid)
	= 219.9993 Imp. gallons
U.S. Gallons of water at 62°F	= 3.7805 kg.
Imperial Gallons of water at 62°F	= 4.5351 kg.
U.S. gallon (Liquid)	= 0.8327 Imp. gallons
Imperial gallons	= 1.201 U.S. gallons (Liquid)

TABLE 14.5
Constants and Conversion Factors useful in Pumping Water and Irrigation Works (Contd.)

Hectare metre	$= 10^4$ cubic metres
	= 2,199,990 Imp. gallons
	= 2,642,000 U.S. gallons
	$= 10^7$ litres
367 gpm. (Imp.)	= 440 gpm. (U.S.) = 1667 litres per min.
	= 1 hectare cm. per hour
Litre	= 0.2642 gallons (U.S.) = 0.2202 gallon (Imp.)
	= 1 kg. of water
H.P.	= 1.014 metric H.P.
Metric H.P.	= 0.9863 H.P.
Hectare metre	= 8.107 acre foot
Acre foot	= 0.123 hectare metre
Theoretical metric water horse power of a pump	$= \dfrac{\text{l. p.m.} \times \text{pressure at pump in metres}}{4505}$
Actual horse power	$= \dfrac{\text{Theoretical horse-power}}{\text{Pump efficiency}}$
Kilowatt input horse power	$= \dfrac{\text{l. p.m.} \times \text{pressure at pump at metres}}{6125 \times \text{pump efficiency} \times \text{Motor efficiency}}$
Cost in Rs. per 1000 litres pumped a pump	$= \dfrac{0.137 \times \text{power cost per K.W. hr} \times \text{Head in metres}}{\text{Pump efficiency} \times \text{Motor Eff.} \times 60}$
Cost per hour of pumping	$= \dfrac{0.000137 \times \text{l.p.m.} \times \text{Head in metres} \times \text{Power cost}}{\text{Pump eff.} \times \text{Motor Eff.}}$
Cost per hectare metre of water	$= \dfrac{27.450 \times \text{Head in metres} \times \text{Power per K.W. hour}}{\text{Pump Eff.} \times \text{Motor Eff.}}$
Pump Efficiency	$= \dfrac{\text{lp.m.} \times \text{Head in metres}}{5481 \times \text{b.h.p. (to pump)}}$;
Head	$= \dfrac{5481 \times \text{Pump Eff.} \times \text{b.h.p.}}{\text{l. p.m.}}$
B.H.P. (Brake horse-power) of pump	$= \dfrac{\text{l. p.m.} \times \text{Head in metres}}{5481 \times \text{Pump Eff.}}$

Source. Punjab Agricultural Hand Book-1972.

Specific fuel consumption per b.h.p. hr. for diesel and Petrol engines :

Diesel engines = 0.18 to 0.26 litre/b.h.p. hour

Petrol engines = 0.37 to 0.46 litre/b.h.p. hour

Belt length

The relation between centre distance and belt length is as follows : (for drives with two sheaves)

$$L = 2C + 1.57\,(D + d) + \frac{(D - d)^2}{4C}$$

where L = effective length of belt, metres,

C = distance between centres of sheaves, metres,

D = effective outside diameter of large sheaves, metres,

d = effective outside diameter of small sheaves, metres.

Notes

1.One hectare metre of water lifted by one metre requires approximately 55 k.w.h. of energy based on an average pump and motor efficiency of 50 per cent.

2.Single-stage centrifugal pumps, under ordinary conditions, vary in efficiency from 50 to 70 per cent. For belt-driven pumps, add 5 to 10 per cent to the actual power requirements to provide for belt slippage.

Points to Remember

1. Match your pump capacity to the yield of your well. The yield of well may be determined by a test pump or by a series of animal operated lifts working simultaneously.
2. If a well is to be used, have the well driller develop the well, test the well and select an appropriate pump and the motor.
3. Select the pump that will give the maximum efficiency under the given total head and power output of an engine or a motor. This selection can be made from the catalogues of the reputed manufacturers.
4. Avoid unnecessary power losses in pumping. Raising the delivery pipe above the point of inlet of irrigation channel is wastage of power. Use the minimum number of valves and fittings in a pumping plant.
5. Determine the power available, whether three phase or single phase and the schedule of rates for pumping by contacting the local electricity authority.

TABLE 14.6

Number of Hectares Irrigated in 10 hours with Pumping of Various Quantities of Water and Irrigating Various Depths :

Litres pumped per minute	*Hectares irrigated in ten hours*						*Correspon-ding Hectare cm.*
	1 cm. deep	*2 cm. deep*	*3 cm. deep*	*5 cm. deep*	*10 cm. deep*	*15 cm. deep*	
25	0.15	0.08	0.05	0.03	0.02	0.01	0.15
50	0.30	0.15	0.10	0.06	0.03	0.02	0.30
100	0.60	0.30	0.20	0.12	0.06	0.04	0.60
150	0.90	0.45	0.30	0.18	0.09	0.06	0.90
200	1.20	0.60	0.40	0.24	0.12	0.08	1.20
250	1.50	0.75	0.50	0.30	0.15	0.10	1.50
300	1.80	0.90	0.60	0.36	0.18	0.12	1.80
400	2.40	1.20	0.80	0.48	0.24	0.16	2.40
500	3.00	1.50	1.00	0.60	0.30	0.20	3.00
750	4.50	2.25	1.50	0.90	0.45	0.30	4.50
1000	6.00	3.00	2.00	1.20	0.60	0.40	6.00
1250	7.50	3.75	2.50	1.50	0.75	0.50	7.50
1500	9.00	4.50	3.00	1.80	0.90	0.60	9.00
1750	10.50	5.25	3.50	2.10	1.05	0.70	10.50
2000	12.00	6.00	4.00	2.40	1.20	0.80	12.00

Formula : Hectares irrigated in 10 hours = $\frac{\text{Litres pumped per minute}}{\text{Depth of water in cm.}} \times 6 \times 10^{-3}$

Capacity of the Pump and Power Required

The capacity of the pump depends upon the supply of the water available from the well, number of hectares to be irrigated, crops to be grown, diversity of crops, length of the growing season and the rainfall. If a well cannot supply enough water, the area to be irrigated must be reduced or another well dug. The crops should be more diversified, so that whole of the area has not to be irrigated at the same time. When the growing season is long, the pump can be operated for a longer time also.

The power required to drive a pump depends on the discharge, the total head against which water will have to be pumped and the efficiency of the pump. It is expressed as :

$$BHP = \frac{Q \times H}{76 \times E}$$

where HP is the brake horse-power (metric),

Q is the discharge in litres per sec.,

H is the total head in metres,

E is the efficiency of the pump,

The total head (H) is the difference in elevation between the water-level and the land to be irrigated plus the friction loss in the pipeline. It represents the suction height plus the delivery height, plus the resistance due to the friction expressed in metres. Where a belt drive or gears are used, efficiency (E) is the product of officiency of the pump and the efficiency of the belt drive or gears.

1. *What is the importance of mechanization of various farm operations under Indian conditions ?*
2. *What costs will you consider while deciding on the purchase of a machine ?*
3. *What points one should keep in mind while making a decision on the size and type of the machine to be purchased ?*
4. *Work out the cost of operation of the following farm machinery and equipment :*
   - *(a) A 35 H.P. tractor,*
   - *(b) Seed cum-fertilizer drills,*
   - *(c) Drummy wheat thresher,*
   - *(d) Maize Sheller.*
5. *How will you find out the break even point of a farm machinery ? Illustrate with example.*
6. *What are the custom rates for different kinds of jobs in your area ? In what situations does it pay to hire the work done ? In what situation does it pay to do the custom work ?*
7. *Illustrate how the principles of substitution, opportunity cost and discounting apply in solving power and machinery problems.*

8. *Estimate the break-even-point of the following farm machinery :*
   (a) *Seed-cum-fertilizer drill.*
   (b) *A combine for harvesting threshing & winnowing of wheat.*
   (c) *A 50 H.P. tractor.*

1. *Punjab Agril. University Ludhiana, "Annual Progress Report" of the College of Agricultural Engineering, year 1965-66 and 1966-67.*
2. *Department of Agronomy—Punjab Agril. University. Annual Report on Reponse of various Maize-germplasm sources to Different Agronomic Practices. (June 1, 1967—May 3, 1968).*
3. *Heady E.O. and Jensen, H.R. "Farm Management Economics" Prentice-Hall (India) Ltd. New Delhi—1961.*
4. *Hunt, D. "Farm Power and Machinery Management", Iowa State University Press; Iowa. U.S.A.*
5. *Package of Practices for Rabi crops—1968-69, P.A.U. Publication, Ludhiana.*
6. *Package of Practices for Kharif Crops—1969-70, P.A.U. Publication, Ludhiana.*
7. *Punjab Agricultural Handbook, 1972 P.A.U. Publication, Ludhiana.*
8. *Sandhu, H.S. and Singh, R. "Economics of alternative choices in selected improved practices for general crop farms in Ludhiana Distt :"* Jour. of Res., *Vol: VI, No. 2 Supp. June 1969.*
9. *Kahlon, A.S. and Gill, D.S. "Economics of Mechanising Farm Operations in Punjab"* Jour. of Res., *Vol : V (3) September 1968.*

15 Farm Buildings Management

In the tropical countries like India where farming is exposed to the severities of the climate and vagaries of nature, buildings occupy an important position on the farms. With the advancement of production technology, the importance of buildings has enhanced because the number of implements, machines, etc., has increased. Yet, every farmer cannot have and should not have every type of buildings. Like all other assets, farm buildings should be constructed only if they add to the profit. Before planning and designing the farm buildings, major objectives of the buildings must be understood. The main purpose of almost all classes of service buildings is to house farm equipment, to maintain and preserve stored products, provide shelter to the livestock and ensure efficiency of operations etc. Economy in construction and management and sanitary and comfortable conditions are essential requirements. Some important steps to follow in attaining these objectives are to : (1) determine the functional requirements of the structure, (2) plan the structure for over-all efficiency of operations, (3) consider all new improvements in structural-designs, (4) consider all new materials from the standpoint of performance and economy, (5) design the structure for flexibility to meet changing demands and (6) design for the most economical method of construction which should meet the standards for particular structure.

For every farm situation, one has to decide : whether to have or not to have the buildings; which building to have ? What should be the optimum size and design of the buildings ? Whether to construct a new building or to remodel an old one ? To what extent the farm buildings should be flexible in design ? After deciding on all these points, careful decisions have to be made on location, orientation with respect to sun and winds, sequence of operations, and hygienic considerations, etc.

Buildings as an input

Buildings, like machinery, livestock, labour and land., are a resource essential to the farm production. As it is with the other resources, marginal investments made on farm buildings must bring the highest returns to the farm. By saving labour and by increasing the quantity and improving the quality and time value of crops and livestock products, farm buildings increase income. As they increase the income of the farm, they must be considered as an input in farming similar to other inputs. First and the foremost consideration for a farm building is its relation to the farm enterprise. Buildings must be provided where the farm operations can be carried on efficiently. Not only must the buildings be structurally sound to support the loads involved, but they must also be planned and laid out for the maximum efficiency of operations. They must give adequate protection to the expensive machinery as well as provide comfortable living conditions for the workers. These buildings must include storage space for raw materials or farm inputs and finished products awaiting marketing. It is important to the farmer that these buildings, in addition to meeting the essential structural requirements, contribute enough income to cover maintenance and amortization and also realise profits.

COST-BENEFIT ANALYSIS

Farm buildings must add to the profits otherwise the farmer should not have them. Additional returns can be calculated by estimations with and without farm buildings.

Example. Suppose we have 25 acres of land on which we may have farm-stead in one acre. Further suppose we can grow I crop of wheat and I crop of potato per year. The cost-returns analysis will be as under :

(*i*) *Income From Wheat Poduction*

Wheat yield per acre	= 12 quintals
Total output from 25 acres	= 300 quintals
Value of Wheat @ Rs. 76 per qtl.	= Rs. 22,800
Cost per acre for wheat	= Rs. 600 (including cultivation, seed, sowing, fertilizer, irrigation and labour, cost etc.)
Total cost for 25 acres of wheat	= Rs. 15,000
Net profit from wheat crop	= Rs. 22,800-15,000
	= Rs. 7,800

(*ii*) *Income From Production of 1 Crop of Potatoes*

Potatoes yield per acre	= 60 qtls.
Total output from 25 acres	= 1,500 qtls.
Value @ Rs. 30/- per qtl.	= Rs. 45,000
Input costs @ Rs. 800/- per acre	= Rs. 20,000
Net profit from potato crop	= Rs. 25,000
Total Returns per year	= Rs. 32,800
Average net returns per acre	= Rs. 1,512

Now suppose we construct the following buildings on the farm :

Farm residence	= 2,800 sq. ft. (40' × 70')
Machinery storage	= 540 sq. ft.(18' × 30')
Grain storage (2 rooms)	= 200 sq. ft.
Poultry house for 25 birds	= 100 sq. ft. (10' ×10')
Dairy shed for 5 animals	= 300 sq. ft. (15' × 20')
Housing for 4 draft animal	= 300 sq. ft. (15' × 20')
Fodder storage	= 100 sq. ft. (10' × 10')

(*a*) *Estimated costs of farm residence*

Area of farm residence	= 2,800 sq. ft. (3 rooms)
Life of farm residence	= 50 years
(*i*) Earth work	Rs. 75.00
(*ii*) Concrete	Rs. 1,078.00
(*iii*) R.C.C. work	Rs 2,018.00
(*iv*) Brick work	Rs. 5,013.00
(*v*) Wood work	Rs. 2,550.00
(*vi*) Steel work	Rs. 1,100.00
(*vii*) Flooring	Rs. 650.00
(*viii*) Roofing	Rs. 460.00
(*ix*) Finishing	Rs. 1,400.00
(*x*) Miscellaneous items & other unspecified costs	Rs. 1,000.00
(*xi*) Estimated total cost of farm residence	Rs. 15,244.00

If the farmer stays outside on rent, in the town 2 miles away, he has to pay Rs. 1,000 per year. Annual depreciation on farm residence is $\frac{15,244}{50}$ = Rs. 305/-.

Interest on Rs. 15,244 @ 10 per cent is 152.44. Total annual costs to the farmer is Rs. 457.44. It, therefore, saves some Rs. 543 per year for the farmer, if he builds his own house on the farm. In addition, he will have the convenience of close supervision on the farm work.

(*b*) *Machinery storage*

If we construct an asbestos sheet (roof) shed of area 540 sq. ft. at the rate Rs. 4/- per sq. ft., total cost of shed will be Rs. 2,160/-. Life of the shed will be 15 years. Life of machinery is expected to increase by 2 years due to better storage. Since the life of machinery without storage is 10 years, after storage it will be 12 years. If we take cost of the tractor as Rs. 25,000, of thresher Rs. 4,000, and seed drill as Rs. 1,000, cost of machinery/yr. without storage will be $= \frac{30,000}{10} =$ Rs.3000.

Cost of machinery/yr. with storage will be $\frac{30,000}{12}$ *i.e.* Rs. 2,500. Saving in machinery cost will be 3,000 – 2,500 = Rs. 500/yr. Cost of storage being $\frac{2,160}{15}$ *i.e.* Rs. 144 per year, net savings in storing machinery will be Rs. 500 – 144 *i.e.* Rs. 356/- per year.

(*c*) *Grain storage*

Suppose space required for two small sized storage bins is 400 sq. ft. Cost of one store of 15 qtls. capacity is Rs. 250/- with a life of 10 years. Cost of 2 such stores shall be Rs. 500.

On 30 quintals storage (to the capacity of the store), losses without proper storage @ 10% are 3 quintals. This loss will be avoided if the grain is stored properly in the new stores. Savings in terms of money @ Rs. 80/- qtls will be Rs. 240 per year. Annual costs of storage are Rs. 50 (depreciation) + Rs. 50 interest = Rs. 100/-. Net saving on storage will be Rs. 140 per year.

Similarly, economics of construction of poultry sheds, dairy buildings and other constructions can be worked out. Net benefits on similar basis from different building at 1970 prices work out to be as under :

(*d*) Poultry house = Rs. 330 per year

(*e*) Dairy shed = Rs. 400 per year

(*f*) Draft animal house = Rs. 200 per year

(*g*) Fodder store = Rs. 80 per year.

Total additional returns and savings on costs due to these farm buildings work out to be Rs. 2,049 on an area of one acre which has alternative production potential of Rs. 1,512/-. Net gain per annum thus works out to be Rs. 537/-.

STORAGE STRUCTURE

The following general information on storage structure can be of help to the farm-families in planning their grain stores :

Small Capacity Storage Bins

(*i*)	Capacity of the Bin	=15 qtls.
(*ii*)	Cost of metal Bin storage	= Rs. 250/-
(*iii*)	Life	= 10 years
(*iv*)	Without storage, losses	= 10%
(*v*)	Annual losses in terms of money @ Rs. 80 per quintal	= Rs. 120/-
(*vi*)	Annual costs	= Rs. 45/-
(*vii*)	Net annual savings	= Rs. 75/-

Metal Bin of Medium Capacity

(*i*)	Capacity of the Bin	= 250 qtls.
(*ii*)	Life of the storage Bin	= 15 years
(*iii*)	Cost of the Bin	= Rs. 6,250/-
(*iv*)	Losses without storage	= 10%
(*v*)	Total loss without storage	= 25 qtls.
(*vi*)	Annual losses without storage @ 80/- per quintal	= Rs. 2,000/-
(*vii*)	Annual costs of storage	= Rs. 616/-
(*viii*)	Net savings per year	= Rs. 1,384/-

Flat Storage Large Size

It is made of brick and concrete work with C.G.I. roofings

(*i*)	Storage capacity of the Bin	= 1000 qtls.
(*ii*)	Life of the storage Bin	= 25 years
(*iii*)	Total cost of the storage Bin	= Rs. 16,000/-
(*iv*)	Losses without storage	= 10%
(*v*)	Total annual losses without proper storage	= Rs. 8,000
(*vi*)	Total annual costs of storage	= Rs. 2,040
(*vii*)	Net savings	= Rs. 5,960

Designs, Flexibility and Durability

Farm buildings are built to last for many years. However, profitability of one enterprise may change in relation to another or the capital and labour proportions on the farm may change. These changes may call for shifts in farm enterprises. As a result, a building that is designed to serve only a specific enterprise/ purpose may become virtually obsolete unless it can be extensively remodelled. Many dairy farmers in India who built expensive dairy barns found them of little value when a declining milk market led them to change to crop-cultivation. Changes in farming methods may also cause buildings to become out of date. The change from bullocks to tractors in recent years is making bullock-houses obsolete. Some are wondering if mechanical drying of maize will make the conventional maize stores out of date in a few years.

In order to deal with such changes, one method is to build low cost structures designed to last only a few years. There is a less chance of short-lived buildings becoming obsolete before they fully depreciate. Another way is to make the building structures flexible. Sheds can, for example, be constructed so that they can be used for either housing the livestock or the machinery or for storing grains. The pen-system of housing for dairy cows can be easily adapted to house other types of livestock.

Attention in recent years has been given to designing buildings that are adaptable to a number of uses. As a result, a number of plans for buildings are available. The inconvenience and cost of providing flexibility of this type must be weighed against the alternative cost of having to remodel a highly specialised building, should the enterprise for which it was designed get eliminated from the production programme.

A highly specialised set of buildings maximises the farm income when (1) A given combination of enterprises for which the buildings were designed is maintained over time, (2) This combination of enterprises is the most profitable, and (3) Price ratios and techniques of production remain unchanged over time. In many cases, technical sacrifice in production with a flexible building is small compared to (*i*) the cost of maintaining an unprofitable enterprise with a specialized building or (*ii*) the overhead cost of a specialized building remaining unused because of discontinuance of an enterprise or (*iii*) the cost of remodelling the specialised building.

Depending upon the degree of flexibility required, different designs of the buildings can be used.

Example 1. If we need a barn of size 36' × 73' having doors and windows, this stall barn can have different designs such as : (1) a single row barn, (2) double row barn face out, (3) double row barn face in, as shown in Figs. 15.1, 15.2 and 15.3.

If the building is made of concrete roof and brick walls and is used as a single-row barn on one side and the rest of space for storage purpose (Fig. 15.1), we can have 16 stalls. In future, if dairy enterprise is to be expanded, it can be converted into a double row barn with face in or face out (Figs. 15.2 and 15.3). This additional row of stalls will be built in the space previously kept for storage.

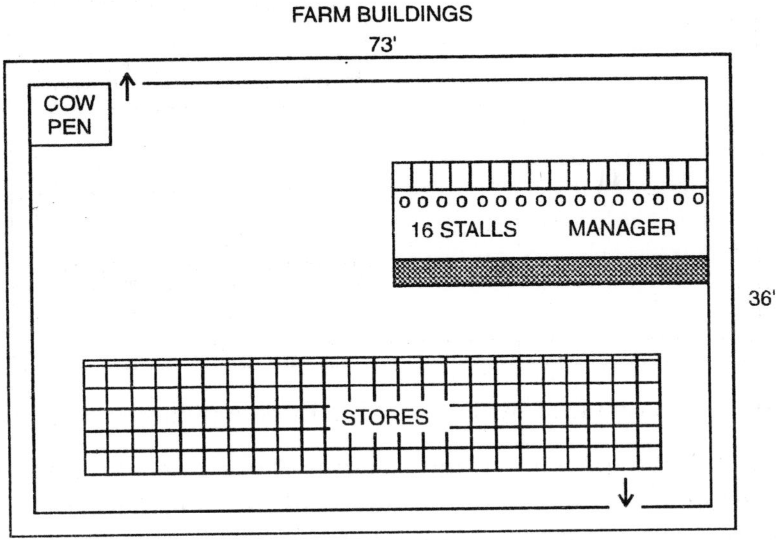

Fig. 15.1. Single Row Face Out System

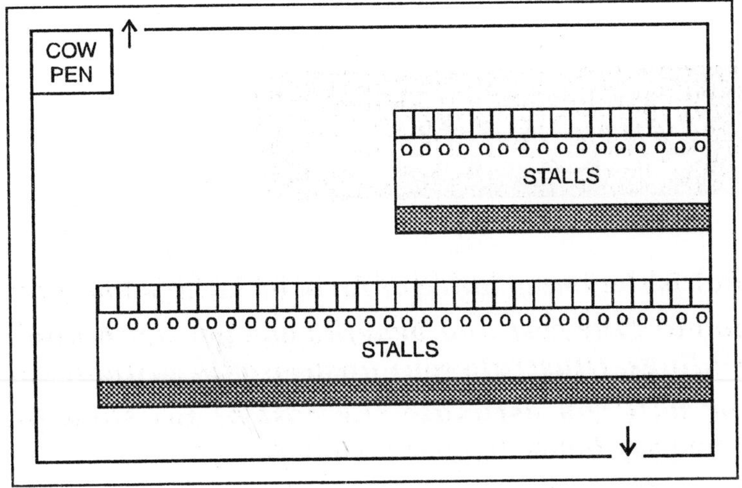

Fig. 15.2. Changed Structure of the Building. Double Row Face Out System.

This barn, if need be, can be used for grain storage or as a machinery shed and can be easily expanded to accommodate more animals.

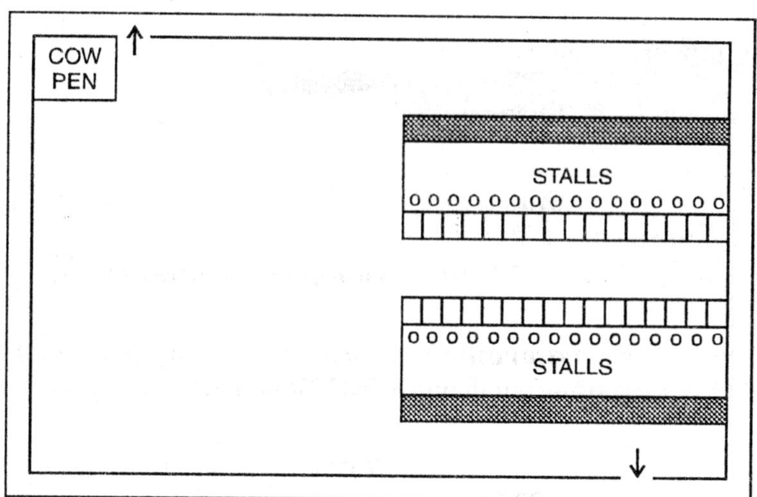

Fig. 15.3. Changed Structure of the Building. Face in System.

Example 2. We have a storage structure for grains of capacity 100 tons on the farm. Its design can be made flexible such that this can be used for other purpose at the time of need. Suppose this is made of concrete floor, with sheet-roofing and having wooden or L-Iron truss structure. It can be changed to have two or more doors instead of one. Roof can be changed and the building can be made a circular bin. Once it is made circular, however, the structure will become inflexible.

1. ***What is the importance of farm buildings to a farm business ?***
2. ***Compare the cost and benefits one gets with and without farm buildings. Illustrate your answer with suitable examples.***
3. ***How will you estimate the cost of (a) shed for machinery (b) poultry house (c) grain-store ?***
4. ***What is the importance of flexibility in building designs ? Suggest some suitable method of providing flexibility in farm structures.***
5. ***When does remodelling of a building become necessary ? How will you decide whether to remodel an old building or rebuild a new one ?***

1. *Adam "Farm Management". McGraw Hill Book Company, Inc., New York, pp. 170-80.*
2. *Ashby, Doge, Shedd, "Modern Farm Buildings", pp. 54-93 and 156-168.*
3. *Bradford, Lawrence A. and Jensen, Harald R. "Farm Management Analysis", John Willey and Sons, London, 1962, pp. 411-422.*
4. *Barre, H.J. Sammet L.L. "Farm Structures", John Willey and Sons, 1958, pp. 207-272; 385-434.*
5. *Tondon, R.K. and Dhondyal, S.P. "Principles and Methods of Farm Management", Achal Prakashan Mandir Parmat, Kanpur, 1967.*
6. *Dutta, B.N., "Estimating and Costing in Civil Engineering", 1969.*
7. *Gray, E. Harold, "Farm Service Buildings". McGraw Hill, New York, 1955.*
8. *Heady and Jensen, "Farm Management Economics", Prentice Hall (India) Ltd. New Delhi, 1964.*
9. *Sane, S. Yashwant, "Planning and Designing Buildings", Poona, 1958.*
10. *Wolley, C.John, "Planning Farm Buildings", McGraw Hill, 1953, pp. 9-24, 200-24-24.*

Risk and Uncertainty

Biological nature of farm enterprises entails some uncertainties in their production and prices, coupled with uncertainties of availability of inputs. Some of them are measurable in their parametres of probability, yet others are more or less a random phenomena that cannot be estimated with any acceptable degree of accuracy. The first category uncertainties lead to the business risks that can be, to a considerable extent, provided for either through adjustments in the production programmes and resource-use planning or through hedging, forward contracts, ensurances etc. The latter category cannot be treated as calculable risks and are not amenable to programmes of production or resource-use adjustments. Insurance at the best will be only a wide-shot. How are these risks and uncertainties accounted for in the production programmes of the farmers is the central objective of this chapter. Discussion here centres around (*i*) how do the farmers in their normative production programmes account for estimable uncertainties (risks) of price fluctuations and yield (production) variabilities of farm products ? and (*ii*) how do they provide for uncertainties of availability of factor-inputs ?

Product-price Uncertainty

Price fluctuations directly affect the returns from an enterprise. Unfortunately the producer-seller normally has no control over the product-prices. The price uncertainty (it is especially true in vegetable cultivation), therefore, is accounted for in his decisions on level and combinations of farm enterprises. Under the situation, a farm-entrepreneur normally faces the following enterprise-alternatives in respect of their returns vis-a-vis price uncertainty (Risk) :

(*i*) high returns enterprise with low price uncertainty.

(*ii*) high returns enterprise with high price uncertainty.

(*iii*) low returns enterprise with low price uncertainty.

(*iv*) low returns enterprise with high price uncertainty.

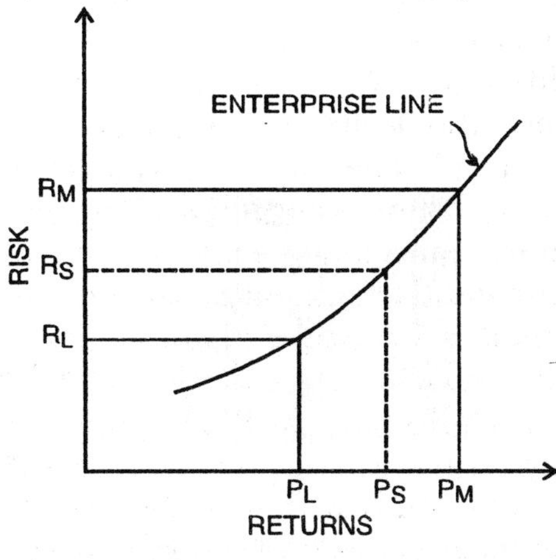

Fig. 16.1

Decisions on situation (*i*) and (*iv*) are obvious; to take up the Ist category enterprise(s) to the maximum permitted by resource-use capabilities and discard the category-four enterprise(s) completely. It is only in enterprise-categories (*ii*) and (*iii*) that rational decisions on level and combination of enterprises would need to be made. In this case, a farm-entrepreneur's resistance line will be in climbing up the risk-ladder. He will move up the risk elevation from R_L to R_M (Fig. 16.1) permitted by his equity, financial shock-absorption-capacity, delimited by his own financial resources and credit-worthiness. Mental attitude on business risks, of course, plays a pivotal role. As the entrepreneur moves up from R_L to R_M, he will travel on returns line from P_L to P_M. Distance moved on R_L to R_M line will depend upon the complementary ratio : $\frac{P_M - P_L}{R_M - R_L}$ or $\frac{\Delta P}{\Delta R}$:

If both R and P are measured in money terms, the optimum point will be where $\frac{\Delta P}{\Delta R}$ ratio gets equated with $\frac{P_r}{P_p}$ ratio. Here R will measure the movement on risk-line, P the corresponding direct change in returns through changes in enterprise-combinations; P_p the weight attached to a unit of returns vis-a-vis P_r cost involved in a unit of risk. Normally, the ratio $\frac{P_r}{P_p}$ had to be taken as next best risk-returns alternative available for investment on the farm. If, for example, price risk-cost is Rs. 100/- to Rs. 200/- between points R_L to R_M and corresponding returns Rs. 300/- to Rs. 500/-, $\frac{\Delta P}{\Delta R}$ ratio will be $\frac{500 - 300}{200 - 100} = 2$. Suppose further, this returns-risk ratio keeps on declining till it is 1 at R_M. If $\frac{P_r}{P_p}$ ratio is 1.5 due to 150% next best returns on alternative risk cost (say on another crop or animal enterprise) the entrepreneur will move on to the point (say R_s), where taking this much price risk will have the same risk-return ratio (1.5) as promised by the next-best alternative. Moving on this line in this context will mean shifting from low risk-low returns enterprise to higher risk-higher returns enterprises.

In most of the enterprises, however, the risk-returns ratio does not remain constant at different levels of adoption. Most of the time, the ratio declines, as higher level of enterprise is included in the production programmes (Fig. 16.2). There is a little possibility of an enterprise with increasing risk-returns ratio for any individual farm entrepreneur, because of too small a volume of his production to influence the market prices and decisions. This is especially true in developing countries. If the lowest-lying enterprise-ratio line (A in Fig. 16.2) does not intersect any other enterprise line, the obvious choice will be to take up this enterprise to the point where $\frac{\Delta P}{\Delta R}$ gets equated to $\frac{P_r}{P_p}$ ratio, as explained in the earlier section.

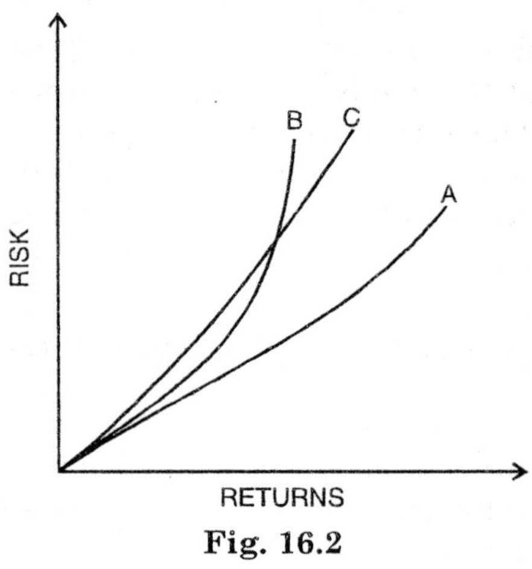

Fig. 16.2

If, however, the lowest-ratio-line intersects the other line(s), the optimum decision will be a combination of enterprises as illustrated in fig. 16.3. Within the framework of limited farm resources, under the normative conditions, the first preference will be for enterprise A upto the point N. Next the enterprise B will be taken up upto the point K and the enterprise-ratio-line C will be followed beyond K. This explains how the farm entrepreneur balances price-risk of and returns from various enterprises and decides on a combination of enterprises.

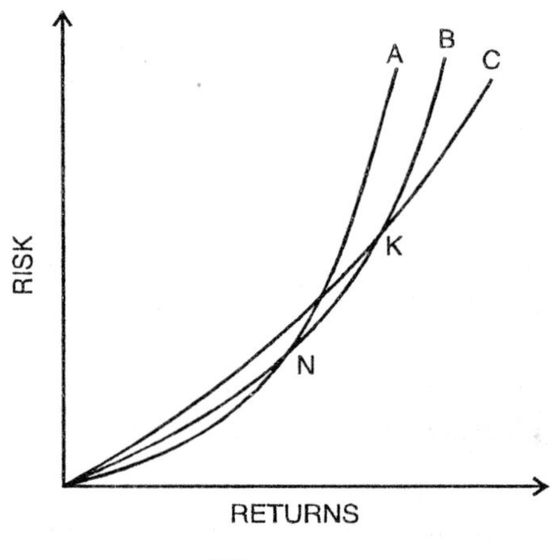

Fig. 16.3

Yield uncertainty

Yield and production also have a probability distribution, the parameters of which can be measured with a fair degree of accuracy from time series data. Here again the following categories of farm enterprises will present alternatives to the farmer :

(*i*) low yield—high risk enterprise(s)

(*ii*) low yield—low risk enterprise(s)

(*iii*) high yield—high risk enterprise(s), and

(*iv*) high yield—low risk enterprise(s).

In respect of category (*i*) and (*iv*), the decisions are again very obvious. The first category enterprise(s) should not be taken up at all (this analysis is irrespective of the levels and changes in prices, which has been discussed in earlier section). The fourth category enterprise(s) would be taken up to the maximum permitted by the farm resource-use capabilities. Decisions in respect of the combination of acceptable yield and uncertainty elements (A point on low yield-low risk to high yield high risk path) will be made exactly in the same way as in case of decisions on price risk-return ratio line. Ratio $\frac{\Delta Y}{\Delta V}$ will be equated to $\frac{P_v}{P_y}$ when ΔY is the change in yield and ΔV the yield variability. P_v is the cost the farmer will put on the yield variability and P_y the value per unit of Y. Here it is a situation of value balancing between increased yield and its variability. The situation becomes more explicitly demonstrated in the developing countries where improvements in production technology are promising higher yields but at the same time involve higher yield variability too, especially in case of new strains of crops like maize, rice and wheat. The adoption of new technology, therefore, varies from place to place, region to region and farmer to farmer depending upon yield uncertainty-returns ratios their situations promise and the values the farmers put on these two variables. The 'yield variability-returns' ratio in turn is influenced by physical, biological and other environmental factors and the value ratio $\frac{P_v}{P_y}$ is affected by the farmer's resource-situation (especially capital and equity), technical-skill-confidence, managerial ability; family structure, social interaction, economic setup and mental outlook.

Profitability–A Catch-all factors

Price and yield levels and their variability ultimately result in enterprise profitability and variability in it. But, it involves an element of cost* also. This will open up following alternative enterprise possibilities for the farmer :

(*i*) Low cost—Low profitability—Low variability enterprises.

(*ii*) Low cost—Low profitability—High variability enterprises.

(*iii*) Low cost—High profitability—Low variability enterprises.

(*iv*) Low cost—High profitability—High variability enterprises.

(*v*) High cost—Low profitability—Low variability enterprises.

(*vi*) High cost—Low profitability—High variability enterprises.

(*vii*) High cost—High profitability—Low variability enterprises.

(*viii*) High cost—High profitability—High variability enterprises.

* In the context of decision making here, the relevant costs to be considered will be variable costs.

Decision again would be obvious in categories 3 and 6. The two points will lie at 'X' and 'Y' in three dimensional Fig. 16.4. Rest of the enterprises will lie on cross-diagonal line XY. At the optimum point, following equations will have to be satisfied :

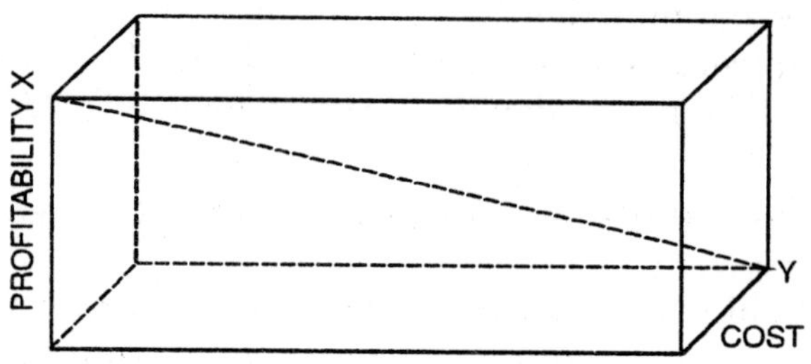

Fig. 16.4

(*i*) $\frac{\Delta Y}{\Delta V} = \frac{P_c}{P_y}$ (*ii*) $\frac{\Delta Y}{\Delta V} = \frac{P_v}{P_y}$

These two equations will solve down to the equation $\frac{\Delta V}{\Delta C} = \frac{P_C}{P_V}$ Again, thus, the balance will be struck where ratio $\frac{\Delta V}{\Delta C}$ will equal to the ratio of the values the farmer puts on additional costs and additional variability. As he shifts to high profitability-enterprise or the higher level of enterprise, he might have to incur higher costs and face higher variability in the profitability of the enterprise(s). As such, there can be three situations : (1) constant variability-cost ratio, (2) increasing ratio, and (3) decreasing ratio (Fig. 16.5). In the event of the constant-ratio, the entrepreneur would go to the extent, he can bear the variability (risk) within the resources available to him. If it is an increasing ratio, the tendency will be not to increase the level of enterprise or shift to new enterprise. This factor often plays a crucial role in holding the rapid adoption of new technology in the developing countries. In case of decreasing ratio, the farmer will be tempted to incur the additional costs to the maximum permitted by their resources in order to increase the level of enterprise(s) or adopt new enterprise(s) to operate at high profitability level of enterprise(s).

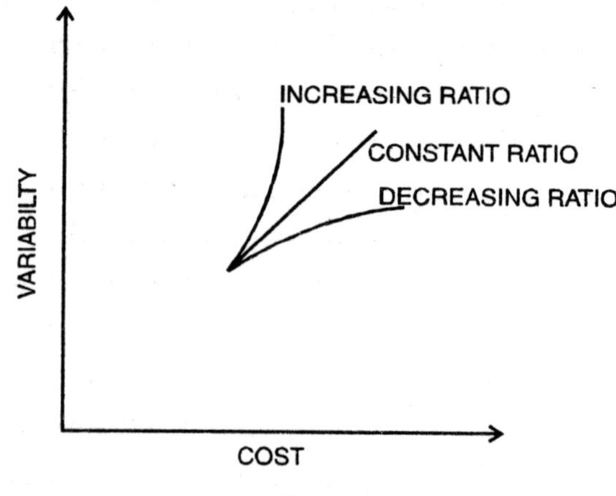

Fig. 16.5

Uncertain Availability of Inputs

It is not very uncommon, especially in the developing countries, that the supplies of some crucial inputs (more so in case of unconventional inputs such as fertilizers, insecticides, hybrid seeds etc.) become uncertain to the farmers. This uncertainty element would get incorporated into the production programmes of the farmers through :

(*i*) adjustments in the levels of enterprises at the time of planting,

(*ii*) adjustments in the planting dates, and

(*iii*) adjustments in application rates of inputs, especially on the growing crops.

Level of Enterprises

Optimally, the level of a crop enterprise is a, cateris paribus, function of availability of the crucial inputs (which are assumed uncertain in this analysis). To take a simple case of one product-one input relationship, this can be of the type Y = $f(x_1 / x_2..............., x_n)$ where 'Y' is the level of enterprise, 'x', the crucial input of which the supply is uncertain and '$x_2........x_n$'other inputs, of which supply is assumed to be sure. If the enterprises are more than one, which have a functional relationship with the same uncertain-availability-input (a situation of diversified farming) and also if there are more than one uncertain inputs, the farm entrepreneur will have alternative programmes at different levels of estimates of availabilities of inputs. Depending upon the estimated input or input-mix available at the planting time, his decision to allocate acreage to different crop-enterprises will be based on his objective to maximise production (more appropriately returns)to the estimated available quantities of these crucial inputs.

The allocation process can be illustrated with the help of diagrams. In Fig. 16.6, functional relationships of two enterprises 'A' and 'B' with the availability levels of one input, separately for each enterprise, are shown. The number of such functions will depend upon the number of enterprise alternatives available to the farmer. These functions (in case of two enterprises) can be converted into production possibility curves as shown in Fig. 16.7. Each curve will show a different level of estimated availability of the input at the planting time. The production possibility curve will thus shift upwards or downwards depending upon

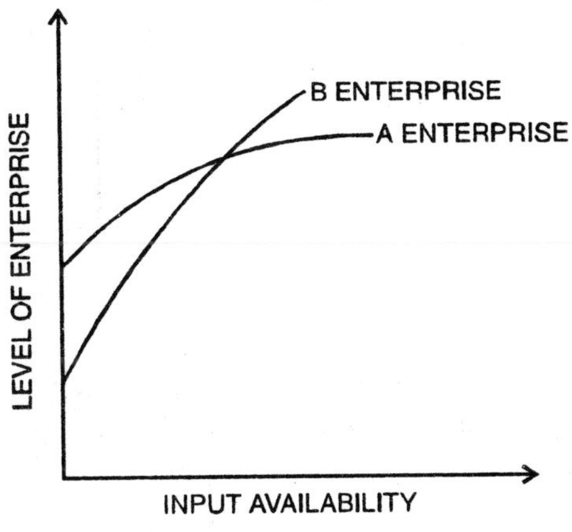

Fig. 16.6

higher or lower estimates of availability of the inputs. Point P here will indicate the level of two enterprises with availability of the input at zero, indicating, of course, that some minimum production of the two enterprises is possible even without any use of the crucial input. As the estimated availability of the input increase, the choice horizon will expand along PL or PK or points on curves located within PL and PK plane. The actual acreage allocation will, however, further depend upon the relative profitability of the two enterprises shown by the iso-revenue line 'pp'. The tangent at point 'M' will be the point of optimum allocation where $\frac{\Delta Y_2}{\Delta Y_1}$ will be equal to $\frac{Py_1}{Py_2}$. Here the combination of enterprises will be Oa and Ob.

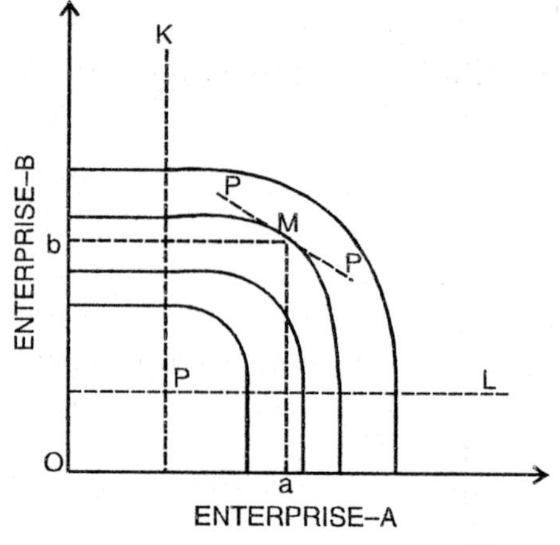

Fig. 16.7

With more than one input being uncertain, the production possibility curves at different levels of estimated availabilities can be constructed for various feasible combination of inputs of practical importance. For a given estimated availability level of resource-mix, the production possibility curve (BCDEA) is illustrated in Fig. 16.8.

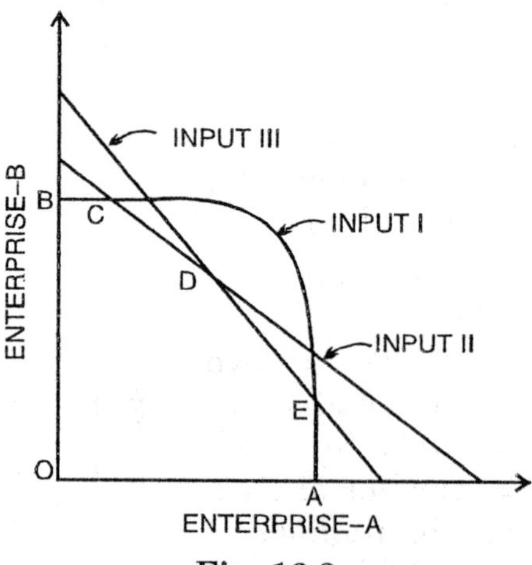

Fig. 16.8

Extending the analysis to more than two products and more than two crucial (as well as uncertain) inputs, the relationship will hold as under :

$$Y_1 = f_1 (x_1, x_2 \ldots\ldots x_k / x_{k+1} \ldots\ldots\ldots\ldots x_{k+n})$$
$$Y_i = f_i (x_1, x_2, \ldots\ldots\ldots\ldots x_k / x_{k+1} \ldots\ldots\ldots\ldots x_{k+n})$$
$$Y_t = f_t (x_1, x_2 \ldots\ldots\ldots\ldots x_k / x_{k+1} \ldots\ldots\ldots\ldots x_{k+n})$$

The decision point at planting time involving more than one product and more than one input will be where :

$P_{Y1}.\ Y_{.1}/\Delta X_1 = P_{Y2}.\ Y_2/\Delta X_1 = ...\ PY_t.\ Y_t/\Delta X_1$

$P_{Y1}.\ Y_{.1}/\Delta X_2 = P_{Y2}.\ Y_2/\Delta X_2 = ...\ PY_t.\ Y_t/\Delta X_2$

$P_{Y1}.\ Y_{.1}/\Delta X_K = P_{Y2}.\ Y_2/\Delta X_K = ...\ PY_t.\ Y_t/\Delta X_K$

For each level of input or input-combination the coefficients of this matrix will change. The farm entrepreneur has to thus keep ready with quite a few of alternative decisions to cope with the uncertain supply situation and make a choice as the situation would prevail at the planting time. This needs careful prior analysis and production planning, but a large majority of the farmers, especially in the developing countries do not have an access to or do such a prior written or even mental planning. As a result, the production programmes often get upset and the farms operate at points lower than the optimum.

Adjustments in planting time. Another way open to the farmers to adjust their production programmes to the elements of uncertain availability of inputs is to delay the planting of crops to gain more time for arranging supplies. This again of course, has a limit on the extent to which planting of a crop can be delayed, because soon decrements in productivity due to late planting would outbalance the increments due to the additional use of the crucial input(s) such as fertilizers. At the same time delayed sowing will involve higher dozes of input(s) and higher accompanying costs. Fig. 16.9 illustrates the point.

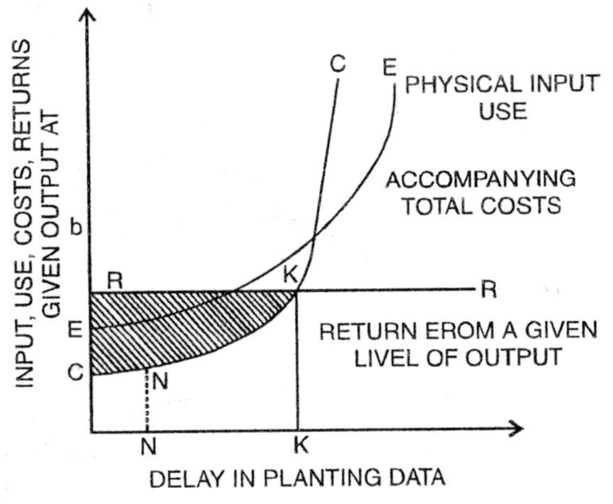

Fig. 16.9

Production possibility of a given level of enterprise is indicated by the curve EE with higher and higher use of input till the curve goes completely elastic, indicating that further delay in sowing time cannot be compensated by the use of additional doses of the input. If the returns from a given level of production is a straight line 'RR', the accompanying costs curve 'CC' will intersect it at a point K. The shaded area RKC will show the profit margin over these costs. So long as costs-curve remains parallel to returns-curve (upto the point N) the entrepreneur will remain indifferent to planting date and can delay the planting without any hesitation to wait for the supplies of the uncertain crucial input(s). As the cost curve moves up, his willingness to delay planting will keep declining. He may not touch the point K, because all profits at this point will be washed off. He will operate between the points N and K. Exact point will depend upon when he is able to secure the supply of the crucial uncertain-availability input(s).

For the purpose of rational decisions on this issue, the farmers need factual information on interaction effects of delays in dates of planting and increases in the use of crucial input(s) such as fertilizers and seed on production of crops. This information is, however, badly lacking for the farmers, especially in the developing countries. Most of the time, the farmers remain indifferent to late-sown crops and do not attempt to compensate for the delay by additional application of inputs. Often, thus late sown crops go without application of crucial inputs and the late procured inputs go unused. Intensive experimental research is, therefore, needed in this direction, especially in the developing countries.

Inputs Application on Growing Crops

No doubt the supplies of uncertain-availability-inputs may restrict the level of enterprise(s) at planting time and also influence the sowing date, the farm entrepreneur sometimes does not, curtail the acreage and/or does not delay the planting of the crop, if the input can be applied after planting (top dressing). How far this method can go to mitigate the adverse effects of uncertain availability, again depends upon how far top-dressing or after application of the input(s) on timely sown crop can give advantage over pre-planting or planting-time application of the input(s) on timely sown crop.

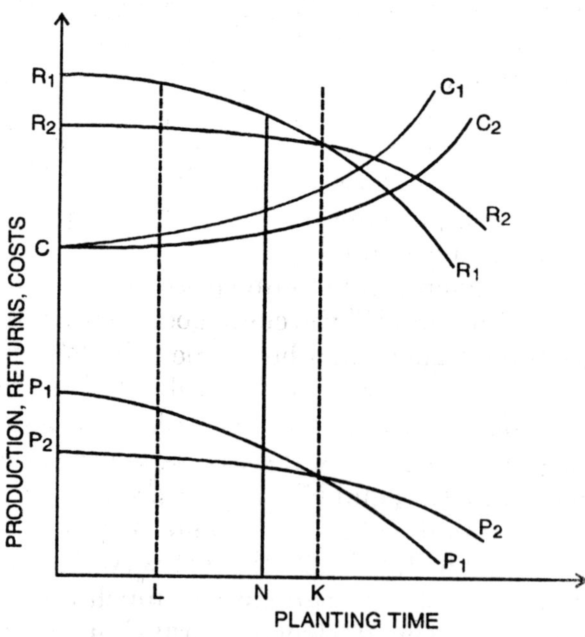

Fig. 16.10

Fig. 16.10 illustrates the point. Curve P_1 P_1 depicts the production of the crop with planting-time application of the input over delayed dates of planting. P_2 P_2 curve indicates production of a timely sown crop, with the (top-dressing) delayed. R_1R_1 and R_2R_2 are the total returns curves and C_1C_1 and C_2C_2 are the corresponding total accompanying costs curves. If the supplies are uncertain to be available beyond point K, the choice of the farmer for definite will be on P_2P_2 curve, with revenue shown by R_2R_2 and costs C_2C_2, because here C_2C_2 and R_2R_2 curves envelop the C_1C_1 and R_1R_1 curves showing larger comparative profits. Upto the date (point) L the choice will be in delayed planting of the crop with planting-time application of the input, because upto this point, all curves run parallel and P_1 has a definite advantage, because there are no decrements in production due to delayed planting. Between date L and K, the choice will be in favour of planting-time application and delayed planting till the gap R_1—R_2 remains greater than the gap C_1—C_2 *i.e.*, till the gain in returns remains to be larger than the disadvantages on cost (point N in the diagram). Beyond N, of course, the choice will be on top dressing on timely sown crops.

All of these, of course, are normative analysis. In actual practice also, the farmers do some mental exercise knowingly or unknowingly, and some make rough written calculations too, on the alternatives open to them under the conditions of risk and uncertainty. Yet, majority of the farmers, do not have any factual information on the elements of risk and uncertainty, their coefficients of probability and the alternative courses of action open to them with estimates of accompanying costs and returns. There is, therefore, a need to gather experimental and field data on risk and uncertainty elements involved in production and prices of outputs and availability of inputs, as they actually mould or would modify the production plans of the farmers.

1. ***What do you understand by risk and uncertainty in Agriculture ? Discuss distinction between risks and uncertainties.***
2. ***What is the importance of risk and uncertainty in Agriculture ?***
3. ***How do the farmers in their normative production programmes, account for estimable uncertainties of price fluctuations and yield variabilities of farm products ?***
4. ***How do farmers provide for uncertainities of availability of factor inputs ?***

1. *Hildrith, Clifford : "Problems of Uncertainty in Farm Planning" Journal of Farm Economics, XXXIX (5) Dec. 1957.*
2. *Simpson, I.G., Hales, A.W. and A.Fletcher : "Linear Programming and Uncertain Prices in Horticulture" Indian Journal of Agricultural Economics XV(4) Dec. 1963.*
3. *Misra, Bidyadhar : "Uncertainty & Adoption of New Farming Practices in India" Indian Journal of Agricultural Economics XV (4) Dec. 1963.*
4. *Malya, (Miss) M. Minakshi & Rajagopalan. "Nature of Risk Associated with Rainfall & its effect on farming—A case study of Kurnool District (A.P.)". Indian Journal of Agricultural Economics XV (4) Dec. 1963.*
5. *Kahlon, A.S &Johl, S.S. "Nature & Role of Risk & Uncertainty in Agriculture'. Indian Journal of Agricultural Economics XV(4) Dec. 1963.*
6. *Vyas, V.S. & Rakhral, K.R. "Uncertainty Crop Planning" Indian Journal of Agricultural Economics XV (4) Dec. 1963.*
7. *Apte, D.P. "Uncertainty in Agriculture & Decisions of the cultivator regarding the crop to be Cultivated" Indian Journal of Agricultural Economics XV (4) Dec. 1963.*

INDEX

A

Accounting period 153, 225
Accruals 269
Additivity 206, 207
Administrative decisions 21, 26-27
Advantages
—of cash flow map 308
—of farm records and accounts 222, 223
—of farm planning 177
Agricultural Finance Officer 315
Agricultural wages and employment 344, 345
Agro-economic research centre 31
Agronomy 18, 19
Algebraic
—form 63
—method 112, 115
Alternative plan 303
Analysis
—in production economics 51
—of the alternative plans 194
Annual
—revaluation 194
—Use of machine 359
Assets 252, 253
Average
—fixed cost 89
—Product 58
—Total cost 90
—variable cost 89

B

Balance sheet 298
Banker's loan folder 317
Basic information for farm machinery 373-375
Basic relationships 125
Basics of farm production decisions 45-61
Best size of the farm 22
Biological sciences 19
Borrower-farmer's credit file 318
Boundary lines 114, 136
Branch manager 313
Break through 7
Break-even point 369
Broader field 16
Budget 189-191
Budgeting 192-205
Buildings as an input 388
Business
—Judgement 42
—skill 146

C

Capital
—changes 266
—efficiency 274-279
—ratios 277
—receipts 307
—turnover 38
Cash and non-cash costs 81
Cash
—flow as a money map 301
—flow chart 307
—relief 266
Casual labour 347
Categories of
—costs 83-84

—Farm efficiency measures 272
Changing the size of machine 365
Characteristics of :
—a good plan 180
—average cost curves 90
—farming as a business 36-43
—farm management 15-17
—Iso-cost line 110
—marginal cost 90
Choice indicators 50
Choice of mode of fertilizer placement 338
Choosing optimum level of output 114
Classification of
—Farm cash records 257
—farm labour 345
Communication and markets 30
Comparative costs of fertilizers 121
Competitive
—crops 124
Complementarity 126
Complementary enterprises 168
Completion of security documents 316
Complete Budgeting 192-205
Composition of farm labour 347
Concept of cost 80
Constant
—marginal returns function 64-66
—productivity principle 152
—rate of substitution 106-108, 129, 158-159, 164-165
Continuous function 49
Cost concept 51
Cost
—accounting 226
—benefit analysis 388
—of fencing 326-327
—of operating a tractor 359
—of operating bullocks 360
—of production 81
—principles 153-156
—ratios 275-277
—return analysis 332
Crop
—competition
—production records 232-233
—rotation 24
—yields index 301
Cropping
—Pattern 231
—system 333
Credit control 307
Current ratio 300

Decisions : 22
—administrative 26
—building 23
—farm labour and machinery programme 22
—How to produce 25
—How much to produce 24
—Irrigation 23
—Marketing 21, 27
—operational 21
—Size of farm 22
—Strategic 22
—What to produce 24
—When to produce 25
Decreasing
—marginal returns function 67
—rate of substitution 130, 159-160, 166
Demand promissory note 316
Depreciation 247-251
Derivation 60
Designs, durability in buildings 392
Desirable organisational change 177
Determination of
—net revenue as a function of output 92
—optimum production combination 139-140
Development of farm management 30

Diminishing
—balance method 248-249
—returns principle 149, 152
Disbursement of loan 317
Discontinuous function 50
Discounting income 170
Discrete function 50
Diversification 24, 145
Diversification Model 215
Divisibility 206
Double entry system 227
Draft and power requirements of machinery 376

E

Economics of fertilizer use 334
Economic :
—analysis 176
—efficiency 20
—feasibility tests 292
—theory 17
—unit 47
—viability 315
Educational :
—process 177
—tool 15
Effect of changes in
—input prices 112
—output prices 97
Efficient farm layout 324
Efficiency measures and business decision 277-278
Elasticity of production 71
Enterprise :
—budget 188-189
—combination 349
—mix 24
—relationships 131
Entrepreneurship 4
Estimation of :
—input requirement of alternate plan 204-205
—labour and power requirement 191
Exact marginal product 60
Executive 4
Expansion path 114, 142

Factor-Factor Analysis 116, 118, 120
Factor-Factor relationship 102-123
Factor-Product relationships 62
Facotr-product price changes and production decisions 97-99
Family :
—satisfaction 1
Farm :
—budgeting 183
—building management 387-394
—business analysis 220-284
—Credit Analysis Kit 317-319
—diary 257
—Efficiency measures 271-277
—entrepreneur 51
—executive 51
—family labour
—Family living Budget 303-306
—Financial Budget 303-306
—Financial Management 286-287
—Income potentials 8-13
—Income statement 262
—Inventory
—Labour management 343
—Machinery management 356-386
—Manager 51
—Managers labour 346
—map 229
—Planning 176
—unit as a whole 17
—work simple function 352-354
Farm Management :
—characteristics 15
—decisions 22-27
—educational tool 15

—extension 6, 32-33
—process 2
—problems 28-29
—relationship with other sciences 17
—research 4, 30-32
—teaching 5, 34
Fear of taxation 225
Feed records 239-240
Fencing 326, 327, 328
Fertilization management programme 335
Field officer 315
Financial
—accounting 226
—records 241
Financing agriculture 39
Fixed activities 200
Fixed cost 82, 153
Fixed and variable costs 39
Fixed and variable cost principle 154
Fixed proportion combination 106
Flexibility in buildings 392
Flow resources 48
Fluctuation in prices 3
Full cost accounting 226

Game theory models 216
Gokhale institute of Politics and Economics 30
Govt. payments 264
Grain storage 390
Graphic
—form 64
—method 112, 115, 116
—presentation 140
Graphs in production function analysis 52

Hiring Vs owning a machine 368
Home and business 39
How farm planning helps 178
Hypothetical data 75

Impact of technological change 77
Imperfect knowledge situation 51
Implementing the plan 194
Importance of
—farm management 6-15
—farm finance
—to farmer 287
—to lender 287
—to adviser 287
Improving the efficiency of farm labour 348
Inadequate capital 28
Income improvement 177
Income statement 261, 262, 300
Increasing
—productivity 152
—rate of substitution 129, 166
Independent enterprises 163
Indian Council of Agricultural Research 30, 32
Indicator-choice 50
Industrial development 14
Inelastic demand for farm products 39
Information needed for planning and Budgeting 182-183
Initial investment in Machines 358
Initiative and ambition 42
Inputs :
—application on growing crops 404
—price changes and least cost combination 116
Integrating science 16
Intensity of cropping 273
Intensive Agril. Distt. Programme 32
Inventory of Limited resources 193
Irrigation capacity 198
Iso
—clines 113, 136
—cost lines 110

—quants 105
—revenue lines 137, 139, 141

Jamabandi Register 309, 310
Joint Product 125, 163

Khasra Girdawari 313-314
Kharif Land 144

Labour
—efficiency 322
efficiency measures 273
—maximum 144
—records 236-237
Land
—Management 322
—use efficiency 271-272
—use capability classification 197
Law of Equi-marginal returns 161
Laws of production economics 46
Layout of felds 325
Learning 41
Least cost combination 111-113
Level of enterprises 401
Levels of farm accountancy 225-229
Liabilities 252, 253
Limitations of :
—principles of farm management 172
Linearity 206
Linear programming Analysis 202
Linear relationships 54-55
Livestock production and disposal records 235

Machinery :
—storage 390
—use record 236-238
Management
—decisions 20
—factor 199
—functions 3
—learning and adjustment 41
—of importance resources 322-342
—of labour 351
Manager 4
Managerial
—ability 42
—skills 29
Marginal
—analysis 295
—cost 90
—cost curve 76
—product 58, 59, 70, 75
—rate of product substitution 134-135
—revenue curves 76
Marketing decisions : 21, 27
—buying 27
—selling 27
Measure of Farm income 277
Mechanics of processing farm credit proposals 308
Mental alertness and imagination 41
Methods of :
—Computing depreciation 247-251
—valuation 245-247
Micro-approach 16
Minimisation of cost on fetilizers 120-122
Minimum loss principle 95-97
Mixed farming 350
Mode of payment 264
Modified programming model 215, 216
Mono-period resources 81
Monotonic relationship 56
Mortgage deed 316
Mutation 310

N

Nature of farm management 15
Net capital rates 254
Net revenue as related to output 93
Net worth statement 252, 253, 254, 256, 299
Non-cash costs 81
Non-linear relationships 55
Non-monotonic relationship 56

O

Objectives of
—farm planning 178
—production economics 46
Off farm work 267
Old Vs New machines 372
Operating cost rates 275
Operational
—decisions 21, 22, 23
—size 22
Opportunity
—cost 83-84
—Cost principle 162-163
—Curve 131
Optimum :
—Combination 141
—Farm Plan 195
—Fertilizer level 335-336
—Point 165
—Product combination 139-143
—Productive decision 94-95
—Time of application of fertilizers 337
Organic Matter 334

Partial
—budge 184-186
—budgeting 184
Parts of a farm record system 228
Perfect knowledge situation 51
Permanent hired labour 346
Personal :
—cash records 257
—interviews 308
—requirements 42
Planning
—and budgeting 182-183
—horizon 2
—period 81
Plant 48
Political Science 19
Poly-period resources 81
Practical Science 15
Pre
—payments 270
—sanction farm inspection 316
Price :
—changes and production decision 97
—line 137-139
Primary forces of production 36
Principle characteristics of a good farm plan 180
Principle of :
—Combining enterprises 163-166
—Comparative advantage 168
—Factor substitution 156-160
—Time comparison 168
—Variable proportion 149
Probabilistic models 216
Problems and difficulties in farm accounts 224-225
Procedure for working out the least cost combination 157
Process of taking inventory 244
Product :
—Mix 24
—price changes and optimum combination of output 141
—price uncertainty 396
Production
—decisions 97-99

—efficiency 20
—function 50, 63-69
—function analysis 183
—period 50
—records 235-237
—relationship 62-79
Production economics
—Field 45-46
—Language 47
—Meaning and scope 45
—Objectives 46-47
Production possibility curve 131-139
Production and disposal of farm produce 234-235
Psychological aspects 19
Purchase of old V/s New Machine 372
Profitability
—a catch-all factor 399
Profit
—maximisation 94
—rule 158
Projected profit and loss statement 308
Proper filling of loan application 309
Punjab board of Economic enquiry 30-32

R

Rate of capital turn over 277
Rational and Irrational zones of production 116
Recommendations of a good layout 325-328
Reducing fraction method 249-250
Regions of production function 72-77
Register of mutations 310-311-312
Relationship between
—Average and marginal costs 91
—average fixed costs, average variable cost and average total costs 89
—Farm management and other sciences 17
—Production function and total cost function 85-86
—Total, average and marginal product 69-71
—Total fixed costs, total variable costs and total costs 86
Remodelling of farm layout 328
Repayment
—capacity the second test 293-295
—plan 297
Requirement in farming profession 41
Resource levels 144
Returns :
—concepts 51
—the first test 292-293
—to fixed farm resources 144
Revenue records
—verification 309
Ridge line 113, 114, 136
Risk-bearing ability—the third test 296-297
Roads 326
Role of credit in production and marketing 288-291

Sanction of advance 316
Scatter diagram 57
Scope of Farm management 4
Security documents 316
Selection of :
—depreciation method 251
—Enterprises 24
—Method of fertilizer application 337-338
—Size of machine to buy 358
—Source of nutrients from fertilizers 339
Semi-skilled labour 347
Shifts in production function 78
Short period 81
Short run-production function 50
Simple
—arithmetical calculation 111
—cash record 258

Single
—enterprise accounting 226
—entry system 227
Skilled labour 347
Slope of
—curve 57
Small size of farm business 28
Social sciences 19
Sociology 19
Soil Management 333
Soil management practices 333
Special
—cases of substitution 160
—features of Indian farm labour 348
—problems in computing depreciation 251
Specialisation 145
Specification of :
—appropriate prices 193
—technical co-efficients 192
Statistics 19
Steps in farm planning and budgeting 192-195
Stock resources 48
Storage structures 391
Store/stock register 236-239
Straight line method 248
Strategic management decisions 22-23
Subsistence farming 224
Substituting machinery for labour 359
Substitution ratio 127
Successful farm manager 3
Supplementarity 128
Supplementary enterprises 167
Supporting sciences 18, 19
Systems of book-keeping 227-228

Tabular
—form 63
—method 115, 139
Taxes 270
Technical
—feasibility report 315
—unit 47
Techniques of farm planning 181
Technological
—change 77
—progress 7
Three
—regions of production function 72
—zones of cost function 94
Time comparison principle 168
Timeliness of operations and machines 367
Time regidities in consumption of Agril. products 40
Tools of farm management analysis 176-219
Topography 324
Total
—budgeting 192
—cost 83, 88
—Cost function 84-85
—Fixed cost 88
—Product 58, 70
—Variable cost 88
Transformation
—function 131
—Period 50
Treatment and Classification of Special transactions 263-270
Trends in custom work 369
Triple role of Indian farmer 224
Turn over 38
Types of
—Cash accounts 257
—Costs 153-154
—Factor-factor relationships 106
—Farm budgting 184
—Farm records and accounts 228
—Product relationship 163-164
Typical farm management decisions 20

Uncertain availability of Inputs 401
Uncertainty and risk 396-405
Underemployment 29
Units of accounting 47
Unskilled labour 348
Uses of Farm Cash Accounts 261-263

Valuation 245-247
Variable costs 85-154
Varying rate of substitution 108
Verification of Revenue records 309

Water channels 326
Weather and price risks 340
Working ratios 254-299

Yield 271
Yield uncertainty 398

Zones of cost function 94.